VoIP Security

VoIP Security

James F. Ransome, CISM, CISSP
John W. Rittinghouse, Ph.D., CISM

ELSEVIER
DIGITAL
PRESS

AMSTERDAM • BOSTON • HEIDELBERG • LONDON
NEW YORK • OXFORD • PARIS • SAN DIEGO
SAN FRANCISCO • SINGAPORE • SYDNEY • TOKYO

Elsevier Digital Press
30 Corporate Drive, Suite 400, Burlington, MA 01803, USA
Linacre House, Jordan Hill, Oxford OX2 8DP, UK

Library of Congress Cataloging-in-Publication Data
A catalog record for this book is available from the Library of Congress.

ISBN: 1-55558-332-6

British Library Cataloguing-in-Publication Data
A catalogue record for this book is available from the British Library.

For information on all Elsevier Digital Press publications
visit our Web site at www.books.elsevier.com

04 05 06 07 08 09 10 9 8 7 6 5 4 3 2 1

Printed in the United States of America

Contents

List of Figures and Tables

Foreword

I am a techno-gadget collector. Early adopter is probably too kind a term for me, as I am positively addicted to the new goodies that are thought up in the garages and minds of the talented people who inhabit the technical industry. I still have my first laptop, a Grid Compass I, which is about 1982 vintage. It has a tiny, nine-inch screen, a yellow phosphor display, a 5-MB hard drive, 256 Kb of bubble memory for RAM, a 300-baud built-in modem, all housed in a magnesium case that is not only a heat sink for the laptop, but can also take an eight-foot drop without damage. It runs a strange operating system called GridOS, still uses XMODEM and Kermit to transmit files back and forth and has an IEEE 488 parallel bus for connection to peripherals, which are enormous compared to today's 1.4 inch hard drives with massive storage capabilities. Oh, and it has a 720 kb floppy drive as well.

Yes, it's a boat anchor compared to the snazzy Sony laptop I drag around with me for work, but it was the first laptop that had the form and function of today's modern laptops. And it was rugged—which was a requirement. I got the Grid Compass I many years ago, when I was employed by an oil company and the geologists and geophysicists were complaining that they did not have remote access to the systems in the data center. After playing with the Grid for a while, we bought a boatload of them and the rest is history—laptop mania had begun.

At about the same time, Craig McCaw of McCaw Cellular (then a new fangled idea) got up at a computer convention (then called the NCC) and said that the day would come when consumers would willingly pay $100 per month or more for wireless voice access. He predicted that cellular phones would evolve from the take-over-your-car models and the new "bag" phone models to something similar to Captain Kirk's tricorder, which would fit in your shand and be small enough that you would not mind carrying it around at all times. And everyone would have them. He was practically laughed off the stage.

Some years later, I got one of the very first digital cameras from Canon. It had a two-inch floppy drive and connected to my desktop system via the serial port. You could only store about 20 pictures per floppy, but the cool thing was that I didn't need a scanner to scan in paper pictures, and I could go directly from camera to inclusion into a word-processing document with pictures of unseemly telco closets and other nasties to prove to customers that their cable infrastructure needed a major makeover.

I also was an early adopter of personal digital assistants. I had the original Apple Newton and then later the Palm Pilot PDA and evolved all the way to the Palm Vx, until I gave it up and moved on to an HP (then Compaq) iPaq running Windows CE (and now Pocket Windows). I even signed up for the original MobilStar wireless service for the Palm, so I could access the Web and check e-mail while running around from city to city.

Along the way, my personal phone got smaller. I went from a bag cellular phone, to a small Mitsubishi handheld cellular, to an assortment of Nokias and Motorolas. I also had a Nextel for a while that was tri-mode: CDMA, TDMA and GSM, all at the same time. A bit big, but nice in those days if you needed to travel internationally and didn't want to have three phone numbers and three phones. Did it work in Japan? Of course not. CDMA-One in Japan is unique and required a unique phone. The cool thing about Japanese cellular phones, though, was that they were so tiny while having an enormous battery life. I noticed once that all Japanese cell phones had a lanyard on them. I was told by a distributor in Tokyo that they had to put lanyards on the phones, as the phones were so small that people would forget they were in their pockets and run them through the wash. The lanyard helped remind people they had a phone in their pocket.

I have always been a proponent of wireless technologies. Being an early adopter, I was one of the first to sign up for a 12-city wireless network called Ricochet when it rolled out in 2000. It provided an always-on, 500-kbps wireless connection in specific cities in the US. When you hit a city where it was available, it worked pretty well. Sadly, after investing a couple of billion in build-out, the company failed due to lack of business. Strangely enough, it came to the rescue, literally, on September 11, 2001 in New York. For several weeks, it was the only operational data network in the area near the World Trade Center that could be used by emergency management personnel. It was actually decommissioned at the time, but someone remembered using it and the emergency management personnel were able to access it.

Of course, when T-Mobile started putting in 802.11 wi-fi "hot spots" in all the American Airlines Admiral's Clubs, I was an early adopter. Anything to download e-mail at a decent speed is a good thing for me (especially since I get more than 500 e-mails a day). The hot spots have spread out to Starbucks coffee shops and other locations (like hotels), and they are a welcome respite from dial-up whenever possible. As a consultant, I have had my hands in the creation of new technology gadgets myself. I have consulted on a variety of projects that have resulted in new goodies that I am proud to use today. The latest is Connexion by Boeing, a broadband wireless network environment to access Internet services in real-time in an always-on configuration, while cruising on a commercial aircraft at 35,000 feet. Working on the security components and architecture of the product was a four-year endeavor that has been interesting, to say the least (for example, how do you keep seat 14B from hacking seat 27J?).

Traditional PBXs have been getting smaller as well. In the Dark Ages, PBX units took up entire floors of larger enterprise companies. Wiring was expensive, phone handsets were expensive and the network was insular in nature. Signaling System 7 (SS7) has traditionally been the realm of voice connectivity only—no data, no video, no other access. As a result, it's remained somewhat secure, mostly through obscurity. Still, the need to have PBX flexibility in much smaller packaging has led to the development of mini-PBX systems and those that provision voice connectivity over a separate frequency range in the data wiring provisioned to cubes and offices. This has especially been an issue where companies spread out into smaller locations, or when telecommuting becomes more the norm than the exception.

Then there was the consulting gig I was involved in a few years ago to examine the security of a cell/data phone—a third generation (3G) cell phone that would be sold in Japan to provide iMode connectivity (basically wireless TCP/IP access). The cool thing about the unit was that it had a browser for Web access and an IP address, in addition to supporting cellular phone protocols. This meant that the phone was not just a phone—it was a data access point as well.

In the meantime, TCP/IP networking grew up and became a mainstay data protocol that most companies cannot live without. Away have gone SNA, DECnet, AppleTalk, ARCNET and all the other strange vendor-specific protocols that got data networks to the desktops of today. The growth of the Internet is now legendary, and the use of networking provisioned by TCP/IP protocols has become the norm for not just Internet access, but internal corporate networking access as well.

It was inevitable that eventually, voice access over data networks would happen. As can be seen by this little walk down memory lane, as components that were traditionally big and bulky got smaller and more compact, the need to exchange information with the components has grown. Add in the additional applications demands that have become integral to the devices provisioned to us and you have the need to mix voice, data and video all at once. As technology has evolved to more compact forms, the consumer has also demanded that the technologies be combined in one—not many—device(s). Users want their phone, television entertainment, Internet access, e-mail collector and application access to be from the same device—preferably one that will fit in a pocket and not cost an arm and a leg to buy and use.

It's only logical that all of this has led to a convergence of networks that service voice, video and data. Previously, these were separate, disparate network environments which provided rudimentary connectivity for the technologies in question—and not much more. All of that has changed. A massive change in network needs in the corporate marketplace, deregulation of the "last mile" access by local telephone companies, miniaturization of access methodologies and a large growth in the need to converge applications into more modular, "smaller" access methods has become the norm. Pushing voice over a TCP/IP network is the obvious next step as networks have become multifaceted in function and form.

At the same time, the access methodologies early adopters have been consuming for a long time are starting to come together. Devices such as Sony's Treo, which combines a PDA, cell phone, and wireless access in a single device, are a small view of what is to come—sooner rather than later.

Cell phone makers are already previewing handsets that provide CDMA, TDMA, CDMA-One, GSM and wi-fi access at the same time. The interesting thing with the wi-fi functionality is that it is primarily for Voice over Internet Protocol (VoIP), when the user is near a wi-fi wireless LAN network, such as in an office. This allows "follow me" calling and receiving of calls by the user, no matter where they go, as the voice systems can locate and forward a call to the user no matter how they are connected. With a little imagination, and the use of a camera-phone capability, the video conferencing our parents saw at Epcot and in the AT&T "future service" commercials could become the norm rather quickly. Add in a high-speed data feed and the phone handset of the near future becomes a multichannel television (with cable and video-on-demand), integrated with full voice capablility, and Internet-application support. And VoIP is a critical component.

Add VoIP to traditional Customer Relationship Management (CRM) applications, and a desktop browser now allows real-time, interactive customer support for applications as well as conversations. Put in technologies such as voice recognition, speech translation and other related goodies that are just now starting to peek out from under the blanket, and the opportunities for VoIP to transform business and communication is astounding.

Drs. Rittinghouse and Ransome have written a tour-de-force work on VoIP that is sure to satisfy the needs of anyone interested in the technology, and any company that is seriously looking at integrated, converged methods to share information with voice technologies. One nice thing about this book is the explanation of traditional voice methodologies (the chapter on telephony 101) and how they apply to VoIP. This information is critical to understanding the proper implementation of VoIP, and it will be immensely helpful to engineers and managers who have traditional data networking experience but little experience with voice networking and traditional telecommunications methods.

Of specific note, the book's emphasis on the security issues of the technology is critical—there are few texts on VoIP security, much less from individuals who are security practitioners with the proper expertise, experience and credentials. This book is a must-read for those considering the implementation of VoIP, to ensure that it becomes part of a master solution and not part of the security problems that IP networks always bring along with them. As converged networking environments are deployed, replacing the traditionally segregated voice and data network environments, the need to carefully consider and manage the security of voice in the VoIP environment is critical.

I am sure that you will learn a great deal about VoIP and VoIP security issues from this tome. I am also sure that it will keep you up at night as there are as many unanswered questions to VoIP security as there are solutions. But this book is a great starting point, and I highly recommend it as a jump-off to your education on the technology. This good book, by two of the smartest men I know, is a must-have for any technical library or team looking into the technologies associated with VoIP.

Dr. William M. Hancock, CISM, CISSP
September 1, 2004

Preface

Much has already been written about the advantages of using the Internet for telephony. In fact, in a short time, one can browse the Internet and find thousands (if not millions) of pages of material that discuss every conceivable aspect of telecommunications, protocol, transport, media, and a thousand other topics. However, finding a cogent presentation of the vital material needed to take someone with little or no background from a zero-knowledge-base on the matter to having a fairly well-versed understanding of something is a difficult challenge. Dr. Ransome and I have attempted to present the topic of voice over Internet from just such a perspective. Our approach was to take the reader from the little-known and lead them into a better understanding of the topic. In approaching this task, we both soon realized that several key knowledge domains needed to be presented. For one to truly understand Internet telephony, the reader must have a solid understanding of digital voice, telephony, networking, Internet protocols, and, most important of all, how all of these technologies are put together to create yet another technology, Voice over Internet telephony. Furthermore, knowing why such technology has evolved to the point of becoming commonplace in enterprise is also important. In presenting the material in this book, our intent has been to introduce the evolution of technologies needed for VoIP processing in such a way that the reader understands how and why it has evolved to the point where we find it today. We believe the reader will gain a strong fundamental understanding of the topic and understand how its application in business has changed the telecommunications industry forever.

In Chapter One, we begin our foray into VoIP with a discussion of why business has migrated to VoIP and what the realities of making a transition can cost, in terms of both tangible and intangible costs. We try to present both the advantages and disadvantages of migrating to VoIP platforms and point out some potential security pitfalls that can be avoided with a little planning beforehand.

Chapter Two presents the concepts of speech and digital voice to the reader. Many steps evolved along the way to enable the human voice to be carried over great distances on copper wire. Issues such as how to take human speech, convert it to a signal, transport that signal from point A to point B, decipher the signal into recognizable speech on the receiving end, and repeat the process from receiver to sender in a duplex fashion are covered in depth. This chapter will help the reader understand the magnitude of the task and what it took in terms of technology evolution to get from the humble beginnings of the telephone to the SIP-phones of today.

Given a solid understanding of speech and digitization techniques, Chapter Three gives the reader a short history lesson on the evolution of the telephone, the basic components needed to conduct a telephone conversation, and how it all evolved. A discussion of signaling is presented in order to help the reader understand how important each aspect of the current telephone system is and how that component evolved out of necessity. Along the way, the reader will gain an understanding of how differences between telephone systems in North America and Europe evolved, why they differ, and what has been done to make them interoperate as they do today.

Before one can truly understand how telephony has evolved, it is essential to understand how data is transmitted over the Internet. Chapter Four presents packet networking and provides an overview of fundamentals of networking, routingm and switching. From this point, the reader is introduced to the many protocols that guide the evolution of the VoIP technology and how voice is transported over Internet. In this chapter, we begin to look at some of the security issues and weaknesses of using Internet for voice and the ways they are dealt with in modern enterprise. VoIP security, transport, and signaling protocols are covered in detail, as well as issues that complicate networking when integrating voice traffic with network traffic.

At this point in the book, the reader should have a solid grasp of the various technologies needed to process Voice over Internet, so Chapter Five introduces the concepts of packetizing voice traffic to accomplish that task. Compression, transport, and routing issues are covered in detail. Also, the chapter discusses the various types of hardware needed to set up and make the calls work. Finally, this chapter will present some of the recent regulatory issues that have been dealt with in the U.S. Congress.

Chapter Six begins with a discussion of quality and reliability and what can be done to achieve acceptable levels of service for VoIP users. Various techniques to achieve an acceptable level of service are presented, along with information needed to help the reader implement VoIP and manage it properly in an organization. Pitfalls that may be encountered along the way to successful implementation are covered, and some techniques to prevent pain during the implementation process are presented.

Chapter Seven discusses most of the known security risks present with a VoIP implementation. The risks are separated into infrastructure risks and attack risks. Each category is covered in great detail, providing the reader with a solid understanding of the vulnerabilities of the technology, along with methods and techniques to avoid becoming a victim of such vulnerabilities. Once the reader has gained a solid understanding of the risks of VoIP, they are ready to take on the task of implementing it in their organization.

Chapter Eight provides a summary of best practices for VoIP and may be unique in that the material herein has been amassed from years of experience and over the course of many implementations. The chapter breaks down best practices into general issues, issues with PBX networks, VoIP networks, protocol issues, addressing and access issues, VPN and IPSec issues, and VoIP phone issues. It provides a comprehensive overview of best practices for nearly every conceivable aspect of VoIP telephony.

Chapter Nine is an overview of VoIP and the law. VoIP, as it relates to current regulations, is a hot topic for lawmakers and the legislative bodies of states and governments are dealing with it from several aspects. Internet commerce, tariffs, transport of funds, and many other issues are just a small part of the can of worms that VoIP has opened up over the last two decades. We try to present a coherent overview of the laws in effect in the U.S. today and explain why they have evolved and what they are meant to accomplish.

In the final chapter of this book, we look to the future and discuss the new breed of telephony devices that are quickly becoming mainstream in today's modern company. The evolution of VoIP continues into the wireless realm, and that evolution presents yet another complex array of security issues that the reader should be aware of when thinking about using VoIP.

We hope the reader finds this book useful and that it helps to make the subject of integrating VoIP with existing technology or infrastructure more approachable. Our goal is to help the reader move forward with confidence and a solid understanding as they explore the pitfalls and potential benefits of using VoIP in their organization. To that end, we encourage the readers to progress through the book in the order presented and digest the material in small chunks. There is a lot of technology to present in a single book, and it is often complex and evolved out of necessity. Do not try to take it all in at once. Let the material slowly soak in, and gain the foundations needed to truly understand the how and why of VoIP. It will be of great advantage to you, the reader, to have the concepts of these converged technologies in your arsenal of knowledge as you move forward in your careers. Best of luck to all of you.

John W. Rittinghouse, Ph.D., CISM

James F. Ransome, Ph.D., CISSP, CISM

Acknowledgments

from James F. Ransome:

I would also like to take this opportunity to give special thanks for the patience of my wife Gail during the many hours that I have spent on the completion of this book and my doctoral dissertation. I would also like to thank Dr. James Cannady, the chairman of my doctoral dissertation committee for teaching me that research is a journey and discipline, not a single point in time. Additional thanks go to Terry Dalby for his technical review of Chapters 7, 8, and 10. I would also like to thank Dr. John Rittinghouse, my co-author, and Theron Shreve of Elsevier/Digital Press for their continued partnership in our series of books and work together.

from John W. Rittinghouse:

Many people besides the authors contribute to the great effort that is required to take an idea from scratch and see it become a finished product. In reality, the author usually depends on quite a few others to help him or her in keeping things in order. This is something that is very true in the case of getting this book out the door and into your hands. My wife, Naree Rittinghouse, is certainly among those I would like to thank for her love and understanding, her encouragement, and most of all, her faith in my work. I would like to thank Dr. Tony Dubendorf for his tireless efforts reviewing each chapter and providing excellent feedback. Bill Hancock is another individual who helped contribute to the success of this book. His expertise in the security realm knows no bounds, and he worked many late nights reviewing, editing, and validating the work herein to ensure its accuracy and relevancy to our cyber-environment of today. Finally, I would like to thank all of the folks at Elsevier/Digital Press for their continued support of my work.

The (Business) Value of VoIP

Have you ever thought to yourself "Why should we do this VoIP thing?" or "What value will voice over Internet provide my company?" or even "What is all this VoIP craze?" Simply put, Voice over Internet Protocol (VoIP) refers to the process of transporting voice communications over Internet Protocol (IP) networks like the Internet. VoIP is somewhat of a misleading term because it implies such a restricted focus on "voice." The term IP Telephony (IPTel) is more general. Telephony over IP (ToIP) describes the transport of real-time text over IP networks. It differs from instant messaging in that ToIP systems transmit bidirectionally one character at a time. This gives the user the feel of real-time communication, just like voice or video systems that transport streaming media over IP. ToIP is a term used to mean the transport of text over IP from a ToIP-enabled IP phone, PC-based client, or a legacy TTY device connected to a Public Switched Telephone Network (PSTN) gateway.

A TTY is also known as a Telecommunications Device for the Deaf (TDD). The TTY consists of a keyboard, which holds somewhere from 20 to 30 character keys, a display screen, and a modem. The letters that the TTY user types into the machine are turned into electrical signals that can travel over regular telephone lines. When the signals reach their destination (usually another TTY), they are converted back into letters, which appear on a display screen, are printed out on paper, or both. Some of the newer TTY devices are even equipped with answering machines. As good as TTY devices are, the innovation that comes from the use of the Internet for communications has far exceeded most expectations when the Internet came into being as a popular new media only a decade or so ago. Now, as with most technologies, VoIP has many potential benefits as well as obstacles that may be encountered. This chapter addresses both the benefits of and obstacles to VoIP.

1.1   Internet Telephony versus Telephony over the Internet

IP Telephony (IPTel) refers to the transport of voice, video, text, and other real-time media over IP networks. IPTel is considered to be a key technology that will provide advances in communication for end users and is expected to completely replace the PSTN over time. According to the International Telecommunication Union (ITU) Web site,[1] the die has been cast for the continued future of IPTel:

> *The Internet and IP-based networks are increasingly being used as alternatives to the public switched telephone network. Internet Telephony Service Providers (ITSPs) can provide voice and fax services which are close to becoming functionally equivalent to those provided by public telecommunication operators (PTOs). However, few ITSPs are licensed by national authorities and they generally do not have any universal service obligations. Many countries ban IP telephony completely, yet IP calls can be made to almost any telephone in the world. Many PTOs are establishing their own IP telephony services, and/or using IP-based networks as alternative transmission platforms. In the longer term, as more and more voice traffic becomes IP data traffic, there will be little to distinguish between IP telephony and circuit-switched telephony. However, many telecommunications regulatory schemes depend upon such a distinction, both physically and as a matter of policy and law. As these trends continue, the telecommunications framework will come under increasing pressure to adapt.*

It is also inevitable that most governments of the world will wrestle with the use of IPTel and determine just how to turn these advances in technology into another form of revenue, for which ordinary users will undoubtably pay, that will be used to create even more forms of bureaucracies, whose specific purpose is to oversee and regulate what is now unregulated and untaxed. Until that time comes, however, the average Internet consumer/user will benefit greatly from such strides in technology.

1.2   The Value of VoIP: Return on Investment (ROI)

ROI is a major selling point for the use of VoIP. Why wouldn't it be? Some of the more attractive components of VoIP are large cost savings (especially in the area of long-distance telephone costs), new features, and converged networks. Bottom-line cost savings are fairly easy to quantify, whereas other VoIP benefits, such as productivity improvements, are more difficult to quantify in terms of ROI. As with most ROIs, there are both hard and soft benefits. Hard benefits are the easiest to sell to management, because they result from clearly defined, tangible cost savings. In contrast, soft benefits are called soft because they don't necessarily save real money, and they are usually harder to quantify from a business perspective. For example, stating that use of XYZ technology will increase productivity because of some inane reason or another is a soft benefit. Clearly, trying to measure productivity increases can become convoluted and subject to interpretation. The inane reason may or may not be something all staff members agree on—the very nature of disagreement that could (and usually does) exist causes this to be considered a soft benefit. Therefore, most organizations focus solely on the hard cost savings, but it is always important to clearly differentiate between hard and soft benefits to improve the credibility of the business case with financial decision makers. The company will not care if it is saving five cents per minute on VoIP calls if their sales productivity is decreasing because of poor-quality or dropped calls.

1.2.1   Getting the Most from VoIP: Cost Savings

The cost of VoIP implementation expenses are an important factor in making IT spending decisions. VoIP implementations can require a significant amount of new equipment and often also require significant infrastructure upgrades. In order to reduce the initial capital outlay necessary for implementing VoIP, many vendor companies are now offering equipment-leasing plans to spread the expense over several years or staging the VoIP deployment gradually as a means of easing the cost burdens. As with any new technology that is introduced into the corporate environment, the ROI scenario may vary across many different site locations. The unique deployment scenarios required for each site usually mean that the cost savings are likely to occur in several business areas, each area seeing individual impact on capital costs, expenses, and user productivity. A successful VoIP implementation will recognize these differences and use them to guide the strategy for inserting VoIP into existing infrastructures. A successful VoIP implementation will be designed as a long-term investment that will provide returns in capital and productivity savings, and help avoid additional security risks.

1.2.2 Capital and Expense Savings

VoIP may be an infrastructure that is already paid for if you own the IP network or are already paying an Internet Service Provider (ISP) for bandwidth. Because long-distance telephone calls are typically a major line item in an organization's budget, the use of VoIP can result in significant capital and expense savings over a PSTN. VoIP users only incur the cost of using the network, in contrast to PSTN users, whose long-distance costs can vary depending on the distance called (location of caller and callee) and the time at which the call occurs.

Centralized call-processing architectures are available from several VoIP manufacturers and can reduce equipment, maintenance, and support costs. These architectures also enable organizations to standardize the voice services that they deliver to their employees. A centralized team can now manage the entire organization's voice services from a single site, rather than requiring internal or outsourced resources to manage each Private Branch Exchange (PBX) or key system.

The use of VoIP can also result in a reduced incremental cost of network ownership. The nearly unlimited capacity of most corporate LANs will allow a new VoIP user to be added at a reduced per-user cost. A VoIP-enabled data network also enables the easy and inexpensive addition of new corporate office networks, which also reduces the expense of incremental costs.

Because of the PSTN toll rate structure, companies with a large number of international sites may find the long-distance phone call cost savings from toll bypass attractive. Bypassing the PSTN and making telephone calls on an IP network is referred to as toll bypass. This occurs when a PBX or an IP PBX is connected to a VoIP gateway, which is then connected to an IP network. Instead of going from the PBX to a PSTN switch, the call traffic goes from the PBX to the VoIP gateway, avoiding the toll or cost of using the PSTN for long-distance calls. In most cases, the long-distance costs associated with PSTN usage should decrease after a VoIP implementation. Some companies may want to keep the PSTN as a fallback network. Many organizations will not convert to VoIP completely or all at once because of disaster recovery and business continuity concerns during the migration phase and proceed in staged implementations.

Rather than absorbing the costs of buying or leasing a PBX and network infrastructure for PSTN calls in addition to an IP network, both voice and data can run on one network, resulting in savings that provide a lower total cost of network ownership for VoIP. Single networks are also easier to expand and change, reduce the wiring costs required for two networks, and can easily incorporate wireless infrastructures.

1.2.3   Productivity Savings

VoIP implementations can also result in quantifiable savings in several areas, including the following:

- Management and support savings
- Enhanced mobility
- Reduced site preparation time

In some cases, infrastructure convergence through the use of VoIP will make it possible to reduce the internal staff required to support and manage the two separate infrastructures. As discussed later in this section, this savings must be balanced with the cost for training, because the management of a converged network requires consolidating existing infrastructure and, in some cases, learning new skills. For example, IT personnel will need to learn telecom skills, and telecom personnel will need to learn data-networking skills.

VoIP offers enhanced mobility, which can allow many organizations to institute more flexible work environments and reduce facilities and real estate costs while increasing employee productivity and morale. This capability allows individuals to log in to any phone within the organization and still have their extension number and any applications or services they use available to them, even though they are away from their desks. For many organizations, this new capability can result in significant cost savings and even revenue growth through increased productivity.

1.2.4   New Features

Some of the most compelling reasons to consider a VoIP implementation are new applications and features, which offer productivity improvements for both end users and IT staff. These fall into the category of soft benefits in that they are not easily quantifiable. These new VoIP applications and features can (1) enable unified messaging through the integration of voice mail, e-mail, and fax, while providing the ability to retrieve your messages anytime, anywhere, and in any way; (2) assist in the elimination of phone tag and provide better support for a remote workforce through advanced call routing that can also include integration with Customer Relationship

Management (CRM) systems to look up customer information and route support calls to the appropriate technical support group; (3) integrate voice, video, and text communications into a single business application; and (4) provide the ability to add new features to VoIP implementation much more quickly and easily than to a traditional PBX because they can take advantage of client/server architecture, open development platforms, and well-known standards to speed deployment of new applications and features.

1.2.5   Convergence of Technologies

Convergence is the consolidation of different types of application traffic such as voice, video, and data on the same IP network. A single network infrastructure and management savings are some of the tangible returns from convergence. If convergence is done correctly, it will provide a single scalable network infrastructure that provides for all of your business communication needs, which will offer both cost and management savings. Although convergence is not an overnight process, it must be started in the concept planning phase of your VoIP deployment project.

Because of its relatively low bandwidth, voice is considered the easiest first step in convergence requirements, to be followed by video and then dedicated Integrated Services Digital Network (ISDN) lines that link conference rooms together for videoconferencing. The addition of video traffic to an IP network can reduce the need for an additional video network infrastructure in support of teleconferencing, corporate training, and distance learning, which provides further benefits in a converged network.

1.2.6   Potential Drawbacks in VoIP Implementations

The potential downsides or obstacles of a VoIP implementation must also be considered when evaluating the ROI. Cost and business risks are major downsides when considering investment in a VoIP implementation. The business risk can be reduced with proper planning and good management. The level of quality and reliability are major challenges when justifying a VoIP ROI, in that you rarely have to worry about these issues with PSTN. In particular, you must be able to meet the challenge or expectation of "five nines" or 99.999% reliabilty when implementing a converged IP network that consolidates voice and data traffic onto one complex subsystem that will most likely also include PSTN fallback. In addition, you must consider what happens if elements of a converged network go down.

A complex network infrastructure upgrade may be required to have VoIP tuned to a level that provides quality levels comparable to those of

PSTN calls. Good voice-quality requirements place strict requirements on the VoIP network traffic, in terms of latency, jitter, and number of lost packets. This will also result in significant costs for the initial deployment of a VoIP infrastructure, in that it will also require new network equipment, servers, IP phones, management software, and diagnostic tools.

VoIP will also requires extensive training for the IT staff and users. This cost must be balanced with the cost for outsourcing some of this expertise. VoIP is a relatively new technology, so personnel with the skills required for successful deployment and management may be difficult to find and expensive to hire. The fear of stepping into the unknown can be overcome by adhering to established IT project principles, such as proper planning, assessment, and management. A VoIP infrastructure deployment should use the same best-practice decision-making and project management processes as any major IT project.

1.2.7 VoIP Implementation Realities of ROI

For the most part, it is unlikely that a VoIP implementation will remove all of the old equipment and replace it with brand-new equipment. To maximize ROI, it is best to deploy VoIP in a staged approach, where the candidate sites or locations are picked at which success is likely and the ROI will be good. A few well-planned quick wins will take advantage of the low-hanging fruit to help you build on your success. Some areas one may consider for achieving VoIP implementation ROI quick wins are the following:

- Implementing VoIP infrastructure in new offices rather than refitting
- Adding VoIP to planned data network upgrades
- Using excess bandwidth capacity where possible for VoIP traffic
- Replacing expiring PBX leases or service contracts with VoIP
- Upgrading voice networks when approaching bandwidth limits
- Using VoIP Virtual Private Networks (VPNs) via IP phones or softphones for remote users
- Leveraging VoIP to converge technologies after a merger or acquisition

1.2.8 What about VoIP Security?

Although there is still a threat of Time Division Multiplexing (TDM) toll fraud in legacy voice systems, the security risks for misuse or attack from individuals or groups outside of a company are low. In contrast, with VoIP you inherit all of the risks of an IP network, including viruses, targeted denial-of-service attacks, and the security of packetized voice conversations, which are possible to intercept. Although revenue growth and cost reduction are always paramount with the senior executives making the business decisions, some industries, including finance and health care, have passed new federal legislation to ensure customer information confidentiality, exposing the company to additional liability. Although considered soft benefits by many, business continuity planning and security are a necessity in the ROI process and will require the participation of the highest-level executives within an organization. Is VoIP technology inherently secure? No. Can it be secured? Yes. The details of why VoIP is not inherently secured and how it can be secured are addressed in Chapters 7 to 9 of this book.

1.3   Summary

VoIP promises to reduce the total cost of ownership of telecommunications and networking through the elimination of various charges and services, by (1) reducing equipment expansion and cutting ongoing costs; (2) avoiding PBX service costs and support contracts; (3) empowering employees with integrated services and increasing productivity; (4) providing cost-effective unified messaging; and (5) reducing systems' downtime and increasing performance; 6) allowing for a flexible call center configuration, improved customer support, reduction in abandoned calls and call times, increased customer satisfaction, and improved security.

These promises may or may not be kept, depending entirely on IT staff leaders who understand how to properly implement and leverage such opportunity; otherwise, welcome to the black hole money pit of corporate project failures. This is a grim reality, but the truth is that VoIP is relatively new and, because of the shortage of case studies on successful deployments, companies struggle to outline the strategic goals, measure tangible benefits, and reduce all of the associated costs and risks.

Cost considerations must also be weighed carefully when planning the deployment of VoIP in your enterprise. Some of the unique costs for VoIP that you must consider include VoIP-specific telecommunication hardware and software, IP phone sets and/or softphones, additional network requirements to achieve acceptable levels of quality of service and performance on par with that provided by PSTN, specialized skill set requirements and costs of having professional services assistance, ongoing support and administration, support and maintenance contracts, initial deployment support calls and potential user downtime losses, training for both IT support and users, and disposal costs for existing infrastructure.

As with all technology, VoIP is not without its risks. Potential risks that should be considered include quality of service/performance, user acceptance, user and staff training, support of varying skill levels and administration resources, and interoperability with existing and future systems, proprietary versus open systems technology, and related interoperability issues. The time is coming to an end where you can have the advantages of gaining a competitive edge from investing in VoIP as an early adopter of this emerging technology. In today's era of tightened spending, the need to build a solid business case is critical and will be necessary to win funding approval. This chapter should serve you well as a general overview of what to look for when making the business case for your investment in VoIP technology.

1.4　Endnotes

1.　　URL reference is: http://www.itu.int/osg/spu/ni/iptel/

1.5　General References

Emmerson, B. (2004). *Convergence: The Business Case for IP Telephony.* Retrieved July 13, 2004 from
www.acaimc.com/downloads/businesscase.pdf

Gartner. (2003). *Business Planning for VoIP and IP–Telephony—train wreck or smooth ride?* Retrieved July 13, 2004 from
www.gartner.com/teleconferences/asset_9148.jsp

NetIQ. (2001). *A Handbook for Successful VoIP Deployment: Network Testing, QoS, and More.* Retrieved July 13, 2004 from
http://itpapers.zdnet.com/abstract.aspx?docid=29619&tag=tu.tk.6587.f1

Pisello, T. (2003). Ask the Expert: Questions and Answers—ROI and IT Investment. Retrieved July 21, 2004 from http://searchcio.techtarget.com/ateQuestionNResponse/0,289625,sid19_cid558148_tax292624,00.html

Roinetworks.com. (2004). *Business case for VoIP, remote agents, and converged communications.* Retrieved July 13, 2004 from
www.roinetworks.com/businessdiscussion.htm

Techabulary. (2004). *Voice over IP (VoIP).* Retrieved July 13, 2004 from www.techabulary.com/v/voip.html

Walker, J. & Hicks, J. (2002). *The Essential Guide to VoIP Implementation and Management*. Retrieved July 13, 2004 from www2.cs.uh.edu/~sujeetv/projects/Ad-Hoc/NetIQ_VoIP_Chapter1.pdf

Walker, J. & Hicks, J. (2004). *Taking Charge of Your VoIP Project*. Indianapolis, IN: Cisco Press.

2

Digital Voice Fundamentals

The most prevalent use of digitized speech today is found in the telephone network. Comprising a global infrastructure and used by hundreds of millions of people, telephony is the most common example of an electronic speech communications system. The networks that connect our phones together are known as Public Switched Telephone Networks (PSTNs). Most PSTN systems use analog communications between our individual telephones and the local switch. Because of the vast scale and the length of time it has taken for speech communications systems to evolve, a significant amount of research has been directed at finding more efficient methods of transferring the spoken word from the point of origination (the speaker's telephone handset) through a copper wire medium and "downwire" to a termination point (the call-receiving handset). Developments in this area over time have resulted in a gradual replacement of analog components with more reliable and modern digital circuits.

Digital communication systems outperform analog systems, especially in the presence of noise, and they provide a means of easily encrypting transmission data for security purposes. However, a trade-off must be made when balancing quality of speech, speed of transmission, and overall line capacity. When such choices are presented, the decision generally evolves into a compromise that balances cost with performance, as is the case in so much of the technology realm we live in today. Speech coding techniques attempt to reduce network bandwidth requirements and simultaneously maintain high-quality speech output during the transmission process. This chapter presents an overview of the major techniques used to accomplish this goal and explains how such techniques have evolved.

An excellent discussion of speech presented in a white paper by Dr. Ciarán McElroy[1] explains how speech signals are inherently analog in nature and, in the process of digitization, a transformation from the continuous domain into a discrete domain must be carried out before any digital coding can be performed. The transformation process uses time sampling techniques followed by amplitude discretization (in a process known as *quantization*, explained later in this chapter). The sampling process, if carried out at a sufficiently high rate, enables information to be preserved without any significant loss of quality. The quantization process, on the other hand, always introduces some distortion into the signal. The primary goal researchers seek to achieve in speech coding processes is to design a low-complexity speech coder that is capable of producing high-quality speech using the lowest data transmission rate possible. The properties of low complexity, high-quality output, and a low bit rate tend to be mutually exclusive, and a trade-off exists in practical coders. In the next section, we describe how human speech is produced and categorized.

2.1   Speech Properties

All human speech sounds are formed by forcing air from the lungs through the vocal tract. The *vocal folds* comprise two membranes located in the larynx. These membranes allow the area of the trachea (the *glottis*) to be varied. In an average man, the vocal tract extends from the opening of the vocal folds to the mouth and is generally about 17 centimeters in length. When air passes through the vocal tract, it introduces short-term variations (approximately 1 millisecond in duration) into the speech signal. These variations can be thought of as a filtering mechanism that introduces resonance qualities into the sound. These resonance qualities are called *formants*. The frequencies produced for formants are controlled by the varying shape of the vocal tract and the movement of the tongue.

An important component found in many speech codecs is a short-term filter that will attempt to mimic the human vocal tract. Because the shape of the vocal tract varies relatively slowly during speech, the transfer function for its modeling filter only needs to be updated relatively infrequently (20-millisecond intervals). The vocal tract filter is excited when air is forced into it through the vocal cords. When breathing, the vocal folds remain open. During speech production, the vocal folds open and close. Each open-and-close cycle of vocal fold vibration is caused both by the subglottal air pressure that has built up sufficiently to separate the folds and by the Bernoulli effect, which, as the air runs through the glottis at an increased velocity, accounts for a sudden drop in pressure against the inner sides of each fold and sucks them together again. The types of sounds that are generated in the speech process can generally be broken into three broad categories:

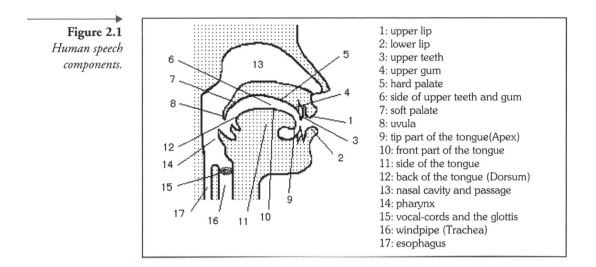

Figure 2.1
*Human speech
components.*

1: upper lip
2: lower lip
3: upper teeth
4: upper gum
5: hard palate
6: side of upper teeth and gum
7: soft palate
8: uvula
9: tip part of the tongue(Apex)
10: front part of the tongue
11: side of the tongue
12: back of the tongue (Dorsum)
13: nasal cavity and passage
14: pharynx
15: vocal-cords and the glottis
16: windpipe (Trachea)
17: esophagus

voiced, unvoiced, and plosive. Figure 2.1 illustrates the components used in production of speech.

2.2   Classes of Speech

There are three basic categories of speech used by researchers to help them consistently describe the types of sounds produced by human beings. *Voiced sounds, unvoiced sounds,* and *plosives* are the most common terms used to describe the types of speech we are able to produce. Each category describes a grouping of sounds that can be produced based on the way we move air through our bodies and how we move specific organs in the process.

2.2.1   Voiced Sounds

During voiced speech, the vocal folds are normally closed. As our lungs force air out, air pressure builds up behind the folds. Eventually, the air pressure is sufficient enough to force the folds to open. The resulting out-flow of air causes the vocal folds to vibrate in a *relaxation oscillation.* Voiced sounds are produced when our vocal cords vibrate open and closed, interrupting the air flow and creating quasi-periodic pulses of air to emanate from the vocal folds. The natural effect of this quasi-periodic opening and closing of the glottis is that air passing through the remainder of the vocal tract forms a quasi-periodic *pulse train.* The frequency generated as a result of this vibration is determined by the length of the vocal folds and their tension. This vibration frequency is known as the *pitch frequency.*

The rate at which the glottis opens and closes determines the pitch of the sound that emanates from the vocal tract. This pitch changes as a result of the varying shape and the tension of the vocal cords and the pressure of the air behind them. Voiced sounds show a high degree of periodicity at the pitch period, which is typically between 2 and 20 milliseconds (ms). For normal speakers, this pitch can be anywhere in the range of 50 to 400 Hertz (Hz). Women and children tend to produce a higher average pitch frequency than do men because the length of their vocal folds is generally much shorter than the length of the average man's vocal folds.

2.2.2 Unvoiced Sounds

During unvoiced speech, the vocal folds are normally open so air can pass freely into the rest of the vocal tract. Unvoiced sounds are generated by forming a constriction at some point along the vocal tract and forcing air through the constriction. Such sounds show little long-term periodicity. The vocal folds do not vibrate in this process. An example of an unvoiced sound is "s" as in "six."

2.2.3 Plosive Sounds

Plosive sounds result when a complete closure is made in the vocal tract and air pressure that is built up behind this closure is released suddenly. Plosive sounds are the result of an explosion of air that creates a sharp noise. Articulation of any plosive sound includes three distinct phases: during the first phase, called the *approach*, the articulators are moving together, preparing to block the airstream; the second stage, called the *hold* or *closure*, occurs when the articulators completely block the speech tract, thereby preventing air from going out and contributing to a buildup of pressure in the airstream; during the third and last stage, called the *release*, or *plosion*, the speech organs move swiftly, releasing the air with an explosion of sound. If the stricture or narrowing of the vocal tract does not completely close and a narrow passageway is left for air to go out, the pressure build necessary for the formation of a plosive is insufficient. The resulting sound that is uttered is not accompanied by this sudden burst of air when pressure is released. Instead, a continuous flow of air is created, and the articulation results in a friction between the airstream and the speech organs. Such sounds created by this friction are called *fricatives*.

Some sounds cannot be considered to fall into any one of the three classes, but are a mixture. For example, voiced fricatives result when both vocal cord vibration and a constriction in the vocal tract are present.

Although many possible speech sounds can be produced, the shape of the vocal tract and its mode of excitation change relatively slowly, so speech can be considered to be quasi-stationary over short periods (approximately 20 ms). Speech signals show a high degree of predictability, sometimes because of the quasi-periodic vibrations of the vocal cords and also because of the resonances of the vocal tract. Speech coders attempt to exploit this predictability in order to reduce the data rate necessary for good-quality voice transmission.

2.3   Sampling

A speech signal is continuous in time. Before it can be processed by digital hardware, it must be converted into a signal that is discrete in time. Sampling is a process that converts a continuous time signal into a discrete time signal by measuring the signal at periodic intervals in time. As the number of samples per second (the sampling rate) increases, the sampled signal approximates the continuous signal more closely. In fact, if the sampling rate is high enough, the sampled signal will contain all of the information that is present in the continuous signal. The *Nyquist Sampling Theorem* states that a signal may be perfectly reconstructed if it is sampled at a rate greater than or equal to twice the frequency of the highest frequency component of the signal. In 1933, Henry Nyquist discovered that the maximum signaling rate of a noiseless channel was twice the number of samples.[2] This can be seen when observing a standard sine wave carrier signal. The natural form of a sine wave allows us to see that every half cycle is a mirror image of the other half of the sine wave. This fact leads to the conclusion that the sampling rate must be twice the highest frequency, because each cycle of the waveform corresponds to two values: one for positive amplitude level and the other for negative amplitude level. If there are w cycles per second (Hertz), then $2w$ signal states exist. Figure 2.2 illustrates this concept (shown on the following page).

If a noiseless communications channel uses N values per signaling state, then the channel's maximum data transmission capacity can be calculated in bits as follows:

Maximum data rate = $2w\mathbf{Log_2}N$ bits per second

where w is the number of cycles (in Hertz) and N is the number of discrete signaling states used.

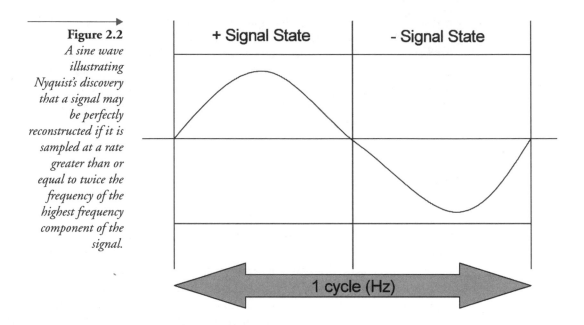

Figure 2.2
A sine wave illustrating Nyquist's discovery that a signal may be perfectly reconstructed if it is sampled at a rate greater than or equal to twice the frequency of the highest frequency component of the signal.

This relationship is known as Nyquist's Sampling Theorem and is the basis for pulse code modulation (which is explained later in this chapter).

2.4   Quantization

Quantization is defined as a process in which the continuous range of values of an analog signal are sampled and divided into nonoverlapping (but not necessarily equal) subranges, and a discrete, unique value is assigned to each subrange. The value of each signal sample is represented by a value selected from a finite set of possible values. The difference between the unquantized input and the quantized output is called the *quantization error* (or *noise*), and it is desirable to minimize the perceived magnitude of this error. In order to achieve this objective, several quantization techniques have been developed (e.g., uniform quantization, logarithmic quantization, nonuniform quantization, and vector quantization). All such quantization schemes can be made to adapt to the input waveform's particular statistics so that the quantizer will always be optimum and provide the highest possible quality with the lowest possible bit rate. Obviously, the operations performed by the quantizer are critical to the overall performance of a digital speech system. Unfortunately, as researchers strive to increase the efficiency of quantizers, complexity and cost factors also increase correspondingly.

2.4.1 **Uniform or Linear Quantizers**

Uniform or linear quantizers are those in which the distances between all of the reconstruction levels are the same. They make no assumptions about the nature of the signal being quantized. For this reason, linear quantizers normally do not provide the best performance. However, they are usually the simplest and cheapest form of quantizer to implement. In order to quantize speech for telephone operations (i.e., analog signals sampled at 8 kHz and bandpass filtered in a frequency range from 300 to 3,400 Hz), a 13-bit uniform quantizer is necessary to provide toll-quality speech.

2.4.2 **Nonuniform (Logarithmic) Quantization**

The problem with uniform quantization is that as the signal amplitude decreases, the Signal-to-Noise Ratio (SNR) decreases. This problem is partially solved by logarithmic quantizers. However, if the Probability Distribution Function (PDF) of the input is known, one can match reconstruction levels to the PDF, so the mean squared quantization error is minimized. This means that most of the reconstruction levels occur in the vicinity of the most likely inputs. It has the effect of minimizing the perceived quantization errors. Speech signals can have a dynamic range exceeding 60 decibels, so a large number of reconstruction levels are necessary for the uniform quantizer to attain high-quality speech. However, quantizer resolution is more important for the low-amplitude parts of a signal than for the high-amplitude parts of a signal. Therefore, it should be obvious that the uniform quantizer is wasteful in reconstruction levels and, hence, wastes bandwidth. The situation could be improved if the distance between the reconstruction levels increased as the amplitude of the signal increased. A simple method of achieving this effect is to pass the signal through a compressor with a logarithmic characteristic before quantization. This compressed signal can then be uniformly quantized. This technique is known as companding.

2.4.3 **Companding**

In the Analog-to-Digital (A/D) conversion process, a compression technique is used to compensate for errors that occur when assigning values to each sample. Such errors can occur when a sampled signal may not correspond exactly to a quantized value. This assignment process is called *companding*. Distortion in quantization occurs as a result of differences between quantized steps. Studies have shown that it takes 2,048 quantizing steps to provide a sufficient level of granularity to represent the human voice accurately.[3] It requires an 11-bit code to represent these 2,048 steps (8,000 × 11 = 88,000 bits per second). Telephonic voice signals are capable of as much as a 30-decibel variation in range, so it made sense to vary the distribution of these 2,048 quantization steps. This helps reduce quantizing noise and provides a better output signal. Nonlinear companding is implemented in a stepwise linear process using either A-law or μ-law coding (explained in following sections).

2.4.4 Vector Quantization

In the quantization methods previously described, each sample was quantized independently from its neighboring samples. Rate distortion theory tells us that this is not the most efficient method of quantizing input data. It is always more efficient to quantize the data in blocks of N samples. The process is simply an extension of the scalar quantization methods described previously. With scalar quantization, the input sample is treated as a number on the real number line and rounded off to predetermined discrete points. For vector quantization, the block of N samples is treated as an N-dimensional vector and is quantized to predetermined points in the N-dimensional space. Vector quantization can always outperform scalar quantization. However, it is more sensitive to transmission errors and usually involves a much greater computational complexity than scalar quantization.

2.5   Waveform Coding

Waveform coders/decoders (*codecs*) attempt to produce a reconstructed signal whose waveform is as close as possible to the original without using any knowledge of how the signal to be coded was generated. This means that, in theory, codecs should be signal independent and work well with non-speech signals. Generally, such codecs are of relatively low complexity and are capable of producing high-quality speech at transmission rates above 16 kilobits (kbits) per second. When the transmission rate is lowered below this level, reconstructed speech quality degrades rapidly. Waveform coders are generally designed to be signal-independent so they can be used to code a wide variety of signals in addition to those produced by speech. These codecs exhibit a graceful degradation in the presence of noise and transmission errors. However, to be most effective, they can only be used at medium bit rates. Waveform coding can be carried out in either time or frequency domains. Various types of waveform coding are discussed in the next several sections.

2.5.1 Time Domain Coding: Pulse Code Modulation (G.711)

The simplest form of waveform coding is Pulse Code Modulation (PCM), which merely involves sampling and quantizing the input waveform. Narrow-band speech is usually band-limited to 4 kilohertz (kHz) and is typically sampled 8,000 times per second (8 kHz). Every speech sample must be quantized. If a linear quantization process is used, then 12 bits per sample are required to create a bit rate of 96 kilobits per second (kb/s). However, this bit rate can easily be reduced by using a process known as *nonlinear quantization*. For the purposes of coding speech with nonlinear quantization, it was found that 8 bits per sample rather than 12 bits per sample was nearly as efficient for reproducing speech with a quality almost indistinguishable from the original sound.

In speech coding processes, it is common practice to implement an approximation to a logarithmic quantizer. Such approximated quantizers produce a Signal to Noise Ratio (SNR) that is nearly constant over a wide range of input signal levels. At a processing rate of 8 bits/sample (or 64 kbits/s), they can produce a reconstructed signal nearly identical to the original and literally indistinguishable to the human ear. Two such nonlinear PCM codecs were standardized in the 1960s: μ-law (pronounced *mu-law*) and A-law.

In America, μ-law coding is the standard used, known as G.711u, while in Europe the slightly different A-law compression standard, G.711a, is used. Because of their simplicity, excellent quality, and low delay, both of these codecs are still widely used today. For example, the .au audio files that are often used to convey sounds over the Web are in fact just PCM files. A discussion of the encoding methodology for both A-law and μ-law standards is presented as follows.

A-law Coding

With **A** set to a constant value of 87.56, the curve for the A-law can be plotted from the following formula:

$$Y = \frac{Ax}{(1+\log A)} \quad 0 \le \frac{V}{A}$$

$$Y = \frac{1+\log(Ax)}{(1+\log A)} \quad \frac{V}{A} \le v \le V$$

where **v** represents instantaneous input voltage and **V** represents the maximum input voltage, **x** has the value of **v/V** and varies between -1 and 1, **Y** has the value of **i/B** where **i** is the number of quantization steps starting from the center of range and **B** is the number of quantization steps on each side of the center of range.

μ-law Coding

The curve for μ-law can be plotted from the following formula

$$\mu = \frac{\log\,(1+\mu x)}{\log\,(1+\mu)}$$

where μ has a value of 255 and x has the value of v/V and varies between -1 and 1.

Both A-law and μ-law define the number of quantizing levels used to describe a sound sample and how those levels are arranged. Under μ-law, the quantization scale is divided into 255 discrete units of two different sizes called *chords* and *steps*.

Chords are spaced logarithmically, with each succeeding chord larger than the preceding one. Within each chord, 16 steps are spaced linearly. Thus, steps are larger in larger chords. In practice, the μ-law uses 16 chords: 8 for the positive side of the signal and 8 for the negative side of a signal. Because there are 16 steps in each chord and zero level is shared, the number of levels used becomes 16 × 16 − 1 = 255. The spacing of chords and steps is shown in Figure 2.3.

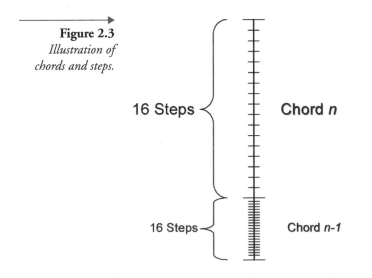

Figure 2.3
Illustration of chords and steps.

16 Steps — Chord *n*

16 Steps — Chord *n-1*

Instead of directly encoding a step to represent the power level of a sample, each PCM word is segmented into three parts: a polarity bit, a three-bit segment for the chord value, and a four-bit segment to represent one of 16 possible steps within a chord. The trisegmented word is illustrated in Figure 2.4.

Figure 2.4
PCM word format.

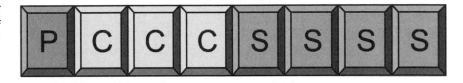

In Figure 2.4, P represents the polarity bit, CCC represents the three-bit chord value, and SSSS represents the four-bit step value. In comparison to μ-law, which uses 16 chord segments, A-law uses 13 segments to format a PCM word. In A-law, six segments are used to represent the positive portion of a signal, and a zero chord represents the 13th segment. In either case, μ-law or A-law, the result is an eight-bit PCM word. With 8,000 samples taken per second, the coding process results in a digital stream of 64 kbps, capable of transporting one PCM analog voice stream. This single digital stream is referred to as a *digital signal, level 0*, or DS0 in the telecommunications industry. It is an essential building block of the PSTN.

PCM Multiplexing

Communications carriers generally encode PCM signals for group transmission because it is much more economical and practical to use transmission lines to capacity than to transmit a single signal at a time. This process, known as *multiplexing*, dates back to the early 1960s and allows a U.S. carrier to transmit 24 voice conversations (or 30 in Europe) simultaneously. Originally, PCM multiplexing was established at the Central Offices (COs) of carriers out of necessity in order to relieve urban congestion. Carriers installed specialized equipment known as *channel banks* in the COs that consisted of a coder-decoder (codec), a Time Division Multiplexer (TDM), and a Line Driver. The purpose of the codec was to simultaneously accept a group of 24 analog voice signals (24 DS0s) and sample each signal 8,000 times per second. This process produced a series of signals known as PAM signals that were quantized and coded into 8-bit bytes. The purpose of the TDM was to combine the digital bit stream created from each of the 24 analog voice streams into a single high-speed serial bit stream. When creating this serial bit stream, a single framing bit was added to every sequence of 24 eight-bit groupings. This framing bit occurs 8,000 times per second and provides synchronization for the transmission. This results in each multiplexed frame consisting of 193 bits ((24 × 8) +1). Because frames are transmitted 8,000 times per second, the multiplexer produces a serial bit rate of 193 bits per frame times 8,000 frames per second, or 1.54 Mbps, the operating rate of a *trunk level 1* circuit, also known as a T-1 line. The channel bank system was a forerunner to the T-carrier system used today for data transmissions.

The purpose of the Line Driver in the channel bank was to convert the serial bit stream into bipolar signals for transmission "down-line." This is equivalent in function to the Channel Service Unit/Data Service Unit (CSU/DSU) used in networking today. A repeater was needed to repropagate the digital signal down-line across copper wire transmission lines at intervals of approximately every 6,000 feet. The use of a repeater ensured delivery of a signal without distortion because it actually regenerated a new pulse at each repeater interval. Repeaters are essentially the digital equivalent of an amplifier, which is used to boost analog signals during transmission.

Using channel banks for voice transmission resulted in better signal quality than analog transmissions. The multiplexing process allowed for each T-1 circuit to carry 24 DS0 voice conversations simultaneously. This method of waveform encoding is used worldwide, with slight differences in the companding process. These slight encoding differences were only one instance of why it was necessary for the International Telecommunication Union (ITU) to evolve in order to respond to continual advances in technology and establish a set of global standards that allow telecommunications carriers around the globe to work interchangeably. What follows is a brief history of the evolution of the ITU (portions extracted from the ITU web site[4]).

Evolution of the International Telecommunication Union (ITU)

On May 24, 1844, Samuel Morse sent his first public message over a telegraph line between Washington and Baltimore and ushered in the telecommunications era. Within 10 years, telegraphy was available as a service to the general public. In those days, however, telegraph lines did not cross national borders. Because each country used a different system, messages had to be transcribed, translated, and handed over at frontiers, then retransmitted over the telegraph network of the neighboring country. Given the slow and unwieldy nature of this system, many countries eventually decided to establish arrangements that would facilitate interconnection of their national networks. However, because such arrangements were managed by each country at a national level, setting up telegraph links often required a huge number of separate agreements. In the case of Prussia, for example, no less than 15 agreements were required for the link between the capital and the frontier localities bordering other German states. To simplify matters, countries began to develop bilateral or regional agreements, so that by 1864, several regional conventions were in place.

The continuing rapid expansion of telegraph networks in a growing number of countries finally prompted 20 European states to meet to develop a framework agreement covering international interconnection. At the same time, the group decided on common rules to standardize equipment to facilitate international interconnection, adopted uniform operating instructions that would apply to all countries, and laid down common international tariff and accounting rules.

On May 17, 1865, after two and a half months of arduous negotiation, the first International Telegraph Convention was signed in Paris by the 20 founding members, and the International Telegraph Union (ITU) was established to facilitate subsequent amendments to this initial agreement. Today, some 135 years later, the reasons that led to the establishment of the ITU still apply, and the fundamental objectives of the organization remain basically unchanged.

Following the patenting of the telephone in 1876 and the subsequent expansion of telephony, the ITU began, in 1885, to draw up international legislation governing telephony. With the invention in 1896 of wireless telegraphy—the first type of radiocommunication—and the utilization of this new technique for maritime and other purposes, it was decided to convene a preliminary radio conference in 1903 to study the question of international regulations for radiotelegraph communications. The first International Radiotelegraph Conference, held in 1906 in Berlin, signed the first International Radiotelegraph Convention, and the annex to this Convention contained the first regulations governing wireless telegraphy. These regulations, which have since been expanded and revised by numerous radio conferences, are now known as the Radio Regulations.

The year 1920 saw the beginning of sound broadcasting at the improvised studios of the Marconi Company, and in 1927, the International Radio Consultative Committee (CCIR) was established at a conference held in Washington, D.C. The International Telephone Consultative Committee (CCIF, set up in 1924), the International Telegraph Consultative Committee (CCIT, set up in 1925), and the CCIR were made responsible for coordinating the technical studies, tests, and measurements being carried out in the various fields of telecommunications, as well as for drawing up international standards.

The 1927 International Radiotelegraph Conference also allocated frequency bands to the various radio services in existence at the time (fixed, maritime, and aeronautical mobile, broadcasting, amateur, and experimental), to ensure greater efficiency of operation in view of the increase in the number of radiocommunication services and the technical peculiarities of each service.

At the 1932 Madrid Conference, the ITU decided to combine the International Telegraph Convention of 1865 and the International Radiotelegraph Convention of 1906 to form the International Telecommunication Convention. It was also decided to change the name of the ITU to International Telecommunication Union. The new name, which came into effect on January 1, 1934, was chosen to properly reflect the full scope of the ITU's responsibilities, which by this time covered all forms of wireline and wireless communication.

In 1947, after World War II, the ITU held a conference in Atlantic City, New Jersey, with the aim of developing and modernizing the organization. Under an agreement with the newly created United Nations, it became a UN specialized agency on October 15, 1947, and the headquarters of the organization in Switzerland were transferred in 1948 from Bern to Geneva. At the same time, the International Frequency Registration Board (IFRB) was established to coordinate the increasingly complicated task of managing the radio-frequency spectrum, and the Table of Frequency Allocations, introduced in 1912, was declared mandatory.

In 1956, the CCIT and the CCIF were merged to form the International Telephone and Telegraph Consultative Committee (CCITT), in order to respond more effectively to the requirements generated by the development of these two types of communication. The following year was marked by the launch of the first artificial satellite, *Sputnik-1*, and the beginning of the space age. In 1963, the first geostationary communications satellite (*Syncom-1*) was put into orbit following the suggestion, made by writer Arthur C. Clarke in 1945, that satellites could be used for the transmission of information.

In order to meet the challenges of new space communications systems, in 1959 the CCIR set up a study group responsible for studying space radiocommunication. In addition, an Extraordinary Administrative Conference for space communications was held in 1963 in Geneva to allocate frequencies to the various space services. Subsequent conferences made further allocations and put in place regulations governing the use, by satellites, of the radio-frequency spectrum and associated orbital slots. In 1992, allocations were made for the first time to serve the needs of a new kind of space service using nongeostationary satellites, known as Global Mobile Personal Communications by Satellite (GMPCS). The same year, spectrum was identified for IMT-2000, the ITU-developed next-generation global standard for digital mobile telephony. Due for commercial implementation early in this new millennium, IMT-2000 will harmonize the incompatible mobile systems currently in use around the world while providing a technical foundation for new, high-speed wireless devices capable of handling voice, data, and connection to online services such as the Internet.

In 1989, the Plenipotentiary Conference held in Nice, France, recognized the importance of placing technical assistance to developing countries on the same footing as its traditional activities of standardization and spectrum management. To this end, it established the Telecommunication Development Bureau to step up efforts being made to improve communications in the developing regions of the world. At the same time, against a background of increasing globalization and the gradual liberalization of world telecommunication markets, the Nice Plenipotentiary Conference initiated a reevaluation of the Union's structures, operation, working methods, and the resources allocated to enable it to achieve its objectives. The conference established a committee of experts whose task was to recommend changes that would ensure that the ITU continued to respond effectively to the needs of its members. In 1992, a plenipotentiary conference, known as the Additional Plenipotentiary Conference, took place in Geneva and dramatically remodeled the ITU, with the aim of giving it greater flexibility to adapt to today's increasingly complex, interactive, and competitive environment.

As a result of the reorganization, the ITU was streamlined into three sectors, corresponding to its three main areas of activity: Telecommunication Standardization (ITU-T), Radiocommunication (ITU-R), and Telecommunication Development (ITU-D). The new system also introduced a regular cycle of conferences to help the ITU rapidly respond to new technological advances.

The Kyoto Plenipotentiary Conference in 1994 adopted the first-ever strategic plan for the ITU, which advocated a more client-oriented approach and a program of activities centered around the changing roles, needs, and functions of ITU members. In addition, the Kyoto conference identified a need for a forum where members could engage in broad, informal discussions on global telecommunication policies and strategies. It thus established the World Telecommunication Policy Forum (WTPF), an ad hoc meeting that encourages the free exchange of ideas and information on emerging policy issues arising from the changing telecommunication environment. The first WTPF was held in Geneva in 1996 on the theme of global mobile personal communications by satellite, and the second in Geneva in 1998, on trade in telecommunication services.

The ITU's most recent plenipotentiary conference, held in Minneapolis, Minnesota, from October 12 to November 6, 1998, focused on strengthening the participation of the private sector in the work of the ITU and adopted several resolutions that enhance the rights of sector members, as well as measures to provide the ITU with the flexibility and latitude needed to match the industry's time frames and operational practices. The conference approved the establishment of a new World Summit on the Information Society, and called for greater ITU participation in the evolution of the Internet as a means of global communication.

2.5.2   G.711 PCM Standardization

The ITU established Recommendation G.711 as the standard for PCM. The companding differences between North American μ-law and European A-Law are so slight that the human ear cannot distinguish a difference, and both allow for a high-quality reproduction of the signal to be produced. With carriers having to spend billions of dollars over the years developing an infrastructure based on this method of waveform coding, it is easy to see why it is still used today, even though technical improvements and advancements have allowed for variations that produce near-toll-quality voice at lower data rates than PCM. These variations include Differential Pulse Code Modulation (DPCM), Adaptive Differential Pulse Code Modulation (ADPCM), and Continuously Variable Slope Delta Modulation (CVSDM).

2.5.3   Time Domain Coding: Differential PCM (DPCM)

PCM makes no assumptions about the nature of the waveform to be coded, hence it works very well for nonspeech signals. However, when coding speech, there is a very high correlation between adjacent samples. This correlation could be used to reduce the resulting bit rate. One simple method of doing this is to transmit only the differences between each sample. This difference signal will have a much lower dynamic range than the original speech, so it can be effectively quantized using a quantizer with fewer reconstruction levels. In this method, the previous sample is being used to predict the value of the present sample. Obviously, the prediction would be improved if a much larger block of the speech were used to make the prediction. This technique is known as *Differential Pulse Code Modulation* (DPCM).

2.5.4 Time Domain Coding: Adaptive Differential PCM (G.721/G.726)

With DPCM both the predictor and the quantizer remain fixed in time. Greater efficiency could be achieved if the quantizer adapted to the changing statistics of the prediction residual. Further gains could be made if the predictor could adapt to the speech signal. This would ensure that the mean squared prediction error was being continually minimized independently of the speaker and the speech signal. There are two methods for adapting quantizers and predictors: feed-forward and feed-backward adaptation. With *feed-forward adaptation*, the reconstruction levels and the prediction coefficients are calculated at the transmitter, using a block of speech. They are then quantized and transmitted to the receiver as side information. Both the transmitter and the receiver use these quantized values to make the predictions and quantize the residual. For *feed-backward adaptation*, the reconstruction levels and predictor coefficients are calculated using the coded signal. Because this signal is known to both the transmitter and the receiver, there is no need to transmit any side information, so the predictor and quantizer can be updated for every sample. Feed-backward adaptation can produce lower bit rates, but it is more sensitive to transmission errors than feed-forward adaptation techniques. Adaptive Differential Pulse Code Modulation (ADPCM) is very useful for coding speech in medium bit rates. The ITU has formalized a standard for coding telephone speech in 32 kb/s, the G.721 standard (superceded by G.726). It uses a feed-backward adaptation scheme for both the quantizer and the predictor. The predictor has two poles and six zeros, so it will produce a reasonable quality output for nonspeech inputs.

2.5.5 Continuously Variable Slope Delta (CVSD) Modulation

CVSD is a type of delta modulation in which the size of the steps of the approximated signal is progressively increased or decreased as required to make the approximated signal more closely match the input analog wave.[5] CVSD modulation is a method of digitizing a band-limited audio signal.[6] The CVSD modulator is, in essence, a 1-bit A/D converter. The output of this 1-bit encoder is a serial bit stream, where each bit represents an incremental increase or decrease in signal amplitude and is determined as a function of recent sample history. A CVSD converter consists of an encoder-decoder pair. The decoder is connected in a feedback path. The encoder receives a band-limited audio signal and compares it to the analog output of the decoder. The result of the comparison is a serial string of ones and zeros. Each bit indicates that the band-limited audio sample's amplitude is above or below the decoded signal. When a run of three identical bits is encountered, the slope of the generated analog approximation is increased in its respective direction until the identical string of bits is broken. The CVSD decoder performs the inverse operation of the encoder and regenerates the audio signal.

2.5.6 Frequency Domain Coding

Frequency domain waveform coders split the signal into several separate frequency components and encode these independently. The number of bits used to code each frequency component can be varied dynamically. The two primary methods discussed in this chapter are subband and transform coding.

Subband (G.722) Coding

This is the simplest of the frequency domain techniques. In the subband coder, the signal is passed through a bank of bandpass filters. Each subband is then lowpass translated, and the sampling rates are reduced to the Nyquist rate for each band. The subbands are then coded using one of the time domain techniques described previously. The number of bits assigned to each band can be varied according to the band's perceptual importance. At the receiver, the sampling rates are increased and the bands are modulated back to their original positions. They are then summed to produce the output speech.

The main advantage of subband coding is that the quantization noise produced in one band is confined to that band. This prevents the quantization noise from masking frequency components in other bands. This means that separate quantizer step sizes can be used for each band. Therefore, bands with lower energy can have lower step sizes and hence are preserved in the reconstructed signal. The confinement of the quantization noise also allows a perceptually weighted distribution of bits. Subband coding has found widespread use in wide-bandwidth, high-quality commentary channels for teleconferencing. These systems commonly use a coder described in the ITU's G.722 standard.

Transform Coding

This is a more complex technique and involves a block transformation of a windowed segment of the input signal. The idea is that the signal is transformed into the frequency or some other similar domain in such a way that the samples are uncorrelated. Coding is then accomplished by assigning more bits to more important transform coefficients. At the receiver, the decoder then carries out the inverse transform to obtain the reconstructed signal.

2.5.7 Vocoding

The Vocoder (**V**oice-**O**perated re**C**or**DER**), developed in 1936 by Homer Dudley, a research physicist at Bell Laboratories, in New Jersey, was a composite device consisting of an analyzer and an artificial voice. The vocoder is an audio processor that captures the characteristic elements of an audio signal and then uses this characteristic signal to alter other audio signals. Vocoding is a method for encoding and reducing the bandwidth of speech signals (*bandwidth* refers to the amount of information either in a signal or that can be carried by a communications channel). Vocoders enable the timbre of one signal to be modified by that of another. The vocoder was initially used in attempts to synthesize speech. The basic component extracted during the vocoder analysis is called the *formant*. The formant describes the fundamental frequency of a sound and its associated noise components. The analyzer detected energy levels of successive sound samples measured over the entire audio frequency spectrum via a series of narrow-band filters. The results could be viewed graphically as functions of frequency against time. Figure 2.5 shows the basic operation of a vocoder.[7]

The synthesizer reversed the process by scanning the data from the analyzer and supplying the results to a feedback network of analytic filters energized by a noise generator to produce audible sounds. The fidelity of the machine was limited because the machine was intended as a research machine for compression schemes to transmit voice over copper phone lines. Werner Meyer-Eppler, then the director of Phonetics at Bonn University, in Germany, recognized the relevance of the machines to electronic music after Dudley visited the university in 1948 and used the vocoder as a basis for his future writings which, in turn, became the inspiration for the German "Electronische Musik" movement.

Figure 2.5
Vocoder components.

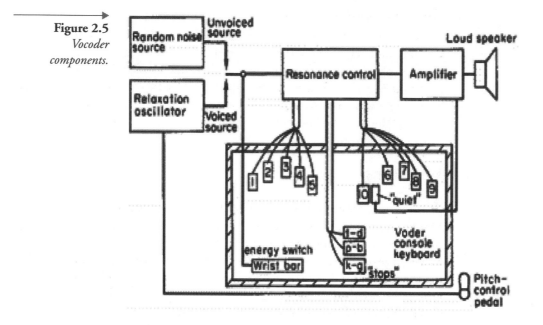

Operation and Types of Vocoders

A vocoder works by taking an input signal and subsequently feeding that signal through a series of Parallel Signal Filters (PSFs) in order to create a Filter Signature (FS), which is based on both the frequency and input level of the frequency components. The resulting signal is then fed into another vocoder input, and the FS created previously is used to filter the synthesized sound. The output signal from the vocoder contains the synthesized sound modulated by the filter. This synthesized sound pulses to the tempo of a voice input signal with tonal characteristics added.

Formant Vocoder   An interesting branch of vocoder research investigated the analysis of formants, or resonances of the voice. The formant vocoder attempted to ascertain the individual formant locations, amplitudes, and bandwidths, as well as the excitation source type (harmonic or noise-like). This resulted in a representation of the voice defined by a compact and efficient parameter set. Difficulties were encountered, however, in the extraction of the formant parameters, and the sound quality of the reconstructed speech was fairly low. Eventually, the formant vocoder for speech coding was surpassed by other coding techniques that provided better sound quality at comparable bit rates. Formant-based techniques have also been explored extensively for parametric voice synthesis, again emphasizing the close relationship of models for coding and synthesis.

Homomorphic Analysis and Coding Homomorphic analysis is a process used to convert a given input into a pseudo-time domain known as *quefrency*, using a transformation called the real Cepstrum. In this domain, convoluted components are spatially separated so that slow-varying components (such as the vocal tract) lie closer to the origin, whereas fast-varying components (such as the glottis) are spread out over the rest of the *quefrency* domain. Consequently, the Cepstrum of an input can be time-segmented into glottal and vocal tract components. This process is particularly useful in speech analysis because it gives a "pure" spectral analysis of the final output without the side effects of the glottal input. The length of the Cepstral window is influential on the quality of the results; if the window is too short, the output will be too smooth to be of any use; if the window is too long, the output will closely resemble the input and again be of little use. Ideally, the window should be a rectangular window of half the length of the speech's pitch (this inherently makes the process more difficult for higher-pitched speakers such as women and children).

The homomorphic vocoder is based on analysis work performed by Alan Oppenheim in 1966 and was implemented by Tom Stockham and Neil Miller for the separation of voice from orchestra and subsequent sound restoration in recordings of solo tenor Enrico Caruso. It is an extension of the principles of the channel vocoder using homomorphic transformations to the Cepstral (inverse log-Fourier) domain. In this domain, what was multiplication in the frequency domain (and thus convolution in the time domain) becomes a simple addition using logarithms. The original voice signal is represented as an addition of excitation and source in the Cepstral domain, and estimation of the separated functions becomes easier. This separation is used for more accurate pitch tracking and spectral estimation and can result in very high-quality reconstruction.

The homomorphic approach is much more robust in that the defining parameter—the maximum window length—can be calculated from fundamental pitch of the input; also, the homomorphic approximation does a superior job of tracing the entire contour of the spectrum, whereas the linear prediction is weighted more heavily on the peaks than on the valleys. However, this weighting may be preferable for processes such as calculating formants. Also, the homomorphic results quickly deteriorate when the pitch is not twice the length of the vocal tract's impulse response (such as the sound emanating from a high-pitched speaker's voice.)

Linear Predictive Coding (LPC) Perhaps the most influential advance in the history of speech coding after Dudley's work was the development of Linear Predictive Coding (LPC) of speech in 1970. LPC is an analysis/synthesis technique that uses the past samples of a voice signal to adaptively predict future samples using linear least-squares estimation. Linear predictive parameters are calculated using well-known autocorrelation or covariance methods. When coupled with an appropriate excitation source model (such as an impulse train or noise for voiced and unvoiced segments, respectively), this technique can result in low bit-rate transmission of speech. Vocal tract filter estimation via LPC also has the benefit of being a closed-form computation, requiring no heuristics to determine parameters. Although computationally intensive, the exponential growth of available computing power has allowed LPC to become the basis of most speech codecs in use today.

In the original LPC vocoder implementation, modeling of the excitation source requires a decision on the type of excitation (voiced or unvoiced) and a pitch estimation of voiced segments. Errors in these decisions usually lead to poor sound quality. Modeling of the excitation source as a periodic impulse train for voiced segments can also result in reconstructed speech that carries a buzzy sound with it. This type of degradation in the LPC vocoder sound quality led to the development of the CELP algorithm. Linear prediction methods attempt to approximate the input with a polynomial of a given order. The number of coefficients in the polynomial plays a role analogous to the window length parameter of homomorphic analysis: if the order is too small, the prediction will be too smooth; conversely, if the order is too large, the prediction will track the input too closely.

2.5.8 Hybrid Coding

Hybrid codecs attempt to fill the gap between waveform and source codecs. As described earlier, waveform coders are capable of providing good-quality speech at bit rates down to about 16 kbits/s, but are of limited use at rates below this speed. Vocoders, on the other hand, can provide intelligible speech at 2.4 kbits/s and below, but cannot provide natural-sounding speech at any bit rate. Although other forms of hybrid codecs exist, the most successful and commonly used are time domain Analysis-by-Synthesis (AbS) codecs. Such coders use the same linear prediction filter model of the vocal tract as found in LPC vocoders. However, instead of applying a simple two-state, voiced/unvoiced model to find the necessary input to this filter, the excitation signal is chosen by attempting to match the reconstructed speech waveform as closely as possible to the original speech waveform. AbS codecs were first introduced in 1982 with what was to become known as the Multi-Pulse Excited (MPE) codec. Later, Regular-Pulse Excited (RPE) and Code-Excited Linear Predictive (CELP) codecs were introduced.

AbS Coding

AbS codecs work by splitting the input speech to be coded into frames, typically about 20 ms long. For each frame, parameters are determined for a synthesis filter, and then the excitation to this filter is determined. This is done by finding the excitation signal that, when passed into the given synthesis filter, minimizes the error between the input speech and the reconstructed speech. Thus the name *analysis-by-synthesis*: the encoder analyzes the input speech by synthesizing many different approximations to it. Finally, for each frame, the encoder transmits information representing the synthesis filter parameters and the excitation to the decoder, and at the decoder, the given excitation is passed through the synthesis filter to give the reconstructed speech. The synthesis filter is usually an all-pole, short-term, linear filter of the form

$$H(z) = \frac{1}{A(z)}$$

where

$$A(z) = 1 - \sum_{i=1}^{p} a_i z^{-i}$$

is the prediction error filter determined by minimizing the energy of the residual signal produced when the original speech segment is passed through it. The order p of the filter is typically around 10. This filter is intended to model the correlations introduced into the speech by the action of the vocal tract.

The synthesis filter may also include a pitch filter to model the long-term periodicities present in voiced speech. Generally, MPE and RPE codecs will work without a pitch filter, although their performance will be improved if one is included. For CELP codecs, however, a pitch filter is extremely important.

The error-weighting block is used to shape the spectrum of the error signal in order to reduce the subjective loudness of this error. This is possible because the error signal in frequency regions where the speech has high energy will be at least partially masked by the speech. The weighting filter emphasizes the noise in the frequency regions where the speech content is low. Thus, minimizing the weighted error concentrates the energy of the error signal in frequency regions where the speech has high energy. Therefore, the error signal will be at least partially masked by the speech, so its subjective importance will be reduced. Such weighting is found to produce a significant improvement in the subjective quality of the reconstructed speech for AbS codecs.

The distinguishing feature of AbS codecs is how the excitation waveform $u(n)$ for the synthesis filter is chosen. Conceptually, every possible waveform is passed through the filter to see what reconstructed speech signal this excitation would produce. The excitation that gives the minimum weighted error between the original and the reconstructed speech is then chosen by the encoder and used to drive the synthesis filter at the decoder. This closed-loop determination of the excitation allows AbS codecs to produce good-quality speech at low bit rates. However, the numerical complexity involved in passing every possible excitation signal through the synthesis filter is huge. Usually, some means of reducing this complexity, without compromising the performance of the codec too badly, must be found.

Regular-Pulse Excited Coding

Like the MPE codec, the Regular-Pulse Excited (RPE) codec uses several nonzero pulses to give the excitation signal $u(n)$. However, in RPE codecs, the pulses are regularly spaced at some fixed interval, and the encoder needs only to determine the position of the first pulse and the amplitude of all the pulses. Therefore, less information needs to be transmitted about pulse positions, so for a given bit rate, the RPE codec can use many more nonzero pulses than MPE codecs. For example, at a bit rate of about 10 kbits/s, around 10 pulses per 5 ms can be used in RPE codecs, compared to 4 pulses for MPE codecs. This allows RPE codecs to give slightly better-quality reconstructed speech quality than MPE codecs. However, they also tend to be more complex. The pan-European GSM mobile telephone system uses a simplified RPE codec, with long-term prediction, operating at 13 kbits/s to provide toll-quality speech.

Code-Excited Linear Predictive Coding

Code-Excited Linear Predictive (CELP) coding is a combination of traditional Linear Predictive (LP) modeling of the resonant qualities of the vocal tract coupled with complex excitation modeling.[8] The CELP codec has proven to be quite successful at transmitting toll-quality speech at low bit rates (down to 4 kbits/sec) and intelligible speech at even lower bit rates. Its use is widespread in today's digital communications devices, such as cellular phones. The general method used to select the excitation is a closed-loop AbS, consisting of a search through a codebook of excitation vectors. The residual error from the LP analysis is compared against the entries of the codebook, filtered by the LP parameters. The entry corresponding to the resulting waveform that best matches (determined via correlation) the residual is chosen, along with a corresponding gain. Because the transmitter and receiver share a copy of the codebook, the codebook entry number and gain are the only values that need to be transmitted for the excitation.

Codebooks vary according to implementation, but they generally contain on the order of hundreds of entries. Variations also exist using multiple codebooks, particularly to model voiced and unvoiced excitations. In this case, however, no voiced/unvoiced decision of the input signal frames is required. The excitation will be composed of some ratio of the deterministic and stochastic vectors, which is established by the gain parameters calculated. Further gains in compression have been achieved using Vector Quantization (VQ), in which excitation vectors are clustered and quantized so that a single excitation vector is chosen to represent an entire cluster. This attempts to capture the wide variance in excitation vectors while limiting overall system complexity by reducing codebook sizes.

This approach was proposed by Schroeder and Atal in 1985 [9], and differs from MPE and RPE in that the excitation signal is effectively vector quantized. The excitation is given by an entry from a large vector quantizer codebook and a gain term to control its power. Typically, the codebook index is represented with about 10 bits (to give a codebook size of 1,024 entries), and the gain is coded with about 5 bits. Thus, the bit rate necessary to transmit the excitation information is greatly reduced—around 15 bits compared to the 47 bits used, for example, in the GSM RPE codec (discussed in a following section).

Originally, the codebook used in CELP codecs contained white Gaussian sequences, because it was assumed that long- and short-term predictors would be able to remove nearly all of the redundancy from the speech signal to produce a random noise-like residual. It was also shown that the short-term probability density function (pdf) of this residual was nearly Gaussian. Schroeder and Atal found that using such a codebook to produce the excitation for long- and short-term synthesis filters could produce high-quality speech. However, in order to choose which codebook entry to use in an AbS procedure, every excitation sequence had to be passed through the synthesis filters to see how close the reconstructed speech it produced would be to the original. This meant that the complexity of the original CELP codec was much too high for it to be implemented in real time. For example, it took 125 seconds of Cray-1 CPU time to process one second of the speech signal. Since 1985 much work on reducing the complexity of CELP codecs, mainly through altering the structure of the codebook, has been done. Large advances have also been made with the speed possible from Digital Signal Processor (DSP) chips, so that now it is relatively easy to implement a real-time CELP codec on a single, low-cost DSP chip. Several important speech coding standards have been defined based on the CELP principle (e.g., the Department of Defense (DoD) 4.8 kbits/s codec and the CCITT low-delay 16 kbits/s codec).

The CELP coding principle has been very successful in producing communications to toll-quality speech at bit rates between 4.8 and 16 kbits/s. The CCITT standard 16 kbits/s codec produces speech that is almost indistinguishable from 64 kbits/s log-PCM coded speech, and the DoD 4.8 kbits/s codec gives good communications-quality speech. Recently, much research has been done on codecs operation below 4.8 kbits/s, with the aim being to produce a codec at 2.4 or 3.6 kbits/s with speech quality equivalent to the 4.8 kbits/s DoD CELP. We briefly describe here a few of the approaches that seem promising in the search for such a codec.

The CELP codec structure can be improved and used at rates below 4.8 kbits/s by classifying speech segments into one of several types (e.g., voiced, unvoiced, and transition frames). The different speech segment types are then coded differently with a specially designed encoder for each type. For example, for unvoiced frames the encoder will not use any long-term prediction, whereas for voiced frames such prediction is vital, but the fixed codebook may be less important. Such class-dependent codecs have been shown to be capable of producing reasonable-quality speech at rates down to 2.4 kbits/s. Multi-Band Excitation (MBE) codecs work by declaring some regions in the frequency domain as voiced and others as unvoiced. They transmit for each frame a pitch period, spectral magnitude, and phase information, and voiced/unvoiced decisions for the harmonics of the fundamental frequency.

Originally, it was shown that such a structure was capable of producing good-quality speech at 8 kbits/s, and since then this rate has been significantly reduced. Finally, Kleijn has suggested an approach for coding voiced segments of speech called Prototype Waveform Interpolation. This works by sending information about a single pitch cycle every 20 to 30 ms and using interpolation to reproduce a smoothly varying quasi-periodic waveform for voiced speech segments. Excellent-quality reproduced speech can be obtained for voiced speech at rates as low as 3 kbits/s. Such a codec can be combined with a CELP-type codec for the unvoiced segments to give good-quality speech at rates below 4 kbits/s.

Federal Standard 1016

In 1991, the DoD standardized a 4.8 kbits/s CELP codec as Federal Standard 1016. The DoD CELP codec divides the speech it is to code into 30-ms frames, each of which is further divided into four 7.5-ms subframes. For each frame, the encoder calculates a set of 10 filter coefficients for the short-term synthesis filter, which is used to model the vocal tract of the speaker. The excitation for this filter is determined for each subframe and is given by the sum of scaled entries from two codebooks. An adaptive codebook is used to model the long-term periodicities present in voiced speech, and for each subframe an index and a gain is determined for this codebook. A fixed codebook containing 512 pseudo-random codes is also searched to find the codebook entry and the gain multiplier for this entry, which minimize the error between the reconstructed and the original speech samples. At the decoder, the scaled entries from the two codebooks are passed through the synthesis filter to give the reconstructed speech. Finally, this speech is passed through a post-filter to improve its perceptual quality.

2.5.9   G723.1 Recommendation

The ITU-T G.723.1 standard specifies a coded representation that can be used for compressing the speech or other audio signal component of multimedia services at a very low bit rate as part of the overall II.324 family of standards. G.723.1 is a speech compression algorithm that has dual coding rates of 5.3 and 6.3 kbps. These types of vocoders process signals with 30-ms frames and have a 7.5-ms look-ahead with very low distortion. The input/output of this algorithm is 16-bit linear PCM samples. Midrange bit-rate G.723.1 vocoders deliver the highest compression ratio of any of the current ITU standards without compromising speech quality. This type of vocoder can perform full duplex compression and decompression functions for multimedia, visual telephony, wireless telephony, and videoconferencing products. This type of coder was optimized to represent high-quality speech at the above rates using a limited amount of complexity. It encodes speech or other audio signals in frames using linear predictive AbS coding. The excitation signal for the high-rate coder is Multipulse Maximum Likelihood Quantization (MP-MLQ), and for the low-rate coder it is Algebraic-Code-Excited Linear Prediction (ACELP).

2.5.10   G.728 Low-Delay CELP Recommendation

The G.728 codec is used to compensate for the fact that at bit rates of around 16 kbits/s and lower, the quality of waveform codecs falls rapidly.

Thus, at these rates, hybrid codecs, especially CELP codecs and their derivatives, tend to be used. However, because of the forward adaptive determination of the short-term filter coefficients used in most of these codecs, they tend to have high delays. The delay of a speech codec is defined as the time from when a speech sample arrives at the input of its encoder to when the corresponding sample is produced at the output of its decoder, assuming the bit stream from the encoder is fed directly to the decoder. For a typical hybrid speech codec, this delay will be on the order of 50 to 100 ms, and such a high delay can cause problems. Therefore, in 1988, the CCITT released a set of requirements for a new 16 kbits/s standard, the chief requirements being that the codec should have speech quality comparable to the G.721 32 kbits/s ADPCM codec in both error-free conditions and over noisy channels, and should have a delay of less than 5 ms and ideally less than 2 ms.

All of the CCITT requirements were met by a backward-adaptive CELP codec, which was developed at AT&T Bell Labs and standardized in 1992 as ITU Recommendation G.728. This particular codec uses backward adaption to calculate the short-term filter coefficients, which means that rather than buffer 20 ms or so of the input speech to calculate the filter coefficients, they are found from the past reconstructed speech. This means that the codec can use a much shorter frame length than traditional CELP codecs, and G.728 uses a frame length of only five samples, giving it a total delay of less than 2 ms. A high-order ($p=50$), short-term predictor is used, which eliminates the need for any long-term predictor. Thus, all 10 bits that are available for each five-sample vector at 16 kbits/s are used to represent the fixed codebook excitation. Of these 10 bits, seven are used to transmit the fixed codebook index, and the other three are used to represent the excitation gain. Backward gain adaption is used to aid the quantization of the excitation gain, and at the decoder a post-filter is used to improve the perceptual quality of the reconstructed speech. All of this leads to a codec at 16 kbits/s with a delay of less than 2 ms, speech quality equal to or better than G.721, and a good robustness to channel errors.

2.5.11 G.729 Recommendation

G.729 is a Conjugate-Structure Algebraic-Code-Excited Linear Prediction (CS-ACELP) codec that models speech based on qualities of the human vocal tract. G.729 is a single-chip, fixed-point, 8-kbits/s, toll-quality speech coding standard for applications, such as VoIP, that require low bit-rate channels. A few months after the original G.729 algorithm was presented for standardization, G.729A was developed to reduce the complexity of the code. Compared with the original algorithm, G.729A requires only half the number of instructions per second. This means the algorithm can run on a slower processor without degrading the quality of the speech. G.729A is a good choice for IPTel applications because it is a low bit-rate and low-complexity algorithm that has a good balance of coding efficiency, speech quality, and stability under extreme conditions.

Speech quality refers to the signal quality and intelligibility of speech that is transmitted over a network. Two main issues affect the quality of speech on packetized networks such as IP: packet loss and delay. Packet loss occurs when a network is congested and/or a routing buffer is exceeded. During packet loss conditions, G.711 (PCM), which codes the waveform of the sound, deteriorates with sound gaps and bursts of noise. G.729 codes the signal based on a model of speech production, and this allows built-in packet loss concealment to produce the same spectral qualities as the missing speech, making gaps in the signal less noticcable to the listener. However, when a significant amount of packet loss occurs, a speaker's voice can sound synthetic. Delay occurs from propagation of the signal across physical wires, encoding/decoding, and processing of digital signals. Delayed signals have two distinct effects on users' satisfaction ratings for telephone connections. First, when there is no echo cancellation and relatively short delay (25 to 150 ms), the speaker will hear his or her voice as an echo. Second, long delay affects the ability to carry on a natural conversation. When delay exceeds 150 ms, callers make awkward interruptions and end up treading on each other's speech. One way to reduce delay is to reduce the size of the speech frame that is processed during encoding and decoding. G.729 uses a 10-ms frame, which makes the encoding delay shorter than G.723.1, for example, which has a 30-ms frame.

Both the G.729 and G.729A coding standards provide a low transmission bit rate with a subjective speech quality rating that is equivalent to G.726, a common 32 kbits/s ADPCM codec. Male speech on a channel using G.729 or G.729A sounds nearly identical on an ADPCM transmission, whereas female and child speech can have a synthetic quality. The gender difference is because the speech coding algorithms are modeled from the male human vocal tract, which is longer and produces lower frequencies when compared to the female vocal tract. As stated previously in this chapter, women and children tend to produce a higher average pitch frequency than do men because the length of their vocal folds is generally much shorter than the length of the average man's vocal folds. Additionally, female speech tends to have a breathy voice quality that results in a broader range of energy around 2500 Hz. These differences aside, in most situations G.729A captures enough qualities of a speaker to satisfy users.

The G.729 codec operates at a peak of 20 million instructions per second (MIPS) and average of 18.5 MIPS, requiring 9,026 words of program memory and 7,262 words of data memory. Each additional distance requires 1,615 words of data memory. When the post-filter is disabled, the total MIPS is reduced to 17.47.

Differences Between G.729, G.729A, and G.729B

Both G.729 and G.729A provide the same speech quality during normal operation; the data rate and frame sizes are the same; and they are fully interoperable. There is confusion between the two standards because they are identical except for complexity. The only detectable performance difference occurs during multiple tandem encoding (encoding and decoding the signal repeatedly). The speech quality of G.729A suffers slightly compared with G.729, but tandem encoding causes speech quality degradation for all CELP codecs and is not enough of a concern to deter anyone from using G.729A. Annex B (G.729B) describes a Speech Activity Detector (SAD) that is used with either G.729 or G.729A. The SAD enables silence suppression (also called *discontinuous transmission*) and generates comfort noise. Silence suppression involves detecting parts of a signal where there is no speech and discontinuing the codec output. Comfort noise is simulated background noise that is played during silence suppression to confirm to the listener that the connection is active. In normal conversation, silence suppression decreases the amount of data sent by 40% to 60%, reducing the long-term average bit rate to about 4 kbits/s. The traditional PSTN contains a two-way channel that is constantly used during a call. The broken line in the packetized network with SAD shows that the talker's channel is not occupied during periods of silence, and the ghosted line represents the receiver's channel, which is not occupied when this person is listening silently. Next to the coding, silence suppression is the best technology for reducing bandwidth.

The G.729 standard is a popular choice for applications such as VoIP that require efficient use of bandwidth and good speech quality. This standard has a good balance of bit-rate and frame size, producing acceptable speech quality under many conditions. Speech coded with G.729 can have a synthetic sound but in most cases this is barely noticeable. G.729A requires less DSP power than G.729, which means that a less powerful DSP can be used, or additional functions may be carried out on the same DSP chip while the codec is running. This saving is gained without degrading the quality of the transmitted speech. Both codecs can be made more efficient with G.729B, which reduces the bandwidth demands by not transmitting silence.

The differences between MPE, RPE, and CELP codecs arise from the representation of the excitation signal $u(n)$ used. In multipulse codecs, $u(n)$ is given by a fixed number of nonzero pulses for every frame of speech. The positions of these nonzero pulses within the frame, and their amplitudes, must be determined by the encoder and transmitted to the decoder. In theory it would be possible to find the best values for all of the pulse positions and amplitudes, but this task is not practical because of the excessive complexity it would entail. In practice, some suboptimal method of finding the pulse positions and amplitudes must be used. Typically, about four pulses per 5 ms are used which leads to good-quality reconstructed speech at a bit rate of around 10 kbits/s.

Although MPE and RPE codecs can provide good-quality speech at rates of around 10 kbits/s and higher, they are not suitable for rates much below this speed because of the large amount of information that must be transmitted about the excitation pulses' positions and amplitudes. If we attempt to reduce the bit rate by using fewer pulses, or coarsely quantizing their amplitudes, the reconstructed speech quality deteriorates rapidly. Currently, the most commonly used algorithm for producing good-quality speech at rates below 10 kbits/s is CELP.

2.5.12 The GSM Codec

The Global System for Mobile communications (GSM) is a digital mobile radio system that is used extensively throughout Europe and in many other parts of the world. The GSM full-rate speech codec operates at 13 kbits/s and uses an RPE codec. For details on RPE codecs, see the earlier section on hybrid codecs. Basically, the input speech is split up into frames 20 ms long, and for each frame a set of eight short-term predictor coefficients is found. Each frame is then further split into four 5-ms subframes, and for each subframe the encoder finds a delay and a gain for the codec's long-term predictor. Finally, the residual signal after both short- and long-term filtering is quantized for each subframe as follows.

The 40-sample residual signal is decimated into three possible excitation sequences, each 13 samples long. The sequence with the highest energy is chosen as the best representation of the excitation sequence, and each pulse in the sequence has its amplitude quantized with three bits. At the decoder, the reconstructed excitation signal is fed through the long-term and then the short-term synthesis filters to give the reconstructed speech. A post-filter is used to improve the perceptual quality of this reconstructed speech. The GSM codec provides good-quality speech, although not as good as the slightly higher-rate G.728 codec. Its main advantage over other low-rate codecs is its relative simplicity: it runs easily in real time on a 66-Mhz 486 PC, for example, whereas CELP codecs need a dedicated DSP to run in real time.

2.6   Digital Speech Interpolation

In digital speech transmission, periods of inactivity or constant signal level are used to increase the transmission efficiency by insertion of additional signals. Human speech is effectively only half-duplex. That is, while one party is speaking, the other is listening. Another property of a typical dialogue is the presence of intermittent silence. From a statistical point of view, the average usage of a voice channel is only 50%. A form of compression can be performed using the aforementioned properties. The use of Digital Speech Interpolation (DSI) is capable of a compression ration of 4:1. This is not actually "true" compression, meaning the actual bit rate of the voice channel is not reduced. The compression is actually done by multiplexing separate channels to a single output channel. Speech interpolation is done by determining whether the channel is active or inactive. This is performed by setting a power threshold. The channel is deemed active if the power falls above the threshold and inactive when the power level falls below the threshold. The threshold setting must be adaptive, because voice characteristics are not constant. Because the threshold setting determines whether the channel is active or not, it affects the performance of the overall compression. A low threshold may detect an inactive channel as active, whereas a high-threshold setting may determine an active channel to be inactive.

Another important aspect of speech interpolation is the signaling required to determine if the channel is active or otherwise. Signal power can fall below the threshold even though the channel is still active. These dips in signal power must also be taken into consideration, because inserting an artificial signal to indicate an inactive channel will make speech sound unnatural. When the channel is inactive, an artificial signal is inserted to simulate the effect of a circuit-switched telephone call. If no signal is injected, the total silence experienced during the inactive period will sound unnatural. DSI allows effective packet-based switching of voice, especially with a variable frame size, because the interval between speech allows more efficient usage of voice channels through speech interpolation.

In the event where high voice activity is encountered, variable-rate ADPCM when coupled with DSI prevents overloading the channel by reducing the output bit rates.

2.7   Summary

The analog network has been the staple technology for more than 100 years, and over time there has been a huge investment in slow, analog, switched voice circuits. The advantages of digital communications over analog communications are vast. Although analog voice technology will always represent the most straightforward way to perfectly reproduce speech signals, digitization has resulted in reduced bulk transport costs and better call processing, although digital voice requires more bandwidth than does analog. An error occurs in 1 in 100,000 analog signals, whereas the error rate for a digital signal is 1 in 10 million.

As more computers, faxes, and other digital devices come into our lives, it makes sense to use a digital signal for cost-effective reasons. When sending digital signals to digital devices, there is no need for analog conversions to take place. In the early days of the telephone, analog made a lot of sense because it simulated how our voices were intended to travel over a copper wire medium. Over time, it has been recognized that a digital signal makes a more reliable and cost-effective way to communicate. Digital-to-analog conversion will continue to be used for the foreseeable future and is by no means going to disappear. Phone companies still have analog systems implemented all over the world, and there is no rush to replace these devices because conversion from analog to digital is possible. Over time, most analog systems will be phased out as they fail and can be expected to be replaced with digital systems. Finally, Table 2.1 summarizes the relevant ITU recommendations for speech encoding and compression.

Table 2.1   *Summary of ITU Recommendations*

ITU Recommendation	Date of Issue	Description
ITU G.711	1988	Pulse Code Modulation (PCM) of Voice Frequencies
ITU G.764	December 1990	Packetization of Voice Protocols
ITU G.722	December 1990	Wideband Coder
ITU G.727	November 1994	5-, 4-, 3-, and 2-bit Sample Embedded ADPCM

Table 2.1   *Summary of ITU Recommendations (continued)*

ITU Recommendation	Date of Issue	Description
ITU G.728	November 1994	Coding 16 kbit/s Speech using Low Delay CELP
ITU G.726	March, 1996	Coding of 40, 32, 24, and 16 kbit/s ADPCM
ITU G.723.1	March 1996	Dual-rate Speech Coder for Multimedia Communications Transmitting at 5.3–6.3 kbit/s
ITU G.723.1 Annex A	March 1996	Silence Compression Scheme
ITU G.723.1 Annex B	March 1996	Alternative Specification Based on Floating-Point Arithmetic
ITU G.723.1 Annex C	March 1996	Scalable Channel Coding Scheme for Wireless Applications
ITU G.729 /G.729 Annex A	March 1996	Speech Coding at 8 kbit/s using Conjugate Structure-Alegbraic CELP (CS-ACELP)

2.8   Endnotes

1. White paper by Dr. Ciarán McElroy, "Principles of Speech Coding," August 2003, Jaynta Ltd, Dublin, Ireland. URL is: www.jaynta.com/technology/principles_of_speech_coding.pdf

2. Michael A. Gallo and William M. Hancock, Computer Communications and Networking Technologies (Pacific Grove, CA: Brooks/Cole Publishing), 2002, p. 88.

3. Uyless D. Black, Advanced Internet Technologies (Upper Saddle River, NJ: Prentice-Hill), 1998, p. 78–80.

4. ITU web site URL is: http://www.itu.int/aboutitu/overview/history.html

5. Definition obtained from http://www.its.bldrdoc.gov/fs-1037/dir-009/_1251.htm

6. IRIG Standard 106-99, "Telemetry Standards", 1999, STEWS-TD-RCC, White Sands Missile Range, NM 88002-5110. URL Reference is:

http://www.spiraltechinc.com/otis/IRIG_Files/
IRIG_Chapter5.htm

7.   URL Reference is:
     http://www.obsolete.com/120_years/machines/vocoder

8.   G. Campos and E. Gouvea, "Speech Synthesis Using the CELP Algorithm," Proceedings of ICSLP, 96(3), 1996.

9.   M. R. Schroeder and B. S. Atal, "Code-excited linear prediction (CELP): high-quality speech at very low bit rates," in Proceedings of the IEEE International Conference on Acoustics, Speech, and Signal Processing (ICASSP), vol. 1, pp. 25.1.1—25.1.4, Mar. 1985.

2.9   General References

Ananthapadmanabha, T. V. & Fant, G. (1982). "Calculation of true glottal flow and its components." *Speech Communication*, 1(3-4):167–184.

Dudley, H. (1936). "Synthesizing speech." *Bell Laboratories Record*, 15:98–102.

Dudley, H. (1950). "The speaking machine of Wolfgang von Kempelen." *Journal of the Acoustical Society of America*, 22(2):151–166.

Dudley, H., Riesz, R. R., & Watkins, S. S. A. (1939). "A synthetic speaker." *Journal of the Franklin Institute*, 2227(6):739–764.

Gersho, A. & Gray, R. M. (1992). *Vector Quantization and Signal Compression*. Germany: Kluwer Academic Publishers.

Lemmetty, S. (1999). *Review of Speech Synthesis Technology*. Master's Thesis, Helsinki University of Technology, Finland.

Moorer, J. A. (1978). "The use of the phase vocoder in computer music applications." *Journal of the Audio Engineering Society*, 26(1):42–45.

Oppenheim, A. V. & Schafer, R. W. (1989). *Discrete-Time Signal Processing*. Englewood Cliffs, NJ: Prentice-Hall.

Spanias, A. (1994). "Speech coding: A tutorial review." *Proceedings of the IEEE*, 82:1539–1582.

Telephony 101

3

3.1 Introduction to Telephony

On the evening of March 10, 1876, at 5 Exeter Place, in Boston, Massachusetts, Alexander Graham Bell uttered these historic words to his assistant Thomas Augustus Watson: "Mr. Watson, come here, I want you." These words were spoken by Mr. Bell using a device that was the earliest known implementation of a telephone, and from the words spoken at this historic event, the telecommunications industry as we know it today was born. Before that moment in time, the road to success had not been easy for Graham Bell (as he liked to be called). Bell had spent several years fooling around with the idea of a harmonic telegraph. Bell believed he could simultaneously transmit six tones across a single wire and cause six reeds attached to the wire at the receiving end to vibrate in response to the frequency of the various tones. The various combinations of sound produced by the vibrating reeds should, he reasoned, simulate the sounds produced by the human voice and allow the vibrations of a voice on one end of the wire to be re-created at the other end, allowing a listener to hear and understand what the speaker was saying.

Bell also integrated a theory that leveraged the varying resistance of a wire. He believed that a diaphragm could be vibrated by the human voice. The diaphragm was attached to a wire that was dipped into a mixture of acid and water. He believed that as the diaphragm moved downward as a result of speaker vibrations, it would force more of the wire into the acid mixture, and the resistance of the wire would be decreased, thereby increasing the conductive properties of the wire. As the diaphragm moved upward, the wire would be withdrawn from the conducting liquid, and its resistance would be correspondingly increased. This device was ultimately successful, and it was used in the telephone industry for many years.

Within a year of Bell's utterance of those now famous words to Watson, on July 9, 1877, the Bell Telephone Company was formed. Alexander Graham Bell became the company's electrician and Watson was in charge of research and manufacturing. Looking ahead with great foresight, Bell realized that the basic patents were due to run out in 16 years, in 1893. He started trying to figure out how to protect his invention and monopolize on the tremendous potential it held. It was not until Theodore Newton Vail was brought in as general manager that a strategy was devised to safeguard Bell Telephone's position as industry leader. Vail immediately began establishing an organization that was strong enough to survive without a monopoly foothold. The first step in Vail's strategy was to obtain a dedicated manufacturing facility. This was accomplished in 1881 when Bell Telephone bought Western Electric Company.

During this time, Vail also sent a bevy of salesmen out into the field to establish telephone exchanges in what was then virgin territory. Promoters local to the area were encouraged to organize a local telephone company and sell stock to raise capital and fund the operations. Successful in promoting this venture to local entrepreneurs, Vail had established a vertically integrated supply division by 1885 that comprised a network of companies licensed under the parent Bell company. The addition of local talent to staff and run the local companies also formed the beginnings of what would become a strong research and development arm, later known as Bell Labs. The expiration of Bell's basic patents in 1893 and 1894 signaled the onset of open competition, and many independent telephone operating companies began to spring up across the country. By 1900, approximately 6,000 independent operators provided service to an estimated 600,000 subscribers. In the last century, over the course of many mergers and acquisitions, the 6,000 independent operators have consolidated to approximately 1,300 local exchange carriers. Bell Telephone, during this time, also changed its name to American Telegraph and Telephone (AT&T).

An unfortunate by-product of all this change over the last century was that all of these telephone systems were not interconnected. Therefore, it was sometimes necessary for a single subscriber to have two or three telephone devices installed to enable communication with other subscribers in other parts of a large city. As impractical as that was, the only reasonable solution at the time to this problem was for AT&T to obtain control of all of the long-distance lines between cities and to refuse other carriers the ability to use them to connect calls. With such a strong monopoly on interstate communications, the competitors were put at bay, and AT&T enjoyed a decade of unbridled prosperity and growth, until the Justice Department filed a federal suit in 1912. By then, the world was angry with AT&T for monopolizing such a public necessity as telephone service. Nathan C. Kingsbury, an AT&T vice president at the time, was fully cognizant of the problem and recognized that the best demonstration of AT&T not being in a monopoly position was to point out to the Justice Department the thousands of independents, all seemingly operating in harmony, to effect nationwide communications. As part of this litigation was settled, it was agreed in 1913 that AT&T would provide interconnection arrangements to all independents. This agreement became known as the Kingsbury Commitment.

By 1934, telecommunications had become so important to the country that Congress passed a Communications Act, which also created the Federal Communications Commission (FCC). The most significant section of this act is what we now refer to as *universal service*. It stated the following:[1] *"For the purpose of regulating interstate and foreign commerce in communication by wire and radio so as to make available, so far as possible, to all the people of the United States a rapid, efficient, nationwide, and worldwide wire and radio communication service with adequate facilities at reasonable charges."*

As a result of this universal service principle, a support structure evolved whereby certain groups of subscribers (such as long-distance users, business subscribers, and subscribers in locations where telephone service could be easily provided) wound up having to pay more than their actual costs. This helped to offset the true costs of providing service to other groups of subscribers (such as those in rural areas or located in other high-cost locations), who would pay less than the actual cost of providing such services. The Justice Department once again filed suit against AT&T in 1949, claiming that Western Electric charged inordinately high prices from their customers, thus forcing the operating telephone companies to charge their subscribers inappropriately high rates to offset such costs. The suit dragged on for nearly seven years until a consent decree was reached in 1956. AT&T won the seven-year struggle, and Western Electric did not have to be divested from AT&T. The settlement decreed that the Bell System would from that time forth engage only in telecommunications, and nonexclusive licenses would be granted to any applicant on equal terms. This was supposedly a final judgment, but the eventual breakup of the Bell System in 1984 was accomplished through a modification of this final judgment, known as the Modification of Final Judgment (MFJ).

Although the Bell System appeared to be the clear winner in this 1956 settlement, it would, over the next two decades, begin to lose many battles.

In November 1974, the Justice Department once again filed suit to break up the Bell System. The case dragged through the court systems until 1978. Judge Harold Greene was appointed to take over the proceedings, and he began to move matters quickly through the system. On January 4, 1982, the Justice Department issued a brief announcement to state that negotiations with AT&T had been reopened. On January 8, 1982, AT&T announced that it had agreed to break up its multibillion-dollar monopoly. It was agreed that AT&T would divest the local parts of the Bell operating telephone companies (called the baby bells). AT&T would be allowed to keep its manufacturing facilities and its long-distance network. The agreement became effective on January 1, 1984. The 22 Regional Bell Operating Companies (RBOCs) agreed to reform into seven regional holding companies.[2] The agreement mandated that the Bell Operating Companies not be allowed to manufacture nor be allowed to conduct long-distance business operations within their regional territories. AT&T was barred from getting into the local-exchange business and was prohibited from acquiring stock and assets of any RBOC as part of this settlement. The 1996 Telecommunications Act overturned most of the rules established in 1984 and left operational implementation of the act to the FCC.

To this day, the FCC struggles to establish a balance between fairness in competition and public interest, which is certainly not an easy task, as indicated by the mountains of paperwork and rendered decisions made in the last decade. The struggle continues, but overall, to the public good. Telephone prices are dictated by open-market competition, and opportunity and challenges are met daily. One such opportunity for businesses and public users is Voice over Internet Protocol (VoIP). Telecommunications companies are struggling to cope with competition over the Internet, and those that have joined the wave appear to be gaining a successful foothold on the market, whereas those that have resisted will likely become footnotes in the telco history pages. Time will tell, but as we creep forward in technological innovation, prices seem to be falling and public ability to instantly communicate with anyone worldwide only improves with SIP-phones and computerized desktop telephony. The rest of this chapter covers the technology, discussing how phones work today and how they evolved into what we take for granted in our offices and homes.

3.2   Call Technology Basics

Human speech is best described as an acoustic, analog waveform signal. In an analog telephone, speech is represented as an electric signal with frequency and amplitude. The frequency of the signal is a measure of the pitch of human speech. The amplitude or height of the signal measures the volume of our speech. Digital voice is simply an analog waveform signal converted to zeros and ones. When speech is transmitted over telephone lines, through local and regional PBXs, and is transmitted across the PSTN, the signal tends to pick up noise and signal distortion. The greater the distance a transmitted voice has to travel, the more likely it is that noise and distortion will increase until the original speech becomes so distorted that it is difficult to understand. In addition, analog voice transmitted over long distances is attenuated, which means that the volume decreases significantly. Many trunk lines used to link central offices are actually digital trunk lines. Telephone companies and carriers use digital lines because they are more dependable and less sensitive to noise and distortions. The inherent benefits of digital voice are that its quality is independent of distance, it can be multiplexed as a single channel to reduce equipment costs and operational expenses, and each digital trunk line has the capacity to replace the cost of six to eight analog trunk lines.

Throughout the early years of the telecommunications industry, up until the early 1960s, voice communications networks were analog based. With the development of digital PBXs, switches, multiplexers, and channel banks, a shift to digital-based technology occurred. A trend toward convergence in voice and data equipment throughout corporate enterprise networks evolved. Such convergence provided lower-cost telephony and business solutions for both corporate enterprise networks and small-office, home-office users. Data networks typically operate at much lower costs and usually have enough bandwidth to carry voice traffic. Integrating voice and data networks by utilizing existing data network infrastructures can provide long-term cost benefits to an organization. Such integration does not come easy, however, and there are many challenges when integrating data and voice on a corporate network. These challenges include the need for toll-quality voice, a reliable and predictable delivery of voice traffic, transmitted with very low delay, and at a low cost.

Additionally, enterprises require a toll bypass capability for long-distance voice traffic and, typically, use of converged networks requires high utilization rates, minimal transmittal delay, very low bandwidth requirements, and very low error rates for simultaneous transmittal of voice and data traffic. There are limitations on some existing data network technologies. A few such technologies can address the low delay and high efficiency requirements of voice traffic. Packet-based technologies such as Frame Relay, Asynchronous Transfer Mode (ATM), and Transmission Control Protocol/Internet

Protocol (TCP/IP), however, are suitable for voice traffic. These technologies bundle data into network-manageable data packets, which are only sent when data or voice traffic needs to be transported from a source to a destination. Silence, noise, and flag-filled data is suppressed to minimize bandwidth use. Frame Relay Access Devices (FRADs), ATM switches, and IP routers all must convert voice traffic into packets for transport over a packet network.

3.2.1 Traditional Handsets

The traditional telephone handset contains a receiver, a transmitter, and a device known as a *hybrid*. The handset houses the earpiece (receiver) and the mouthpiece (or transmitter). We speak into the mouthpiece, and our speech is transmitted over one pair of wires. We listen through the earpiece and receive sound from another pair of wires. In total, four wires make up the handset. The telephone connects to the PBX using a separate, dedicated pair of wires, which are designated as the *subscriber loop*. The receiver/transmitter, which is composed of four wires, must interface with the PBX, which uses two wires. The hybrid device makes this four-wire to two-wire conversion. This hybrid device evolved out of necessity. The use of two-wire circuitry to connect a telephone instrument to a serving telephone company switch or corporate PBX was based on economic considerations. A two-wire circuit is less expensive than a four-wire circuit, and it provides a full-duplex transmission path suitable for a variable distance based on the wire gauge of the conductor. Usually, two-wire circuits can be used at a distance of up to approximately one to two miles.

When the telephone company established initial networks across the country, call routing between exchanges required the transmission of voice over much greater distances than those used in the local loops. Because a signal attenuates as it traverses a line, the telephone company inserted amplifiers along the path of the long-distance circuits to rebuild and propagate the attenuated signals. Because these amplifiers were unidirectional, voice had to be separated into two different paths for transmission between central office switches, with one path used for transmission and the other used for reception. This signal splitting resulted in the use of a four-wire circuit for transmitting voice between central offices, with the circuit commonly referred to as a *trunk*.

On a four-wire circuit connecting PBXs or central office switches, the transmit path conductors are referred to as *Tip* and *Ring*, while the receive path conductors are referred to as *Tip/1* and *Ring/1* to differentiate them from the transmit path. To alleviate echo that sometimes results from a portion of speech energy being reflected back toward the talker, communications carriers use echo suppressors. Such devices are designed to minimize the effect of reflected speech energy.

3.2.2   Switch Hook

The switch hook is located directly below the handset. When you lift the handset out of the cradle, the switch hook closes, and an electrical current flows through the phone. When this condition occurs, the phone is said to be *off-hook*. The PBX supplies the electrical power necessary to operate the telephone device. When you place the handset back into the telephone cradle, the switch hook is placed into an opened position, and the electrical current is unable to flow through the telephone. This condition is referred to as *on-hook*.

3.2.3   Side Tone

Side tone is essentially an intentional feedback signal that is an output of a phone's hybrid device. The device allows a small portion of the speech signal to process though the earpiece as an audible signal that is used to help the speaker judge how loud he or she is talking.

3.2.4   Dialer

The dialer is a device one uses to enter a phone number for the party to be called. The phone number is, in essence, a digital address. In a rotary dialing device, the caller spins the dial and the distance the dial spins represents a corresponding digit to be sent out as part of the address to be processed by the PBX. For a push-button phone, the caller would press buttons that each generate a unique tone pair (known as Dual-Tone Multi-Frequency (DMTF) and explained later in this chapter) used to represents each digit.

3.2.5   VoIP and VoIP Phones

VoIP is the term commonly used to refer to support of voice transmissions encapsulated and transmitted within the IP packets of a network. VoIP has received a lot of attention in the last few years because many corporate networks use the TCP/IP protocol for networking over the Internet. Almost every company in operation today has an existing IP data network. Transmitting their voice traffic over their existing IP backbone or local area network (LAN) enables a company to significantly reduce their long-distance and international telephone costs.

VoIP can offer users advantages such as long-distance toll bypass, interactive e-commerce, global online customer support, and much more. IP is a connectionless packet-switching protocol. IP is connectionless because data is sent without having the sender establish a direct connection with the recipient. Data is encapsulated within an IP packet and sent over the network using a source and destination address, typically of the form 123.456.789.0. IP is called a network layer protocol because it provides the network layer addressing information. There is no guarantee that the IP packet will reach the destination, and there is no guarantee that each successive packet between the same source and destination will follow the same path. For this reason, IP provides only a *best-effort* service for packet delivery.

Because IP can only provide us with a best-effort service for packet delivery, we use another protocol, called Transport Control Protocol (TCP), which implements a more reliable transport service on top of the routing delivery service provided by IP. TCP implements a sequential packet delivery and error recovery methodology that can account for duplicate or lost packets. If an IP packet is lost and an error is detected, TCP will send a message to the source and ask for a retransmit of the lost or error-detected packet. TCP is connection based, so it establishes a direct connection with the TCP stack on the receiving side of the transmission before sending any packets. Sending IP as a part of the TCP is where the term TCP/IP originates.

Yet another transport layer protocol, User Datagram Protocol (UDP), makes a best effort to deliver packets to destinations as quickly as possible with minimal overhead and minimal delay. Because it is a best-effort service, UDP does not guarantee reliable delivery. Voice traffic is most often transported via these UDP packets. Just as IP uses TCP for transport services, UDP uses another protocol, Real-Time Protocol (RTP), to provide fast, end-to-end delivery of real-time traffic such as interactive voice and video. RTP features include time stamping, packet sequencing, and monitored delivery of a voice packet. When using one or more of these transport protocols to provide a means of delivery, an IP encapsulated voice packet will have header information added to it during the transport process. The receiving end uses this header information to process the packets and route traffic accordingly.

Combining voice over an existing corporate IP network provides many advantages, such as (1) the ability to retain and use the existing data network infrastructure to reduce long-distance toll costs between branch offices and the corporate headquarters, (2) remote local dialing and cost-effective telecommuting operations; (3) direct PC-to-PC, PC-to-phone, and phone-to-phone calls over an IP LAN; and (4) interactive PC-to-PC voice calls, online chat sessions, and white-boarding or document sharing, making daily operations more cost-effective for an organization.

The new breed of digital telephones used in these scenarios are called IP phones. Rather than having a four-line telephone connector in the back, they usually have an Ethernet LAN connector (typically, an RJ-45 jack). An IP phone connects directly to an IP telephony server within the organization's infrastructure. The IP telephony server does all of the call setup and call processing that was once performed by the PBX. Desktop computers can also now serve as IP phones (called softphones). All that is needed is a headset and a microphone attached to the computer's audio card. The computer's CPU runs the softphone software and performs all of the call-processing functions over the computer's LAN connection to the corporate data network. Just like an IP phone, the softphone relies on an IP telephony server somewhere on the network to do all of the call setup and call processing.

3.3   Understanding Signaling

Signaling protocols are used to establish and control call sessions activated for such activities as multimedia conferencing, telephone conversations, providing or receiving distance learning, and similar collaborative applications. The IP signaling protocols used today connect clients to each other through a LAN or through the Internet. The main functions of call setup and control are looking up the user location, performing a name and address translation, establishing a direct connection setup, negotiating available features, managing participant activities (such as invitation, logon, logoff), and terminating the call. Some other services, such as billing, security, session announcement, and directory services, may be included in the session when using one of the more recently developed call session protocols. Although signaling is related to data stream transmission protocols, the actual data transmission functions are not part of the set of functions supported by current signaling protocols.

The call session capabilities we enjoy today all have their roots in analog circuit-switching technology that started in the early 1960s. That technology was the basis for modern packet-based network telephony used today. Even today, analog trunk circuits are in use that connect to automated systems such as a PBX over the network, which, in turn, connects to a central office (CO). The most common form of analog trunking used is the E&M interface. Many people believe that E&M signaling derives its name from "ear and mouth," but its true origin is from the terms *Earth* and *Magnet*. Earth represents an electrical ground and magnet represents the electromagnet used to generate tones. For each connection used, E&M signaling defines a trunk circuit side and a signaling unit side. Often, the PBX is seen as the trunk circuit side and the CO is seen as the signaling unit side. E&M signaling is the most commonly used method of analog trunk signaling.

3.4   Subscriber Loop Signaling

Signaling processes are categorized into three basic types: supervision, addressing, or call-progress (alerting). Supervision involves the detection of changes to the status of a loop or trunk. Once these changes are detected, the supervisory circuit will generate a predetermined response such as closing a circuit (loop) to connect a call. Addressing involves the passing of dialed digits (pulsed or tone) to a PBX or CO. These dialed digits provide the switch with a connection path to another phone or customer premises equipment. Alerting provides audible tones to the user, indicating certain conditions such as an incoming call or a busy phone.

3.4.1   Supervisory Signaling

Supervisory signaling is used to monitor the status of a line. The status of a line can either be idle (on-hook) or active (off-hook). Supervisory signaling types are generally broken into three categories: loop-start, ground-start, and E&M signaling. Each signaling type is discussed in greater detail in the following section.

Loop-Start Signaling

A phone line or trunk is "started" or "seized" by sending a supervisory signal. That signal is typically generated when a user lifts the receiver off the phone. Simply by taking your phone off-hook results in the physical closing of the switch hook, and flow of current begins when the circuit is completed. The two ways that this can be accomplished are through a loop-start or a ground-start. With a loop-start, a line is seized by bridging the tip and ring leads (both wires) of your telephone line when the handset is lifted out of the cradle. This action signals the off-hook condition by allowing DC current to flow through the local loop. The current that flows from the handset through the local loop is detected by the switch or PBX, which responds by providing a dial tone to indicate readiness to accept an address.

When the switch or PBX generates dial tone, it also places the specific port connected to the telephone via a local loop in an off-hook indication mode. This action results in the local loop becoming active. When a call is terminated by a subscriber placing the handset back into the cradle, the switch hook opens, stopping the flow of the current, and the local loop returns to its on-hook state. The terms *on-hook* and *off-hook* are universally used to describe the state of the local loop with respect to the presence or absence of current. Loop-start signaling is used primarily on local loops, but it can also be used on trunks. However, its use on certain types of trunks can result in problems. Just as with local loops, trunks require supervisory signaling. When loop-start signaling is used, only the originating instrument can release the connection.

Some problems result with the loop-start process when it is used as a two-way interface between two switches, such as is the case for a connection to CO lines from a PBX or Central Office\Voice Frame Relay Access Device (CO\VFRAD). There is a period of up to 4 seconds before the calling switch actually applies a ringing voltage for the first time after a loop-start line has been seized. During this interval, the called switch doesn't know that the line is in use, and it could attempt to make a call using the same line. This results in a condition called *glare*. When glare occurs, it prevents the line from being used by either side. When both sides of the line are operating in an unattended mode, glare becomes an important issue. With an attendant present at either side of the line, the glare condition can be easily resolved. Most often, the problem occurs when neither side has an attendant present and the line becomes unusable by both sides. To contend with this problem, switch-to-switch communications use the ground-start interface because it has proven to be a better process to seize a line than the loop-start process.

Although glare conditions can be tolerated when used on dedicated local loops, the occurrence of this condition on trunk lines shared among users each contending for use of lines cannot be tolerated. To circumvent problems in this situation, a two-way handshaking mechanism is used to coordinate access to a trunk line. The end requesting access waits for an acknowledgment from the remote end before seizing the trunk. Trunk supervisory signaling methods such as start-dial, ground-start, and E&M signaling have been developed to alleviate the problems associated with loop-start signaling as it is applied to trunks.

Ground-Start Signaling

Ground-start signaling is a method of signaling used on subscriber trunks whereby one side of the two-wire trunk (typically the "ring" side of the tip and ring) is grounded in order to get a dial tone. Ground-start trunks are typically used for PBXs because of the intermittent nature of local loops when used in a PBX environment. Many PBX systems use ground-start signaling because it is less prone to glare than a loop-start process. Local loop lines are typically used for ordinary single-line phones.

E&M Signaling

E&M signaling is the most commonly used method of analog trunk signaling. It is a type of supervisory signaling that is often used between PBXs. E&M supervisory signaling differs from loop-start and ground-start signaling in that it uses separate paths for voice and signaling. For the voice path, the trunk can consist of either two or four wires. There are five basic methods of E&M signaling that can be used, referred to as Types I through V, and a sixth method has evolved as a British Telecom standard used in the United Kingdom (see Table 3.1). The variations that are found in E&M signaling types occur because of the way in which grounding is performed with the E or M leads.

In the E&M signaling process, a PBX requests use of a trunk by raising its M lead. The distant end honors the request by sending an electrical current flowing down to the requestor on the E lead. This particular method of signaling is used by all types of E&M signaling. Differences occur in the manner in which the flow of electrical current is used to differentiate one type of signaling from another.

Connector block positions used years ago to install this type interface were marked alphabetically as E and M rather than having been numbered. These E and M designations were written into a standard instruction set used by telephone company personnel, and the designations carried forward over time. The M lead is used to transmit and the E lead is used to receive signaling information. E&M leads may consist of either two wires (plus ground lead) or four wires (two balanced circuits). However, these wires are not the wires referred to when calling an E&M interface two-wire or four-wire. E&M interfaces are characterized as two-wire or four-wire by the nature of the voice path, not the signaling path. In other words, voice can be carried on either a single loop of one pair of wires or on a separate wire pair transmitting in each direction. E&M modules are available to support both two-wire and four-wire voice paths. There are five different

Table 3.1 *E&M Signaling Types*

E&M Signaling Type	Description
I	E&M Type I is commonly used in North America. Under E&M Type I signaling, the battery for both E and M leads is supplied by the PBX, an on-hook condition results in the M lead being grounded and the E lead open. In comparison, an off-hook condition results in the M lead providing the battery and the E lead being grounded.
II	E&M Type II is commonly used in Canada and Europe. One of the problems found with Type I signaling is that the interface can cause a high return current through the grounding system. If two PBXs were improperly grounded, this could result in current flowing down the M signaling lead, which results in a remote PBX detecting the current on the E lead. This in turn results in the occurrence of a false seizure of a trunk. To address this problem, E&M Type II signaling added two additional signaling leads: Battery (SB) and signal ground (SG). Under Type II signaling, the E lead works in conjunction with the SG lead, while the M lead is strapped to the SB lead. This results in the grounding of the trunk at each end and eliminates potential grounding problems from occurring.
III	Type III signaling is similar to Type I, the key difference being in the use of transmission equipment to supply the battery and ground source, which results in loop current flowing on the M lead when an off-hook condition occurs. Type III signaling was primarily used with older CO equipment and is now in very limited use because most older CO switches have been replaced.
IV	Type IV signaling is similar to Type II, but the operation of the M lead differs. In Type II signaling, the M lead states are "open" and "battery." Under Type IV signaling the states are "ground" and "open." The key advantage of Type IV signaling is the fact that an accidental shorting of the SB lead will not result in an excessive current flow.
V	Under Type V signaling, both the switch and the transmission equipment supply a battery. Here the battery for the M lead is located in the signaling equipment, while the battery for the E lead is located in the PBX. Under Type V signaling, the PBX side grounds its M lead to seize the trunk. In comparison, a voice port on a router, FRAD, or voice gateway supporting Type V signaling would ground its E lead to seize the trunk. Type V signaling is the ITU E&M signaling standard and represents the most common method of E&M signaling outside of North America.
VI	E&M Type VI is a British Telecom Standard used in the UK.

types of E&M signaling circuits, as mentioned previously. The number of physical wires used for signaling depends on the particular E&M type.

In addition to the five types of E&M signaling shown in Table 3.1, there are also two types of audio signaling, two-wire and four-wire. Although this can add confusion to an already large number of combinations, the fact is that a four-wire E&M interface cable can actually consist of six to eight physical wires. This is because the difference between two-wire and four-wire circuits depends on whether the audio path is full-duplex on a single pair of wires or if it operates at full-duplex on two pairs of wires. Voice transmissions can be carried over either a two-wire or four-wire path. When a four-wire path is used, the Tip/Ring leads transmit voice traffic, while Tip1/Ring1 receives voice traffic. Signaling information is transmitted on the M lead and received on the E lead. Four-wire E&M Type I trunks are used to connect PBXs. From a PBX, the Tip and Ring leads transmit voice traffic, while Tip1/Ring1 is used to receive voice traffic. Signaling information is transmitted on the M lead and received on the E lead. Voice and signaling wires do not run directly from PBX to PBX. Instead, a tie-trunk is terminated on the terminating end of the E&M tie-trunk. When the signal traverses the lines from one end to the other, the transmission equipment crosses over the appropriate leads: T/R to T1/R1, M lead to E lead, and so on, until it reaches its destination.

Seizing a Trunk using E&M Signaling

A PBX seizes the trunk when it asserts the M signal and the E lead is not asserted (E is asserted when the trunk is busy, or seized from the other end), the far switch responds by asserting its M lead, and the originating switch will see that response signal on its E lead. Assuming that there is another switch at the other side of the transmission trunk, the E&M interface will be defined from the switch to transmission equipment. When the dialing information is transmitted between the switches, the called end may indicate its readiness to receive digits by either a wink-start, a delay-dial trunk, or immediate-start. Each method is briefly described as follows:

- ■ **Wink-start**. Wink-start signaling represents a commonly used trunk-signaling method. Under this signaling method, the originating trunk is placed in an off-hook condition, which results in the remote switch responding by transmitting an off-hook pulse of between 140 and 290 milllisecons (ms) in duration, after which the switch returns to an idle or on-hook state. When the called end is ready to receive dialing information, it sends back a *wink*, which is a signal of at least 140 ms that is asserted on the far-end M lead and appears on the originating end's E lead. An audible dial tone on the voice path may also be returned by the called switch at the same time. EIA-464, the American National Standards Institute (ANSI) standard for PBXs, allows for a dial tone on the voice path to be substituted for the wink signal. However, a configuration issue will result if the other PBX accepts it. In this case, the calling end then dials, either by toggling the M lead or by transmitting DTMF tones on the voice path. This off-hook pulse is referred to as a wink-back, which, when detected by the originating switch, results in the switch waiting for at least 210 ms and then transmitting the address digits to remote switch. The remote switch then returns to an on off-hook condition to answer the call.

- *Delay-dial trunk.* The called end will immediately (less than 300 ms) assert its M lead (go off-hook) until it is ready to receive dialed digits when it sees the E lead active. When it is ready to return to on-hook, the calling end then dials using either a pulse or tone. Both the wink-start and delay-dial will behave similarly when the called switch is not busy and can respond quickly, but may be difficult to tell them apart. Regardless of the trunk signaling type, a busy switch will be ready to receive dialing at a certain time. In other words, a delay pulse will be longer than a wink pulse, but both will end at the same time.

- *Immediate-start.* This start method is a trunk-signaling type called an immediate-start, but it doesn't offer acknowledgment to a seizure condition. Immediate-start signaling represents one of the most basic trunk-signaling methods. When an immediate-start signaling method is used, the originating switch places the trunk off-hook and maintains that condition for a minimum of 150 ms, after which the switch outputs the address digits. The originating end starts dialing after a short time after seizing the trunk and dial tone from the called switch is optional. Because there is no real handshake between switches, this type of trunk signaling is appropriate only when a dedicated logical or physical trunk is used between switches.

In all three of these cases, the called PBX will assert its M lead when the called extension answers, and the calling PBX will see this on its E lead. There is also no hard rule against any of these three trunk types having an interface with any of the five types of E&M. However, it would be difficult—perhaps impossible—for two switches to use delay-dial on any E&M interface because of the delay across a frame-based network. Delay-dial requires a quick response to each seizure, in a time that may be less than the round-trip propagation delay across the frame relay backbone. After the near end has seized a trunk and it has been acknowledged by the far end and the trunk type is wink-start or delay-dial, the originating end will transmit dialing. After the called station (telephone) answers (goes off-hook), the called switch asserts the M signal lead, which appears on the E lead at the calling end. Both E and M remain asserted while the call is in progress. When either switch detects an on-hook from its station, it drops its M signal (causing E to drop at the other end). The second switch, if its phone is not hung up, should give a dial tone and behave as if a call were originating. There is also the possibility that asserting a signal lead might result in ending a signaling tone on the voice path, happens with interoffice alalog circuitry.

The timing of events can be critical for signaling between E&M interfaces. For instance, a wink's length is closely controlled to distinguish it from a disconnect (hang-up) that is followed immediately by another call request. The ratio of on to off may also have to be preserved when replicating dial pulses. This ratio varies by country, and in the United States, the break (open-loop circuit, on-hook state) is held close to 61% of the pulse times, whereas in other countries the make-to-break ratio can be closer to 1:1.

3.4.2 Address Signaling

Address signaling provides the telephone number that enables a call to be routed to its appropriate destination using the phone numbering system that identifies each phone in a voice network. All PBXs, COs, or switches will use address signaling to determine how to establish a call to the correct destination. This is called *switching the call*. To complete the remote call, the switch must find a path to logically connect the local and remote switch. There are two commonly used methods of address signaling: dial pulse and Dual-Tone Multi-Frequency (DTMF) signaling.

Dial Pulse

Dial pulse is a term associated with rotary dial phones. With dial-pulse signaling, digits are sent over the subscriber loop as pulses. On a rotary phone, when you choose a digit and turn the dial, a spring winds, and when the dial is released, the spring rotates the dial back to its original position, during which time a cam-driven switch opens and closes the loop. Under dial-pulse signaling, digits are transmitted from the originating telephone instrument by the opening and closing of the local loop. In actuality, as you turn the rotary dial, this action winds up a spring. When you release the dial to select a digit, the spring rotates back to its originating position and opens and closes the loop several times, which corresponds to the value of the dialed digit. The number of consecutive openings and closings represents the dialed digit. To ensure that any PBX or switch can receive and understand the digits, the digit pulses are produced at a specific rate and are within a certain tolerance. Note that each dialed digit must be generated at a specific rate and must be within a predefined tolerance for it to be recognized.

To accomplish this system, each pulse consists of two parts referred to as *make* and *break*. The make segment represents the period when the circuit is closed, and the break segment represents the period when the circuit is placed in the open condition during a dialed-digit period. In North America, the make-to-break ratio is 39 percent make to 61 percent break, whereas in the United Kingdom the ratio used is 33 percent make to 67 percent break. In North America, digits are pulsed at a constant rate of 10 pulses per second (PPS). The rate may vary in other locations. Dial pulse addressing is a very slow process because the number of pulses generated equates to the digit being dialed. So, dialing digit 9 generates nine make and break pulses. Dialing digit 0 generates 10 make and break pulses. To increase the speed of dialing, a new dialing technique called DTMF was developed.

Dual-Tone Multi-Frequency (DTMF) Signaling

DTMF provides the push-button dialing signals and is much faster than rotary dialing. Switches today most often use DTMF rather than toggling the M lead on switches. DMTF is most often supported on a push-button phone. Many phones use tones instead of pulses to send the digits to the PBX. The keypad has 12 keys. As shown in Figure 3.1, each key or number has a pair of tones: a low-frequency tone and a high-frequency tone, hence the name dual-tone multi-frequency. For each row of keys, there are individual low-frequency tones. A different high-frequency tone represents each column.

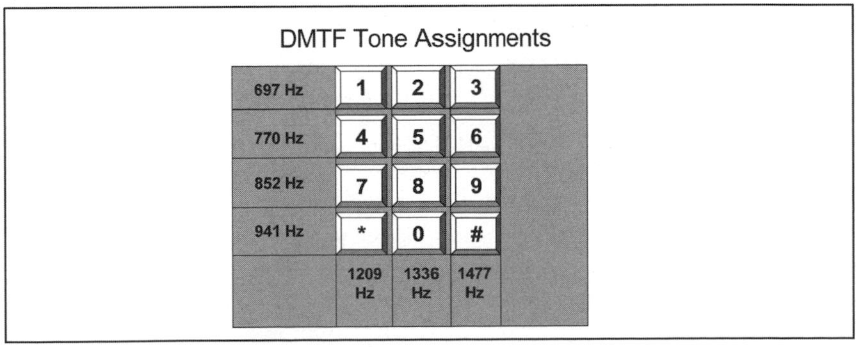

Figure 3.1
DTMF tone assignments.

DMTF Tone Assignments

	1209 Hz	1336 Hz	1477 Hz
697 Hz	1	2	3
770 Hz	4	5	6
852 Hz	7	8	9
941 Hz	*	0	#

When you press a key, the phone sends the digit as a low- and high-frequency tone. For instance, the number 5 is represented by two tones: 770-and 1209-Hz tone. The keypad has been standardized, but the tone tolerances may vary. The PBX or switch will recognize the two tone frequencies and know that the number 5 was dialed.

3.4.3 Call-Progress Signaling

Informational signals are generated by the PBX or switch to tell the user about the call's progress. There are different types of informational signals, such as the busy signal, fast busy, dial tone, and ringback. Table 3.2 shows a summary of alerting tones that could be generated by the CO switch during a phone call. The call-progress tones seen in the table are used for North American phone systems. International phone systems often use a different set of progress tones. Everyone should be familiar with most of these call-progress tones, especially dial, busy, and ringback. Congestion progress tone is used between switches. Receiver off-hook is the loud ringing that occurs when the phone is left off the hook for an extended period. No such number occurs when the number dialed can't be found in the routing table of a switch.

Table 3.2 *Network Call Progress Tones.*

Type of Tone	Frequency (Hz)	On-time	Off-time
Dial	350 + 440	Continuous	n/a
Busy	480 + 620	.5	.5
Normal ringback	440 + 480	2	4
PBX ringback	440 + 480	1	3
Congestion (toll)	480 + 620	.2	.3
Reorder (local)	480 + 620	.3	.2
Receiver off-hook	1400 + 2060 + 2450 + 2600	.1	.1
Unknown number	200 + 400	Continuous	Freq Mod 1 Hz

3.5 Components of the Phone System

3.5.1 Phone

The phone is the instrument used to place and receive calls. We use the phone as our point of entry into the phone system, signaling the CO that a call is desired or receiving signals from the CO that we have an incoming call. How this works is explained in the section entitled "Making the Basic Telephone Connection."

3.5.2 PBX

PBX is the acronym used for **P**rivate **B**ranch e**X**change, a private telephone network used within an enterprise that switches calls between enterprise users on local lines while allowing all users to share a certain number of external phone lines. The main purpose of a PBX is to save the cost of requiring a line for each user to the telephone company's CO. Users of the PBX share a certain number of outside lines for making telephone calls external to the PBX. The PBX is owned and operated by the enterprise rather than the telephone company. PBXs once used analog technology, but today's modern PBX systems use digital technology. Most medium-sized and larger companies use a PBX because it's much less expensive than connecting an external telephone line to every telephone in the organization. In addition, it's easier to call someone within a PBX, because the number you need to dial is typically just three or four digits.

A new variation on the PBX theme is the centrex, which is a PBX with all switching occurring at a local telephone office instead of at the company's premises. PBX systems usually include components that create one or more telephone trunk (multiple phone) lines that terminate at the PBX. The PBX system is often composed of a computer with sufficient memory to manage call switching within the PBX as well as in- and outbound calls. The network of lines within the PBX terminates at a console or switchboard staffed by a human operator. In some situations, alternatives to a PBX include centrex service (in which a pool of lines are rented at the phone company's CO), key telephone systems, and, for very small enterprises, primary-rate Integrated Services Digital Network (ISDN).

3.5.3 Subscriber Loop

A subscriber loop is simply a telephone line that extends between a CO and a telephone station, PBX, or other line-end equipment. The previous section on loop-start signaling discussed how the subscriber loop is used between the CO and the user phone device.

3.5.4 Trunk and Access Lines

The term *trunk line* refers to the direct line connecting two telephone switches to each other. The term originated from the use of "trunk lines" in railway systems, and the concept remains much the same: a single line used to directly transport from point to point between main stations. Connections between exchanges comprise the *trunk network*. From each station, *access lines* connect to the subscribers using the local exchange. Each access line connects a subscriber to a station, which is interconnected to one or more trunk lines that connect to other stations. Traffic is routed from exchange to exchange, starting with a call from the local loop subscriber over the access line to the local exchange and across a trunk line that terminates at the destination exchange. From the destination exchange, the signal is routed onto the correct destination access line to the phone device whose address was dialed by the caller. The *access network* is said to be that part of a telecommunications network that connects the subscribers with their local exchange.

3.6 Making the Basic Telephone Connection

3.6.1 On-hook

Before a phone call is initiated, the telephone set is in a ready condition waiting for a caller to pick up the handset. This state is called *on-hook*. In this state, the 48-VDC circuit from the telephone set to the CO switch is open. The CO switch contains the power supply for this DC circuit. Having the power supply located at the CO switch prevents a loss of telephone service when the power goes out at the location of the telephone set. Figure 3.2 shows the on-hook phase.

3.6.2 Off-hook

The off-hook phase occurs when the telephone customer decides to make a phone call and lifts the handset off the switch hook of the telephone set. The switch hook closes the loop between the CO switch and the telephone set and allows current to flow. The CO switch detects this current flow and transmits a dial tone (350- and 440-hertz [Hz] tones played continuously) to the telephone set. This dial tone lets the customer know that dialing can start. There is no guarantee that the customer will get a dial tone right away. If all of the circuits are being used, the customer might have to wait for a dial tone. The access capacity of the CO switch being used deter-

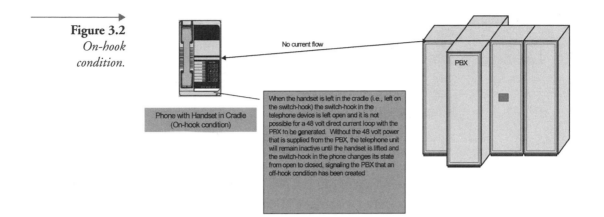

Figure 3.2
*On-hook
condition.*

No current flow

PBX

Phone with Handset in Cradle
(On-hook condition)

When the handset is left in the cradle (i.e., left on the switch-hook) the switch-hook in the telephone device is left open and it is not possible for a 48 volt direct current loop with the PRX to be generated. Without the 48 volt power that is supplied from the PBX, the telephone unit will remain inactive until the handset is lifted and the switch-hook in the phone changes its state from open to closed, signaling the PBX that an off-hook condition has been created

mines how soon a dial tone will be sent to the caller's phone. The CO switch generates a dial tone only after it has reserved registers to store the incoming address. Therefore, the customer can't dial until a dial tone is received. If there is no dial tone, then the registers are not available. Figure 3.3 shows the off-hook phase.

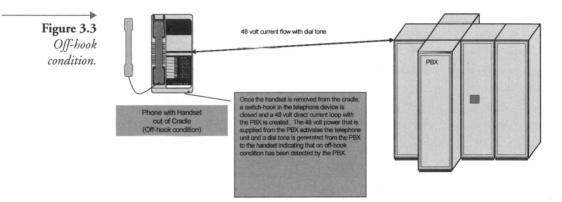

Figure 3.3
*Off-hook
condition.*

48 volt current flow with dial tone

PBX

Phone with Handset
out of Cradle
(Off-hook condition)

Once the handset is removed from the cradle, a switch-hook in the telephone device is closed and a 48 volt direct current loop with the PBX is created. The 48 volt power that is supplied from the PBX activates the telephone unit and a dial tone is generated from the PBX to the handset indicating that on off-hook condition has been detected by the PBX.

3.6.3 Dialing

At this point, the phone handset has been picked up and a dial tone has been established. The dialing phase allows the customer to enter a phone number (address) of a telephone at another location. The customer enters this number using either a rotary phone that generates pulses or a touch-tone phone that generates tones. These pulses or tones are transmitted to the CO switch across a two-wire, twisted-pair cable (tip and ring lines). Figure 3.4 illustrates the dailing phase.

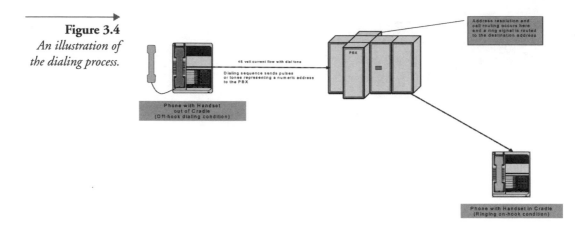

Figure 3.4
*An illustration of
the dialing process.*

3.6.4 Switching

As the phone number is dialed, the tones or pulses are transmitted to the PBX, where switching (address resolution) occurs. In the switching phase, the CO switch translates the pulses or tones into a port address that connects to a telephone set of the called party. This connection could go directly to the requested telephone set (for local calls) or through another switch or several switches (for long-distance calls) before reaching its final destination.

3.6.5 Ringing

Once the CO switch connects to the called line, it sends a 20-Hz 90V signal to this line. This signal rings the phone of the called party. While ringing the called party's phone, the CO switch sends an audible ringback tone to the caller. This ringback lets the caller know that ringing is taking place at the called party's phone. The CO switch generates a ringback by transmitting 440- and 480-Hz tones to the caller's phone. These tones are played for a specific on time and off time. If the called party's phone is busy, the CO switch sends a busy signal to the caller. This busy signal consists of 480- and 620-Hz tones.

3.6.6 Talking

In the talking phase, the called party hears the phone ringing and decides to answer. As soon as the called party lifts the handset, an off-hook phase starts again, this time on the opposite end of the network. The local loop is closed on the called party's side, so current starts to flow to the CO switch. This switch detects current flow and completes the voice connection back to the

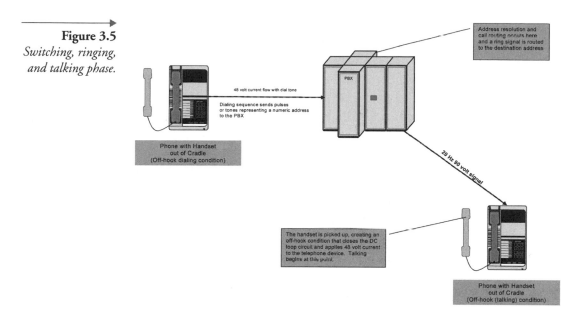

Figure 3.5
Switching, ringing, and talking phase.

calling party's phone. Now voice communication can start between both ends of this connection.

Figure 3.5 illustrates the switching, ringing, and talking phase.

3.7   North American Numbering Plan (NANP)

The North American Numbering Plan (NANP) uses 10 digits to represent a telephone number. These 10 digits are divided into three parts: the area code, office code, and station code. In the original NANP, the *area code* consisted of the first three digits of the telephone number; it represented a region in North America (including Canada). The first digit was any number from 2 to 9, the second digit was 1 or 0, and the third digit was any number from 0 to 9. The *office code* consisted of the second three digits of the telephone number; it uniquely identified a switch in the telephone network. The first digit was any number from 2 to 9, the second digit was any number from 2 to 9, and the third digit was any number from 0 to 9. The area code and office code could never be the same because the second digit of each code was always different. With this numbering system, the switch was able to determine whether this was a local call or long-distance call by looking at the second digit of the area code. The *station code* consisted of the last four digits in the telephone number. This number uniquely identified a port within the switch that was connected to the telephone being called. Based on this 10-digit numbering system, an office code could have up to 10,000 different station codes. In order for a switch to have more than 10,000 connections, it would have to have more office codes assigned to it.

An increase in the number of phone lines installed in homes, Internet access, and fax machine usage dramatically reduced the number of phone numbers available. This scenario prompted a change in the NANP. The present plan is basically the same as the old plan except for the area code and office code sections of the telephone number. The three digits for the area code and office code are now selected in the same fashion. The first digit can be any number from 2 to 9, and the second and third digits can be any number from 0 to 9. This scenario dramatically increases the number of area codes available, in turn increasing the number of station codes that can be assigned. If the call is a long-distance number, a 1 must be dialed before the 10-digit number.

3.8   International Numbering Plan (ITU-T E.164)

The International Numbering Plan is based on ITU-T specification E.164, an international standard that all countries must follow. This plan states that the telephone number in every country cannot be greater than 15 digits. The first three digits represent the country code, but each may or may not use all three digits. The remaining 12 digits represent the national specific number. For example, the country code for North America is 1. Therefore, when calling North America from another country, 1 must be dialed first to access the NANP. Then the 10 digits required by the NANP are dialed. The 12 digits of the national specific number can be organized in any manner deemed appropriate by the specific country. Also, some countries may use a set of digits to indicate an outgoing international call. For example, 011 is used from within the United States to place an outgoing international call.

3.9   CCS, CCIS, CAS, and SS7

Two methods can be used to transmit supervisory signaling over a T-1 circuit. Those methods are referred to as Common Channel Signaling (CCS) and Common Associated Signaling (CAS). Under the CCS method, signaling information is transmitted along the same path as the voice signal; however, it flows on a separate channel that is multiplexed with the digitized voice signals. CCS systems are usually High-level Data Link Control (HDLC)–based message-oriented signaling systems. Signaling information is transmitted along the same path as the voice signal in CCS, but it flows on a separate channel that is multiplexed with the digitized voice signals. It is used primarily on the 30-PCM-channel circuit known as an E1 circuit line and uses one channel for signaling and another for frame alignment, resulting in the E1 circuit having 32 channels, with each operating at 64 Kbps for a composite transmission rate of 2.048 Mbps. CCS signaling is used primarily on European E1 circuits and some limited use on T-1 circuits. CCS requires one voice slot to be dedicated to transmitting signaling information when it is used on a T-1 circuit. Within the United States, PSTN, the original implementation of CCS, started in 1976 and was known as Common Channel Interoffice Signaling (CCIS). This signaling is similar to ITU-T's Signaling System 6 (SS6). The CCIS protocol operated at relatively low bit rates (2.4K, 4.8K, 9.6K) but transported messages that were only 28 bits long. However, CCIS could not adequately support an integrated voice and data environment. Therefore, a new HDLC-based signaling standard and ITU-T recommendation was developed called Signaling System 7 (SS7).

CAS signaling is primarily used on T-1 circuits to eliminate the requirement for a voice slot. The seventh bit position in frames 6 and 12 in a 12-frame framing sequence are "robbed" to convey signaling information, which is also why CAS signaling is informally referred to as *bit robbing*. Supervisory signaling between PBXs is conveyed on a private voice network between a PBX and a communications carrier's CO switch or between two switches or two PBXs through bit position 7 in frames 6 and 12. The bit 7 pattern represented in frames 6 and 12 is based on the type of signaling, such as loop-start, ground-start, or E&M, and the signaling being conveyed. In CAS signaling, such signaling information as loop open, loop closed, ring present, and ring removed must be conveyed under loop-start signaling. E&M signaling is different from CAS signaling in that it only has two states: idle and busy. The seventh bit in the sixth frame is referred to as the "A" bit, while the signal bits in the twelfth frame are referred to as the "B" bits to differentiate between the signal bits.

The establishment of a telephone call requires several different types of signaling: (1) to inform network devices that a telephone is off the hook; (2) to supply destination information so that the call may be routed properly; and (3) to notify both caller and callee that a call has been placed. SS7 is a relatively new signaling technology and the ITU standard that provides for signaling, call setup, and management of PSTN calls. A separate network is typically is used for SS7 flows, and it is sometimes referred to as *out-of-band signal* because the data transfer for SS7 does not occur on the same path as the call. This is why SS7 is considered the architecture for performing out-of-band signaling in support of the call-establishment, billing, routing, and information-exchange functions of the PSTN. It identifies functions to be performed by a signaling-system network and a protocol to enable their performance.

An SS7 network is made up of two key components: the Signal Transfer Point (STP) and the Session Control Point (SCP). The STP provides routing through the SS7 network and could be thought of as the IP router of the SS7 network. The SCP provides a variety of management features to include 800-number lookup, in a similar manner to how Domain Name System (DNS) and Dynamic Host Control Protocol (DHCP) provide address lookup and management for IP networks. VoIP systems have a corresponding set of rules for call signaling. SS7 was first defined by the ITU-T in 1980; the Swedish Post, Telephone, and Telegraph (PTT) started SS7 trials in 1983; and some European countries are now entirely SS7-based. Within the United States, Bell Atlantic began implementing SS7 in 1988, among the first Bell operating companies, if not the first, to do so.

Currently, most of the long-distance networks and local-exchange-carrier (LEC) networks have migrated to implementations of ITU-T's SS7. By 1989, AT&T had converted its entire digital network to SS7; and US Sprint is SS7-based. However, many LECs are still in the process of upgrading their networks to SS7 because the number of switch upgrades required for SS7 support impacts the LECs much more heavily than the international carrier. The slow deployment of SS7 within the LECs is also partly responsible for delays in incorporating Integrated Services Digital Network (ISDN) within the United States. There are three versions of SS7 protocols at the present time: ITU-T version (1980, 1984) detailed in ITU-T Q.701–Q.741, the AT&T and Telecom Canada Version (1985), and the ANSI (1986) version. SS7 currently provides support for Plain Old Telephone Service (POTS) through the use of a Telephony User Part (TUP), which defines the messages that are used to support this service. An additional ISDN user part (ISUP) has been defined that supports ISDN transport. Eventually, because the ISUP includes translations from POTS to ISDN, the ISUP is expected to replace the TUP.

3.10 Summary

With the lines beginning to blur between voice and data infrastructures, IT managers and administrators today must know how to integrate telecom devices of varying stages of technology into their modern networks.

Digital switches and digital transmission capabilities have opened the floodgates for more voice traffic to be sent over existing phone lines, for better sound quality, and for simplified management of the public switched voice network. As indicated in this chapter, the use of DTMF has greatly increased network capacity and paved the way for myriad telephony software applications, such as automated voice access to bank accounts and voice-enabled e-mail.

Support and management of telecom technologies is likely becoming a critical part of the IT worker's job description. Many IT workers have only a basic understanding of the voice side of IT operations. An introduction to key telephony devices and technologies is essential to avoid potential pitfalls in computer–telephony integration. In order to truly understand how to secure a VoIP network, such knowledge is absolutely essential. This chapter is the first of several chapters in this book intended for readers who are not familiar with the basic concepts essential to understanding VoIP and VoIP security. It is also intended to be a quick refresher for those readers needing a review of basic telephony and VoIP fundamentals in order to obtain full value out of the material presented in the second half of this book.

3.11 Endnotes

1. "Communications Act of 1934: 50th Anniversary Supplement," Federal Communications Law Journal (Los Angeles), January 1985.

2. These companies were Bell Atlantic, BellSouth, Southwestern Bell, NYNEX, Ameritech, US WEST, and Pacific Telesis.

3.12 General References

Alexander, John, et al, "Cisco CallManager Fundamentals: A Cisco AVVID Solution," Cisco Press, July 2001, 720 pages.

Bates, Regis J., Gregory, Donald W., "Voice and Data Communications Handbook," McGraw-Hill, August 2001, 1032 pages.

Bellamy, John C., "Digital Telephony," Wiley, March 2000, 643 pages.

Caputo, Robert, "Cisco Packetized Voice & Data Integration," McGraw-Hill, September 1999, 352 pages.

Collins, Daniel, "Carrier Grade Voice Over IP," McGraw-Hill, September 2000, 496 pages.

Davidson, J., et al, "Voice over IP Fundamentals," Cisco Press, March 2000, 373 pages.

Edgar, Bob, "The VoiceXML Handbook: Understanding and Building the Phone-Enabled Web," CMP Books, April 2001, 481 pages.

Farmer, J., Large, D., and Ciciora, W., "Modern Cable Television Technology: Video, Voice, & Data Communications," Morgan

Kaufmann Publishers, January 1999, 873 pages.

Gonzalo Camarillo, Jonathan Rosenberg, "SIP Demystified," McGraw-Hill, August 2001, 320 pages.

Johnston, Alan, "SIP: Understanding the Session Initiation Protocol," Artech House, January 2001, 228 pages.

Keagy, Scott, "Integrating Voice and Data Networks," Cisco Press, October 2000, 779 pages.

4

Packet Technologies

4.1   Packet Networking Overview

Packet switching (networking) refers to a set of processes whereby specific protocols are used when processing messages. Such messages are divided into packets before they are sent. Each packet is then transmitted individually and can even follow different routes to its destination. Once all of the packets forming a message arrive at the destination, they are recompiled into the original message. Most modern Wide Area Network (WAN) protocols, including TCP/IP, X.25, and Frame Relay, are based on packet-switching technologies. In contrast, normal telephone service is based on a circuit-switching technology, in which a dedicated line is allocated for transmission between two parties. Circuit switching is ideal when data must be transmitted quickly and must arrive in the same order in which it is sent. This is the case with most real-time data, such as live audio and video. Packet switching is more efficient and robust for data that can withstand some delays in transmission, such as e-mail messages and Web pages. Another technology, ATM, attempts to combine the best of both worlds— the guaranteed delivery of circuit-switched networks and the robustness and efficiency of packet-switching networks. We will discuss ATM later in this book. For now, let's focus our attention on the components needed in a packet (switched) network.

4.1.1   ISO/OSI Network Model

The standard model for networking protocols and distributed applications is the International Standard Organization's Open System Interconnect (ISO/OSI) model. It defines seven network layers. The OSI reference model is a hierarchical structure of seven layers that defines the requirements for communications between two computers. It was conceived to allow interoperability across the various platforms offered by vendors. The

Figure 4.1
*OSI model as
applied to network
devices.*

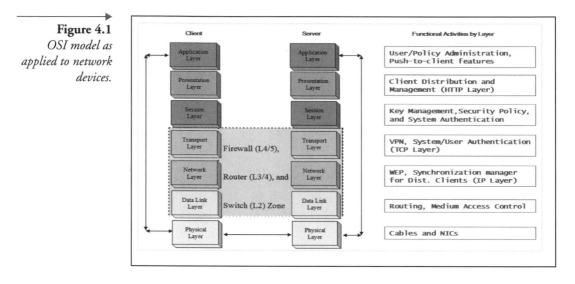

model allows all network elements to operate together, regardless of who built them. By the late 1970s, ISO was recommending the implementation of the OSI model as a networking standard, but unfortunately, TCP/IP had been in use for years.

The OSI reference model provides a set of general design guidelines for data communications systems and also gives a standard way to describe how various portions (layers) of data communications systems interact. The hierarchical layering of protocols on a computer that forms the OSI model is known as a *stack*. A given layer in a stack sends commands to layers below it and services commands from layers above it. TCP/IP was fundamental to ARPANET and the other networks that evolved into the Internet. Only a subset of the whole OSI model is used today. It is widely believed that much of the specification is too complicated and that its full functionality has taken too long to implement, although many people strongly support the OSI model. Figure 4.1 (above) depicts the OSI model.

Layer 1: Physical

Protocols at the physical layer are responsible for establishing, maintaining, and ending physical connections (point-to-point) between computers. These protocols are manifested in the media across which transmission occurs. These protocols do not specify the various cables and connectors, and these specifications are sometimes said to belong to layer 0. Physical layer defines the cable or physical medium (e.g., thinnet, thicknet, unshielded twisted pairs). All media are functionally equivalent. The main difference is in convenience and cost of installation and maintenance. Converters from one media to another operate at this level.

Layer 2: Data Link

Data link protocols provide logical link control and medium access control. These protocols provide reliability to the physical layer transmission by ordering the data into frames and adding error checking and addressing information. The network interface card assembles the data link layer frames. The data link layer actually defines the format of data on the network. A network data frame (a.k.a. packet) includes checksum, source and destination address, and data. The largest packet that can be sent through a data link layer defines the Maximum Transmission Unit (MTU). The data link layer handles the physical and logical connections to the packet's destination, using a network interface. A host connected to an Ethernet would have an Ethernet interface to handle connections to the outside world, and a loopback interface to send packets to itself.

Ethernet addresses a host using a unique, 48-bit address called its Ethernet address or Media Access Control (MAC) address. MAC addresses are usually represented as six colon-separated pairs of hex digits (e.g., 8:0:20:11:ac:85). This number is unique and is associated with a particular Ethernet device. Hosts with multiple network interfaces should use the same MAC address on each. The data link layer's protocol-specific header specifies the MAC address of the packet's source and destination. When a packet is sent to all hosts (broadcast), a special MAC address (ff:ff:ff:ff:ff:ff) is used.

Layer 3: Network

The network layer protocols establish, maintain, and terminate end-to-end (network) links. These protocols route messages across the network(s) between two computers. Different network operating systems often have their own network layer protocols, but can also use other protocols. This flexibility is essential when communicating accross multiple client/server platforms. Internetwork Protocol (IP) is used as a network layer interface. IP is responsible for routing, directing datagrams from one network to another. The network layer may have to break large datagrams—larger than MTU—into smaller packets, and the host receiving the packet will have to reassemble the fragmented datagram. The IP identifies each host with a 32-bit IP address. IP addresses are written as four dot-separated decimal numbers between 0 and 255 (e.g., 129.79.16.40). The leading one to three bytes of the IP identify the network, and the remaining byte identifies the host on that network. The network portion of the IP is assigned by InterNIC Registration Services, under contract to the National Science Foundation, and the host portion of the IP is assigned by the local network administrators, locally by noc@indiana.edu. For large sites, usually the first two bytes represents the network portion of the IP, and the third and fourth bytes identify the subnet and host, respectively.

Even though IP packets are addressed using IP addresses, hardware addresses must be used to actually transport data from one host to another. The Address Resolution Protocol (ARP) is used to map the IP address to its hardware address.

Layer 4: Transport

Transport layer subdivides user-buffer into network-buffer-sized datagrams and enforces desired transmission control. Two transport protocols, Transmission Control Protocol (TCP) and User Datagram Protocol (UDP), sit at the transport layer. Reliability and speed are the primary difference between these two protocols. TCP establishes connections between two hosts on the network through sockets, which are determined by the IP address and port number. TCP keeps track of the packet delivery order and the packets that must be present. Maintaining this information for each connection makes TCP a stateful protocol. UDP, on the other hand, provides a low overhead transmission service, but with less error checking. Transport layer protocols are responsible for the reliability of end-to-end connections. These protocols assemble multiple network layer packets into a coherent message. This layer also provides flow control and error recovery.

For example, the Network File System (NFS), which is an essential building block of modern networks, is built on top of UDP because of its speed and statelessness. Statelessness simplifies the crash recovery process. NFS is used to allow host machines to mount partitions on a remote system and use them as though they are local file systems. This allows a system administrator to store resources in a central location on the network, providing authorized users with continuous access to them. Currently, there are two versions of NFS in use. NFS version 2 (NFSv2), which has been around for several years, is widely supported by various operating systems. NFS version 3 (NFSv3) has several more features, including a variable file handle size and better error reporting.

Layer 5: Session

The session protocol defines the format of the data sent over the connections. NFS uses the Remote Procedure Call (RPC) for its session protocol.

RPC may be built on either TCP or UDP. Login sessions use TCP, whereas NFS and broadcast sessions use UDP. Protocols at this layer are necessary for establishing, maintaining, and ending sessions between user applications. Such protocols are designed to make the differences, across various platforms, transparent to the user.

Layer 6: Presentation

External Data Representation sits at the presentation level. It converts local representation of data to its canonical form and vice versa. The canonical form uses a standard byte-ordering and structure-packing convention, independent of the host. The presentation layer protocols deal with data syntax during transfer between two application processes. If the client and server are using different file formats, this layer has conversion protocols. Therefore, computers using different file formats can still communicate with each other. Data encryption and decryption protocols also exist at the presentation layer.

Layer 7: Application

The application layer provides network services to the end users. Mail, ftp, telnet, DNS, NIS, and NFS are examples of network applications. This layer has protocols that support user applications, but it does not include the applications themselves. There is an opinion that the network operating system should be included in this layer, but this is open to disagreement. Strictly speaking, this layer deals with file access and management and includes the OSI X.400 and X.500 e-mail protocols. X.400 allows interoperability between different e-mail software, and X.500 synchronizes e-mail across different systems.

4.1.2 TCP/IP Network Model

Although the OSI model is widely used and often cited as the standard, TCP/IP has been used by most Unix workstation vendors. TCP/IP is designed around a simple four-layer scheme. It does omit some features found under the OSI model, and it also combines the features of some adjacent OSI layers and splits other layers apart. The four network layers defined by the TCP/IP model are as follows:

- **Layer 1: Link**. This layer defines the network hardware and device drivers.

- **Layer 2: Network**. This layer is used for basic communication, addressing, and routing. TCP/IP uses IP and ICMP protocols at the network layer.

- **Layer 3: Transport**. This layer handles communication among programs on a network. TCP and UDP fall within this layer.

- **Layer 4: Application**. End-user applications reside at this layer. Commonly used applications include NFS, DNS, arp, rlogin, talk, ftp, ntp, and traceroute.

4.2   Routing and Switching

4.2.1   Routing Basics

The process of routing traffic over the Internet is essentially the implementation of a method of path selection. The routing process assumes that the addresses stored in the IP data packets it processes have been assigned to facilitate data delivery. The routing process assumes that these addresses convey at least a minimal amount of information about where a host is located. This addressing assumption permits routers to forward packets without having to rely on broadcasting or referencing a complete listing of all possible destinations. Because the Internet was designed to accommodate large networks where broadcasting or use of huge routing tables would not be practical, routing at the IP level is used as a primary means of forwarding data packets from source to destination. Three prerequisites must be met to perform routing:[1]

1.   Design

2.   Implementation

3.   Enforcement

Design

An organizational structure or top-level design plan of some sort must exist that maintains which addresses are allocated and to whom they are assigned. Most often, these addresses are segmented into fields that correspond to various levels in a physical hierarchy. At each level of the hierarchy, only the corresponding field in the address is used, permitting addresses to be handled in blocks. In the world of IP, the most common designs are IP address classes, subnetting, and Classless Interdomain Routing (CIDR).

IP Addresses and Address Classes   An IP address is a unique identifier for a node or host connection on an IP network. An IP address is a 32-bit binary number usually represented as four decimal values, each representing 8 bits, in the range 0 to 255 (known as octets) separated by decimal points. This is known as "dotted decimal" notation.

It is sometimes useful to see these values represented in binary form.

Example: 179.220.140.200

```
    179 = 10110011
    220 = 11011100
    140 = 10001100
    200 = 11001000
```
or
```
    179.    220.    140.    200  (dotted decimal form)
10110011.11011100.10001100.11001000 (binary form)
```

Every IP address consists of two parts: one identifying the network and one identifying the node. The class of the address and the subnet mask determine which part belongs to the network address and which part belongs to the node address. Now, let's discuss the five different types of address classes. One can determine which class any IP address belongs to by examining the first four bits of the IP address.

```
Class A addresses begin with 0xxx, or 001 to 126 decimal.
Class B addresses begin with 10xx, or 128 to 191 decimal.
Class C addresses begin with 110x, or 192 to 223 decimal.
Class D addresses begin with 1110, or 224 to 239 decimal.
Class E addresses begin with 1111, or 240 to 254 decimal.
```

Addresses beginning with binary 01111111 (127 decimal) are reserved for loopback and internal testing on a local host. Class D addresses are reserved for multicasting, and Class E addresses are reserved for future use. They should never be used for host addresses. Now we can see how the class determines, by default, which part of the IP address belongs to the network (N) and which part belongs to the node (n).

```
Class A — NNNNNNNN.nnnnnnnn.nnnnnnn.nnnnnnn
Class B — NNNNNNNN.NNNNNNNN.nnnnnnnn.nnnnnnnn
Class C — NNNNNNNN.NNNNNNNN.NNNNNNNN.nnnnnnnn
```

In the previous example, 179.220.140.200 is a Class B address. Therefore, the network address is defined by the first two octets (179.220.xxx.xxx). The node part of the address is defined by the last two octets (NNN.NNN.140.220). The node section of the address is set to all zeros when it is necessary to specify the network address for any given IP address. In our example, 179.220.0.0 specifies the network address for 179.220.140.200. When the node section is set to all ones (10110011.11011100.11111111.11111111), it represents a broadcast address that is meant to be used to send to all hosts on the network. In this case, the full address reflecting a node setting for broadcast would be 179.220.255.255.

Subnetting   A subnet allows the flow of network traffic between hosts to be segregated based on a network configuration. By organizing hosts into logical groups, subnetting can improve network security and performance. Three IP network addresses are reserved for private networks. The addresses are 10.0.0.0/8, 172.16.0.0/12, and 192.168.0.0/16. They can be used by anyone setting up internal IP networks, such as a lab or home LAN behind a Network Address Translation (NAT) or proxy server or a router. It is always safe to use these addresses because routers on the Internet will never forward packets coming from these addresses. These addresses are defined in RFC 1918.[2]

Subnetting an IP network can be done for a variety of reasons, including organization, use of different physical media (e.g., Ethernet, FDDI, WAN), preservation of address space, and security. The most common reason is to control network traffic. In an Ethernet network, all nodes on a segment see all of the packets transmitted by all of the other nodes on that segment. Performance can be adversely affected under heavy traffic loads because of collisions and the resulting retransmissions. A router is used to connect IP networks to minimize the amount of traffic each segment must receive.

Subnet Masking   Perhaps the most recognizable aspect of subnetting is the subnet mask. Like IP addresses, a subnet mask contains four bytes (32 bits) and is often written using the same dotted decimal notation. A common subnet mask in binary form is:

```
11111111 11111111 11111111 00000000
```

Most often, the dotted decimal form is shown as 255.255.255.0. When using the subnet mask, it should be considered as an attribute of an IP address. The combination of the IP address and the subnet mask are intended to work in tandem, both helping to segment the address into two parts: an "extended network address" and a host address. For a subnet mask to be valid, its leftmost bits must be set to 1. For example, the mask

```
00000000 00000000 00000000 00000000
```

is an invalid subnet mask because the leftmost bit is set to 0. Conversely, the rightmost bits in a valid subnet mask must be set to 0, not 1. Therefore, this address is also invalid:

```
11111111 11111111 11111111 11111111
```

Any valid subnet mask will contain two pieces: the left side with all mask bits set to 1 (representing the extended network portion) and the right side with all bits set to 0 (the host node portion). Subnetting allows network administrators a greater degree of flexibility in designing network architectures. Host machines that exist on different subnets can only communicate with each other by using network gateway devices such as routers. The ability to filter traffic between subnets can make more bandwidth available to applications and can limit access in desirable ways. The reader is encouraged to consult RFC 1918 for more details about these special networks.

Classless Interdomain Routing (CIDR) Classless Interdomain Routing (CIDR) was invented several years ago to keep the Internet from running out of IP addresses. The address class system defined previously can be wasteful when allocation of IP address space is processed. Before CIDR, literally anyone who could reasonably show a need for more than 254 host addresses was given a Class B address block of 65,533 host addresses. What was even more of a horrid waste of available IP address space was the allocation of Class A blocks that have more than 16 million address spaces to certain companies and organizations that likely would never use that number of IP addresses. Studies have shown that only a small portion of allocated Class A and Class B address space has actually been assigned to a host computer on the Internet.

CIDR, described in a group of Internet RFCs[3] (1467, 1481, 1517, 1518, 1519, and 1520), is intended to increase the efficiency of the Internet routing tables. Part of this efficiency would be gained from just reducing the size of the number of entries required in the routing tables. By enforcing a policy of allocating IP addresses in a way that allows routing information for multiple networks to be aggregated into a single routing table entry, this effort is meeting with success. ISPs today are being assigned Class C address space in contiguous blocks that they, in turn, will use to reallocate to their customer base. By using variable-length netmask information in the routing protocols, it enables multiple Class C networks to be represented by a single routing table entry. This process is referred to as *classless* because it enables routing to occur at intermediate levels that fall between the traditional eight-bit boundaries of IP network class spaces. An unavoidable drawback, however, is the need to renumber existing domains to take advantage of CIDR. This can result in a high administrative cost if the networks involved are very large.

People realized that addresses could be conserved if the class system was eliminated. By accurately allocating only the amount of address space that was actually needed, the address space crisis could be avoided for many years. This was first proposed in 1992 as a scheme called *supernetting*. Under supernetting, the classful subnet masks are extended so that a network address and subnet mask could, for example, specify multiple Class C subnets with one address. RFC 1519[4], released in September 1993, details the process of supernetting, which is beyond the scope of this section. Suffice it to say that with the implementation of CIDR and supernetting, the address shortage that was expected to occur years ago will not occur for years to come. At that point in the future, IPv6, which is implemented with 128-bit addresses, will become the de facto standard. Under IPv6, address allocation could allow 1 billion unique IP addresses for every individual on Earth!

Implementation

The design plan must be implemented in switching nodes, which must be able to extract path information from the addresses. Because router programming is generally not under a designer's control, designs must be limited by the features provided by manufacturers. Subnetting's great appeal lies in its flexibility, while using a fairly simple implementation model.

Enforcement

The plan must be enforced in host addressing. A design is useless unless addresses are assigned in accordance with it. Addressing authority must be centralized, possibly with subsets of the available addressing space delegated to subordinates.

Routing is almost always used at the IP level in the Internet environment. Bridging is almost always used at the data link layer. For new network installations, it is best to plan for routing even if it's not planned for use during the initial phase of network operation. It requires advanced planning to design an addressing scheme that will satisfy organizational needs and work properly. However, remember that your hardware won't know the difference between an organized, planned addressing scheme and a haphazard addressing scheme. It is recommended that an organization plan for the ability to put routers in strategic locations, even if those locations will initially use bridges or concentrators. Planning for their eventual use will allow routers to be easily added later. There are few things more frustrating than knowing exactly where a router should be added and, because of a lack of prior planning, knowing that a hundred network addresses must be changed before the router can be added.

4.2.2 Routing Tables

Internet hosts use routing tables to compute the next hop for a packet. Routing tables can take many forms, but here is a simple model that can explain most Internet routing. Each entry in a routing table has at least two fields: the IP Address Prefix and the Next Hop address field. The Next Hop is the IP address of another host or router that is directly reachable via a physical connection (most often it is Ethernet). The IP Address Prefix specifies a set of destinations for which the routing entry is valid. In order to be in this set, the beginning of the destination IP address must match the IP Address Prefix, which can have from 0 to 32 significant bits. For example, an IP Address Prefix of 128.18.0.0/16 (routing address/mask) would match any IP Destination Address of the form 128.18.X.X.

Bridged networks are regarded as single connections for routing purposes. If no routing table entries are found that match a packet's Destination Address, the packet is discarded as undeliverable. If more than one routing table entry matches a Destination Address, the longest match Destination Address is preferred. The longest match is defined as the entry with the most 1 bits present in its Routing Mask. In order to avoid the need for specifying route entries for every possible Internet destination, most hosts and routers often use a default route. In many instances, especially for single connections, the routing tables will contain nothing but a single default route. Default routes are common on networks with only a single link connecting to the global Internet. A default route has a Routing Address/Mask pair of 0.0.0.0/0.0.0.0. In other words, it matches every IP address, but because there are no 1 bits in its Routing Mask, any other match would be selected by the longest match rule. The default route is used only if no others matches are in the routing table. Often, on single connection networks, routing tables will have entries for local nets and subnets, as well as a single default route leading to the outbound link. However, remember that all Next Hops must be directly reachable, so the default routes won't necessarily point to the same IP address.

4.2.3   Distance-Vector Routing Protocols

This particular type of routing protocol requires each router to inform its neighbors of its routing table. For each network path, the receiving routers pick the neighbor advertising the lowest cost, then add this entry into its routing table for readvertisement. Hello and RIP are common distance-vector (D-V) routing protocols. Common enhancements to D-V algorithms include split horizon, poison reverse, triggered updates, and hold down. You will find a good discussion of D-V, or Bellman-Ford algorithms, in RIP's protocol specification, RFC 1058.[5]

4.2.4   Switching

An electrical switch physically directs electrical current to one of several wires. Once the connection is made, the switch appears to become a part of the wire. It introduces little to no resistance, attenuation, or delay. A networking switch is designed to behave in much the same way. Its primary feature is speed and, just like an electrical switch, it is designed to appear much like a straight piece of wire when relaying data signals.

Switches must implement a normal path selection algorithm; they just do it faster. Layer 2 switches bridge; layer 3 switches route. Normal bridges and routers will receive an entire packet, analyze its headers, make a forwarding decision, and then transmit the packet. The packet is stored in RAM while being processed. These RAM buffers can become bottlenecks in a busy network. Switches use specialized onboard processing chips than can enable them to forward packets directly from source to destination without passing packet data through RAM buffers.

Consider a typical Ethernet switch, which acts much like a standard IEEE 802.1d bridge. The difference is that as soon as an incoming packet's header has been received, a forwarding decision is immediately made, before the packet is completely received. If the destination Ethernet segment is idle, the packet begins transmission there immediately. As bits are received, they are shunted through the switch fabric to the destination interface. On a 10-Mbps Ethernet, the net delay is perhaps 1 or 2 microseconds, as opposed to several milliseconds for a typical bridge. This is termed *cut-through switching*. ATM switches provide a good example of layer 3 switching. When a connection is set up, a routing decision is made based on the ATM NSAP address. A virtual path identifier (VPI) is assigned and used in the header of subsequent cells for that connection. The switch fabric is configured to transmit cells bearing that VPI directly to the destination interface.

4.3   IP Networks

4.3.1   Address Resolution Protocol (ARP)

Address Resolution Protocol (ARP) resides in the bottom half of the network layer. It can be considered a mechanism for mapping addresses between the network logical addresses and MAC layer physical addresses. For example, the network layer protocol IP is not aware of 48-bit MAC addresses such as Ethernet. Likewise, the MAC layer protocol such as Ethernet is not aware of 32-bit IP addresses. ARP provides the mechanism to map MAC addresses to IP addresses in a temporary memory space called the *ARP cache*.

The ARP cache is a dynamic cache, and the information is stored only for 120 seconds (then it is discarded). In this manner, the ARP cache remains small. The ARP cache can be viewed by using the "ARP -a" command at a command prompt. This should display the current ARP cache. If nothing is displayed, then most likely your computer hasn't communicated on the network (for the past 120 seconds). Ping another device on the network and see if the ARP cache has changed.

The basic operation of ARP is as follows: when the IP layer wants to communicate with another device on the network, it checks the ARP cache (to see if there is a match with an Ethernet address). If there is no matching entry in the ARP cache, an ARP broadcast datagram is sent out that basically says: "Does anybody know whose Ethernet address belongs to this IP address?" The receiving station (that has the IP address) responds with an ARP datagram that says: "This is my IP address and here is my Ethernet address." The ARP cache is updated, and the original IP layer information is passed on to the MAC layer for processing.

4.3.2   Understanding IP, TCP, UDP, and ICMP Packets

An excellent discussion of IP header packets is found on the Web, written by Roamer[6] (an alias). Much of the information that follows was originally posted to the Web by that person but is presented here in slightly modified format for clarity and quality. Written in three parts, Roamer's article provides a good basic overview of IP packets and will help the reader quickly understand their significance in firewall processing.

IP Packets

The IP header, as defined in RFC 791[7], looks like this (Figure 4.2):

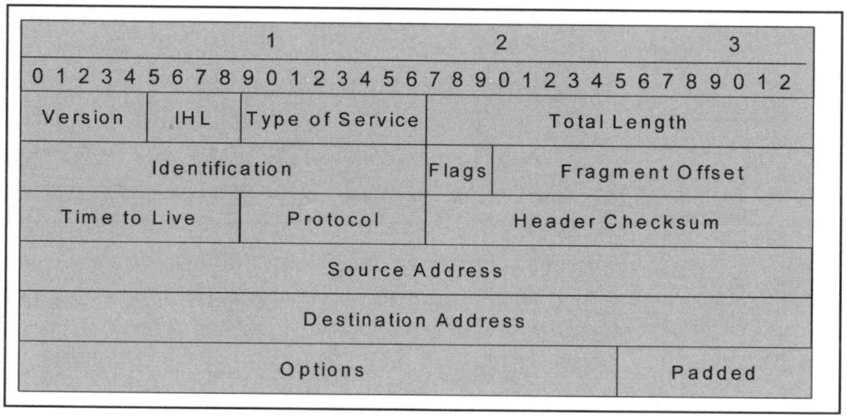

Figure 4.2
IP packet header.

The first four bytes are the header version. The next four bytes define the IP header length. An example of this in a dump would look like this:

```
0x000  45c0  005c e857 0000 3f01 5a93 aa81 3534
```

Let's look at the bold fields above. The four indicates that this is IP version 4. The five indicates that the header length is five double words or 20 bytes long. Coincidentally, this is the smallest possible size for an IP header. Next let's look at the total length field.

```
0x000  45c0 005c  e857 0000 3f01 5a93 aa81 3534
```

The bold text above (bytes 2 and 3) are set to 0x005c. This converts to 92 decimal and indicates that the entire length of the packet, including the

header, is 92 bytes. Because we know that the header is 20 bytes, we now
know that there are 72 bytes of data. The next two bytes represent the IP
identification number.

```
0x000 45c0 005c e857 0000 3f01 5a93 aa81 3534
```

The IP identification number is mainly useful for identifying anomalous
signatures. This is essentially a random number, but it is generated in different ways depending on the IP stack that is used. It is also used in conjunction with the next two bytes (flags and offset) to control fragmentation.

```
0x000 45c0 005c e857 0000 3f01 5a93 aa81 3534
```

The first bold byte above (**3f**) indicates the time to live (TTL). After the
TTL is the Protocol Field (**01**). This indicates the type of protocol that this
packet encapsulates. For the purpose of this example, we will focus on
0x01, 0x06, and 0x11 or decimal 1 (**ICMP**), 6 (**TCP**), and 17 (**UDP**). The
above example indicates an ICMP packet.

The next eight bytes give the source (**aa81 3534**) and destination (**5804
003d**) IP addresses. These (as well as all information in a packet header) are
encoded in Network Byte Order. This means that aa813534 decoded is the
IP address 170.129.53.52.

```
0x000 45c0 005c e857 0000 3f01 5a93 aa81 3534
0x010 5804 003d 0303 4a7d 0000 0000 4500 002c
```

The next three bytes indicate any options for this packet, and the final
byte of the header is padding. As you can see, once broken down, an IP
header is not just a random collection of numbers. Each part of the IP
header has a specific function.

TCP Packets

The TCP header is shown in Figure 4.3.

This header would follow the IP header if the protocol byte is set to 6.
The first two bold fields below represent the source and destination ports:

```
0x010 ca82 1233 fdb9 0050 bd51 a0f4 0000 0000
```

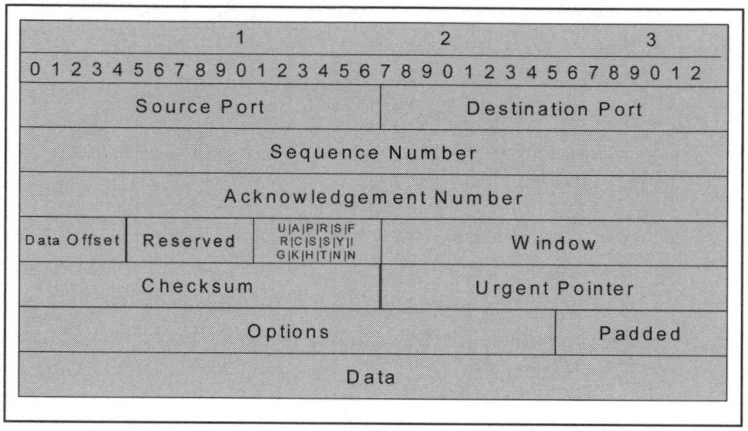

Figure 4.3
*TCP packet
header.*

Figure 4.3 TCP packet header.

fdb9 indicates a source port of 64473, and **0050** represents a destination port of 80 or HTTP.

The next two 32-bit values are the sequence numbers. The first value is the sequence number of this packet, and the second value is the sequence number that is being acknowledged.

```
0x010 ca82 1233 fdb9 0050 bd51 a0f4 0000 0000
```

This gives us a sequence number of 3176243444 and an acknowledgment number of 0. Next we come to the data offset:

```
0x020 7002 4000 785d 0000 0204 05b4 0101 0402
```

Here we have a size of 7. Multiply this by 4 bytes to get a length of 28 bytes. The shortest possible length for a TCP header is 20 bytes, which is represented by a 5 in this field. Next we have the code bits:

```
0x020 7002 4000 785d 0000 0204 05b4 0101 0402
```

In order to understand the code bits, we need to look at this section of the TCP header.

```
                 2   1    8   4   2   1
   We have :  |  U  |  A  |  P  |  R  |  S  |  F  |
```

In our case (02) would mean that neither the 2 or 1 (U or A) are set in the first two bits, and the 2 (S) is set in the second four bits. These bits represent Urgent, Ack, Push, Reset, Syn, and Fin. So in our case, the Syn bit is the only one set.

The window size is used to implement flow control, which is how much data is sent through at a time.

```
0x020 7002 4000 785d 0000 0204 05b4 0101 0402
```

In our case the window size is 0x4000 or 16,384. This means that the other end can send up to 16,384 bytes. Once this size has been sent, the other side will wait for an Ack or an adjustment in the window size before sending more data. The urgent pointer is only useful if the URG bit is set. In our case it is not, so we have a value of 0000.

```
0x020 7002 4000 785d 0000 0204 05b4 0101 0402
```

If it were set, this would indicate where the urgent data is within the packet. Finally, we have the TCP options. This field is not required and will only appear when the header is larger than five. If there are any options present, they must be stated in a multiple of four bytes in this field.

```
0x020 7002 4000 785d 0000 0204 05b4 0101 0402
```

After the options comes the actual data to be transmitted. This concludes our look at TCP packets. In the next section, we teach you how to decode UDP and ICMP packets to understand how data is transmitted via those protocols.

UDP and ICMP Packets

The UDP header is shown in Figure 4.4.

The first two bold fields below represent the source and destination ports:

```
0x010 ca82 1233 05ab 0035 0032 2dc1 0000 0000
```

05ab indicates a source port of 1451, and **0035** represents a destination port of 53 or DNS. Next is the message length. This field will be analogous to the datagram length field in the IP header.

Figure 4.4
*UDP packet
header.*

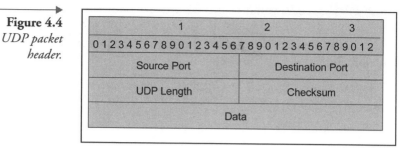

```
0x010 ca82 1233 05ab 0035 0032 2dc1 0000 0000
```

The UDP checksum, like all IP checksum values, is used by the destination machine to check the validity of the packet.

The ICMP header (Figure 4.5) has only three parts:

Figure 4.5
*ICMP packet
header.*

Now, let's look at how to deconstruct ICMP packets. ICMP is a messaging protocol used to test connectivity, handle error correction, and make notifications. Ping is the most common use of ICMP. Let's examine this line from a dump file:

```
0x010 7002 4000 785d 0800 c3ee 05b4 0101 0402
```

The first two bytes (**08**) tell us that this is an echo request or ping packet. The code (**00**) tells us there is no code. The table seen on the following page can be used to decode ICMP types and codes. **c3ee** is the checksum, which is used to test validity. Table 4.1 contains all IMCP codes.

Table 4.1   *ICMP Decode Table*

Type	Name	Code(s)
0	Echo reply	0—none
1	Unassigned	

Table 4.1 *ICMP Decode Table (continued)*

Type	Name	Code(s)
2	Unassigned	
3	Destination unreachable	0—Net unreachable
		1—Host unreachable
		2—Protocol unreachable
		3—Port unreachable
		4—Fragmentation needed and DF bit set
		5—Source route failed
		6—Destination network unknown
		7—Destination host unknown
		8—Source host isolated
		9—Communication with destination network is administratively prohibited
		10—Communication with destination host is administratively prohibited
		11—Destination network unreachable for TOS
		12—Destination host unreachable for TOS
4	Source quench	0—none
5	Redirect	0—Redirect datagram for the network
		1—Redirect datagram for the host
		2—Redirect datagram for the TOS and network
		3—Redirect datagram for the TOS and host
6	Alternate host address	0—Alternate address for host
7	Unassigned	
8	Echo	0—None
9	Router advertisement	0—None
10	Router selection	0—None

Table 4.1   *ICMP Decode Table (continued)*

Type	Name	Code(s)
11	Time exceeded	0—Time to live exceeded in transit
		1—Fragment reassembly time exceeded
12	Parameter problem	0—Pointer indicates the error
		1—Missing a required option
		2—Bad length
13	Timestamp	0—None
14	Timestamp reply	0—None
15	Information request	0—None
16	Information reply	0—None
17	Address mask request	0—None
18	Address mask reply	0—None
19	Reserved (for security)	
20-29	Reserved (for robustness experiment)	
30	Traceroute	
31	Datagram conversion error	
32	Mobile host redirect	
33	IPv6 where-are-you	
34	IPv6 I-am-here	
35	Mobile registration request	
36	Mobile registration reply	
37-255	Reserved	

This concludes our look at IP packets. This section was not designed to make you an expert at decoding packets but was geared toward providing you with a basic understanding necessary for decoding packets as they come across your network.

4.4 VoIP Security Protocols

4.4.1 H.235 and Security Profiles

In November 2000, the ITU-T defined different security profiles and began the process of establishing some semblance of interoperability with the release of the H.235 Version 2 standard. Security profiles were necessary because the standard does not mandate any particular set of features. The profiles defined provide varying security levels and describe a subset of security mechanisms offered by security standard H.235, which should be considered as mandatory items of inclusion. Because the subset of features can be implemented with various options enabled (or not) for protection of H.235 communications, the result was that the impact of an implementation could vary largely dependent on how many of the features were implemented. The following sections, originally presented in NIST SP 800-58,[8] provide a brief overview of the various profiles used across different organizations.

4.4.2 H.235v2

H.235v2 is the successor to the H.235 version that was approved in November 2000. This updated version of the standard included enhancements such as support for elliptic curve cryptography and Advanced Encryption Standard (AES), as well as the addition of several security profiles that were defined to support product interoperability. These new security profiles are defined in several annexes to H.235v2. These include:

- **Annex D:** Shared secrets and keyed hashes
- **Annex E:** Digital signatures on every message
- **Annex F:** Digital signatures and shared secret passing on first handshake followed by keyed hash usage

Each of these security profile annexes are discussed in the following paragraphs.

4.4.3 H.235v2 Annex D: Baseline Security Profile

The baseline security profile defined in H.235v2 Annex D relies on symmetric encryption techniques. Shared secrets are used to provide authentication and validation of message integrity. The three supported scenarios for this profile are (1) endpoint to gatekeeper, (2) gatekeeper to gatekeeper, and (3) endpoint to endpoint. For this particular security profile, gatekeeper-routed signaling (i.e., hop-to-hop security) is the favored technique. Using gatekeeper-routed signaling for a direct call model is possible, although it is limited in capability because a shared secret must be established between parties before any actual communication can take place. This approach might be feasible in smaller environments, but it can lead to huge administrative effort when implemented in larger environments. This profile supports secure fast connect and H.245 tunneling, and it may be combined with a voice encryption option. This profile is easy to implement, but it is not highly scalable for use as a global IP telephony solution because of the restricted methods of key management.

4.4.4 H.235v2 Annex E: Signature Security Profile

The signature security profile relies on asymmetric encryption techniques. Certificates and digital signatures are used to provide authentication and message integrity. The signature security profile mandates the gatekeeper-routed model. Because this profile relies on a public key infrastructure rather than relying on a preestablished shared secret, it scales for larger, global environments. In addition to the baseline security profile, it provides nonrepudiation; this security profile supports secure fast connect and H.245 tunneling and may be combined with the voice encryption option described in the next section. Usage of this protocol may have a significant, critical impact on overall system performance because it requires the use of digital signatures for every message processed. It requires signature generation and verification on both the sender and receiver side of the transaction.

4.4.5 Voice Encryption Option

The H.235v2 Annex D: Voice Encryption Option offers confidentiality for voice stream data and may be combined with the baseline security profile or with the signature security profile. The voice encryption option describes the master key exchange during an H.225.0 call-signaling process. The generation and distribution of media stream keys during H.245 call control also requires a master key exchange. The encryption algorithms are intended to be used in CBC mode, and the new profile provides support for AES encryption. The following security mechanisms are described within the voice encryption security profile:

- Encryption of RTP packets using various methods and modes
- Key management with key and security capability exchange
- Key update mechanism and synchronization

Encryption and key management for RTCP and authentication and integrity for RTP and RTCP are not covered by this profile. In order to counter potential denial of service and flooding attacks on open or discovered RTP/UDP ports, the H.235 standard defines a media antispamming procedure. This antispamming procedure provides a lightweight RTP packet authentication and integrity mechanism intended for use on selected fields through a computed Message Authentication Code. The algorithms used to compute the Message Authentication Code are either triple-DES-MAC or the SHA1 function. Media antispamming uses the padding mechanism of RTP. For this feature, no special security profile was specified in H.235 as was done for the voice encryption security profile for RTP encryption. However, media antispamming features may be used in combination with media encryption to enhance the overall security protection profile.

4.4.6 H.235v2 Annex F: Hybrid Security Profile

The hybrid security profile relies on both asymmetric and symmetric techniques. The hybrid profile is a combination of the baseline security profile and the signature security profile. Certificates and digital signatures are used to provide authentication and message integrity (as in the signature security profile) for the first handshake between two entities. During this handshake process, a shared secret is established that is used later on in the process in just the same way as was described for the baseline security profile. The hybrid security profile mandates the use of the gatekeeper-routed model. Because this profile relies on a public key infrastructure instead of preestablished shared secrets, it is suitable for use in larger, global environments where scalability may be a concern. This profile supports secure fast connect and H.245 tunneling, and it may be combined with the voice encryption option to further protect voice streaming media. It provides a relatively high level of security without relying on preestablished shared secrets. Because key management uses digital signatures, it is scalable and suitable for use in global IP telephony deployments. Moreover, it does not suffer from the same performance requirements as the signature security profile.

4.4.7   H.235v3

Version 3 of H.235 supersedes H.235v2 and features a new procedure for encrypted DTMF (touch tone) signals, supports object identifiers for the AES encryption algorithm (used for media payload encryption), and supports enhanced stream-cipher encryption modes (OFB/EOFB) for encryption of media streams. It introduces an authentication-only option in Annex D, which is used for NAT/firewall traversal, and it provides better security support for direct-routed calls in a new annex, Annex I. There is also improved error reporting in the new version.

4.4.8   Baseline Security Profile Enhancements

Using this profile, either message authentication and integrity are achieved by calculating an integrity check value over the complete message, or an authentication-only process is achieved by computing an integrity check over a special part of the message. The latter option is useful in environments where NAT and firewalls are implemented. The specific version used is distinguished by a predesignated identifier.

4.4.9   Draft H.235v3 Annex G: SRTP and MIKEY usage

Annex G discusses the incorporation of key management to be used for supporting the Secure Real-time Transport Protocol (SRTP). This annex is still not standardized because the referenced IETF documents for key management (MIKEY) and media data security (SRTP) are still in draft form at the time of this writing and are not yet available as a formal standard. The SRTP provides confidentiality, message authentication, and replay protection for RTP/RTCP traffic. The RTP standard provides the flexibility needed to adapt to application-specific requirements, with the possibility to define various security profiles in companion documents. SRTP is defined as such a profile for the RTP, and it is currently in draft status. The draft is expected to be a standard soon, but it was not finalized at the time of this writing. SRTP may be used within multimedia sessions to ensure a secure media data exchange. It can be used with several session control protocols (e.g., with H.323 or SIP). SRTP does not define key management by itself. It uses a set of negotiated parameters from which session keys for encryption, authentication, and integrity protection are derived. The key management is not fixed. Within the IETF, the working group MSEC discusses key management solutions to be used beyond other protocols with SRTP. The preferred solution is MIKEY, which is also part of the group key management architecture.

MIKEY describes a key management scheme that addresses real-time multimedia scenarios (e.g., SIP calls and RTSP sessions, streaming, unicast, groups, multicast). The focus lies on the setup of a security association for secure multimedia sessions, including key management and update, security policy data, and so on, such that requirements in a heterogeneous environment are fulfilled. MIKEY also supports the negotiation of single and multiple crypto sessions. This is especially useful for the case where the key management is applied to SRTP, because RTP and RTCP may need to be secured independently. Deployment scenarios for MIKEY include peer-to-peer, simple one-to-many, and small-size interactive group scenarios.

MIKEY supports the negotiation of cryptographic keys and security parameters for one or more security protocols. This results in the concept of crypto session bundles, which describe a collection of crypto sessions that may have a common Traffic Encryption Key (TEK), Traffic Generation Key (TGK), and common belonging-session security parameters. MIKEY defines three options for the user authentication and negotiation of the master keys (all as two-way handshakes). They are:

- Symmetric key distribution (preshared keys, MAC for integrity protection)
- Asymmetric key distribution
- Diffie-Hellman key agreement protected by digital signatures

Although a fourth version does exist, it is not part of the MIKEY specification. It is specified as an extension to MIKEY, and it describes the Diffie-Hellman key agreement, which is protected by use of symmetric, preshared keys. The default and mandatory key transport encryption methodology is AES in counter mode. MIKEY uses a 160-bit authentication tag, generated by HMAC with SHA-1 as the mandatory algorithm as described in RFC 2104.[9] When asymmetric mechanisms are used, support of X.509v3 certificates for public key encryption and digital signatures is mandatory. Annex G discusses use of MIKEY to integrate a key management scheme suitable for SRTP in three profiles:

- **Profile 1:** Uses symmetric techniques to protect the key management data in gatekeeper-routed scenarios

- **Profile 2:** Uses asymmetric techniques to protect the key management data in scenarios with a single gatekeeper instance

- **Profile 3:** Describes Profile 2 for multiple intermediate gatekeepers.

The basic concept of all three protection profiles is the protected transmission of key management data as a self-encapsulated module.

4.4.10   Draft H.235v3 Annex H: RAS Key Management

Key management negotiation processes that occur during the RAS gatekeeper discovery phase comprise the basic premise formulated in H.235 Annex H. During gatekeeper discovery, a shared secret is established between the endpoint and the gatekeeper. The negotiation of the shared secret may be protected using PINs or passwords (*a.k.a.* shared secrets). The draft document references two protocols used for Encrypted Key Exchange using a shared secret to obfuscate a Diffie-Hellman key exchange process. The first protocol referenced is the Encrypted Key Exchange (EKE), whereby a shared secret is used to encrypt the Diffie-Hellman public keys with a symmetrically encrypted algorithm. The second protocol mentioned is the Simple Password-authenticated Exponential Key Exchange (SPEKE) methodology, where a shared secret is used to create a key generator for use with the Diffie-Hellman public key group. Use of these protocols for RAS key management helps create a strong Diffie-Hellman key exchange with the use of a common, shared secret. A potential disadvantage when using these particular protocols is that they are subject to patent protections under U.S. law (*and thereby they are also subject to protection under international World Intellectual Property Agreements*).

The draft discusses utilization of a PIN (or password) for protection of an exchange of the public part of a public key system (i.e., Diffie-Hellman or elliptic curves) encrypted using a symmetric encryption algorithm in CBC mode. To be more specific, the password or PIN is used to derive the initialization vectors for the encryption algorithms. The negotiated keys and algorithms are subsequently used to further protect the RAS and call-signaling phase.

One particular option that is used to protect the call-signaling phase is Transport Layer Security (TLS), which is discussed in the draft Annex H. Under this option, the RAS negotiation is substituted for the initial TLS handshake process. Obviously, this is only useful if the call-signaling process is gatekeeper-routed. This approach is especially useful for intergatekeeper authentication and signaling using the Location Request/Location Confirmation (LRQ/LCF) exchange. In this case, there is no third RAS message by which the calling gatekeeper can authenticate itself to the called gatekeeper using prenegotiated key data. However, the caller can be implicitly authenticated when it successfully establishes the call-signaling channel using the correct TLS session parameters. TLS can be deployed without using a costly handshake simply by using the recode layer of TLS in conjunction with the previously negotiated key data and algorithms that were obtained during the RAS negotiation phase.

4.4.11 H.235v3 for Direct-Routed Scenarios

Both Annex D and Annex F are intended to be used in gatekeeper-routed environments. Annex I of H.235 enhances both the baseline security profile and the hybrid security profile with the option to be applied in an environment where direct-routed calls (endpoint-to-endpoint) are made using the gatekeeper for address resolution. Because endpoints do not initially possess a shared secret, a Kerberos-like approach is taken to establish a shared secret between the two communicating endpoints. Here, the gatekeeper serves as the key distribution center, issuing two "tickets" (tokens): one containing the key material secured with the caller's encryption key and the other one secured with the called party's encryption key. The encryption keys are derived from the shared secret between the caller and the gatekeeper using a pseudo-random function defined in H.235 Annex I. The pseudo-random function is basically the same as the one used in TLS.

The gatekeeper also generates a session key used for communication between the two endpoints involved in the call. The gatekeeper encrypts this key data using the previously derived encryption keys. The encrypted session keys are then transmitted back to the caller. The caller utilizes one of the encrypted session keys while the other encrypted session key is sent to the called party. The messages exchanged between the gatekeeper and the calling endpoint carrying the tickets are secured with either H.235 Annex D or H.235 Annex F protocols. The shared secret established via the "ticket" (token) exchange between caller and called party may be used in subsequent direct messages to provide message integrity protection in accordance with H.235 Annex D.

4.4.12 **SIP Security**

Session Initiation Protocol (SIP) is the IETF-specified protocol used for initiating a two-way communication session. It is considerably less complex to implement than H.323 when simple calls are to be performed. SIP is text based, so it avoids certain ASN.1-associated parsing issues the H.323 protocol suite must contend with if S/MIME is not used. Also, SIP is an application-level protocol. It exists independently from the protocol layer it is transported across. It can be based in TCP, UDP, or with several different IPs. UDP may be used to decrease overhead and increase speed and efficiency, or TCP may be used if SSL/TLS is incorporated for security services. Unlike H.323, only one port is used in SIP (note that H.323 may also be used in a way that uses only one port: direct-routed calls). The default value for this port is 5060.

The architecture of an SIP network is different from the H.323 structure. A SIP network is made up of endpoints, a redirect server, a proxy server, a location server, and a registrar. In the SIP model, a user is not bound to a specific host. The user initially reports his or her location to a registrar, which may be integrated into either a proxy or a redirect server. This information is in turn stored in the external location server. Messages from endpoints must be routed through a proxy or redirect server. The proxy server intercepts messages from endpoints or other services, inspects their "To:" field, contacts the location server to resolve the username into an address, and forwards the message to the appropriate endpoint. Redirect servers perform the same resolution function, but the onus is placed on the endpoints to perform the actual transmission. That is, redirect servers obtain the actual address of the destination from the location server and return this information to the original sender, which then must send its message directly to the resolved address.

SIP is modeled on the three-way handshake method implemented in TCP. The call setup process is similar with a redirect server, but with the extra step of returning the resolved address to the source endpoint. During the setup process, communication details are negotiated between the endpoints using Session Description Protocol (SDP), which contains fields for the codec used, the caller's name, and so on. Here is an example:

- If Bob wishes to place a call to Alice, he sends an INVITE request to the proxy server containing SDP info for the session.

- The proxy server then takes the INVITE request and forwards it to Alice's client via Bob's proxy, which could even be her proxy server.

- Eventually, assuming Alice wants to talk to Bob, she will send an "OK" message back containing her call preferences in SDP format.

- Bob will respond with an "ACK." SIP provides for the ACK to contain SDP instead of the INVITE, so that an INVITE may be seen without protocol-specific information.

- After the "ACK" is received, the conversation may commence along the RTP/RTCP ports previously agreed upon.

Notice that all of the traffic was transported through one port in a simple (text) format, without any of the complicated channel/port switching associated with H.323. Still, SIP presents several challenges for firewalls and NAT.

4.4.13 Existing Security Features in the SIP Protocol

RFC 3261[10] describes several security features for SIP and deprecates several security features which were advocated in the original RFC 2543,[11] such as the usage of Pretty Good Privacy (PGP) and HTTP Basic Authentication. Because of its weak security, and to avoid attacks by downgrading the required security level of the authentication, the HTTP Basic Authentication was deprecated in the current document RFC3261.

4.4.14 Signaling Authentication using HTTP Digest Authentication

The digest authentication scheme is based on a simple challenge-response paradigm. The digest authentication scheme challenges the remote end using a nonce (once-only) value. SIP digest authentication is based on the digest authentication defined in RFC2617.[12] Here, a valid response contains a checksum (by default, the MD5 checksum) of the username, the password, the given-once value, the HTTP method, and the requested URL. In this way, the password is never sent in the clear.

4.4.15 S/MIME Usage within SIP

SIP messages carry MIME bodies. MIME defines mechanisms for the integrity protection and the encryption of the MIME contents. SIP may utilize S/MIME to enable mechanisms such as public key distribution, authentication and integrity protection, or confidentiality of SIP signaling data. S/MIME may be considered as a replacement for PGP used in RFC2543 to provide means for integrity protection and encryption of SIP messages. To be able to protect SIP header fields as well, tunneling of SIP messages in MIME bodies is specified. Generally, the proposed SIP tunneling for SIP header protection will create additional overhead. S/MIME requires certificates and private keys to be used, whereas the certificates may be issued by a trusted third party or may be self-generated. The latter case may not provide real user authentication but may be used to provide a limited form of message integrity protection. The following sections explain the usage of S/MIME more in-depth.

The current document RFC3261 recommends that S/MIME be used for User Agents (UAs). Moreover, if S/MIME is used to tunnel messages (described as follows), it is recommended to use a TCP connection because of the larger messages, to avoid problems that may arise by the fragmentation of UDP packets. Services such as authentication, integrity protection, and confidentiality of signaling data are possible.

4.5   Confidentiality of Media Data in SIP

SIP does not consider the encryption of media data. Using the RTP encryption as defined in RFC1889[13] may provide confidentiality for media data. Another option for media stream security is the use of SRTP [DSRTP]. For key management, SDP (cf. RFC2327[14]) may be used. SDP can convey session keys for media streams. Note that using SDP for the key exchange provides no method to send an encrypted media stream key. Therefore, the signaling request should be encrypted, preferably by using end-to-end encryption.

4.5.1   TLS Usage within SIP

RFC3261 mandates the use of TLS for proxies, redirect servers, and registrars to protect SIP signaling. Using TLS for UAs is recommended. TLS is able to protect SIP signaling messages against loss of integrity, confidentiality, and replay. It provides integrated key management with mutual authentication and secure key distribution. TLS is applicable hop-by-hop between UAs/proxies or between proxies. The drawback of TLS in SIP scenarios is the requirement of a reliable transport stack (TCP-based SIP signaling). TLS cannot be applied to UDP-based SIP signaling.

4.5.2   IPSec Usage within SIP

IPSec may also be used to provide security for SIP signaling at the network layer. This type of security is most suited to securing SIP hosts in an SIP VPN scenario (SIP user agents/proxies) or between administrative SIP domains. IPSec works for all UDP-, TCP-, and SCTP-based SIP signaling. IPSec may be used to provide authentication, integrity, and confidentiality for the transmitted data and supports end-to-end as well as hop-by-hop scenarios. At this time, there is no default cipher suite for IPSec defined in SIP. *Note*: RFC3261 does not describe a framework for the use of IPSec. Especially, no information is given as to how the key management is to be realized or which IPSec header and mode is to be used.

4.5.3   Security Enhancements for SIP

Currently within the IETF, several drafts concerning security are being discussed, with a view toward providing a general security solution to SIP scenarios. Several drafts have been produced concerning authentication, integrity, and confidentiality for SIP. The following subsections provide a short overview of Internet drafts, which may be of interest for a discussion of security enhancements for common SIP scenarios. The list of Internet drafts considered here is not complete and should rather reflect that this is an important topic, where work remains to be done.

4.5.4   SIP Authenticated Identity Body

SIP Authenticated Identity Body (AIB) defines a generic SIP authentication token. The token is provided by adding an S/MIME body to a SIP request or response in order to provide reference integrity over its headers. The document defines a format for this message body named as AIB. This is a digitally signed SIP message (sip/message) or message fragment (sip/frag).

4.5.5   SIP Authenticated Identity Management

The existing mechanisms for expressing identity in SIP often do not permit an administrative domain to verify securely the identity of the originator of a request. This document recommends practices and conventions for authenticating end users, and proposes a way to distribute cryptographically secure authenticated identities within SIP messages by including an authentication token (as an MIME body). This token is then added to the message. There are basically three ways to add an MIME body to a request. They are:

1.   Redirection

2.   Authentication service acts as B2BUA

3.   Content indirection

4.5.6   SIP Security Agreement

SIP has several security mechanisms. Some of them have been built into the SIP protocol directly, such as HTTP authentication. These mechanisms even have alternative algorithms and parameters. The idea originates from the Third Generation Partnership Project (3GPP), a collaboration of telecommunications companies, and provides a mechanism for selecting which security mechanisms to use between two entities. RFC3261 does not provide any mechanism agreement options. Moreover, even if some mechanisms such as OPTIONS were used to perform a mechanism agreement, the agreement would be vulnerable to bidding-down attacks. Three header fields are defined for negotiating the security mechanisms within SIP between an SIP entity and its next SIP hop. Five mechanisms are currently supported:

- TLS
- HTTP digest
- IPSec with IKE
- Manually keyed IPSec without IKE
- S/MIME

Connection Reuse

Connection reuse defines a method to reuse TCP connections that have already been established between a user agent and a proxy for the backward direction from the proxy to the client. The TLS security approach can also leverage this, because clients often do not possess a certificate and corresponding private key. Thus, it would not be possible to open a TLS connection to these clients (except via TLS anonymous mode).

4.5.7 SIP End-to-Middle, Middle-to-Middle, Middle-to-End Security

Currently, two drafts are being discussed within the IETF dealing with end-to-middle, middle-to-middle, and middle-to-end security. The first of these drafts, "End-to-middle Security in the Session Initiation Protocol (SIP)," was created to address the need to enable intermediaries to utilize some of the SIP message header and body when end-to-end security is applied. Examples include logging services for enterprise use, firewall traversal, transcoding, and early media extortion. Intermediaries may not be able to trace the SIP message body for certain information (e.g., port numbers to be opened) if the body is encrypted. There is still a discussion about this draft within the SIPPING group.

The second draft, "A Mechanism to Secure SIP information Inserted by Intermediaries," discusses what the title implies, and has a strong relation to the history-inserted draft. Proxies sometimes need to delete a message body in a request in order to delete user authentication data (e.g., proxy authorization) that is protected with S/MIME, but the SIP standard (RFC3261) does not allow this action. RFC3261 is designed so that a proxy does not break integrity of the body.

The security requirements between both approaches are slightly different, because here information is added by intermediaries and used by intermediaries. Nevertheless, they share the same fundamental problems to be solved in SIP. It is anticipated that there will be further discussion on this item, because certain scenarios exist where this functionality is needed.

4.5.8 SIP Security Issues

The text encoding of SIP makes it easier to analyze using standard parsing tools such as Perl or lex and yacc. Still, some new requirements are placed on the firewall in a SIP-based VoIP network. First, firewalls must be stateful and monitor SIP traffic to determine which RTP ports are to be opened and made available to which addresses. This responsibility is similar to the task firewalls on an H.323-based network perform, except the call setup and header parsing is much simpler. The other issues SIP-based VoIP encounters with firewalls are associated with RTP traffic and incoming calls. As with H.323, the big problem for SIP is NAT.

NAT inhibits SIP's registration and communication mechanisms and requires innovative solutions to resolve. The problems exist because in a

SIP-based network, the SIP proxy is normally outside the NAT device. There are three main scenarios for using a SIP proxy:

1.   The proxy is within the corporate LAN and the teleworker connects from outside

2.   The proxy is at the telecom side and clients from, for instance, smaller companies connecting to this proxy for VoIP service

3.   Two administrative domains are connected, both have their own proxy

So the problem is bartering communication between a proxy server that deals with global IP addresses and a machine that has been assigned a private network address. Rosenberg & Schulzrinne[15] classify three different sets of problems SIP traffic has in such an architecture: originating requests, receiving requests, and handling RTP. We have already dealt with the incompatibilities of RTP with NAT and now we will see the issues NAT presents to the call setup process.

To initialize a session from behind the NAT, a caller can simply send an INVITE message as always. The outgoing port number (5060) will be preserved by the NAT, but response communication could be disturbed. If SIP is implemented over UDP (recall that SIP is protocol independent), the proxy server must send the UDP response to the address and port the request arrived on. A simpler solution is to use the standard practice of routing SIP communication over TCP. With TCP, the response from the callee will come over the same channel as the original INVITE, so NAT will not present a problem.

We have already discussed some of the problems with incoming VoIP connections against NAT. Now we will look more in-depth at the SIP-specific problems with incoming calls. Rosenberg & Schulzrinne[16] trace the problem back to the registration process. When users contact the registrar, they provide their IP address as their reachable address, and this is stored in the location server. Unfortunately, this is their private IP address. The proxy server deals only with global IP addresses, so when a message comes in for username@domain.com, it will attempt to route this call to the registered address, but in the public domain. For instance, if username@domain.com is registered to an internal IP address of 10.7.34.189, then the proxy server will attempt to forward the traffic to this address, but in the public domain. This address is unreachable for the proxy server, and the connection will be refused. The solution to this problem is a delicate manipulation of IP addresses and an expansion of the responsibilities of the SIP proxy server.

4.5.9 MGCP

Media Gateway Control Protocol (MGCP) is used to communicate between the separate components of a decomposed VoIP gateway. It is a complementary protocol to SIP and H.323. The MGCP protocol was derived from version 1.1 of the SGCP protocol, which was a fusion of the SGCP version 1 and IP Device Control (IPDC). MGCP is currently being maintained by PacketCable TM (called NCS (Network Call-signaling Protocol)) and the Softswitch Consortium TM. In October 1999, MGCP was finally converted into an informational RFC2705[17]. There are plans for the MGCP specification to be enhanced by international standards bodies. One is the IP Cablecom activity proposing J.162 (NCS) and J.171 (Trunking Gateway Control Protocol, a variant of J.162). A similar version of these proposals will also be provided within ETSI as EuroPacketCable specifications. At the present time, MGCP is the de facto industry standard and has not yet been superseded by MEGACO/H.248.

4.5.10 MGCP System Architecture

Within MGCP, the MGC server or "call agent" is mandatory and manages the calls and conferences and supports the services provided. The MG endpoint is unaware of the calls and conferences and does not maintain call states. MGs are expected to execute commands sent by the MGC call agents. MGCP assumes that call agents will synchronize with each other, sending coherent commands to MGs under their control. MGCP does not define a mechanism for synchronizing call agents. MGCP is a master/slave protocol with a tight coupling between the MG (endpoint) and MGC (server).

RTP data is exchanged directly between the involved MGs. The call agent uses MGCP to provide the gateways with the description of connection parameters such as IP addresses, UDP port, and RTP profiles. These descriptions follow the conventions delineated in the SDP from RFC2327. SDP is used for multimedia sessions, which also run on UDP connections.

4.5.11 MGCP Security Considerations

Regarding security, there are no mechanisms designed into the MGCP protocol. The informational RFC2705 refers to the use of IPSec (either AH or

ESP) to protect MGCP messages. Without this protection, a potential attacker could set up unauthorized calls or interfere with ongoing authorized calls. Beside the usage of IPSec, MGCP allows the call agent to provide gateways with session keys that can be used to encrypt the audio messages, protecting against eavesdropping. The session key will be used later in RTP encryption. The RTP encryption, described in RFC1889, may be applied. Session keys may be transferred between the call agent and the gateway by using the SDP (cf. RFC2327).

4.6   Voice Transport Protocols

4.6.1   Real-time Transport Protocol (RTP)

The Real-time Transport Protocol (RTP) provides end-to-end network transport functions suitable for applications transmitting real-time data, such as audio, video, or simulation data, over multicast or unicast network services. RTP does not address resource reservation, and it does not guarantee quality of service (QoS) for real-time services. The data transport is augmented by a control protocol (RTCP) to monitor the data delivery in a manner scalable to large multicast networks, and to provide minimal control and identification functionality.[18] RTP and RTCP are designed to be independent of the underlying transport and network layers. The protocol supports the use of RTP-level translators and mixers.

There are no changes in the packet formats on the wire, only changes to the rules and algorithms governing how the protocol is used. The biggest change is an enhancement to the scalable timer algorithm for calculating when to send RTCP packets in order to minimize transmission in excess of the intended rate when many participants join a session simultaneously.

4.6.2   Transport Control Protocol (TCP) and User Datagram Protocol (UDP)

Because IP can provide only best-effort service for packet delivery, one might be tempted to ask the question: "Why would anyone want to encapsulate voice in IP packets?" Another protocol, TCP, implements a reliable transport service on top of the routing delivery service provided by IP. TCP implements sequential packet delivery and error recovery for duplicate or lost packets. So if an IP packet is lost and an error is detected, TCP will send a message to the source device and ask it to retransmit the packet. In addition, TCP is connection based; it first establishes a connection with the TCP protocol stack on the other side before sending any packets.

Another transport layer protocol, UDP, makes a best effort to deliver packets to destinations, with minimal overhead and delay. Because it is a best-effort service, UDP does not guarantee reliable delivery. Voice is usually transported via UDP packets.

RTP resides on top of UDP and provides fast, end-to-end delivery of real time-traffic such as interactive voice and video. RTP will time stamp, add sequence numbering, and monitor delivery of the voice packet. With one or more of these transport protocols providing the delivery mechanism, the IP-encapsulated voice packet will have header information added to it. RTP provides multicast capability and carries the timing and payload type.

4.6.3 Real-Time Control Protocol (RTCP)

RTCP is based on the periodic transmission of control packets to all participants in the session, using the same distribution mechanism as the data packets. The underlying protocol *must* provide multiplexing of the data and control packets (e.g., using separate port numbers with UDP). According to Schulzrinne et al.,[19] RTCP performs the following four functions:

1. *Provides feedback on the quality of the data distribution.* This is an integral part of the RTP's role as a transport protocol and is related to the flow and congestion control functions of other transport protocols. The feedback may be directly useful for control of adaptive encodings, but experiments with IP multicasting have shown that it is also critical to get feedback from the receivers in order to diagnose faults in the distribution. Sending reception feedback reports to all participants allows one who is observing problems to evaluate whether those problems are local or global. With a distribution mechanism such as IP multicast, it is also possible for an entity such as a network service provider who is not otherwise involved in the session to receive the feedback information and act as a third-party monitor to diagnose network problems. This feedback function is performed by the RTCP sender and receiver reports.

2. *Carries a persistent transport-level identifier for an RTP source called the canonical name (CNAME).* Because the SSRC identifier may change if a conflict is discovered or a program is restarted, receiv-

ers require the CNAME to keep track of each participant. Receivers may also require the CNAME to associate multiple data streams from a given participant in a set of related RTP sessions (e.g., to synchronize audio and video). Intermedia synchronization also requires the Network Time Protocol (NTP) and RTP time stamps included in RTCP packets by data senders.

3. *The first two functions require that all participants send RTCP packets, therefore the rate must be controlled in order for RTP to scale up to a large number of participants.* By having each participant send its control packets to all of the others, each can independently observe the number of participants. This number is used to calculate the rate at which the packets are sent.

4. *Conveys minimal session control information* (this is an optional function). For example, participant identification to be displayed in the user interface. This is most likely to be useful in loosely controlled sessions, where participants enter and leave without membership control or parameter negotiation. RTCP serves as a convenient channel to reach all of the participants, but it is not necessarily expected to support all of the control communication requirements of an application.

Functions 1 to 3 should be used in all environments, but particularly in the IP multicast environment. RTP application designers should avoid mechanisms that can only work in unicast mode and will not scale to larger numbers. Transmission of RTCP may be controlled separately for senders and receivers for cases such as unidirectional links, where feedback from receivers is not possible.

4.6.4   Stream Control Transmission Protocol (SCTP)

SCTP is a reliable transport protocol operating on top of a connectionless packet network such as IP. According to Stewart et al.,[20] SCTP offers the following services to its users:

- Acknowledged error-free nonduplicated transfer of user data

- Data fragmentation to conform to discovered path MTU size

- Sequenced delivery of user messages within multiple streams, with an option for order-of-arrival delivery of individual user messages

- Optional bundling of multiple user messages into a single SCTP packet

- Network-level fault tolerance through supporting of multihoming at either or both ends of an association

The design of SCTP includes appropriate congestion-avoidance behavior and resistance to flooding and masquerade attacks. SCTP is designed to transport PSTN signaling messages over IP networks but is capable of broader applications.

4.6.5 Trivial File Transfer Protocol (TFTP)

TFTP is a simple protocol to transfer files, and therefore was named the Trivial File Transfer Protocol (TFTP).[21] It has been implemented on top of the Internet User Datagram Protocol (UDP or Datagram), so it may be used to move files between machines on different networks implementing UDP. It is designed to be small and easy to implement. Therefore, it lacks most of the features of a regular File Transfer Protocol (FTP). The only thing it can do is read and write files (or mail) from and to a remote server. It cannot list directories, and it currently has no provisions for user authentication. In common with other Internet protocols, it passes 8-bit bytes of data.

Any transfer begins with a request to read or write a file, which also serves to request a connection. If the server grants the request, the connection is opened and the file is sent in fixed-length blocks of 512 bytes. Each data packet contains one block of data and must be acknowledged by an acknowledgment packet before the next packet can be sent. A data packet of less than 512 bytes signals termination of a transfer. If a packet gets lost in the network, the intended recipient will timeout and may retransmit the last packet (which may be data or an acknowledgment), thus causing the sender of the lost packet to retransmit that lost packet. The sender has to keep just one packet on hand for retransmission, because the lock step acknowledgment guarantees that all older packets have been received. Notice that both machines involved in a transfer are considered senders and receivers. One sends data and receives acknowledgments, and the other sends acknowledgments and receives data.

Most errors cause termination of the connection. An error is signaled by sending an error packet. This packet is not acknowledged and not retransmitted, so the other end of the connection may not get it. Therefore, timeouts are used to detect such a termination when the error packet has been lost. Errors are caused by three types of events:

1.   Not being able to satisfy the request (e.g., file not found, access violation, or no such user)

2.   Receiving a packet that cannot be explained by a delay or duplication in the network (e.g., an incorrectly formed packet)

3.   Losing access to a necessary resource (e.g., disk full or access denied during a transfer)

TFTP recognizes only one error condition that does not cause termination—the source port of a received packet being incorrect. In this case, an error packet is sent to the originating host. This protocol is restrictive, in order to simplify implementation. For example, the fixed-length blocks make allocation straightforward, and the lock step acknowledgment provides flow control and eliminates the need to reorder incoming data packets.

4.7   Signaling Protocols

4.7.1   SIGTRAN

The SIGTRAN protocols are designed to carry signaling messages for telephony services.[22] The carriers may be different and may use other transport network providers. The security requirements for these situations may be different. SIGTRAN protocols involve the security needs of several parties, the end users of the services, the service providers, and the applications involved. Additional security requirements may come from local regulation. Although having some overlapping security needs, any security solution should fulfill all of the different parties' needs. The SIGTRAN protocols assume that messages are secured by using either IPSec or TLS.

4.7.2   H.248/MEGACO

The ITU (specifically, ITU-T SG16) adopted MEGACO version 0.1 in April 1999 as the starting specification for H.GCP (H-series, Gateway Control Protocol), later known as H.248. The IETF started to work on MEGACO as a compromise protocol between MGCP and MDCP. In June 1999, the IETF MEGACO WG and ITU-T came out with a single document describing a standard protocol for interfacing between Media Gateway Controllers (MGCs) and Media Gateways (MGs): MEGACO/H.248. MEGACO/H.248 is expected to win wide industry acceptance as the official standard for decomposed gateway architectures released by both the IETF and ITU-T. Because MEGACO/H.248 is derived from MGCP, many similarities can be found,[23] for instance, the following:

- Similarity between the semantics of the commands in the two specifications. The use of ABNF grammar for syntax specification and the Session Description Protocol (SDP) to specify media stream properties is the same as in MGCP.

- The processing of signals and events in media streams is the same in MEGACO as in MGCP.

- The concept of packages containing event and signal definitions that permits easy extension to the protocol is borrowed from MGCP.

- The MEGACO specification for transport of messages over UDP is the same as specified in MGCP. The three-way handshake and the computation of retransmission timers described in MGCP are also described within the ALF definition specified in Annex E of MEGACO.

MEGACO/H.248 introduces several enhancements compared with MGCP, including the following:

- Support of multimedia and multipoint conferencing enhanced services

- Improved syntax for more efficient semantic message processing

- TCP and UDP transport options

- Allows either text or binary encoding (to support IETF and ITU-T approach)

- Formalized extension process for enhanced functionality

- Expanded definition of packages

MEGACO is described as Gateway Control Protocol Version 1 within the RFC3525.[24] It has basically the same architecture as MGCP. MEGACO/H.248 commands are similar to MGCP commands, but the protocol models are quite different. MEGACO was defined by having a media gateway connection model that has two entities:

- **Terminations:** Source or sink for (one or more) media streams
- **Context:** Grouping of terminations connected in a call

In contrast, MGCP uses the following two entities:

- **Endpoints:** Source or sink of data
- **Connection:** Association between two endpoints

Taking a multipoint conference as an example, MEGACO simplifies the connection setup by adding terminations to a context, whereas MGCP has to establish several connections to the conference server. The context in this scenario may cover multiple media streams for enhanced multimedia services. With MEGACO/H.248, the primary mechanism for extension is by means of packages. MEGACO/H.248 packages include more detail than MGCP packages. They define additional properties and statistics, along with event and signal information that may occur on terminations.

4.7.3   MEGACO Security Considerations

MEGACO (RFC3525[25]) recommends security mechanisms that may be in underlying transport mechanisms, such as IPSec. H.248 goes even a step further by requiring that implementations of the H.248 protocol implement IPSec if the underlying operating system and the transport network support IPSec. Implementation of the protocol using IPv4 is required to implement the interim Authentication Header (AH) scheme. H.248 states that implementations employing the AH shall provide a minimum set of algorithms for integrity checking using manual keys (compliant to RFC2402[26]).

The interim AH scheme is the usage of an optional AH, which is defined in the H.248 protocol header. The header fields are exactly those of the SPI: SEQUENCE NUMBER and DATA fields as defined in RFC2402. The semantics of the header fields are the same as the "transport mode" of RFC2402, except for the calculation of the Integrity Check Value (ICV). For more details on the calculation of the ICV, check H.248. The interim AH scheme does not provide protection against the eavesdropping and replay attacks.

For MEGACO, a manual key management is assumed and the replay protection, defined for IPSec, may not be used in this scenario. Furthermore, H.248 states that implementations employing the ESP header shall provide a minimum set of algorithms for integrity checking and encryption. Moreover, implementations should use IKE (RFC2409[27]) to permit more robust keying options. Implementations employing IKE should support authentication with RSA signatures public key encryption.

4.8   DNS and DNSSEC with VoIP

The Domain Name System (DNS)[28] is one of the Internet's primary building blocks. It is basically the distributed host information database used for translating names into addresses and routing mail to its proper destination. When a user visits Web site www.xyz.com, the browser queries the local DNS server to perform a database lookup of the IP address of www.xyz.com. DNS returns the IP address of www.xyz.com as 123.45.67.8. The user's Web browser uses the dotted decimal address to traverse the Internet and find the address requested. DNS Security Extensions (DNSSEC) is a technique for securing the Domain Name System. It is a set of extensions to DNS, which provide end-to-end authenticity and integrity and was designed to protect the Internet from certain attacks. All responses in DNSSEC are digitally signed; therefore, by simply checking the signature of a response, the receiver is able to validate if the data is identical to the data on the authoritative server.

4.8.1   DNSSEC and Identity

DNSSEC is a set of extensions to DNS, which provide end-to-end authenticity and integrity. In an article in the *Business Standard,*[29] Paul Mockapetris, the inventor of DNS, talks about DNSSEC and why he thinks DNS is the answer to many of the identity problems on the Internet. Quoting from the article:

> *Mockapetris argues that a work-in-progress extension to the DNS specification called DNSSEC is what makes the DNS up to the task of solving most of the identity-related issues on the Internet. Unfortunately, since DNSSEC isn't bulletproof (and, according to some, could result in other vulnerabilities), the specification has been a work-in-progress since*

November 1993, when the DNS working group of the Internet Engineering Task Force (IETF) held its first DNSSEC design meeting. Despite the imperfections of DNSSEC, Mockapetris says that it's time to go for it. "The DNS has been growing for twenty years, but during that time, no progress has been made on securing it."

Mockapetris claims that the real problem is that the committee is trying to solve the problem perfectly rather than doing what can be done now. Many people believe that the 80% part of the problem can be solved with a DNS-like mechanism for Web services, whereas the committees can expound forever on the other 20% of the problem. The basic idea behind DNSSEC is simple: provide an authentication mechanism for DNS lookup so that it's harder (but not impossible) to forge DNS information. That means that you can be relatively certain that the e-mail that claims to have come from *wherever.com* actually did, or that the HTTP request you're processing is actually from your partner at *wherever.com* and is not an imposter.

The technology behind these confidence checks uses digital signatures and public key cryptography. DNSSEC uses secure hash algorithms for the digital signing of the records—called RRSets—that appear in the DNS database. Using its private key, the site could digitally sign the domain mapping information that appears in the DNS database, and any application that depends on that information could subsequently retrieve the matching public key from a special key record stored under the DNS entry. Using the public key, the application can then verify that the domain mapping information was signed with the private key and use the data with confidence that it was not spoofed by an attacker or imposter.

4.9   MPLS and VoIP

Multiprotocol Label Switching (MPLS) is a QoS-enabling technology deployed by several of the largest service providers worldwide to provision Service-Level Agreements (SLAs). It provides a mechanism for engineering network traffic patterns independent of routing tables. Unlike IP, which routes via IP addresses, MPLS assigns short labels to network packets that describe how to forward them through the network. It employs protocols such as Open Shortest Path First (OSPF), Internet Group Multicast Protocol (IGMP), Constraint Routed—Label Distribution Protocol (CR-LDP) and Resource ReSerVation Protocol—Traffic Extensions (RSVP-TE). MPLS performs the following functions:

- Specifies mechanisms to manage traffic flows of various granularities, such as flows between different hardware, machines, or even flows between different applications

- Remains independent of the layer 2 and layer 3 protocols

- Provides a means to map IP addresses to simple, fixed-length labels used by different packet-forwarding and packet-switching technologies

- Interfaces to existing routing protocols, such as RSVP and OSPF

- Supports IP, ATM, and Frame Relay layer 2 protocols

In MPLS, data transmission occurs on Label-Switched Paths (LSPs). LSPs are a sequence of labels at every node along the path from the source to the destination. LSPs are established either before data transmission (control-driven) or upon detection of a certain flow of data (data-driven). The labels are underlying protocol-specific identifiers.

Several label distribution protocols are used today, such as Label Distribution Protocol (LDP) or RSVP, or piggybacked on routing protocols such as Border Gateway Protocol (BGP) and OSPF. Each data packet encapsulates and carries the labels during their journey from source to destination. High-speed switching of data is possible because the fixed-length labels are inserted at the very beginning of the packet or cell and can be used by hardware to switch packets quickly between links.

MPLS is a versatile solution to address the problems faced by present-day networks-speed, scalability, QoS management, and traffic engineering. MPLS has emerged as an elegant solution to meet the bandwidth-management and service requirements for next-generation IP-based backbone networks.

4.9.1 Label Distribution Protocol (LDP)

In MPLS version 2, Label-Switching Routers (LSRs) must agree on the meaning of the labels used to forward traffic between and through them. LDP is a new protocol that defines a set of procedures and messages by which one LSR informs another of the label bindings it has made. The LSR uses this label-switching protocol to establish LSPs through a network by mapping network layer routing information directly to data-link layer switched paths. These LSPs may have an endpoint at a directly attached neighbor (like IP hop-by-hop forwarding), or they may have an endpoint at a network egress node, enabling switching via all intermediary nodes. A Forwarding Equivalence Class (FEC) is associated with each LSP created. This FEC specifies which packets are mapped to that LSP.

Two LSRs that use LDP to exchange label mapping information are known as LDP-peers. LDP-peers conduct LDP sessions between them. In a single session, each peer is able to learn about the other's label mappings because the protocol is bidirectional. There are four types of LDP messages shared between peers:

- Discovery messages
- Session messages
- Advertisement messages
- Notification messages

Using discovery messages, the LSRs announce their presence in the network by sending Hello messages periodically. This hello message is transmitted as a UDP packet. When a new session must be established, the hello message is sent over TCP. Apart from the discovery message, all other messages are sent over TCP. The notification messages signal errors and other events of interest. There are two kinds of notification messages:

1. *Error notifications.* These signal fatal errors and cause termination of the session.

2. *Advisory notifications.* These are used to pass on LSR information about the LDP session or the status of some previous message received from the peer.

All LDP messages have a common structure that uses a Type-Length-Value (TLV) encoding scheme. This TLV encoding is used to encode much of the information carried in LDP messages. The Value part of a TLV-encoded object (TLV) may contain one or more TLVs. Messages are sent as LDP Protocol Data Units (PDUs). Each PDU can contain more than one LDP message.

4.9.2 Constraint-based Routing—Label Distribution Protocol (CR-LDP)

CR-LDP is one of the protocols found in the MPLS architecture. CR-LDP contains extensions for LDP to extend its capabilities (such as setup paths) beyond what is available for the routing protocol. For instance, an LSP can be set up based on explicit route constraints, QoS constraints, or several other similar constraints. Constraint-based Routing (CR) is a mechanism used to meet traffic engineering requirements on a network. These requirements are generally met by extending LDP to include support of Constraint-based Routing—Label-Switched Paths (CR-LSPs). Other uses for CR-LSPs include MPLS-based VPNs. CR-LDP is the same as LDP, but it does have some additional TLV parameters to help transfer and speed up the overall routing process. The applicability of CR-LSP Setup using LDP is discussed at length in the Network Working Group (NWG) Request for Comments: 3213.[30] The NWG document discusses possible network applications and extensions to the LDP that are required in order to implement CR. It also provides some guidelines for deployment and states some of the known limitations of the existing protocol. According to this NWG document, it is a prerequisite to advancing CR-LDP on the standards track. The reader is encouraged to reference this document for further discussion of CR-LDP, as it is beyond the scope of this chapter.

4.9.3 RSVP and RSVP-TE

RSVP is a resource reservation setup protocol for the Internet. A host uses RSVP to request a specific QoS from the network on behalf of an application data stream. RSVP carries the request through the network, visiting each node the network uses to carry the stream. At each node, RSVP attempts to make a resource reservation for the application data stream. In order to make a resource reservation while at the node, the RSVP daemon communicates with two local decision modules, known as *admission control* and *policy control*. Admission control determines whether the node has sufficient available resources to supply the requested QoS. Policy control determines whether the user has administrative permission to make the reservation. If either check fails, the RSVP program returns an error notification to the application process that originated the request. If both checks succeed, the RSVP daemon sets parameters in a packet classifier and packet scheduler to obtain the desired QoS. The packet classifier determines the QoS class for each packet, and the scheduler orders packet transmission to achieve the promised QoS for each stream.

A primary feature of RSVP is its scalability. RSVP scales to very large multicast groups because it uses receiver-oriented reservation requests that merge as they progress up the multicast tree. The reservation for a single receiver does not need to travel to the source of a multicast tree; rather, it travels only until it reaches a reserved branch of the tree. Although the RSVP protocol is designed specifically for multicast applications, it may also make unicast reservations.

RSVP is also designed to utilize the robustness of current Internet routing algorithms. RSVP does not perform its own routing; instead, it uses underlying routing protocols to determine where it should carry reservation requests. As routing changes paths to adapt to topology changes, RSVP adapts its reservation to the new paths wherever reservations are in place. This modularity does not rule out RSVP from using other routing services.

Current research within the RSVP project is focusing on designing RSVP to use routing services that provide alternate paths and fixed paths. RSVP runs over IP, both IPv4 and IPv6. Among RSVP's other features, it provides opaque transport of traffic control and policy control messages, and provides transparent operation through nonsupporting regions.

The RSVP-TE protocol is an addition to the RSVP protocol for establishing LSPs in MPLS networks. The extended RSVP protocol (RSVP-TE) supports the instantiation of explicitly routed LSPs, with or without resource reservations. RSVP-TE also supports smooth rerouting of LSPs, preemption, and loop detection. RSVP-TE defines a session as a data flow with a particular destination and transport layer protocol. When RSVP and MPLS are combined, a flow or session can be defined with greater flexibility and generality. The ingress node of an LSP uses several methods to determine which packets are assigned a particular label. Once a label is assigned to a set of packets, the label effectively defines the flow through the LSP. Such an LSP is an LSP tunnel because the traffic through it is opaque to intermediate nodes along the LSP.

New RSVP Session, Sender, and Filter Spec objects, called LSP Tunnel IPv4 and LSP Tunnel IPv6, have been defined to support the LSP tunnel feature. In some applications, it is useful to associate sets of LSP tunnels, such as during reroute operations or in spreading a traffic trunk over multiple paths, which sets are called traffic-engineered tunnels. To enable the identification and association of the LSP tunnels, two identifiers are carried. A tunnel ID is part of the Session object. The Session object uniquely defines a traffic-engineered tunnel. The Sender and Filter Spec objects carry an LSP ID. The Sender (or Filter Spec) object, together with the Session object, uniquely identify an LSP tunnel.

4.10 Voice over Frame Relay Access Devices (VFRADs)

Frame Relay is commonly used in corporate data networks because of its flexible bandwidth, widespread accessibility, support of a diverse traffic mix, and technological maturity. Of the three popular packet/cell technologies (i.e., Frame Relay, IP, and ATM), Frame Relay is the most widely deployed. Frame Relay service is based on Permanent Virtual Connections. Frame Relay is appropriate for closed user groups and is also recommended for star topologies and when performance needs to be predictable. Voice over Frame Relay (VoFR) is a logical progression for corporations that are already running data over Frame Relay.

Voice over Frame Relay Access Devices (VFRADs), such as RAD's MAXcess, integrated bandwidth manager, integrate voice into the data network by connecting the router (or using the integrated router available on certain MAXcess models), SNA controller, and the PBX at each site in the corporate network to the Frame Relay network. Many VFRADs, such as RAD's MAXcess, employ sophisticated techniques to overcome the limitations of transporting voice over the Frame Relay network without the need to add costly bandwidth.

Prioritization

The VFRADs' prioritization schemes "tag" different applications according to their sensitivity to delay, assigning higher priority to voice and other time-sensitive data such as Systems Network Architecture (SNA). The VFRADs let the higher-priority voice packets go first, keeping the data packets waiting. This has no negative effect on data traffic, because voice transmissions are relatively short and, being compressed, require very little bandwidth. They can therefore slip into the data network alongside the heavy graphics, payroll information, e-mail, and other data traffic without perceptibly encumbering overall network performance.

Frame Relay service providers have also begun to offer different QoS. Users can purchase the highest quality of service, Real-Time Variable Frame Rate, for voice and SNA traffic. The second quality Frame Relay service, Non-Real-Time Variable Frame, is typically purchased for LAN-to-LAN and business class Internet and intranet traffic. The lowest quality of service, Available/Unspecified Frame Rate, is used for e-mail, file transfer, and residential Internet traffic. In addition, the VFRAD can be configured to assign less-sensitive traffic with a Discard Eligibility bit. These frames will be dropped first in case of network congestion.

Fragmentation

The VFRADs incorporate fragmentation schemes to improve performance. Data packets are divided into small fragments, allowing higher-priority voice packets to receive the right-of-way without waiting for the end of long data transmissions. The remaining data packets in the data stream are momentarily halted until the voice transmission gets through. The downside of fragmentation is that it increases the number of data frames, thereby increasing the number of flags and headers. This increases overhead and reduces bandwidth efficiency.

Controlling Variable Delay

Variation in the arrival times between packets, also called jitter, causes unnatural-sounding voice instead of a smooth voice stream. If a packet does not arrive in time to fit into the voice stream, the previous packet is replayed. This can seriously detract from voice quality. To avoid the effect of jitter, VFRADs detain each packet in a jitter buffer, giving subsequent packets time to arrive and still fit into a natural voice flow. Because the jitter buffer adds to the overall delay of voice transmissions, the optimal jitter buffer should fit the network's differential delay. Better access devices employ adaptive jitter buffering, which continuously monitors the network delay and adjusts the queuing period accordingly.

Voice Compression

Voice compression allows the packet-switching network to most effectively carry a combination of voice and data sessions without compromising voice quality. Because Frame Relay access is usually at data rates of 56/64 kbps, low bit-rate voice compression algorithms such as ITU G.723.1 and G.729A permit the greatest number of simultaneous multiple calls while maintaining high-quality voice. Vendors that have implemented voice compression algorithms in their FRADs can offer greater bandwidth savings, reduced network congestion, and high-quality voice transmissions.

Silence Suppression

In a telephone conversation, only about 50% of the full duplex connection is used at any given time, because, generally, only one person talks while the other person listens. In addition, voice packets are not sent during inter-word pauses and natural pauses in the conversation, reducing the required bandwidth by another 10%. Silence suppression frees this 60% of bandwidth on the full duplex link for other voice or data transmissions.

Echo Cancellation

Echo cancellation improves the quality of voice transmissions. It eliminates the echo that results from the reflection of the telephony signal back to the caller, which can occur in a four-wire to two-wire hybrid connection between the VFRAD and the telephones or PBX. The longer it takes the signals to return to the caller, the more perceptible the echo will be.

4.11 Voice over ATM (VoATM)

Asynchronous Transfer Mode (ATM) is a multiservice, high-speed, scalable technology. It is a dominant switching fabric in carrier backbones, supporting services with different transfer characteristics. ATM simultaneously transports voice, data, graphics, and video at very high speeds. On the downside, ATM services are expensive and not yet universally available. Large enterprises are increasingly connecting headquarters and main offices to the WAN via broadband links such as ATM to accommodate their vast amounts of voice and data transmissions, such as heavy graphics, payroll information, and voice and video conferencing.

Fragmentation is built into ATM, with its small, fixed-size, 53-byte cells. Very fast ATM switches speed data through the ATM network. The high bandwidth associated with ATM reduces congestion problems, providing extremely reliable service. Carriers can therefore promise customers QoS, as stipulated in SLAs.

ATM prioritization is implemented through QoS parameters. ATM was designed from the outset to carry voice as well as all types of data. ATM Adaptation Layer 1 (AAL1) protocol in ATM's Constant Bit Rate (CBR) service was the de facto standard for VoATM. However, this protocol proved inefficient for voice applications. CBR, the highest-quality class of ATM service, provides Circuit Emulation Service (CES), which transmits a continuous bit stream of information. This allocates a constant amount of bandwidth to a connection for the duration of a transmission. Although it guarantees high-quality voice, CES monopolizes bandwidth that could be used for other applications. In addition, in the interest of reducing delay, CES might send the fixed-size ATM cells half empty rather than waiting 6 milliseconds for 47 bytes of voice to fill the cell. This wastes more than 20 bytes of bandwidth per ATM cell. Dynamic Bandwidth Circuit Emulation Service (DBCES) is a variation of CES. DBCES does not send a constant bit stream of cells, but transmits only when there is an active voice call (off hook). However, like in CES, the cells might remain partially empty.

Therefore, using AAL1 for VoATM increases the overhead of voice transmissions and wastes bandwidth.

AAL2's Variable Bit Rate (VBR-RT) service, as specified in ITU-T recommendation I.363.2, emerged as the standard of choice for VoATM. The structure of AAL2 allows for the packing of short packets (1 to 45/64 bytes), also called *minicells*, into one or more ATM cells. (This resembles Frame Relay's and IP's variable-sized fragments.) In contrast to AAL1, which has a fixed payload, AAL2 enables a variable payload within cells. This functionality provides a dramatic improvement in bandwidth efficiency over structured or unstructured circuit emulation using AAL1. In addition, AAL2 supports voice compression and silence suppression and allows multiple voice channels with varying bandwidth on a single ATM connection.

Voice compression is not necessary in pure-ATM networks, which enjoy ample bandwidth. However, in hybrid ATM–Frame Relay networks (e.g., with ATM headquarters and Frame Relay branches), voice compression is required because Frame Relay uses voice compression. ATM must therefore be equipped to support voice compression that will work with VoFR equipment at the remote site.

4.12 Summary

Packet networking has been around since the advent of networking. In this chapter, we have provided the basics necessary for the reader to understand the next generation of this technology as it is applied to VoIP technology. We began with an overview of packet networking fundamentals, TCP/IP, the ISO/OSI model, and the basics of routing and switching. Next, we described the basics of IP networks to include Address Resolution Protocol and an overview of IP, TCP, UDP, and ICMP packets. We described the voice security, transport, and signaling protocols that are now helping to accelerate the march toward convergence of voice and data and are being designed to enable mixed-media communications over packet networks. This advance allows networks to handle voice, data, and video over common media, which is the essence of convergence.

The description provided for each protocol also helps the reader understand how all of the next-generation network protocols, such as SIP, MGCP, Megaco, and H.323, provide services for all products, services, applications, and solutions that utilize packet-based voice, data, and video communications technologies, regardless of transport medium—wireless, copper, broadband, or fiber optics. DNS and DNSSEC, MPLS, Voice over

Frame Relay Access Devices, and Voice over ATM and the interrelationship and enhancing effects on VoIP closed out our discussion of packet networking. With a basic understanding of packet networking technologies, the reader will possess the necessary comprehension to move to and understand VoIP processing, the topic of our next chapter.

4.13 Endnotes

1. Anonymous, "Routing," http://www.networkingnews.org/networking/routing.html

2. Rekhter, Y. et al. (1996). RFC 1918: Address Allocation for Private Internets. Retrieved July 26, 2004 from http://rfc.sunsite.dk

3. RFCs may be obtained from http://rfc.sunsite.dk

4. Fuller, V. et al. (1993). RFC 1519: Classless Inter-Domain Routing (CIDR): An Address Assignment and Aggregation Strategy. Retrieved July 26, 2004 from http://rfc.sunsite.dk

5. Hedrick, C. et al. (1988). RFC 1058: Routing Information Protocol. Retrieved July 26, 2004 from http://rfc.sunsite.dk

6. Roamer and Chris Hurley, "Understanding IP Packets", Parts 1-3, April 8, 2001. URL is http://www.securitytribe.com

7. RFC 791, "Internet Protocol—DARPA Internet Program Protocol Specification," September 1981

8. Kuhn, D., Walsh, T., Fries, & Steffen. (2004). Special Publication 800-58: Security Considerations for Voice Over IP Systems Recommendations of the National Institute of Standards and Technology. National Institute of Standards and Technology, Technology Administration, U.S. Department of Commerce.

9. Krawczyk, H. et al. (1997). RFC 2104: HMAC: Keyed-Hashing for Message Authentication. Retrieved July 26, 2004 from http://rfc.sunsite.dk

10. Rosenberg, J. et al. (2002). SIP: Session Initiation Protocol. Retrieved July 26, 2004 from http://rfc.sunsite.dk

11. Handley, M. et al. (1999). RFC 2543: SIP: Session Initiation Protocol. Retrieved July 26, 2004 from http://rfc.sunsite.dk

12. Franks, J. et al. (1999). RFC 2617: HTTP Authentication: Basic and Digest Access Authentication. Retrieved July 26, 2004 from http://rfc.sunsite.dk

13.   Schulzrinne, H. et al. (1996). RFC 1889: RTP: A Transport Protocol for Real-Time Applications. Retrieved July 26, 2004 from http://rfc.sunsite.dk

14.   Handley, M. et al. (1998). RFC 2327: SDP: Session Description Protocol. Retrieved July 26, 2004 from http://rfc.sunsite.dk

15.   Schulzrinne, H., Casner, S., Frederick, R., & Jacobson, V. (2003). Network Working Group Request for Comments: 3550 (Obsoletes: 1889), Category: Standards Track, RTP: A Transport Protocol for Real-Time Applications. Retrieved July 2, 2004 from www.faqs.org/rfcs/rfc1889.html

16.   Rosenberg, J. & Schulzrinne, H. "The Session Initiation Protocol: Providing Advanced Telephony Services across the Internet." Bell Labs Technical Journal, Vol. 3, No. 4, October/December 1998, pp. 144–160.

17.   Arango, M. et al. (1999). RFC2705: Media Gateway Control Protocol (MGCP) Version 1.0. Retrieved, July 26, 2004 from http://rfc.sunsite.dk

18.   Vanguard Managed Solutions. (2003). Understanding Voice Technology—Vanguard Technical Reference. Mansfield, MA: Vanguard Managed Solutions.

19.   Schulzrinne, H., Casner, S., Frederick, R., & Jacobson, V. (2003). Network Working Group Request for Comments: 3550 (Obsoletes: 1889), Category: Standards Track, RTP: A Transport Protocol for Real-Time Applications. Retrieved July 2, 2004 from http://www.faqs.org/rfcs/rfc1889.html .

20.   Stewart, R. et al. (2000). Network Working Group Request for Comments: 2960, Category: Standards Track: Stream Control Transmission Protocol. Retrieved July 2, 2004 from www.ietf.org/rfc/rfc2960.txt

21.   Loughney, J., Tuexen, M., Pastor-Balbas, J., & Ericsson Espana, S. (2004). Network Working Group Request for Comments: 3788, Category: Standards Track, Security Considerations for Signaling Transport (SIGTRAN) Protocols. Retrieved July 2, 2004 from www.ietf.org/rfc/rfc3788.txt

22.   Kuhn, D., Walsh, T., Fries, & Steffen. (2004). Special Publication 800-58: Security Considerations for Voice Over IP Systems Recommendations of the National Institute of Standards and Tech-

nology. National Institute of Standards and Technology, Technology Administration, U.S. Department of Commerce.

23.   Groves, C. et al. (2003). Request for Comments—3525: Gateway Control Protocol Version 1. Retrieved July 18, 2004 from ftp://ftp.isi.edu/in-notes/rfc3525.txt

24.   Groves, C. et al. (2003). Request for Comments—3525: Gateway Control Protocol Version 1. Retrieved July 18, 2004 from ftp://ftp.isi.edu/in-notes/rfc3525.txt

25.   Kent, S. et al. (1998). RFC 2402: IP Authentication Header. Retrieved, July 26, 2004 from http://rfc.sunsite.dk

26.   Harkins, D. & Carrel, D. (1998). RFC 2409—The Internet Key Exchange (IKE). Retrieved July 18, 2004 from www.faqs.org/rfcs/rfc2409.html

27.   DNSSEC. (2004). DNSSEC—DNS Security Extensions Securing the Domain Name System. Retrieved July 2, 2004 from www.dnssec.net

28.   Windley, P. (2003). DNSSEC and Identity. Retrieved July 2, 2004 from www.windley.com/2003/08/19.html#a781

29.   Ash, J. et. al. (2002). Network Working Group Request for Comments: 3213, "Applicability Statement for CR-LDP."

30.   Ash, et. al. (2002). Network Working Group Request for Comments: 3213, "Applicability Statement for CR-LDP."

4.14   General References

Arango, M. et al. (1999). *RFC2705: Media Gateway Control Protocol (MGCP) Version 1.0*. Retrieved July 26, 2004 from http://rfc.sunsite.dk/

Archer, K. et al. (2001). *Voice and Data Security*. Indianapolis, IN: SAMS Publishing.

Bellovin, S., Ioannidis, J., Keromytis, A. & Stewart, R. (2003). *RFC 3554: On the Use of Stream Control Transmission Protocol (SCTP) with IPsec*. Retrieved July 18, 2004 from www.ietf.org/rfc/rfc3554.txt

Biran, G. (2004). *Voice over Frame Relay, IP and ATM: The Case for Cooperative Networking*. Retrieved July 12, 2004 from www.protocols.com/papers/voe.htm

Coene, L. (2002). *RFC 3257: Stream Control Transmission Protocol Applicability Statement.* Retrieved July 18, 2004 from www.faqs.org/rfcs/rfc3257.html

ENSC. (2004). *ENSC 835 Final Project Report.* Retrieved July 12, 2004 from www.ensc.sfu.ca/~ljilja/ENSC835/Projects/e.chan/Report.pdf

Franks, J. et al. (1999). RFC 2617: *HTTP Authentication: Basic and Digest Access Authentication.* Retrieved, July 26, 2004 from http://rfc.sunsite.dk

Fuller, V. et al. (1993). RFC 1519: *Classless Inter-Domain Routing (CIDR): An Address Assignment and Aggregation Strategy.* Retrieved July 26, 2004 from http://rfc.sunsite.dk

Groves, C. et al. (2003). *RFC 3525: Gateway Control Protocol Version 1.* Retrieved July 18, 2004 from ftp://ftp.isi.edu/in-notes/rfc3525.txt

Handley, M. et al. (1998). *RFC 2327: SDP: Session Description Protocol.* Retrieved July 26, 2004 from http://rfc.sunsite.dk

Handley, M. et al. (1999). *RFC 2543: SIP: Session Initiation Protocol.* Retrieved July 26, 2004 from http://rfc.sunsite.dk

Harkins, D. & Carrel, D. (1998). *RFC 2409: The Internet Key Exchange (IKE).* Retrieved July 18, 2004 from www.faqs.org/rfcs/rfc2409.html

Hedrick, C. et al. (1988). *RFC 1058: Routing Information Protocol.* Retrieved, July 26, 2004 from http://rfc.sunsite.dk

Jungmaier, A., Rescoria, E., & Tuexen, M. (2002). *RFC 3436: Transport Layer Security over Stream Control Transmission Protocol.* Retrieved July 18, 2004 from www.ietf.org/rfc/rfc3436.txt

Kent, S. et al. (1998). *RFC 2402: IP Authentication Header.* Retrieved, July 26, 2004 from http://rfc.sunsite.dk

Kiser, C. (2003). *Regulatory Considerations for Cable-Provided IP Telephony.* Retrieved July 12, 2004 from www.mintz.com/images/dyn/publications/Kiser-IPTelephony.pdf

Krawczyk, H. et al. (1997). *RFC 2104: HMAC: Keyed-Hashing for Message Authentication.* Retrieved July 26, 2004 from http://rfc.sunsite.dk

Management Information Base. Retrieved July 12, 2004 from www.ietf.org/internet-drafts/draft-ietf-ccamp-gmpls-lsr-mib-05.txt

McDermott, R. (1999). *Voice Over IP.* Research Paper. Retrieved July 12, 2004 from http://people.bu.edu/rjm123/VoIP.htm

Nadeau, T., Srinivasen, C., Farrel, A., Hall, T., & Harrison, E. (2004). Internet Draft: Generalized Multiprotocol Label Switching (GMPLS) Label Switching Router (LSR). Retrieved July 15, 2004 from http://www.ietf.org/proceedings/02nov/I-D/draft-ietf-ccamp-gmpls-lsr-mib-00.txt

National Cable & Telecommunications Association. (2004). *Balancing Responsibilities and Rights: A Regulatory Model for Facilities-Based VoIP Competition—An NCTA Policy Paper.* Retrieved July 12, 2004 from www.ncta.com/PDF_files/VoIPWhitePaper.pdf

NexTone Communications, Inc. (2003). *Enterprise Voice Services.* Retrieved July 12, 2004 from www.nextone.com/pdfs/enterprise.pdf

Ong, L. & Yoakum, J. (2002). *RFC 3286: An Introduction to the Stream Control Transmission Protocol (SCTP).* Retricved July 18, 2004 from www.faqs.org/rfcs/rfc3286.html

Rekhter, Y. et al. (1996). *RFC 1918: Address Allocation for Private Internets.* Retrieved July 26, 2004 from http://rfc.sunsite.dk

Rosenberg, J. et al. (2002). *RFC 3261: SIP: Session Initiation Protocol.* Retrieved July 26, 2004 from http://rfc.sunsite.dk

Samhassan.com. (2004). *Voice-Over-IP.* Retrieved July 12, 2004 from www.samhassan.com/Voice-Over-IP.htm#latency

Schulzrinne, H. et al. (1996). *RFC 1889: RTP: A Transport Protocol for Real-Time Applications.* Retrieved July 26, 2004 from http://rfc.sunsite.dk

Stewart, R., Ramalho, M., Xie, Q., Tuexen, M., & Conrad, P. (2004). *RFC 3758: Stream Control Transmission Protocol (SCTP) Partial Reliability Extension.* Retrieved July 18, 2004 from http://rfc.sunsite.dk/rfc/rfc3758.html

Stone, J., Stewart, R., & Otis D. (2002). *RFC 3309: Stream Control Transmission Protocol (SCTP) Checksum Change.* Retrieved July 18, 2004 from www.ietf.org/rfc/rfc3309.txt

Villalona, S. & Lee, C. (2002). *Voice Over IP.* Retrieved July 12, 2004 from http://webcomposer.pace.edu/CL78352N/IPTelePP.ppt

Walker, J. & Hicks, J. (2004). *Taking Charge of Your VoIP Project.* Indianapolis, IN: Cisco Press.

Sollins, K. (1992). Network Working Request Group For Comments: 1350 (Obsoletes: RFC 783), *The TFTP Protocol (Revision 2).* Retrieved July 2, 2004 from www.faqs.org/rfcs/rfc1350.html

5

VoIP Processing

5.1   Voice Packetization

In order to transmit voice data over a data network, the voice data must first be digitized and then compressed into small, discrete units we refer to as *packets*. The compression algorithm (usually referred to as a *codec*) determines the size and the transmission interval of these packets. In order to transport these voice packets over the network, they are encapsulated as Real-time Transport Protocol (RTP) packets using another protocol, User Datagram Protocol (UDP) as the transport medium. The use of these protocols comes at a slight cost, an overhead of 40 bytes, for each packet sent. Voice packetization is the process used to take a digital bit stream and segment it into discrete packets. Several methods can be used to accomplish packetization of voice data, including Voice over IP (VoIP), Voice over Frame Relay, and VoIP carried on ATM.

Analog voice transmission usually requires a dedicated physical facility to handle each voice call. The equipment used remains in use during the entire duration of the transmission, and is thus unavailable for use by any other signal during this time. This can result in severe limitations on both the speed and volume of information that can be transmitted. Digitization (e.g., DS1, DS3, OC-3) has overcome some of the speed and volume limitations that are evident with analog transmission, but some other limitations still remain. Digitization helps by allowing multiple dedicated channels to be placed on a single physical media by sampling and digitizing the voice and then multiplexing the resulting bit stream in time or in frequency. *Multiplexing* is the process of allocating a signal to a particular time slot or frequency band on a single transmission path such that more information/signals can be carried through the media. Packetization can also result in higher efficiency for transmission. Such gains include eliminating the need for a dedicated channel for each voice call and allowance for easier integration of voice and data traffic convergence on a network. Compression can also be used to decrease the number of bits per second required from the standard 64 kbps commonly used today.

Given sufficient bandwidth, appropriate compression, and low-delay transmission media, packetized voice can be comparable to the toll-quality voice of PSTNs. When used with a different set of engineering parameters and a variable-delay transmission media such as the Internet, the present results have not completely realized the same level of quality because of delay, echo, and dropouts. Even when the voice quality is engineered to be almost as good as the toll-quality voice telephony of today, the services provided by the existing customer premise equipment associated with packetized voice simply do not rival the vertical features provided by traditional LEC circuit switches. In addition, packetizing voice can impact data that is normally carried on the voice network in tone form via fax or computer modems. The net effect is to limit the speed of these modems.

As additional high-bandwidth services are brought to the customer's premises (e.g., cable modems, ADSL), carriers may "give away" packetized voice or offer it at reduced prices compared with normal LEC services. This will motivate additional customers to switch from traditional telephone service to the high-speed packet-switched network.

Carriers use packetized voice to gain network efficiencies. Residential and business customers have used packetized voice as an option to save money on international long-distance and domestic long-distance calls. Additionally, business customers may use packetized voice to eliminate their private voice networks by merging the voice traffic onto their data network, because voice can traverse the higher-speed, higher-capacity data networks of the future fairly inexpensively. Customers may also switch to packetized voice to get bundled, value-added services such as unified messaging or video conferencing. Today, although packetized voice services already have some features and functionality comparable to that provided through traditional circuit switches, they are expected to surpass traditional circuit-switched methods in the next few years.

5.2   Compression

Voice compression is vital in VoIP because traffic often travels over relatively low-speed (e.g., dial-up, DSL) links. The bandwidth savings for the voice services can come in several forms and work at different levels. For example, further digital compression from the higher working layers of the media gateway application is not needed if the analog compression is part of the encoding scheme (algorithm). Silence suppression is the process of not sending voice packets between the gaps in human conversations and is another way to save bandwidth. Significant bandwidth savings can result through the use of compression and/or silence suppression.

Some applications, such as those used for modem functions, can be adversely affected by compression. Compression schemes can interfere with the functioning of modems by confusing the encoding algorithms used. The result is modems that never synchronize or they exhibit very poor throughput. There is also the possibility that intelligence built into some gateways could detect modem usage and automatically disable compression. Low-bit-rate speech compression schemes such as G.729 and G.723.1 could also be problematic in that they try to reproduce the subjective sound of the signal rather than the shape of the waveform. A greater amount of packet loss (or *severe jitter*, explained later) is more noticeable in compressed waveforms than in a noncompressed waveform. Interleaving and other techniques employed by some standards might minimize the effects of packet loss. Codecs output data streams that are put into IP packets and transported across the network to an endpoint. Unintelligible communication will result when different standards or parameters are used on the endpoints rather than using consistent standards and a common set of codec parameters.

5.3   VoIP Packet Processing Issues

5.3.1   Packet Timing Jitter

The timing of packet transmission is of paramount importance in a VoIP implementation, and a predictable, acceptable quality of service must be maintained. *Jitter* is the measure of time between when a packet is expected to arrive to when it actually does arrive. In other words, with a constant packet transmission rate of every 25 milliseconds (ms), every packet would be expected to arrive at the destination exactly every 25 ms. This situation, unfortunately, is not always the case. The greatest culprit of jitter is queuing variations caused by dynamic changes in network traffic loads. Buffering incoming packets and holding them long enough to allow the slowest packets to arrive in time to be played in the correct sequence is required to remove jitter. Jitter is of utmost concern on networks such as IP that do not guarantee that packets will arrive in the same sequence as they were transmitted. Most of the schemes designed to achieve a balance between the conflicting goals of minimizing overall delay and removing jitter center around varying the jitter buffer size in order to optimize the transmission process. One approach to dynamically varying the jitter buffer size is to measure the variation of the number of packets in the buffer over time and to incrementally adjust the buffer size to match the calculated jitter. Another approach used is to sum the number of late packets and calculate a ratio of these packets to successfully processed (i.e., on time) packets. This sum is used to adjust the size of the jitter buffer to achieve an (predetermined) allowable late-packet ratio. This method is preferred for networks with highly variable interpacket arrival times such as IP.

Media gateways often use a *play-out buffer* to buffer a packet stream so that the reconstructed voice waveform is unaffected by packet jitter. Play-out buffers used in media gateways mitigate packet jitter by buffering a packet stream so that the reconstructed voice waveform is not affected. If the media gateway discards packets arriving out of order, it may result in severe jitter, which can cause voice-quality issues by starving its play-out buffer and cause gaps in the reconstructed waveform. In general, the play-out buffer will minimize the effects of nominal jitter, but it does not eliminate the effects of severe jitter.

5.3.2 Packet Timing Latency

In VoIP, latency is the measure of time it takes a talker's voice to reach a listener's ear. The sound quality of a phone call is not necessarily degraded by large latency values. However, a lack of synchronization between speakers can result in hesitations in speaker interaction. The total delay that a signal or packet exhibits is a summation of all the latency contributors. When designing a multiservice network, it is generally accepted that the end-to-end latency necessary for maintaining toll-quality phone calls should be less than 150 ms. The five major sources of latency are packetization delays, data-to-physical-link interconnecting delays, propagation delays, queuing delays, and packet-switching delays.

Packetization delays

Packetization delays are caused by the amount of time it takes the end-points to fill a packet with data to be used in voice services. In most cases, the larger the packet size, the greater the amount of time it takes to fill it. The codec standard that is used will govern the packetization delay. Because the media gateway must remove and further process the packet data, this problem also exists on the receiving side. Although it depends on the exact hardware and software implementation of the media gateway, the amount of delay that occurs in both directions is usually quite small if the packets are kept small.

Data-to-Physical-Link Interconnecting Delays

A nominal delay is associated with the time it takes to serialize (or spool) the digital data onto the physical links of the interconnecting equipment. The delay is inversely proportional to the link speed, which means that the faster the media, the shorter the latency. This value is also somewhat dependent on the link technology used and its access method. Regardless of the bandwidth used, this delay is unavoidable. However, by keeping the number of intervening links to a minimum and by using high-bandwidth interfaces, one can reduce the overall latency to acceptable levels.

Propagation Delays

Propagation delay is the time it takes an electrical or photonic signal to traverse the length of a conductor. Although propagation delays will always exist, they only become an issue when the signal or packet travels a great distance. Distance is a factor because of the need to traverse more physical links, each at a slight cost in terms of processing delay. Over great distances, the delay can cause undesirable effects such as echo, signal loss, and so on.

Queuing Delays

A queuing delay is the amount of time that a packet remains buffered in a network while it awaits transmission. Network traffic loads result in variable queuing delays. When the queue buffer is a configurable parameter, a smaller number will result in better latency values. It is important to set aside adequate bandwidth and resources for voice traffic, because this delay is also based on the amount of traffic the system is trying to pass through a given link. Therefore, more traffic causes an increase in the overall network load. If the queue for voice traffic is allowed to grow too large and it is not serviced fast enough, then the effect is greater latency. Queuing delay is a large source of latency in VoIP networks.

Packet-Switching Delays

Packet-switching delay is the time it takes a router or switch to buffer a packet and make the decision about on which interface the packet is to be directed. It is yet another source of end-to-end latency. If a packet must be further buffered as part of its processing, a greater latency is incurred. This is why the architecture of the router or switch is a critical deciding factor in whether this delay remains small.

5.4   VoIP Call Setup Protocols

Several higher-layer protocols can accomplish call setup and takedown, including H.323, SIP, SCCP, MGCP, and MEGACO/H.248. Call setup protocols use TCP and UDP to transfer data during the setup and takedown phases of a telephone call. They handle functions such as mapping phone numbers to IP addresses, generating dial tones and busy signals, ringing the receiving party, and hanging up. There are two families of call setup protocols: one set for the telephony community and the other for the data-networking community.

5.4.1   Call Setup Protocols from the Telephony Community

The call setup protocols H.323 and Media Gateway Control Protocol (MGCP) come from the telephony community by way of the ITU. H.323 is the oldest and most widely deployed call setup protocol. H.323 is actually a family of telephony-based standards for multimedia, including voice and videoconferencing for use over packet-switched networks. Because the family of H.323 protocols has been refined for many years, it is robust and flexible. The cost of this robustness is high overhead caused by the number of handshakes and data exchanges required for each function that is performed in a calling session. The MGCP is the less flexible of the two protocols, and it is used for controlling telephony gateways from external call control elements known as *media gateway controllers* or *call agents*. A telephony gateway is a network element that provides conversion between the audio signals carried on telephone circuits and data packets carried over the Internet.

5.4.2   Call Setup Protocols from the Data-Networking Community

Session Initiation Protocol (SIP) and Media Gateway Control (MEGACO) are lightweight protocols developed by the Internet Engineering Task Force. SIP is more attractive than a heavyweight protocol such as H.323 because it will get the job done *most of the time*. SIP is supported by Cisco and Nortel, and Microsoft ships SIP client interfaces with its Windows XP operating system. The MEGACO protocol is used between elements of a physically decomposed multimedia gateway. This protocol creates a general framework suitable for gateways, multipoint control units, and interactive voice response units. Vendors have also provided their own proprietary protocols.

For example, Skinny Client Control Protocol (SCCP) is a simple, light-weight call setup protocol for Cisco devices. Although the H.323 family of call setup protocols is predominant today, it is likely that H.323, MGCP, MEGACO, SIP, and SCCP will be used by VoIP equipment in varying degrees for quite some time.

5.5   Voice Streaming Protocols

The voice streaming protocol is responsible for the transition of a telephone conversation, in that it provides for the exchange of actual encoded voice data that occurs after the call setup and before the call takedown, using two data flows, with one in each direction to let both users speak at the same time. Each of these two data flows uses RTP, which is encapsulated in UDP as it travels over the network. Widely used for streaming audio and video, RTP is designed for applications that send data in one direction with no acknowledgments. The header of each RTP datagram contains a time stamp, so the application receiving the datagram can reconstruct the timing of the original data. It also contains a sequence number so that the receiving side can deal with missing, duplicate, or out-of-order datagrams.

The two RTP streams carrying the bidirectional conversation are the primary elements in determining the quality of the voice conversations. It is helpful to understand the composition of the RTP datagrams, which transport the voice datagrams. All of the fields related to RTP sit inside the UDP payload. So, like UDP, RTP is a connectionless protocol. The software that creates RTP datagrams is not commonly part of the TCP/IP protocol stack, so applications are written to add and recognize an additional 12-byte header in each UDP datagram. Two-thirds of the RTP datagram is the header. The sender fills in each header, which contains the following four important fields:

- *RTP payload type.* This indicates which codec to use. The codec conveys the type of data (such as voice, audio, or video) and how it is encoded.

- *Sequence number.* This helps the receiving side reassemble the data and detect lost, out-of-order, and duplicate datagrams.

- *Time stamp.* This is used to reconstruct the timing of the original audio or video. It also helps the receiving side determine variations in datagram arrival times (also known as *jitter*). The real value of RTP is in the time stamp, which is contained in each datagram. The RTP application notes when each datagram actually arrives at the receiving side and compares this to the time stamp. If the time between datagram arrivals is the same as when they were sent, there is no variation. If there is variation in datagram arrival times, the receiving side can easily calculate the jitter using the time stamp.

- **Source ID.** This lets the software at the receiving side distinguish among multiple, simultaneous incoming streams. The real bandwidth consumption used by VoIP calls is higher than it first appears and, depending on the size of the data payload, the accumulation of headers can add a significant amount of overhead.

5.6   IP Telephony Servers, PBXs, and Gatekeepers

Although an IP telephony call occurs via a direct IP connection between two points, the functions of call control, call routing, and billing must be performed by an IP telephony server application and, in the case of large networks, a network of IP telephony servers.

The terms used to describe the server(s) that perform these functions depends on whether we're discussing H.323, SIP, or a vendor-specific solution. In the case of H.323, this set of functions is performed by an application called a *gatekeeper*. The gatekeeper is used by the H.323 protocol to provide Call Admission Control (CAC) and other management functions, such as address lookup, for multimedia services. The gatekeeper uses a set of signaling flows and Registration, Admission, and Status (RAS) to interoperate with VoIP devices. The CAC function of a gatekeeper can be especially important for networks with limited bandwidth, because the gatekeeper can track the number of calls in progress and restrict calls based on current bandwidth consumed. The goal of CAC is to limit new calls (or reroute them to the PSTN) if they may adversely impact the quality of calls that are already in progress on the VoIP network. Vendor solutions will provide these gatekeeper-like functions and may also include support for additional features such as voice messaging, voice conferencing, and click-to-call in the same IP telephony server offering. Each vendor has a unique IP telephony server offering; you will need to go through the process of making sure that each required feature is supported by any given vendor (e.g., Cisco, Nortel, Lucent) before choosing a particular telephony vendor and service.

An IP PBX typically serves as the core IP telephony server. On the PSTN, the PBX is often a closed-box system that provides all of the voice functions and features needed, usually in a proprietary manner. Management of the closed-box platform is left up to the PBX vendor. With VoIP, an IP PBX can be built on a PC platform running an operating system such as Microsoft Windows, Linux, or Sun Solaris. Although parts of the IP PBX are inherently proprietary, the platforms can be managed through specific application programming interfaces provided by the vendor and standard ones included with the operating system.

An IP PBX provides functions and features similar to those of a traditional PBX. Although the standard PBX of the PSTN offers multiple features developed over decades, such as call transfer and call forwarding, IP PBXs are already providing the same kinds of features and more, and their development is advancing quickly. Cisco CallManager is an example of a full-featured IP PBX.

Another new concept introduced along with IP telephony servers is clustering, in which several of these servers are grouped together in a cluster to offer increased scalability, reliability, and redundancy. Clustered servers function together and can be managed as a unit, providing combined processing power while logically appearing as a single server. Clustering is not available with traditional PBXs in the PSTN.

5.7   VoIP Gateways, Routers, and Switches

VoIP gateways, routers, and switches are equipped to handle origination, transport, and termination of VoIP traffic. Because the lower-layer media used is transparent to an IP infrastructure, VoIP technology transcends the differences among these transport media. The underlying technology for a VoIP infrastructure might be ATM, Frame Relay, point-to-point lines, or the public Internet. VoIP gateways and IP routers move RTP voice datagrams through an IP network. VoIP gateways provide a connection between the VoIP network and the PSTN and play a key role in the migration path toward VoIP. IP routers make the necessary decisions to move packets to the next router or hop along the path to the destination.

Despite the increasing popularity of exclusive VoIP phone networks, there are still demands to connect to the PSTN to place calls to PSTN users. When a phone call originates from the VoIP network and the receiving party is on the PSTN, VoIP gateways must use the SS7 protocol to signal switches in the PSTN. VoIP gateways can also provide for *transcoding*, which is the conversion between different codecs. For a codec other than G.711, such as G.729, to be used on the VoIP network, the voice data must be converted to G.711 format before being transferred to the PSTN.

VoIP gateways are powerful computers that enable real-time, two-way communication between a circuit-switched network (PSTN) and a packet-switched network (Internet). They provide functions such as compressing and converting voice to data, as well as transmitting and receiving data packets over the IP network. The VoIP gateway sits between a PBX and a router. When the packets arrive at the destination gateway, the voice data is depacketized and sent out over the PSTN to complete the transmission. Some of the key VoIP gateway functions are the following:[1]

- Act as a phone line on one end and computer network on the other

- Digitize the input telephone signal

- Perform conversion between different codecs

- Compress and packetize data for Internet transmission

- Route data to a given destination over Internet

- Reverse the entire operation for packets coming from a phone line

VoIP gateways can also add latency in that end-systems take time to digitize voice signals, and they must add a "de-jitter" buffering delay to compensate for any variable delay remaining in the system. That can add up to 80 ms, and because the acceptable delay level for toll-quality VoIP is 150 ms, the net that IT managers are left with is just 70 ms for providing a quality call.

VoIP gateways can interconnect with traditional PBXs to provide a migration path and allow for staged VoIP deployments within a corporate environment. VoIP gateways are complex devices that are typically capable of operating many different protocols to handle the variety of signaling and data protocols that are required to communicate between the VoIP network and the PSTN. IP routers make the decisions necessary to move packets to the next router and hop along the path to the destination by examining the IP packet headers. Problems can be identified and diagnosed by using the router functionality to trace the route of a voice packet through the network.

Switches have been traditionally categorized as being either edge or core in nature, although in reality contemporary switches are often hybrids serving both functions as required. When protocol conversions such as circuit-switched voice to compressed VoIP are involved, switches act as highly intelligent routers known as *gateways*. Although each switch may act independently, their individual activities are generally coordinated by a higher-level signaling and control system. In this case, the originating edge switch, the various core switches, and the terminating edge switch act in concert to establish, maintain, and terminate a call.

The advantages of a switched network are considerable in comparison to a dedicated network. A switched network is highly flexible. In the voice PSTN, for example, any-to-any connectivity is supported, because any telephone can connect to any other telephone in the world. Some key examples of the advantages of switched over dedicated networks are as follows:[2]

- *A switched network is shared.* The switches respond on a call-by-call basis if their resources and the circuits that interconnect them are available. A predetermined path is set up for all data associated with the call in a true connection-oriented environment, such as that in a traditional voice call over the PSTN. No path is set up in a connectionless environment such as a TCP/IP packet network. Instead, each data packet works its way through the network over any facilities that are available hop-by-hop (i.e., switch-by-switch).

- *A switched network is highly scalable.* There are no extreme increases in the cost associated with modest increases in connectivity because the cost difference when expanding or contracting a network is generally proportionate to the increase or decrease in functionality.

- *Switched networks are not nearly as susceptible to catastrophic failure as are dedicated networks.* Switched networks typically boast large numbers of switches interconnected to many other switches over circuits that follow diverse physical routes, providing the redundancy and the elimination of single points of failure required to provide good business continuity and disaster recovery planning. If a disaster or failure should occur in a given switch or circuit, many alternative ways to establish or maintain connectivity will exist.

- *Switched networks can be configured and reconfigured much more quickly than can dedicated networks.* There are no long-haul circuits to be set aside and dedicated to private use.

It is also important to understand that there are also some disadvantages of switched networks. Dedicated circuits are always on, and VoIP call setup delays may be considerable in comparison. If a usage-sensitive pricing algorithm is in effect, costs may be higher than with dedicated circuits that are billed on a flat-rate basis if there is a large volume of traffic between sites, because the user can be charged for traffic by call, by minutes of use, or by packet.

5.8   IP Phones and Softphones

Digital telephones are called *IP phones*, which also have the codes located in the telephones. Rather than having a four-line telephone connector in the back, they usually have an Ethernet LAN connection. An IP phone makes data connections to an IP telephony server, which also does the call setup processing. Codecs are located in the IP PBX if analog telephones are used, and the incoming calls are digitized there before being forwarded onto the IP network.

Desktop computers can serve as IP phones on your desk and are also called *softphones*. The computer has a LAN connection into the data network, the CPU runs the codec processing software, and it may be possible for the computer to use an IP telephony server to do call setup processing. Another advantage of softphones is that a headset and microphone can be plugged into the computer's audio card.

5.9   VoIP and Converged Network Regulatory Issues

VoIP services will create many consumer benefits and business opportunities, and the industry is devoting capital, personnel, and other resources to make facilities-based VoIP services a marketplace reality. Resources and rapid technological development, however, are not the only factors that will affect the availability of VoIP services. Regulatory uncertainty and the potential for application of unnecessary or overly burdensome regulation will also affect whether, when, and how VoIP services are deployed.

Much of the public policy discussion surrounding VoIP has centered on the appropriate regulatory classification of such services. Such an approach, however, has several shortcomings, because each regulatory category carries with it a history of regulatory assumptions that may or may not be appropriate for new technologies such as VoIP and the services they spawn. Protecting VoIP services from unnecessary regulation does not require that important public policies be neglected. Even under a generally deregulatory regime, any VoIP service that meets a baseline test should meet certain public policy responsibilities and requirements,[3] such as the principles set forth in the Communications Assistance for Law Enforcement Act, the offering of 911/E911 emergency access, access for the disabled, and appropriate contributions to universal service. But the overall direction of public policy should be toward a deregulatory environment in which even the most vital public policy objectives are secured through the lightest possible regulation, so as not to forestall the many benefits of these new services. Similarly, several legacy utility requirements should not be imposed on VoIP service providers. Most such requirements date from the era of a single provider of phone service and are inappropriate for competitors using nascent technologies that offer alternatives to incumbent providers. In particular, some legacy requirements relate to billing, payment, credit and collection, and quality of service standards. Competitive marketplace forces, rather than prescriptive rules, can address these issues much more effectively for nonincumbent providers of VoIP services. Regulators should make a comprehensive effort to review and eliminate such regulatory requirements for VoIP services.

VoIP service providers, particularly facilities-based providers, do, however, require certain rights irrespective of whether the provider's service is ultimately determined to be an information service, a telecommunications service, or another type of service. These rights relate generally to interconnection and the exchange of traffic, the right to obtain telephone numbers and have them published in telephone directories, the right to access the facilities and resources necessary to provide VoIP customers with full and efficient 911/E911 services, the right to be compensated fairly for terminating traffic delivered from other entities, and the right to nondiscriminatory access to universal service support. In addition, facilities-based VoIP providers need access to poles, ducts, conduits, and rights-of-way, regardless of the ultimate regulatory classification of VoIP services. In the final analysis, facilities-based VoIP services can be the breakthrough that fulfills the vision of the Telecommunications Act of 1996[4] for vast numbers of residential consumers. Support will occur most rapidly and ubiquitously if federal and state policy makers affirmatively promote VoIP services as an important policy objective and adopt a predominantly deregulatory approach to VoIP services.

If policy makers embrace and promote VoIP services and keep them free of unnecessary and inconsistent regulation, the result will be to attract additional investment and propel rapid deployment. The broadband explosion that has occurred since the Telecommunications Act of 1996 has created a pro-competitive framework of deregulatory policies that work for 18 million cable modem subscribers. Conversely, public benefits will inevitably be reduced and delayed if unnecessarily restrictive regulations from the monopoly telephone era are applied. The choice seems clear.

5.10   The VoIP Regulatory Freedom Act of 2004

In an attempt to prohibit state regulatory agencies from regulating the VoIP technologies and to prevent such regulation from stifling technological advances, Senator John Sununu of New Hampshire proposed Senate Bill S.2281,[5] entitled the VoIP Regulatory Freedom Act of 2004. The bill reserves solely to the federal government the responsibility and authority to regulate the offering or provision of a VoIP application (an application that uses the Internet or any successor protocol to offer two-way or multidirectional voice communications). Furthermore, the bill prohibits any state regulation, or delegation to the states, of any such authority. In other words, if any regulations are to ever come, they will be from the federal government, not at the state level.

S.2281 also prohibits the offering or provision of a VoIP application from being subject to access charges under FCC regulations, but it allows the FCC to establish a compensation mechanism for providers of VOIP applications based on the recovery of costs. Recovery of costs is an important factor to innovators of technology, because it allows varied levels of pricing and helps the provider sustain universal service by charging varying rates for urban or rural areas using the more populous regions to support development in the less populous regions of the country. This is similar to the agreements the federal government signed with AT&T in the early 20th century when the technology was still in its infancy.

S.2281 prohibits the FCC from imposing a compensation mechanism based on the mutual recovery of costs through reciprocal obligations unless the FCC has established a single unified regime to send and receive all data and voice communications. It allows connected VoIP application providers to enter into private negotiations for the mutual recovery of costs to send or receive voice communications of a connected VoIP application. Furthermore, the bill directs the FCC to do the following:

1.   Ensure that all providers of a connected VoIP application contribute to the preservation and advancement of federal universal service programs based on a flat fee

2.   Require such providers to provide access to necessary information to law enforcement agencies not less than that required of information service providers

It also requires the FCC to appoint an appropriate representative industry organization to develop guidelines, protocols, or performance requirements pertaining to the offering or provision of connected VoIP applications for the following:

1.   Providing comparable capabilities to 911 services

2.   Improving use by the disabled community

3.   Improving reliability of VoIP applications

4.   Ensuring appropriate security for the application and voice communications

Most important of all, the bill prohibits a state or political subdivision from imposing a tax or other charge on the offering or provision of a VoIP application.

5.11   Summary

This chapter discussed how voice data is converted into digital traffic and transmitted from one point to another. Salient to this process is a solid understanding of the difficulties that VoIP designers and implementers have to contend with, including timing jitter, timing latency, processing, and propagation delays. In order for equipment to interoperate successfully, common rules, or protocols, must be adhered to. We have discussed these rules as call setup protocols from the perspective of the telephony community and the networking community, each of which has different problems to contend with when processing VoIP traffic.

The problems encountered when sending or receiving VoIP traffic require specialized equipment and applications, which were discussed. Among these were VoIP gateways, routers, and switches, as well as IP telephony servers, PBXs, and gatekeepers. From the endpoints, we discussed IP phones and softphones and how they have evolved to provide more features and functionality over time, to the point where they rival traditional PSTN-type services. Finally, this chapter discussed some of the many regulatory issues for VoIP and what the future may hold in terms of greater benefits the public may obtain from VoIP.

5.12 Endnotes

1. Villalona, S. & Cho-Shun. (2002). Voice Over IP. Retrieved July 28, 2004 from webcomposer.pace.edu/CL78352N/IPTelePP.ppt

2. Horak, R. (2001). Dedicated vs. Switched Networks. Retrieved July 28, 2004 from www.commweb.com/shared/article/ showArticle.jhtml?articleId=8704429&pgno=2

3. *Balancing Responsibilities and Rights: A Regulatory Model for Facilities-Based VoIP Competition—An NCTA Policy Paper.* Retrieved February 2004 from www.ncta.com/PDF_files/VoIPWhitePaper.pdf

4. Kiser, C. (2003) Regulatory Considerations for Cable-Provided IP Telephony. Retrieved March 2003 from www.mintz.com/images/dyn/publications/Kiser-IPTelephony.pdf

5. Senate Bill S.2281, electronic document available from www.thomas.loc.gov

5.13 General References

Archer, K. et al. (2001). *Voice and Data Security.* Indianapolis, IN: SAMS Publishing.

Biran, G. (2004). *Voice over Frame Relay, IP and ATM: The Case for Cooperative Networking.* Retrieved July 12, 2004 from www.protocols.com/papers/ voe.htm

ENSC. (2004). *ENSC 835 Final Project Report.* Retrieved July 12, 2004 from www.ensc.sfu.ca/~ljilja/ENSC835/Projects/e.chan/Report.pdf

Kiser, C. (2003). *Regulatory Considerations for Cable-Provided IP Telephony.* Retrieved July 12, 2004 from www.mintz.com/images/dyn/publications/ Kiser-IPTelephony.pdf

McDermott, R. (1999). *Voice Over IP.* Research Paper. Retrieved July 12, 2004 from http://people.bu.edu/rjm123/VoIP.htm

National Cable & Telecommunications Association. (2004). *Balancing Responsibilities and Rights: A Regulatory Model for Facilities-Based VoIP Competition—An NCTA Policy Paper.* Retrieved July 12, 2004 from www.ncta.com/PDF_files/VoIPWhitePaper.pdf

NexTone Communications, Inc. (2003). *Enterprise Voice Services.* Retrieved July 12, 2004 from www.nextone.com/pdfs/enterprise.pdf

Samhassan.com. (2004). *Voice-Over-IP.* Retrieved July 12, 2004 from www.samhassan.com/Voice-Over-IP.htm#latency

Villalona, S. & Lee, C. (2002). *Voice Over IP.* Retrieved July 12, 2004 from http://webcomposer.pace.edu/CL78352N/IPTelePP.ppt

Walker, J. & Hicks, J. (2004). *Taking Charge of Your VoIP Project.* Indianapolis, IN: Cisco Press.

6

VoIP Implementation Basics

6.1   Stages of VoIP Implementation

Planning is the first step required in any major project. With a VoIP implementation, you must decide what you need and what you are going to buy to meet that need. Once that has been accomplished, the next step is to get everything installed, running, and integrated. If you know where you are starting from, you will have a better idea of what is involved in reaching your objective. Ideally, such change will result in an overall improvement in the quality of the services you provide to your users. During the planning stage of this process, you must ensure that your existing network is ready. This requires that you assess any possible negative effects to the applications currently running on the network, evaluate the potential performance issues that occur with VoIP traffic after installation or upgrade, and prepare for what happens if the network goes down. It is also wise to explain to your users and the management team what they can expect from these changes, along with the benefits they will receive from the new project.

The next stage in the VoIP implementation process is the evaluation and purchase of equipment, software, and services, which is sometimes called the *bake-off*. If you are evaluating products from multiple vendors, it is very important to run consistent and repeatable tests to ensure that you are comparing what you want with what you will actually get and to ensure that your metrics match the performance statistics provided by the vendor. Testing is also vital to verify that each vendor's products will interoperate in your network with your current equipment when you are making purchasing decisions that affect a significant portion of your budget.

Deployment and verification are also very important processes in a VoIP implementation. Deploying multimedia applications will challenge a networking team that is only familiar with transaction-oriented applications. For example, they may not discover that the IP routers are configured improperly until after the verification of testing has pointed out slowdowns or failures, or they may discover bandwidth limitations only after users complain. They may also discover the impact VoIP has on other applications only after they begin to field new help desk complaints. As with most IT projects, proactive management from the start of a staged rollout will lead to user satisfaction and will be a welcome change to the thankless firefighting resulting from severe mismanagement that is so common in today's IT environments.

It is important to keep your VoIP network running well by managing the reliability of telephone calls, which will be judged by how well you are reaching your "five nines" uptime target and the quality of the telephone calls, to ensure that they sound as good over the IP network as they do when using the PSTN. The two goals of uptime and reliability may encompass hundreds or thousands of components, including the following:

- The data network equipment along the path between the parties in a conversation, to include routers, switches, network interface cards (NICs), and cabling

- The complete range of telephony components to include VoIP servers and their hardware and software

- Whatever users come in contact with, to include IP phones, desktop computers, and their unique software and configurations

In the past, those in the telephony community have been accustomed to managing costly, high-quality devices that use dedicated telephone wiring, so managing telephone systems was a relatively straightforward process when compared to managing VoIP. In general, telecom management had the luxury of having a specialist to call if something went wrong. There was always someone who maintained key hardware by making a few visits per year to install the latest updates. In contrast, management activities for VoIP need to be proactive, just as they must be with any other major IT applications. Some of these management activities that are essential to successfully manage a VoIP network are discussed in the following paragraphs.

For most enterprises, network performance is vital to the success of the business. For businesses using VoIP, it is a critical factor. The complexity of today's applications and networks drives the absolute requirement for monitoring and event management to ensure the performance of specific devices, LAN segments, or applications. Not all of the products providing monitoring capabilities can tell you the level of quality or performance your VoIP users are experiencing. In today's IT environments, the mix of protocols, applications, and dispersed intelligence makes problem determination much more difficult than when applications and networks consisted of terminals accessing mainframes. Therefore, having different teams that specialize in either network or application troubleshooting is critical to ensuring rapid, accurate fault isolation and diagnosis.

Service-Level Agreements (SLAs) are used to provide a standard for measuring the performance your team is delivering against the expectations of your users. Ideally, such performance should exceed, or at a minimum, be equal to the level of service the users are currently receiving. This is critical to proper service-level and contract management. By establishing trends that show network behavior and performance over time, you can fine-tune your existing infrastructure and plan future investments for future growth.

As you grow, it will be necessary to change your existing system planning and analysis for improvements to be made. Good network management requires reporting systems to report on what is happening across the many components involved. This is especially true when managing a VoIP implementation. Enterprise changes can drastically affect performance factors quickly. An example of such may be the addition of many more users to a call center. Such load increases could lead to performance issues cropping up on the VoIP network because of congestion or bandwidth limitations. These types of changes drive the need for good benchmarking and ongoing assessment of network performance as a routine part of the day-to-day VoIP management process.

More than likely, your VoIP project will have dependencies on other IT projects. A prerequisite for most VoIP deployments will often include Quality of Service (QoS) and a possible network infrastructure upgrade to support it. This will require careful planning and coordination to keep the projects on track. It may require different teams to handle the network upgrade and the VoIP rollout. It is always important to reduce your project dependencies where possible to keep things simple. A VoIP deployment is complicated enough without compounding factors to reduce your chances of success.

6.2 Achieving VoIP Quality and Reliability

Most corporate decision-makers have serious concerns about making the migration to VoIP because it introduces such a vast degree of change into an organization just to be accomplished successfully. Concerns about the quality of VoIP calls, the reliability of IP networks, and (usually) a lack of expertise in voice-over-data deployment are among the more relevant issues today's decision-makers must face. Inferior sound quality and service reliability are major concerns for potential subscribers to VoIP services. Although VoIP service has improved dramatically in recent years, subscribers can still experience poor quality and reliability, even in the best of circumstances. Such variations in quality have brought about the need for providers to establish a minimum level of performance, or a *quality of service*, subscribers can depend upon when using VoIP services.

6.2.1   The Need for Quality of Service (QoS)

Quality of Service (QoS) and performance tuning techniques can help make a VoIP deployment successful. QoS refers to choices about how different users or different application traffic are prioritized on the network. This prioritization process helps administrators to manage demands from competing users, applications, or traffic when they are all sharing the same network. Performance tuning refers to various methods network administrators use for increasing efficiency or making tradeoffs among resources or network attributes. When there are many people or devices that share a resource such as a network, the resources on that network can be either over-provisioned or over-subscribed. Over-provisioning means that more resources are made available than can be consumed. In this case, there is so much of a resource made available that if every subscriber requested it at the same time, there would still be plenty of it to go around. Over-provisioning is usually expensive because it requires lots of reserve capacity. Over-subscribing is a term for situations where a resource has many users or subscribers who, for the most part, don't all ask for use of the resource at the same time. It is usually cheaper than over-provisioning and is much more commonly seen in VoIP. When too many subscribers request service simultaneously, the service may become quite slow or even become unavailable, simply because too many concurrent users consume all of the available resources. Over-subscription can occur whenever there are many inputs and few outputs, as in any situation where a bottleneck or funnel emerges. Unfortunately, every juncture in a network is a potential bottleneck. The total of all the inputs in network devices such as routers and switches can greatly exceed the capacity of a router queue. Because networks are shared and can be over-subscribed, QoS mechanisms are needed to protect users and applications from each other and to provide differentiation of service.

QoS can be used to alleviate occasional network over-subscription. When the network traffic increases enough that performance declines because of over-subscription, an administrator may choose to give some classes of network traffic better treatment than others. The decisions that are made here will mean some users or applications will be given priority over others. This decision will depend on how administrators classify network traffic (i.e., What kind? What are the different classes? Who is authorized for each class of service?) and how they handle each class of traffic (i.e., How should this class of traffic be treated? How is the handling of this class different from that of other classes of traffic?). The classification of the traffic is usually done at the edge of a network, and the handling is usually done in the middle. Decisions about the classifying and handling of network traffic are important business decisions involved in deployment of QoS.

Networks operating without QoS treat all traffic as *best effort* and the network devices do their best to deliver frames from senders to their receivers. Even if a network is not a good candidate for QoS, it is still worth exploring the alternatives when such alternatives involve cheaper bandwidth and a network design with fewer bottlenecks. Even though more bandwidth does give network traffic more throughput and capacity, it does not always help where delay and jitter are involved. QoS is not without its difficulties. Not only is it difficult to set up, but it also involves political decisions to determine who is in each class of traffic and how they get treated. In fact, there are situations where the fear of making the wrong political decision prevents the use of QoS. For example, giving priority to an internal IT VoIP QoS monitoring system by sacrificing the executive staff's traffic will not be as easy politically as using VoIP QoS for a business-critical application. In order to be classified, network traffic needs to be segregated. In general, network applications can be easily identified because they use a unique IP port number. QoS techniques comprise a mix of classification and handling mechanisms to include link-layer QoS techniques, IP QoS techniques, queuing techniques, and traffic shapers.

6.2.2   Link-layer QoS techniques

Link-layer QoS techniques influence the traffic handling on individual data links. For example, ATM has QoS incorporated into its core architecture. IEEE 802.lp/Q is used to insert bytes into Ethernet frames that indicate each frame's priority. The frame priority is used by Ethernet switches to decide which frames get switched ahead of others. There must be some correlation to a higher-layer QoS mechanism to provide any value to application users whose traffic needs to be handled consistently across all the data links in a connection because both of the previously described schemes only work at the lower layers. Most commonly, large packets are broken up by using Cisco Link Fragmentation and Interleaving (LFI). LFI is a Layer 2 technique in which all Layer 2 frames are broken into small, equal-size fragments and transmitted over the link in an interleaved fashion. When fragmentation and interleaving are put into effect, the network device fragments all frames that are waiting in the queuing system. The network device sends these fragments over the link and it reduces the queuing delay of small frames since they are sent almost immediately. Link fragmentation reduces the effects of delay and jitter by normalizing packet sizes of larger packets in order to offer more regular transmission opportunities to the voice packets.

6.2.3 Queuing Techniques

Routers and switches offer ways to prioritize traffic and handle congestion better than using QoS at Layers 2 and 3. This is done through a variety of queuing option techniques to include Weighted Fair Queuing (WFQ), Class-based Weighted Fair Queuing (CBWFQ), Low-latency Queuing (LLQ), and Weighted Random Early Detection (WRED). WFQ is used to improve the handling of low-volume connections in high-volume traffic and is particularly beneficial when VoIP traffic is mixed with heavy file transfers. CBWFQ and LLQ work in combination to provide priority to delay-sensitive VoIP traffic. WRED is used to avoid the mass slowdown of all the TCP connections passing through a router when the network is experiencing congestion. These options have value in smaller networks where they provide their effectiveness rather quickly, but their ability to administer on a consistent basis diminishes rapidly with even a moderate increase in the quantity of network devices present on a network.

CBWFQ and LLQ are used for VoIP traffic priority handling. Traffic match criteria uses DiffServ bits to define the classifying technique for VoIP. WRED is used when congestion occurs to improve the handling of marked DiffServ traffic. Additional VoIP bandwidth must be reserved if congestion problems are encountered in the LLQ. WFQ may help the VoIP traffic compete better with the other traffic if you have a a small percentage of VoIP on a network with a wide mix of traffic. Of course it is best to test WFQ as you deploy it to make sure it really achieves the effect you want.

6.2.4 IP QoS Techniques

There is an increasingly popular set of QoS mechanisms found at Layer 3 in the TCP/IP protocol stack. These mechanisms include the Resource Reservation Setup Protocol (RSVP), Differentiated Services (DiffServ), and

Multiprotocol Label Switching (MPLS). Collectively, these mechanisms are called IP QoS because their purpose is to assist in meeting application IP network requirements from end to end by taking advantage of specific features of the IP protocol.

Resource Reservation Setup Protocol (RSVP)

RSVP reserves resources to meet requirements for bandwidth, jitter, and delay for a particular connection through a series of routers. RSVP sends IP control flows from one end of the network to the other. These IP packets instruct intermediate routers to reserve a portion of their resources, such as bandwidth and queues for forthcoming TCP/IP traffic. RSVP suffers a significant drawback in that it also requires more bandwidth and router resources. The ideal operational conditions for use of RSVP are when the connections are long, such as those used by streaming video, and when only a few connections at a time require reserved resources. RSVP is not a good technique to use for VoIP traffic. However, it should be considered for use with long-running video streams that may be present in your network traffic.

Differentiated Services (DiffServ)

The Precedence Priority Model, also known as Differentiated Services, IP Precedence Type of Service (TOS), or IEEE 802.1pQ, takes aggregated traffic, segregates the traffic flows into classes, and provides preferential treatment of classes. It is only during periods of congestion that any noticeable differentiated services effects are ever realized. Packets are marked or tagged according to priority. Switches read these packet markings and treat the packets based on their priority. The interpretation of the markings must be consistent within the network domain. DiffServ provides IP QoS by using the Type of Service (ToS) byte. In the IP version 4 header specification, DiffServ involves setting the bits in this ToS byte to a non-zero value and it uses the first 6 bits of the TOS byte, which is designated as the Differentiated Services Code Point (DSCP). The 6 bits of the DSCP allow for 26 or 64 different classes of service. The Differentiated Services model defines eight classes, from highest precedence to lowest: Expedited Forwarding (EF), Assured Forwarding 1-4(AF), and Best Effort (BE). Within each class, there are eight drop precedence settings, which indicate to the switch which packets are more important than others within that class. This results in a total of 8x8=64 Differentiated Services Code Points (DSCP). DiffServ marks a relative priority in each IP packet, to be honored by each router that handles the frame. Routers look at IP bits all the time so there is little overhead involved with DiffServ classification. VoIP gateways commonly set this byte as they generate VoIP packets for calls based on the PSTN. Most IP phones and VoIP gateways set the ToS byte to a nonzero value to denote the priority needed for VoIP.

VoIP traffic will need a way to be distinguished from the other application traffic at the edges of the network requiring classification such as that based on port numbers, RTP headers, the DiffServ field, or packet sizes. One way to do this is to use DiffServ bits to classify the traffic as close to its origin as possible. You can also use other QoS techniques such as CBWFQ that can use the DiffServ-marked packets to identify traffic classes. You will need to configure the network devices, particularly the routers, to give traffic with different DiffServ markings different classes of handling. As with all cross-network configuration changes, using DiffServ will require careful planning and good tools.

Although the DSCP field created an efficient scheme for classifying different types of traffic, it is only as good as the weakest network link. Even though DiffServ is generally thought of as "better than best-effort" service, the entire path can only be considered best-effort if every single segment in the path from one codec to the other either does or does not support DSCP handling. In other words, it is either all or none for DSCP. Diffserv is generally used on Ethernet networks and configured on the switches where the volume of VoIP traffic is likely to grow. A separate VLAN for VoIP traffic is also created. Plan to upgrade shared hubs because they cannot provide the service required for VoIP traffic. IP phones or softphone NICs that can set the 802.lp priority field to a nonzero value are used from the phone to the switch. The switches are then configured to provide priority to VoIP traffic that has the 802.1p Priority field set.

Multiprotocol Label Switching (MPLS)

Multiprotocol Label Switching (MPLS) sets up a virtual circuit through an IP network by prefixing each frame with four bytes that tell how to get to the next router in the path. This technique is better suited for very large network backbones with many routers. MPLS is often used by network carriers and Internet service providers, but its complexity makes it impractical for most enterprise networks. MPLS is much more than a QoS technique in that it also provides network operators with a way to offer different classes of service. When packets enter an MPLS-aware network, they are "tagged" with a label that can contain a variety of information. Within an MPLS network, Label Switched Routers (LSRs) are capable of forwarding the packet through the network using the label rather than traditional address fields in the IP header. Label Switched Paths (LSPs) can be configured for different label values to set up routes for different classes of data traffic from different users.

MPLS as a handling technique can be used in tandem with other QoS techniques such as DiffServ, which provides a classifying technique. In this case, MPLS labels can be assigned based on the bit settings of the DSCP so that the MPLS-enabled network provides different paths for traffic with different bit settings. IP QoS techniques treat different classes of traffic differently, and they don't necessarily make one class of traffic move faster than another. These techniques will provide the capability for premium class traffic to get a better guarantee of bandwidth to include better priorities within routers or a better route through a network than traffic routed in a lower class. VoIP traffic needs networks that are tuned for dedicated paths that have low delay, jitter, and loss, as provided by MPLS in ISPs with large, complex networks. In this case, MPLS is the technique of choice, as it gives selected traffic dedicated paths through the backbone of a network. ISPs may also want to use MPLS to internally implement premium VoIP service.

Application Programming Interfaces (APIs)

Application Programming Interfaces (APIs) can be used to enable applications to do their own prioritizing. Recent versions of Windows offer TCP/IP applications an API for requesting the QoS they desire, but these APIs are likely to be little used or ignored for network IP QoS, because applications cannot necessarily be trusted. Even so, the aggregate needs of all the applications running on a network are important considerations when determining the use of QoS techniques.

Traffic Shaping Techniques

Traffic shaping devices, also known as bandwidth managers, are a category of network device that stand at the ingress and egress points in a network. Traffic shapers are the first network devices to begin implementing policies for the traffic they handle, and they can act as local agents for a broad set of rules implemented by policy servers. TCP/IP provides all network traffic with a best-effort delivery service when the network is moderately loaded. As the network load increases, QoS mechanisms help meet specific application requirements to improve on TCP/IP's best-effort delivery. This is particularly important since new applications have their own respective requirements for bandwidth, delay, jitter, and packet loss. Traffic shapers are appropriate if there are clear concentration points in your network. They can decide how much bandwidth to give to each different kind of flow because they look at many different attributes of the network traffic.

6.2.5   QoS Issues

Digital Voice that travels over the PSTN is usually of very high quality because the circuit-switched architecture provides a dedicated circuit for that voice traffic to travel over. The phone company creates a circuit for your call every time you pick up the phone and make a call. Voice traffic is encoded into digital format when that circuit crosses from an analog circuit onto a digital circuit. As previously explained, the encoding of voice or sound data is accomplished through the use of a codec. A codec is a standardized scheme for transforming sound data into binary representations of the sound data in a compressed format. Codecs are required to decode binary data back into voice at the end of the digital circuit. All codecs used in voice over network systems use standards laid out by the International Telecommunications Union G-series recommendations discussed previously. Voice over Network protocols are efficient in their use of bandwidth because they only use it when the parties are actually speaking and they use different codecs for voice traffic. In addition to compression, these codecs also can of save bandwidth by not achieving the quality of sound level comparable to a switched circuit 64Kbps codec. A Mean Opinion Score or MOS rating is typically used to measure sound, using a numeric rating between 1 and 5. MOS will differentiate between a a high-quality call as in comparison to a local call made over an ISDN-type circuit. A MOS rating between 3.5 and 4 is referred to as toll quality and is a reference for what is experienced on most PSTN calls. A toll quality call is an MOS rating between 3 to 3.5 and similar to what you experience on a mobile phone. A MOS rating below the 3 refers to a level where it is typically difficult to communicate. A higher MOS typically indicates that a higher bandwidth will be used by the codec. The following codecs are used in VoIP applications:

- G.711: The standard codec that all VoIP systems must provide support for. G.711 uses 64 Kbps of bandwidth to carry a stream of audio traffic and typically has a MOS score of 4.4.

- G.722: This codec samples audio from 0-7KHz at 48, 56, and 64 Kbps and is used for high-quality voice application.

- G.723.1: The baseline codec for narrowband H.323 communications and operates at 5.3 or 6.4 Kbps. G.723.1 has a MOS of 3.5 and 3.98 respectively.

- G.726: This codec uses an Adaptive Differential Pulse Code Modulation (ADPCM) to encode speech. G.726 can be used at 16, 24, 32, or 40 Kbps and typically has a MOS of 4.2.

- G.728: This codec has a MOS rating of 4.2 at a 16 Kbps bit rate.

- G.729 and G.729a: This codec has a 4.0 MOS at an 8 Kbps bit rate.

In general, VoIP terminals accept multiple codecs and virtually all of them fall back to G.711 if they cannot agree upon the use of a more efficient codec. It is important to have equipment that supports similar or multiple codecs to help move voice traffic as efficiently as possible, and the choice of one codec over another can be an implementation issue. G.711 can affect the quality of the sound heard from the perspective of the limitations of the codec. Also, a codec using bandwidth more efficiently may be the better choice when considered for use on network links that are experiencing significant congestion. Different codecs vary in their degree of packet loss; all IP networks will typically suffer from some packet loss because they work by compressing the audio data in different ways. A codec using less compression is resilient to lost frames because it loses very little time in a dropped frame. A lost frame can cause more damage to the quality of the call, because a more advanced codec will use less bandwidth through compression and other techniques.

6.2.6 QoS in a Voice Over Packet System

QoS is one of the tasks built into the ATM protocol that allows devices to show that their traffic is susceptible to latency problems or is tolerant of latency. QoS allows ATM routing devices to perform traffic shaping on the circuit to control congestion. There can be problems with QoS when too much traffic is designated as sensitive to latency, resulting in network congestion. There is also an underlying network architecture for Voice over Frame Relay that helps it achieve good voice quality. Since Frame Relay is typically implemented on private networks, administrators can combat congestion by adding additional bandwidth. The Committed Information Rate and Burstable Information Rate (CIR/BIR) bandwidth control features found in Frame Relay are generally specified in the SLAs when service is established with a provider. The Committed Information Rate guarantees the amount of bandwidth that can be sent across the link and the Burstable Information Rate is the amount by which the Committed Information Rate can be exceeded. This functionality allows administrators of Frame Relay circuits to know exactly how much bandwidth they are guaranteed and how much over that amount they can periodically exceed for traffic management purposes.

TCP/IP traffic is designed for reliable transmission of data but is not intended to manage the time it takes for round-trip transmission of traffic. Although the latency time for round-trip transmission has very little effect on data, it can be disastrous for real-time voice transmission. A voice link requires slightly less than 250 milliseconds of end-to-end delay to approach toll quality. Since almost all public networks will drop some packets, a redundancy sending technique is used to achieve this level of latency. Although this will help, it does add a certain amount of overhead to the circuit. All traffic is treated equally since there is no integrated QoS in IP networks. This means that a larger packet from another protocol could delay a small VoIP packet. Individual VoIP protocols will deal with each of these issues in a slightly different manner.

Built-in Quality of Service is required for circuits that use the H.323 protocol. Although H.323 is designed to be tolerant of network congestion issues, a network with enough congestion will still cause problems. The RTP protocol is used by H.323 for actual media streams and, within RTP, there is the control protocol RTCP, which includes the Sender Reports and Receiver Reports. Active senders use Sender Reports that contain information about transmission and reception of the media stream itself. Receiver Reports are only used for terminals that listen to the stream. There are three parts to the Sender Reports. The packet is identified as the SR, which identifies the originating host. The data on the timestamp is contained in the second section. This section includes the sender's packet count and sender's octet count from the beginning of the stream. Data that is relevant to the quality of the call is contained in the third section which includes:

- The source identifier for the media source
- The inter-arrival jitter that indicates the percentage of packets that are arriving out of sequence
- The last sender report timestamp identifying the timestamp of the last sender report received
- The last sender report delay used by the sender to calculate round trip delay
- The total number of packets lost
- The fraction of packets lost

■ The highest sequence number received that identifies the last RTP packet received

Network congestion is controlled by adjusting the sending rate of the RTP stream through the use of the Sender and Receiver Reports. Using these reports will add some degree of improvement on a network where packet loss is likely when combined with using a method to provide for a redundancy of frames across the network. However, it will not help overly congested network links. A gatekeeper can also be employed to control Quality of Service with H.323 calls. Authorization can be used to allow the call to proceed, and it can also be used in conjunction with a parameter called allowed bandwidth. Allowed bandwidth tells the terminals what bandwidth the gatekeeper will allow them to use without sending a bandwidth request to the gatekeeper.

The SIP protocol is also susceptible to Quality of Service issues but they are different for Voice Over Packet. SIP uses RTP/RTCP for sending and controlling the actual media streams, and the same codecs, sender reports, and receiver reports used in H.323 are used with SIP. Although SIP can throttle the sending rate to deal with network congestion (just as can be done with H.323), SIP does not have any provision for a gatekeeper and cannot control the bandwidth consumed by the call. If a significant number of VoIP terminals are on the same network, significant bandwidth savings can be realized when using SIP since it has the capability to set up a call with a minimum amount of traffic.

6.3 Tuning for VoIP QoS

Network tuning is used to improve the efficiency of your network and improve the quality of your VoIP deployments. When tuning your network, consider the trade-offs that will likely be practical choices, such as increased CPU utilization for less RAM, more delay for less risk of lost data, or configuration change to the routers, switches, VoIP servers, or IP phones. Efficiency improvements may also require adjustments to default configuration values. Tuning can even improve the performance of the operation of the highly efficient TCP/IP protocol stack generally. Some the areas that can be adjusted are as follows:

■ **TCP window size:** The size of the TCP window determines the amount of data that can be sent before the sender has to stop and wait for an acknowledgment. You can improve the throughput by increasing the window size if you are using a very reliable network where the chances for data loss are very small. A larger window size would force more data to be re-transmitted when packets get lost, resulting in lower throughput. The window size is dynamically adjusted over a wide range of network conditions by TCP/IP stacks to optimize performance.

- **MTU sizes and low latency:** A data network Maximum Transmission Unit (MTU) or maximum frame size is usually 1500 bytes which, at an extremely slow speed (such as 56 kbps), takes longer than 200 ms just to put the packet on the wire. At the cost of just a small amount of data efficiency, you can set a smaller MTU size to be forwarded through the slower-speed links and do not need to change anything other than one router configuration command in order to avoid breaking your delay budget for VoIP.

- **Concurrent sessions per URL:** TCP/IP connections are opened to retrieve data when a URL is requested from a Web browser. A typical Web page may consist of many files of information to retrieve. TCP/IP applications developers make a tuning choice when they determine the optimal number of connections to be opened to retrieve the data in a relatively small time frame. Often, extra memory and programming complexity is the trade-off made for concurrent downloads, and the benefit is a faster response time.

- **Codec:** The codec that you choose will have a significant impact on call quality. Higher-quality codecs such as G.711 will generally consume more bandwidth than G.729; however, G.711 provides a higher MOS when it is used in the same network conditions. A trade-off of quality versus bandwidth consumption will occur when choosing a codec.

- **Silence suppression:** Silence suppression is offered by certain IP phones and softphones and can reduce the bandwidth required for a VoIP call by 50 percent or more, but the resulting speech may sound choppy or clipped. The periods of silence may be irritating for users. Just as with the codecs, silence suppression will result in a trade-off of quality versus bandwidth consumption.

- **Jitter buffer size:** Variations in packet arrival times introduced by the network are smoothed out with the use of a jitter buffer. A larger jitter buffer can hide the jitter problem and should be as large as the maximum jitter experienced. Some phones can configure the size of their jitter buffers dynamically. Jitter buffers add delay that will effect the overall delay budget and reduce call quality. This can produce a situation where a trade-off between increased delay and call quality will have to be made.

- **Speech packet size (delay between packets):** The speech packet size reflects the size of the payload that is sent in each VoIP packet. The greater the size of the payload, the greater the increase in the amount of the voice data that is transferred in a single packet. This results in a reduction in header overhead. A large packet that is lost will have a greater impact on the quality than a smaller packet size that is lost. This tuning parameter should be reserved for advanced tuning, since most of the current IP phones have codecs that optimize the speech packet size. The resulting trade-off is quality versus bandwidth consumption.

There are other possible trade-offs that can be made when tuning VoIP implementations which entail making choices between quality or risk against a limited resource such as bandwidth. Other VoIP tuning possibilities and their trade-offs are Call Admission Control and UDP checksums, which will be explained below:

- **Call Admission Control (CAC):** Access to a resource can be constrained through the use of a tuning technique known as Call Admission Control (CAC). WAN links have a finite amount of bandwidth and networks are often oversubscribed. CAC is used to address this problem. This results in a trade-off in VoIP deployments with call quality versus allowing all users the opportunity to make a phone call at the exact same time. CAC uses a device known as a *gatekeeper* as part of the H.323 standard for multimedia transmissions to provide control admission of VoIP calls into a network. Assuming that allowing too many calls over a single link degrades the quality of all calls, the gatekeeper's job is to prohibit a new call from being made if the network can't provide adequate bandwidth. The gatekeeper must keep track of calls in progress and the bandwidth available. It is important to consider the forecasted calls per user as this data will be used by each gatekeeper for call control purposes when planning your VoIP network.

- **UDP checksum:** The UDP header contains a UDP checksum that checks for data integrity. It serves to detect any errors that may have occurred during transmission. The UDP Checksum value in VoIP datagrams is set to a value of 0 in some IP phones and VoIP gateways. This improves the efficiency of the RTP header compression process and will save time during the checksum computation. Normally, checksum values in UDP will change for every datagram, but by using the value of 0, it will not change throughout the VoIP call and it will enhance the performance of the RTP algorithms. This, of course, results in a VoIP tradeoff between the risk of data error and better compression with a slightly reduced delay speed.

6.4　Configuration and Testing

The configuration of QoS for your network can be very difficult due to implement. Some of the reasons for the difficulties include the following:

- There are many QoS schemes, parameters, and tuning techniques in use today which are new to most network personnel and have their own terminology, parameters, and peculiarities.

- QoS is new technology. More than likely, their will be a lack of knowledge and experience on the part of the network IT staff, because there is not much information or data on techniques made available. QoS changes are also discouraged in many networks, which results in a lack of opportunity for network personnel to gain first-hand knowledge or experiment.

- Most large QoS plans involve many device interconnections and interactions that involve changes in devices and applications through-out a network, moving far beyond just a single router, segment, or piece of software. Mismatches in device setup and cross-product issues are just two of the potential problems that make the setup prone to error.

As with all testing, the testing environment must mirror actual stress conditions as close as possible. QoS handling effects can generally only be observed against the heavy traffic that creates the stress conditions QoS is designed to help mitigate. QoS testing requires the use of a stressed network to detect and test its behavior, test the configuration, improvement of the handling of classes, post-change operational functionality, and whether or not you achieved the improved handling you sought.

Policy-based network management software provides the ability to make QoS feasible. The alternative would be the nearly impossible, error-prone task in a large network of configuring the network devices one at a time by hand. Policies make it much easier to understand the QoS choices you are making and which devices are affected. Of course, this doesn't negate the need for solid QoS experience in determining how the network behaves and performs, both correctly and incorrectly. As with all good IT projects, the QoS team needs to test its work, in settings small and large, before applying its changes network-wide. Since QoS configuration is very complex and involves the interaction of many different network components, it will require testing is to make sure it is functioning or failing as expected. Reliable and repeatable tests for each time a parameter is changed slightly will be required for QoS and tuning changes.

There is a major challenge in the testing of QoS mechanisms to be used in your network. The testing lab must simulate the congestion that accurately represents the production traffic as it exists in the production network and must do all of this in a reliable, repeatable manner, so that when QoS goes into production, it functions exactly as expected. There are two basic approaches to QoS testing that should be included in your testing plan, "before and after" and the "mix of classes."

The "before and after" technique compares the results against the baseline results. In this case, you would conduct a baseline test the proper background traffic and traffic in the class that is to get special handling and then another with the QoS handling technique activated. During the testing process you will need to ensure that the background traffic variables have not changed so that the affected traffic class will actually shows the effects of improved handling.

The "mix of classes" will start with the QoS handling technique activated and inject identical traffic with different classifications into the network. The traffic measurement results will be in terms of the network statistics you are interested in to ensure that the traffic in different classes is handled differently, such as throughput, response time, delay, lost data, and jitter. Tests should be run every time you change any QoS parameter, both before enabling QoS changes and after making any QoS changes. QoS and tuning techniques applied to VoIP traffic should result in a higher MOS as a result of lower delay, lower jitter, and fewer lost packets. QoS should be testing and tuning until you are sure that you have reached your MOS target under congested conditions.

Although QoS is a non-negotiable requirement for a successful VoIP deployment, it is important to understand that QoS is not a replacement for VoIP-quality devices and adequate bandwidth. You should only roll out QoS, after you have added all of your anticipated VoIP traffic to existing data network traffic, and your network monitoring system is reporting that you are encountering congestion infrequently during the workday. The recommended threshold for cumulative congestion per eight-hour day is less than ten minutes. If your congestion exceeds theses numbers, you must go back and upgrade the network by adding more bandwidth, changing your architecture, upgrading your devices, etc. The QoS techniques you use on your network will depend on currently existing infrastructure and the other application traffic.

6.5   VoIP Management

A discussion of VoIP management assumes a reasonably mature data network. It also assumes that you are successfully managing your network components, users, and their applications. Deploying VoIP means you are adding a new, complex application to your network and that your management goals and tasks will change after VoIP is running on the network. The goal during the deployment stages of your VoIP project was to satisfy your first group of VoIP phone users by providing high levels of availability and call quality. Transitioning to the VoIP management stage will change your goals to user availability and management. Such ongoing changes might include managing the need for additional phone users, new network applications, different network components, and daily security intrusions. Managing your VoIP system properly involves the following:

- *Operations.* The smooth handling of the day-to-day changes to the network, applications, and users
- *Availability.* The insuring of high levels of uptime for the overall phone system
- *Call quality.* Making sure that every phone call sounds good
- *Accounting.* Insuring the calls are being charged properly to the right people and departments

Each of the previous four topics has an integral aspect of security to it. For example, tight control over who is permitted to make changes to any VoIP component is a security element that affects operations. Availability and quality due to degraded performance can result from unauthorized access to the phone system or data network. Accounting can also be affected by a lack of security for data such as telephone records that contain private information such as who called whom, for how long, and when.

Understanding the broad set of tools, techniques, and processes used to ensure the reliability and availability of a VoIP implementation addressed through proper VoIP management is important due to its associated ongoing cost. A VoIP application that your business depends on for day-to-day operations will be a business-critical application on your network. VoIP management to ensure good quality, performance, and security is required to maintain a successful VoIP deployment. One of the common misconceptions is that once the challenge of deploying VoIP has been met, the problem is solved. The fact is, the challenge is not over and a good management system will be required to simplify day-to-day operations of a VoIP implementation. Some of the benefits of VoIP management are as follows:

- **Ensuring toll-quality telephone calls:** The Mean Opinion Score (MOS) is a measurement standard for the distinction between good and bad. A good management system can describe precisely whether the current quality is good, acceptable, or poor and can help you recognize performance trends that can lead to lower-quality calls.

- **High expectations for reliability:** There has been an expectation of a high degree of availability throughout the years due to PSTN usage from public phone systems. In fact, most public carriers provide approximately five nines of availability when they pick up a handset. A management system must be in place to maintain a state of high availability.

- **Avoiding failures:** The best way to achieve low downtime is to be proactive in avoiding failures. This is accomplished by deploying hardware correctly, watching trends, replacing failing components before they crash, and upgrading hardware and software in a timely manner in order to eliminate bottlenecks before they degrade quality such as with CPUs, bandwidth, and routers. Good management tools can help you avoid problems entirely rather than worrying about being good at finding and fixing them.

- **Knowing when failures occur:** It is very important to know whether it is a gateway that provides access to the PSTN or a critical server that routes all of your VoIP calls when a component fails on your VoIP system. A good management system monitors and detects failures in key components as it is impractical to manually inspect all components for a failure. Management tools can take automated actions once a failure is detected, such as notifying IT staff of the problem via a pager or e-mail.

- **Pinpointing and diagnosing problems quickly:** Locating and then diagnosing the problem is the next step to take once you know that a failure has occurred. Quick problem resolution to ensure customer satisfaction is the primary result you should be seeking in a good VoIP management system.

- **Ensuring that Moves, Adds, and Changes (MACs) are accomplished smoothly:** This needs to be done in a non-disruptive and timely manner for users and other network applications while not compromising existing security measures.

- **Maintaining privacy:** Information such as who was called, by whom, and when the call was made are all considered private information. A search warrant is normally required in the U.S. to examine the telephone records of an individual or an enterprise. Call Detail Records (CDRs) in a VoIP system containing this information may sit in the database of a VoIP server on your premises. Only approved individuals or programs should be able to read, delete, or modify this data, and they need to be protected from unauthorized access.

- **Filtering relevant management data:** Large amounts of data are generated for VoIP servers and devices in log files and CDRs. Although useful, the sheer volume of data can make it difficult to find what you are looking for. A large amount of performance data can be quickly filtered by a good management system to find the relevant information.

- **Regular and scheduled system checks ensure housekeeping tasks are run:** Web servers and database systems that are part of a VoIP system typically have jobs automatically scheduled to find out whether or not your backup has failed.

- **Future planning for upgrades and purchases:** More than likely, there is a management team in your organization that focus on the bottom line, rather than the details of the technology. They will most likely ask questions such as "What is your budget and what is your purchase schedule as the network, users, and applications change over time?" Plan ahead for these questions and have the correct answers ready when asked.

6.6 Service Level Agreements (SLAs)

A Service Level Agreement (SLA) is an agreement between two parties about the delivery of a certain level of service. If the delivered service doesn't meet expectations, it will cost you time and money. The purpose of an SLA is to help you recover some of the cost incurred during a period of degraded or unavailable service. An SLA is the guaranteed level of quality and availability that you agree to provide to your VoIP phone users. An effective SLA defines what is to be measured when evaluating both the level and quality of service and the expectations that your network's users have for the services you provide. SLAs are also the target to strive for when measuring the actual performance that your VoIP system delivers. In any case, the level of service that was provided to a PSTN user can be considered the baseline for performance and the user experience. It should be the starting point and used as the basis for success in your VoIP deployment. Otherwise, you just traded five nines level service for something less, and you know that will not go over well with your users.

Since a VoIP SLA can involve a large variety of performance metrics to be monitored, your VoIP SLA can be defined in a variety of ways. The best way to start the process of defining your internal and external SLAs is to determine whether or not you will need an internal or external SLA, or both. An internal SLA focuses on those relationships and expectations *within your enterprise*, such as that between users of the system and another internal organization. An external SLA focuses on those relationships and expectations between your company or organization *and a third-party* service provider such as an ISP, carrier, or other VoIP outsource provider. The decision as to whether you need an internal or external SLA or both will be determined by business needs and user expectations. Whether you use one or two SLAs, they will both define metrics that will be measured based on your overall business goals. SLA metrics can be categorized into four key groups—Availability, Call Setup Performance, Call Quality, and Incident Tracking. A discussion of each follows.

- **Availability:** PSTN users expect to hear a dial tone 99.999% of the time and have the same expectation with a VoIP SLA. Availability means that you hear a dial tone when you pick up the phone (i.e., no dial tone means non-availability) and that when you dial a phone number you expect the call to go through and while you're talking, you expect to be able to complete the call without being disconnected. The bottom line is that downtime is unacceptable for customer satisfaction. In addition to directly measuring downtime, there are also important SLA submetrics used to monitor and track availability, including those metrics commonly associated with IP PBX, network, and network service availability, such as call completion percentage, abnormal disconnections, and line busy statistics (number of busy call attempts caused by oversubscription of resources). Availability metrics are basic to maintaining users' satisfaction levels and ensuring the overall health of your system, and they should therefore be the first group of statistics to place in a VoIP SLA.

- **Call Setup Performance:** Call setup metrics must be considered in any VoIP SLA. After you initiate a VoIP call, a complex series of events must occur in sequence and without error. The call setup phase is the first of this series of events. Call setup arranges for and acquires a dial tone, dials the phone number, and gets the result of either ringing at the desired location or a busy signal. Several different call setup protocols (i.e. H.323, SIP, MGCP, and MEGACO) are used for call setup in various VoIP implementations, and all could experience poor performance. These protocols operate principally using the TCP protocol, sending a large number of different flows between the IP phones and VoIP server to establish a call between two parties. If the normal sequence of tones and responses is not provided quickly enough, the poor call setup performance will affect the user's initial perception of the call and they may get impatient and hang up. Call setup metrics are normally divided into two subphases called **dial tone response time** and **call setup response time**. Dial tone response time is the time elapsed from the moment you pick up the phone until you hear a dial tone. If the delay is long enough, users may think the system is unavailable. Call setup response time, also referred to as "post dial delay," this is the amount of delay between the time you dial the phone number and the time you hear ringing or get a busy signal.

- **Call Quality:** As discussed previously, users have established expectations for a VoIP system; they expect it should sound as good as PSTN, resulting in call quality being a key component of a VoIP SLA. MOS is the standard metric for user perception of call quality. Generally, the SLA for all calls should be drafted in terms of the MOS scale, from 1.0 to 5.0. Remember that a MOS of 4.0 or higher is considered toll quality or equivalent to the PSTN, 4.0 is good, 3.6 and above is acceptable, and that anything below 3.6 is not be considered acceptable for business-quality calls. You also need tools that can monitor the performance of calls on your network and calculate a MOS from what is measured, and this functionality and the parameters around it should be spelled out clearly in the SLA. Network performance metrics that make up the MOS include delay, jitter, and lost packets. The codec is the fourth component of the MOS and is not something that is measured in real time, because it is usually a fixed parameter per call. The call quality portion of your SLA should specify the MOS. You may choose to set up your own monitoring thresholds for these metrics rather than use those found in standard tables, so you can trigger early warnings whenever quality is perceived as declining.

- **Incident Tracking:** When the availability, call setup, or call quality SLA metrics decline, you must determine why. Incident tracking metrics come into play whenever an SLA metric deteriorates and falls below or above a pre-determined threshold as stated in the SLA. These incidents can be a result of an outage or severe degradation that needs to be repaired. Scheduled changes and ongoing maintenance are also tracked as incidents. Mean Time to Repair (MTTR) and Mean Time Between Failures (MTBF) are the most common metrics usually included in an SLA to deal with incident tracking. A good VoIP SLA should include incident-tracking metrics to give you an expectation for how rapidly your service provider will respond when service levels are not being met. In turn, incident-tracking metrics help to guarantee the high availability, call setup performance, and call quality already specified in the SLA. Thresholds should be set to be proportional to the SLA metrics, so that alerts can be sent when more downtime or low call quality thresholds are crossed. Event correlation is also important, so this information and alert status should be tied into your fault management and event response systems. Early warnings through event correlation can serve as preventative maintenance, prevent SLA violations for the crucial VoIP network metrics, and possibly avoid triggering violations of incident tracking metrics.

6.6.1 Implementing VoIP SLAs

As with the other areas of implementation discussed, implementing VoIP SLAs is a staged process. In the SLA development process you must first define who is responsible for each role in the SLA implementation process, then identify the right VoIP service levels for your enterprise, negotiate the SLA agreement, choose the correct tools to measure compliance or non-compliance, and then manage the compliance and enforcement of the SLA. Here are some tips on how to best accomplish this.

Define Responsibilities

It is very important to identify the roles and responsibilities of those involved in the implementation, monitoring, and enforcement of an SLA. In larger organizations these roles may be spread out over several people who need to communicate well with each other, while in smaller organizations many of these roles may be handled by the same person. Each implicit task should be completed by someone when an internal SLA is being developed, and must also remain someone's responsibility once the SLA is in force. Some of the tasks will include who defines, decides, writes, manages, measures, responds, conducts accounting, enforces compliance, determines penalties, and who makes the hard decision of getting a new provider if necessary.

Service Level Identification for VoIP and Other Applications

Prior to negotiating an SLA contract, your measurement, metrics, and target SLA values should be identified. The relevant metrics for an SLA were discussed above. Availability, call quality, and call setup performance are the most important to the business, as they are end-user/end-to-end measurements. Other important measurements to be considered are problem repairs such as mean time to repair and how incident management problems are identified, submitted, and communicated to the other team members.

VoIP traffic added to a system near its capacity may significantly increase the response time of other business-critical applications. You may want to consider SLAs for other business-critical applications that may interact with or be affected by VoIP services, including e-mail, groupware, e-commerce, and industry-specific business programs. In most cases, application performance is just as important as network performance. As a starting point, SLA targets are established by establishing performance baselines for your most important applications. It is important to know where MOS, response time, and throughput stands in relation to your baseline. This will prevent writing an SLA where there isn't enough bandwidth or other resources to support a number of calls and MOS that exceeds the capacity to do so.

Your VoIP call quality baseline should start from the last assessment where the MOS met your standards and was conducted after you'd done all the necessary upgrades and eliminated all the bottlenecks or other problems that were identified. The same methodology should be used to acquire baselines for the network performance of other applications, such as response time, throughput, or packet loss. Using baselines of the expected and observable behavior to create your SLA targets will be reap long term benefits.

Service-Level Agreement Negotiation

The SLA will spell out which services are to be provided, how they will operate, and what happens if their expected performance service levels are not met. Walker & Hicks[1] identified the following ten topics that you should address when negotiating a VoIP SLA:

1. Specify the SLA metrics and their target values

2. Describe how the SLA metrics are measured and who measures them

3. Describe the SLA reports and their schedule

4. Allow requests to review SLA compliance information on demand

5. Specify the turnaround times for change requests, by severity

6. Specific support-staff and help-desk levels

7. Schedule periodic reviews and adjustments to contract provisions

8. Describe the rewards for great compliance and penalties for non-compliance

9. Discuss transition assistance for services should the service provider fail or suffer a setback

10. Create a procedure for terminating an SLA contract

The SLA will undoubtedly require negotiations and compromise just as with any other contract. It is important to remember that SLAs don't guarantee the level of service but rather the compensation and other consequences if something goes wrong.

SLA Measurement Tools

Network monitoring tools are a valuable method to perform consistent SLA monitoring and to check SLA compliance with the metrics specified in your contract. Of course, these tools can also be used to avoid SLA infractions altogether. Performance values are monitored on an ongoing basis with these tools, and events are triggered when the target SLA value is about to be crossed. These monitoring tools may be deployed and managed by the service provider, the enterprise team, a third party, or some combination thereof. There are a variety of SLA monitoring tools available to help monitor your VoIP SLAs. Some are focused on specific areas of compliance, and others look at compliance as an end-to-end process. For example, some tools can be used to define the baseline performance for a service while others can be used to monitor it on a day-to-day basis.

SLA Compliance and Enforcement

SLA contracts should establish a system of rewards and penalties for compliance. Penalties for SLA non-compliance may include automatic credit or reimbursement of your charges, withholding payment, or cancellation of the contract. Penalties must be significant to have real consequences for a larger provider. SLAs should be reviewed on a regular basis as they can quickly become outdated, often demanding service levels far below existing technological capabilities. The rapid pace of technology development and user expectations may change frequently for availability and the response time of business transactions. An annual review is normally specified in contracts that require updating of the SLAs to reflect any changes.

You should always try to avoid getting into the enforcement or penalty stage of an SLA contract. Avoiding disputes and legal actions is almost always cheaper and less stressful than pursuing them. In cases of unavoidable noncompliance, SLA contract cancellation may be the most effective penalty. Proactive testing and monitoring described earlier in this chapter is perhaps the best way to have advance warning that something is beginning to go wrong.

6.7   Other VoIP Implementation Issues

As stated previously, the needs of voice and data networks are very different and each business needs to investigate and understand QoS and service. QoS is the most overriding issue affecting the implementation of any voice-based network including H.323, but many other issues factor into the successful implementation of H.323 services. You should execute a QoS audit of your existing system to determine the ability of your existing infrastructure to support both the additional traffic load and the protocols as a first step in implementing a VoIP solution.

There are strict standards for Quality in VoIP implementations that must be met. In a perfect world, the listener and the talker must not be able to differentiate between the normal, toll quality, telephone call through POTS, and the call made using VoIP. The VoIP implementation is not satisfactory if the user can differentiate between the POTS and VoIP call. The ITU has come up with its own standards for VoIP, and the standard VoIP protocol is named H.323. As discussed previously, it is actually a combination of various compression algorithms and some other control protocols. In order to be characterized as H.323 compliant, a VoIP implementation must adhere to these ITU standards. Of course, H.323 compliancy means that a device can communicate with any other H.323 compliant device. H.323 is an industry standard that ensures interoperability between products from different vendors.

Implementing VoIP requires adding real-time capabilities to the existing network and may also require the installation of new devices dedicated to the VoIP structure. A number of new network protocols will be implemented as part of the VoIP deployment. Routers and switches must be capable of understanding the new protocols separating the voice from the data traffic. You must understand your current data traffic patterns and what projects you have planned for the future that will affect them. It is important to make realistic estimates of the impact of VoIP on the volume of data traffic and network capacity. As you need to upgrade or replace network components, make sure they are compatible with VoIP networks. Some of the VoIP implementation issues that you are most likely to face are delay, echo, packet loss, jitter, VoIP overhead, and the fact that standards are lacking for call control information. Each is discussed below.

6.7.1 Delay

The UDP protocol has some inherent flaws, but it is also used to transmit voice, which is problematic once QoS is considered for VoIP. UDP packets may reach the destination out of order, late, or not at all. ITU has set a maximum allowable limit for all these quality determinants to be governed by QoS. One method employed to guarantee deliver by many routers/gateways is to use RSVP. RSVP behaves in a similar manner as the POTS. Once you dial the destination number (or IP address) the RSVP compatible device requests that a certain guaranteed CBR be reserved for the call which is determined by the calling application. This CBR is requested by every router/gateway in the way. If all of the devices agree agrees to this request, a call is established. The method for guarantees proper Quality of Service and eliminates any excessive delays. If the CBR request is denied by even one router/gateway in the way the caller will receive a "busy tone" and all the other routers/gateways who had committed to the CBR will revoke their commitment. Even though not all the routers/gateways are RSVP-ready, this is an acceptable method of guaranteeing good QoS for private networks.

6.7.2 Echo

Echoes result when the caller hears their own voice delayed by as little as 30 ms. The time it takes for a caller's transmit (spoken) audio to travel to the receiving caller and return to their phone receiver is the called the round-trip delay and is important with regards to echo. The greater the round trip delay and impedance mismatch, the worse the potential echo. There are very complex digital signal processing devices called echo cancellers that can rid VoIP of any echo issues. G.164, G.165, and G.168 are in the recommendation set approved by the ITU-T to ensure proper performance of echo cancellers.

6.7.3 Packet Loss

The acceptable packet loss is a function of packet size. A high-value packet size will decrease the end-to-end delay, but you will risk losing it. A degradation of the sound quality will increase with the size of the lost packet. Although a greater packet loss can be tolerated as the packet-size reduced, the smaller packet size has the potential of increasing the end-to-end delay. Since there is no simple answer to creating an appropriate packet size, it must be fine-tuned according to the specific need of the user and the network congestion levels.

6.7.4 Jitter

Jitter is due to the uneven sequence of arrival of UDP packets. This varying inter-packet delay causes jitter and, given the nature of packet switched networks, it is difficult to get the VoIP packets to arrive at their destination at a constant rate. VoIP packets are sent at a constant rate and arrive at their destination at the end of the TCP/IP network at slightly different intervals. Another related issue is the artificial regeneration of silence or background noise which, coupled with the algorithmic delay, creates a little overlap between the time the voice starts and the time the silence ends This may clip the voice, producing an undesirable effect called sound clipping. New sophisticated algorithms on the latest hardware may eliminate this problem.

6.7.5 VoIP Header Overhead Problem

All VoIP packets are made up of two components; the payload (voice data) and the IP/UDP/RTP header data. Although the appropriate algorithms can achieve tremendous compression, the size of the TCP/IP header is still an annoying problem. Using cRTP, these headers can be compressed to two or four bytes and can offer significant VoIP bandwidth savings. In comparison, voice samples compressed by the digital signal processor (DSP) vary in size based on the codec used, but their headers are a constant 40 bytes. Unfortunately, cRTP compresses VoIP calls on a link-by-link basis, and both ends of the IP link need to be configured for cRTP. Assuming you can guarantee the millions of devices used over the Internet will be compatible with cRTP is not a valid assumption. If you use the Internet for VoIP, you will have no choice but to stay away from any header compression, and your header size will remain fixed at 40 bytes.

6.7.6 Standards are Lacking for Call Control Information

For VoIP to completely replace POTS, it will need to provide all the services that modern telephone companies provide. H.323 is an excellent standard for normal voice transmission, but there is no equivalent for Call Control transfer. H.323 converts the Channel-C information (in PRI) to VoIP, but it does not encompass the Channel-D information. The value-added services that we have become accustomed to are implemented through the information passed along Channel-D (in PRI-ISDN). H.323-compliant devices will implement VoIP, but will not pass on the CLI information. For this reason, many vendors have come up with proprietary solutions to this problem. The ITU has come up with their own standard, H.248, which encompasses the call control information across the Internet. A device that is both H.323- and H.248-compliant can communicate with any other H.323-/H.248-compliant device with ease. Once the H.248 standard gains popularity, VoIP technology will be capable of replacing the existing POTS.

6.8   Endnotes

1.   Walker, J. & Hicks, J. (2002). The Essential Guide to VoIP
     Implementation and Management: Ch. 6: Establishing VoIP
     SLAs. Retrieved July 18, 2004 from
     http://www.lstech.org/members/tad/
     netiq_guide_to_voip_implementation_and_management__ch._
     6%2C_voip_implementation_and_management.htm

6.9   General References

Archer, K. et al. (2001). *Voice and Data Security.* Indianapolis, IN: Sams
Publishing.

Gardner, D. (2004). *Study: Consumers Still Worried About VoIP Quality And
Reliability.* Retrieved July 15, 2004 from
http://www.techweb.com/wire/story/TWB20040614S0001

Garifo, C. (2001). *No Downtime: SLA Assurance Growing in Importance for
Providers, Customers.* Retrieved July 18, 2004 from
www.xchangemag.com/articles/152back.html

Manzoor, K. (2001). An Introduction to Voice-Over-IP (VoIP). Retrieved
July 18, 2004 from http://www.homepages.com.pk/kashman/voip.htm

Network Associates. (2003). Is VoIP Right for Your Medium-Sized Business? Retrieved July 18, 2004 from http://www.intelli-net.net/
is%20voip%20right%20for%20your%20small%20business.pdf

Stanley, B. (2002). *Strengthen service-level agreements.* Retrieved July 18,
2004 from www.nwfusion.com/careers/2002/0506man.html

Walker, J. & Hicks, J. (2002). *The Essential Guide to VoIP Implementation
and Management: Chapter Six: Establishing VoIP SLAs.* Retrieved July 18,
2004 from
http://www.lstech.org/members/tad/
netiq_guide_to_voip_implementation_and_management__ch._6%2C_vo
ip_implementation_and_management

Walker, J. & Hicks, J. (2004). *Taking Charge of Your VoIP Project: Strategies
and Solutions for Successful VoIP Deployments.* Indianapolis, IN: Cisco Press.

7

VoIP Security Risks

Organizations that are implementing VoIP technologies in a bid to cut communications costs shouldn't overlook the security risks that can crop up when the voice and data worlds converge. Most companies implementing VoIP are concerned about quality-of-service (QoS) considerations, such as voice quality, latency, and interoperability, rather than security.

The convergence of the voice and data worlds—and the inheritance of IP security risks into the traditional voice side of the network through the implementation of VoIP—require that VoIP implementation also include measures such as encrypting voice services, building redundancy into VoIP networks, locking down VoIP servers, and performing regular security audits to secure the network. As with traditional IP networks, it is also important that VoIP equipment is properly locked down, placed behind firewalls, patched against vulnerabilities, and frequently monitored using intrusion detection systems.

For VoIP security, you want to identify vulnerable areas and then make the cost to the attacker higher than the value. The first step is to identify what you are trying to accomplish when implementing VoIP security measures. Collectively, this is called *risk identification* and identifies what and why you are avoiding, preventing, protecting, or securing. For instance, you want to avoid disruptions to your VoIP phone service, prevent unauthorized calls, protect sensitive phone conversations and records, secure VoIP servers and other network devices so they don't become launch points for attacks against other devices, and so on.

The next step is to identify what a potential attacker is trying to accomplish. For example, what are they after? Are they internal employees, corrupt administrators, external terrorists, or script kiddies? Some examples of identification of risk are as follows:

- A potential attacker may want to disrupt your business by disrupting the IP network or causing phone outages. As little as a 200-ms delay in VoIP traffic flow will cause the conversation to suffer.

- An attacker may want to use your network to obtain long-distance phone calls free and at your cost.

- An attacker may want to obtain confidential, proprietary, or insider information through the capture of voice data. For example, a tool known as Voice Over Misconfigured Internet Telephones (VOMIT) doesn't capture VoIP traffic itself but accepts a capture file from a TCPDUMP, etc., and converts it to a plain audio file.

- The Address Translation Table tracks IPs and phone numbers. This can be subverted and lead to improper connections. An attacker may want to hack into VoIP servers to redirect calls or obtain call details.

There are many reasons why a potential attacker may target your network: to access your organization's financial data; to make unauthorized calls on your network so they can save money; or to damage your company through disruption of key business services. The potential attackers could be end users, internal or external unauthorized users, disgruntled employees, competitors, and possibly corrupt administrators.

7.1 **VoIP Infrastructure Risks**

7.1.1 **VoIP Inherits the Same Threats as the IP Data Network**

VoIP security is typically only as good as that provided for any IP service, such as Web and e-mail services. As with all critical services, VoIP has security vulnerabilities, and they are often targeted for attack. Because of VoIP, voice services are now vulnerable to worms, viruses, and Denial-of-Service (DoS) that were not previously issues with the circuit-switched network. In addition to inheriting the risks of IP, VoIP also inherits the number of individuals who know how to attack an IP system. Because VoIP resides on a shared IP network, it is also accessible by users on the Local Area Network (LAN) and, directly or indirectly, by users on the Internet.

As discussed in the first half of the book, VoIP requires more components and software than a traditional circuit-switched network. More components mean greater potential for vulnerability and include IP Private

Branch Exchanges (PBXs), supporting servers, media gateways, switches, routers, firewalls, cabling, IP phones, and softphones. General-purpose operating systems used by components of VoIP tend to have more vulnerabilities than purpose-built operating systems. IP PBXs use databases and Web servers that may also have vulnerabilities.

VoIP also has many standards, including the Session Initiation Protocol (SIP), H.323, the Media Gateway Control Protocol (MGCP), H.248, and vendor-proprietary protocols and versions. Many of these standards are complex, and their implementations will have flaws that will lead to vulnerabilities that are only compounded by the vendors' "rush to market." Protocols purchased from a "stack" vendor can be problematic in that the vulnerabilities are shared with any system using the stack. Unlike the closed switches of the past, IP PBXs include many layers of software that can create vulnerabilities that could be exploited through both adjacent LANs and the Internet.

An implementation flaw is a programming mistake that when exploited could result in unauthorized remote access, malformed request Denial of Service (DoS), load-based DoS, operating system attack, support software attack, protocol attack, application attack, application manipulation, unauthorized access, and DoS. An explanation of each is as follows:

- *Unauthorized remote access* is when an attacker obtains remote and often administrator-level access.

- *Malformed request DoS* is a a carefully crafted protocol request (a packet) exploiting a vulnerability, which results in a partial or complete loss of function.

- *Load-based DoS* is a "flood" of legitimate requests overwhelming a poorly designed system. IP PBXs are the primary target for attackers because of their critical role in providing voice service and the complexity of the software running on them.

- An *operating system attack* exploits vulnerabilities in operating systems.

- A *support software attack* exploits vulnerability in a key supporting software system, such as a database or Web server.

- A *protocol attack* exploits vulnerability in a protocol implementation, such as SIP or H.323.

- An *application attack* exploits vulnerabilities in the underlying voice application not filtered by the protocol implementation.

- An *application manipulation* exploits a weakness in security, such as weak authentication or poor configuration, to allow abuse of the voice service, such as registration hijacking or toll fraud.

- *Unauthorized access* occurs when an attacker obtains administrative access to a component or software.

- A *Denial of Service* can result from either an implementation flaw that results in loss of function or a flood of requests that overwhelms a component or software.

In the end, a risk is a risk. The first step is to identify that you are susceptible to the risk, and the next step is to assess the cost versus benefit of protecting against the exploitation of the risk. The following chapter deals with the latter and identifies some of the potential security risk areas that need to be addressed before or after a VoIP implementation, but ideally before. As you will see, not all security risks are inherited from IP. Some actually carry over from POTS because they have traditionally always been closed networks, whereas others are unique to VoIP. These are all areas that you want to make sure to secure.

7.1.2 Operating System Vulnerability

Within the VoIP environment, operating systems exist on gatekeepers, call managers, media servers, IP phones, and so on. These are frequently applications running on Windows or Unix servers and as such are subject to various vulnerabilities that are discovered with operating systems on a weekly basis. We will use IP phones as an example of VoIP operating system vulnerability risks. IP phones can be in the form of hardware or software. Hardware IP phones typically run embedded operating systems and, therefore, their operating systems are generally considered to be more secure than softphones. With softphones, someone can potentially install a software phone on any computer on your data network, which presents a rather unique security challenge. Web server software can also be integral to both IP phones and softphones. The Web servers that are running with your phones will offer many vulnerabilities and access points to potential hackers. Softphones have all of the vulnerabilities associated with off-the-shelf operating systems and Web servers, including exposure to viruses and worms. Although the possibility of making free phone calls provides some incentive to hackers, a bigger target and issue for VoIP security is the private, confidential, and proprietary phone call information that is now traveling on your data network in a VoIP network.

7.1.3 **Human Vulnerability**

Recent computer crime statistics[1] indicate that organizations are still more likely to be attacked by their own employees than by outsiders. Core intellectual property, key knowledge, and information on core processes reside in the minds of employees and can be transferred to other companies as employees take new employment opportunities.

This knowledge is rarely captured adequately in databases, human resource records, and organizational accounting information. Many recent industrial espionage cases[2] point to human errors in gathering or searching for information, corrupt or disgruntled employees, and miscommunication or misunderstandings. Information security is a system-level problem and can only be adequately addressed if both technological and organizational issues are considered simultaneously. In this section, we will discuss the human or organizational issues.

Within the VoIP environment, the key target is the exploitation of IP phone and/or the equipment and software that supports or is connected to it, including the human associated with it. The exploitation of humans for information that can be of use to a potential attacker is called *social engineering* and *human exploitation*.

The phone number of the modem and target are key bits of essential elements of information required by a VoIP attacker. For instance, if an attacker or disgruntled employee finds out the phone number of the modem, they could use a default account or brute force their way into the PBX using an automated script to guess the administrative login and password and, if successful, take control of the company's voice communications. Minimal effort is required to discover the phone number of the target, sometimes in a matter of minutes. Various departments in the company may be called by the attacker to obtain the information. The attacker may pose as an employee and say the right things in order to obtain the number or other essential elements of information required for the reconnaissance phase of a successful attack, such as usernames, passwords, and pertinent nonpublic network information. This is a successful and easy method to use to obtain proprietary company information. Entire networks—voice and data—have been compromised by attackers simply calling and asking for information such as remote-access numbers, login and password information, and network IPs. As stated earlier, this effective method of obtaining attacker reconnaissance phase information is known as social engineering.

Another way attackers may obtain this type of attacker reconnaissance phase information is to go through the company's trash cans and dumpsters, looking for internal phone numbers, e-mails that contain user IDs and possibly passwords, or information that may have been scribbled on a sticky note. Shredding company proprietary and other sensitive information, as well as locking up dumpsters, compactors, and other trash facilities, will help deter any possible dumpster divers.

Perhaps the biggest and most quickly exploited security threat to a company is staff, particularly the help desk staff, when they have not received basic corporate security training that includes social engineering methods, countermeasures, and the correct handling of sensitive and proprietary information.

7.1.4   Toll Fraud

Toll fraud is the unauthorized use of your telecommunications system by an unauthorized party (e.g., persons other than your company's employees, agents, subcontractors, or persons working on your company's behalf). A survey of 130 telcos by the Federation of International Irregular Network Access counted the cost of toll fraud at $40 billion per year, with about 40% of this total representing fraud against PBXs.[3] Unlike cell phone fraud, where wireless carriers often absorb the cost of fraud, long-distance landline toll fraud hits the bottom line of companies because they are directly responsible for all calls made on their telecom equipment. This problem can literally bankrupt a small to medium-sized business if it goes undetected for more than a few days. A PBX is usually compromised for fraudulent purposes such as free long distance, free conference calls, or helping a friend make a little extra money with their 900 number.

A recent toll fraud scam involving PBX systems, which can lead to high long-distance charges, was reported on a California Department of Corrections awareness Web page.[4] In this scam, the fraudster claims to be a telephone service technician performing a test on the line. He asks that you transfer him to an operator by pushing 9, 0, # and then hanging up. On some business systems, this can give the caller an outside line that can be used to make long-distance calls. Toll charges will then be billed to the owner of the PBX as directly dialed calls. This cannot occur on residential phone lines. This is a classic social engineering scheme. It is also an example of a popular method for obtaining free phone calls without doing any of the work involved in taking over a system.

7.1.5   Easy Access

Unlike traditional Public Switched Telephone Networks (PSTNs) that required physical access to a phone to make phone calls, an attacker or unauthorized user doesn't necessarily need to be physically present to use a VoIP phone. VoIP provides both easy access and a much more mobile capability to plug-and-play the IP phone into the network as needed to make a call with the charges going to your VoIP system. Worse yet, the capabilities inherent in the VoIP phone can provide a launching point for attacks or exploitation against the network or networks to which the phone is connected.

7.1.6   Service Use and Abuse

VoIP service use and abuse risks can be grouped into two broad categories: insiders and outsiders. Even though intrusions or attacks by outsiders seem to gain the majority of media headlines, the larger problem is actually abuses by insiders. The insider normally has the best knowledge about where the important information is located, physical access to facilities and equipment, and in most cases, the time to be cautious and patient. In most cases, the insider also has a better chance to avoid detection or suspicion. Some insider threats are deliberate and others are not. One of the most significant insider threats is that of the poorly or undertrained individual.

7.1.7   Unintentional and Inadvertent Risks

An important distinction to make is that in the case of the poorly trained individual, the insider is not the individual who is abusing his or her authority on the system or who is attempting to break into the system. Instead, the individual is facilitating another individual conducting the intrusive activity. This is also true for the other type of insider threat (i.e., an individual who deliberately disregards an established security practice). For example, an employee may ignore the company's internal security policies and set up an unauthorized modem on the network for remote access from home. This action is in violation of policy, but the employee is not attempting to break into a system or to access a system that he is not authorized to access. However, in this case, the actions of the employee are making it easier for an outsider to gain unauthorized access by simply calling phone numbers until a computer connected by a modem answers a number, which is also known as *wardialing*.

It is generally acknowledged that most intrusions come as a result of poorly configured systems or as a result of established security policies, such as password management, not being followed. For example, poor password selection can result in successful breaches of security and can be easily prevented if individuals simply follow established practices regarding password selection and protection.

Another problem that can lead to a security breach are those administrators who do not install the latest patches to operating systems. This could be a result of inadequate training on the importance of security patches or a lack of time. Attackers often take advantage of administrators not installing patches that will allow for the exploitation of known holes.

7.1.8   Deliberate Threats

The insider who is deliberately attempting to circumvent security controls for dishonest reasons is a much more serious threat to the organization than the one described in the previous section. Insiders who fall into the deliberate threat category can be further subdivided into two categories: (1) the government or corporate spy conducting espionage activities and (2) the disgruntled or ex-employee. The disgruntled employee often knows where the most sensitive or important data resides in the organization and also what actions will cause the most damage. Sometimes their actions involve selling information to a competitor, but often it is simply an act of sabotage. Recent cases involving disgruntled and former employees indicate that the idea of giving a person a two-week notice and then expecting him to continue working without having the event affect his attitude is usually unrealistic.

7.1.9   Nonemployee or Temporary Employee Granted Access

There is also the risk that an insider who poses a threat to an organization is the nonemployee or temporary employee who has been granted access. Although it is usually limited access, partners, consultants, and contingency workers are frequently granted access to company computing assets in order to work on specific projects. These individuals can attempt to circumvent internal security controls and gain access to information they have not been granted permission to see just as easily as regular employees.

Many large companies may also outsource their security and custodial services. It is more obvious the serious damage that a security person gone bad could do to a company than that of the custodial service personnel.

There are cases where individuals have targeted specific corporations to obtain temporary employment with custodial companies specifically to gain after-hours unauthorized access to machines and information. Nonemployees can gain unauthorized access to corporate information-processing assets by exploiting situations where careless employees leave their systems connected without logging off at night or write their passwords and user access codes down on a piece of paper they store in their desk.

7.1.10   Phreakers Using Phone Systems

Another unique aspect of IP telephony is the IP phone, which has more intelligence than the dumb terminals used in traditional telephony. An IP phone can become an access point to the network—unlike in legacy systems, where the switch that's connected to the phone is a more likely target. Through the increasingly popular SIP call control standard, an IP phone also has enough intelligence to interact with servers and other components on the network, opening the door for attackers to access those components through the phone.

In February of 2004, Cisco Systems and Nortel Networks issued fixes for some of their IP telephony products after the CERT Coordination Center, a Pittsburgh-based research and development group that tracks Internet security problems, issued an alert on multiple vulnerabilities in some implementations of SIP that could invite DoS attacks, service interruptions, or unauthorized access.

Capitalizing on such security holes, hackers and phreakers can subject a converged network to traditional threats, such as viruses and DoS attacks, as well as risks better known to the telephony world, including toll fraud, eavesdropping, and impersonation—and their reasons for doing so aren't always clear.

7.1.11   Hackers Using Computer Systems

Although VoIP is often touted for its ability to save money by eliminating the need to support separate voice and data networks, this also creates a situation where if data systems go down, the voice system could follow. As VoIP sweeps across the high-technology landscape, many IT managers are lulled into a dangerous complacency because they see Internet phoning as a relatively secure telecommunications technology and not as an IP service that is susceptible to the same worms, viruses, and other pestilence that threatens all networked systems. The traditional voice model utilized PBXs, which were stable and secure, but if the VoIP infrastructure isn't properly protected, it can easily be hacked and recorded calls can be eavesdropped. Converged networks utilized to transmit VoIP, including routers, servers, and even switches, are more susceptible to hacking than is traditional telephony equipment. IP telephony has distinctive characteristics that make it more susceptible to attacks than traditional voice. For example, the signaling information that establishes and manages an IP call and the voice samples run over the same network, whereas on the PSTN the signaling information is carried on a different network that's physically separated from the voice samples.

The network components and servers used to support IP telephony infrastructure are also well-known to hackers, unlike the proprietary systems of the legacy voice world. It's all open standards, which means IP telephony is open to attacks. It's also relatively easy to launch an attack against a VoIP network because the software tools available to hackers and others bent on invading a network are more available and easier to use. With access to both the signaling information and the voice packets, hackers could add themselves to a call, divert the call to a third party, or inject packets into the call so that one or both parties would hear the voice samples that the hackers play. Capitalizing on such security holes, hackers can also subject a converged network to traditional threats such as viruses and DoS attacks.

7.1.12   Service Disruption and Denial of Service

A service disruption or a DoS attack is an attack designed to deprive a user or organization of services or resources that are normally available. Most DoS attacks cause the inability to use a particular network service, such as e-mail, or the temporary loss of all network connectivity and services. These attacks can be as localized as a dial-up user's network connection being flooded with useless data to severe attacks that can force a Web site accessed by millions of people to temporarily cease operation. An example of the latter situation was witnessed in the early February 2000 strikes that hit Amazon, Buy.com, CNN.com, eBay, E*Trade, Yahoo!, and ZDNet and crippled these major sites for several hours by a large number of unknowingly compromised computers across the Internet flooding the sites with massive amounts of traffic. Rather than harm the actual server or result in the theft of information or control of the targeted system, DoS attacks generally cause loss of productivity, time, and money. In order to understand how a distributed denial of service (DDoS) works, it is necessary to understand how some common types of DoS attacks work. Common forms of DoS attacks are discussed in the following paragraphs.

7.1.13   Buffer Overflow Attacks

A buffer is a temporary data storage area with a finite amount of space. A buffer overflow occurs when a program or process tries to store more data in a buffer than it was intended to hold. Because buffers are created to contain a finite amount of data, the extra information that has to go somewhere can overflow into adjacent buffers, corrupting or overwriting the valid data held in them.

In buffer overflow attacks, the extra data may contain codes designed to trigger specific actions, in effect sending new instructions to the attacked computer that could, for example, damage the user's files, change data, or disclose confidential information. This is one of the most common kinds of DoS attacks, resulting from more information than the system or service can handle being sent. The "ping of death," one of the most common forms of this attack, overflows a buffer by sending oversized Internet Control Message Protocol (ICMP) packets larger than the 65,536-byte maximum allowed by the IP standard. When certain systems receive a packet of this size, they may reboot, hang, or crash.

7.1.14   SYN Flood

The Transmission Control Protocol (TCP) devices on the Internet assume a trust with the devices that try to connect to them using TCP. There is no authentication or verification of the client trying to establish a TCP connection with another device. A TCP connection is established when a three-way handshake completes the connection. A client sends a TCP packet to a server with the synchronization (SYN) flag set. The server will reserve memory for this connection. The server then returns a TCP packet with both the SYN and acknowledgment (ACK) flags set. The client, in order to complete the handshake, responds to the SYN-ACK packet with an ACK packet. The server reserves memory to accommodate the sessions.

Several SYN packets with spoofed source IP addresses are sent to the targeted server in a SYN flood attack. Because the addresses are spoofed, a reset (RST) message will not be returned, freeing the memory allocated by the original SYN packet. A SYN-ACK will be sent from the server to the spoofed IP address. This SYN-ACK message will time out and the server will resend it, keeping memory allocated. With enough half-open TCP connections, the server will run out of memory. Legitimate TCP connections will be not be able to connect, and some servers will crash because of a lack of memory. A variation of this attack is the reflected SYN flood attacker, where the attacker spoofs the address of the target and sprays SYN packets to multiple relay systems. The relay systems flood the target (the spoofed source IP from the attacker) with SYN-ACKs. The target will respond with an RST because it was unaware of the original SYN. This reset tears down the "connection," but it is CPU- and network-intensive, especially if a high number of relays are used.

7.1.15 UDP Flood

The User Datagram Protocol (UDP) flood DoS attack takes advantage of the UDP chargen and UDP echo services. The UDP chargen service generates a series of characters for each packet it receives and is used for testing purposes. The UDP echo service echoes any character it receives in an attempt to test network programs. The UDP flood attack connects one system's chargen service with another system's echo service, causing a circular flood of useless data between the systems.

7.1.16 Fragmentation Attacks

The IP requires that a packet of excessive size be divided into fragments. The fragment packet identifies an offset to the beginning of the first packet that enables the receiver to put the packet back together. A fragmentation attack sends an invalid offset value in the second or later fragment. This type of fragmentation attack can cause a system to crash if the operating system cannot handle the packet.

Teardrop is the most common form of this attack. A *teardrop attack* consists of an attacker sending a series of fragmented IP datagram pairs to the target system. The amount of pairs required depends on the operating system. For example, Windows NT can take up to 50, whereas Linux can be crashed with one pair. The first fragment is sent with an offset of zero telling the IP that it is the first fragment in the list and a payload of size N. Subsequent fragments are sent with an offset that tells the IP that it should overlap inside the previous fragment; however, the fragment's payload is either nonexistent or very small (1 or 2 bytes), which will result in either a crash or restart of the affected systems. Some of the other variations of this attack are "NewTear," "Nestea," "SynDrop," and "Bonk."

7.1.17 Smurf Attack

A smurf attack results from a network connected to the Internet that is swamped with replies to ICMP echo (ping) requests. A smurf attacker sends ping requests to an Internet broadcast address. These are special addresses that broadcast all received messages to the hosts connected to the subnet. Each broadcast address can support up to 255 hosts, so a single ping request can be multiplied 255 times. The return address of the request is spoofed to be the address of the attacker's victim. All of the hosts receiving the ping request reply to this victim's address instead of the real sender's address. This will cause a large flood of ping replies to be sent to the target IP address. If the flood is large enough, the target IP will not be able to receive traffic. A single attacker sending hundreds or thousands of these ping messages per second can fill the victim's T-1 (or even T-3) line with ping replies, bringing the entire Internet service to its knees.

7.1.18   General Overload

A server can be overloaded by too many requests for legitimate resources, and this is always a possibility because every network has its limitations. Typically, this is a capacity planning issue, but it becomes a security issue when a site is getting several legitimate connections and several thousand connections generated by an attacker. This type of DoS can happen maliciously or accidentally. If the server or network is not fast enough to handle incoming loads, it will experience outages. For example, a Web server can be overloaded by too many requests for Web content.

This type of attack is much more difficult to catch in comparison with other attacks because of the traffic patterns that could lead to it being a more popular DDoS where sophisticated attack-detection sensor technology is being used. For example, it is much simpler to catch several ICMP, UDP, or SYN flood attacks than it is to sort legitimate and illegitimate users who are performing the same type of tasks.

7.1.19   Distributed Denial-of-Service Attacks

Programs such as Tribe Flood Network, tfn2k, trinoo, and Stacheldraht introduce a new aspect of DDoS attacks. Early attempts at distributed attacks involved groups of attackers coordinating attacks against targets that were too formidable for just one attacker. DoS attacks have now evolved and become more sophisticated and complex than some of the first attacks. Through the use of client/server technology, an attacker can dramatically multiply the effectiveness of an attack by utilizing the resources of multiple compromised machines serving as attack platforms. The development of these types of programs makes it possible for an attacker to coordinate massive attacks from several machines with little skill or effort.

There are currently two basic types of distributed attack models. One model requires commands to be sent directly to attacking machines and also requires the direct observation of results. The attacker connects or directly sends a command to each of the machines used in the attack. In response to these commands, each machine will launch the desired attack.

The second model incorporates a second layer of machines between the attacker and the attacking machines. The attacker sends commands from the client to a handler, which acts as a "middle man." The handler sends the commands from the client to the agents that perform the attack. This approach has an advantage for the attacker. The traffic between the handler and agent does contain information about where the attack originated. This makes locating the perpetrator much more difficult. These programs can launch hundreds or even thousands of agent programs within seconds. In both models of DDoS attacks, the perpetrator needs to break into several (sometimes hundreds or thousands) machines all over the Internet. A perpetrator will target poorly secured sites, using well-known exploits in common services, and operating systems.

The most risky and difficult part of the DDoS attack, involving the penetration of these poorly protected machines, has become easier with the availability and use of automated tools. In some cases, automated scanners will search Class C or larger networks looking for a specific vulnerable service, allowing an attacker to find several machines that can be penetrated using just one exploit. Tools of this nature have lowered the skill level required to gain control of several machines, making it easier to target acquisition. DDoS software is installed after the attacker has penetrated a system, which allows the attacker to remotely control the compromised machines and launch coordinated attacks on victim sites. These attacks commonly disrupt network connectivity by consuming bandwidth, router processing capacity, and Web server or other services' capacities.

Common commands for running processes may be displayed with versions that do not reveal the intruders or they may simply install a "root kit" to hide both their processes and the DDoS program's process running on the server. Logs may also be altered, deleted, or in some cases, shut off to hide the attacker's tracks. Sadly for the IT security community, some sloppy or inexperienced attackers do not even take these steps to hide themselves and often go unnoticed.

An experienced attacker will successfully cover his or her intrusion after it has been compromised and a program has been installed that allows the machine to be commanded remotely. The program will listen on a certain port and accepts commands from over the Internet, and once it receives the commands, it launches an attack on the target site. After attacking several poorly defended sites and installing the attack software on each one, the IP address of the machine with the attack client installed on it will be noted for future use. Large-scale attacks across the Internet may utilize several hundreds (if not thousands) of co-opted machines. An attacker needs only to run a single command to start or stop a DDoS attack. The agents can launch one of several types of flood attacks, such as ICMP, SYN, or UDP floods. DDoS attacks are relying more on the spoofing of IP addresses to increase the effectiveness of the attack, making it more difficult to stop and determine the original source of the attack.

7.1.20 Modems

One of the biggest risks from unauthorized modems in the enterprise is not the lack of policies to control the usage of modems but rather the unwillingness or inability of some companies to enforce these policies. Enforcement of these policies can be accomplished through the use of telephone firewalls that monitor and control traffic entering and exiting the network via the telephone system.

Another risk is the result of someone coming from outside the corporate network and using that modem to access internal networks or computer systems. Because data can be transferred in both directions, if a corporate computer is connected via modem, a malicious attacker can put files on your computer and possibly on your network without your permission. If an attacker is successful, the entire security infrastructure can be circumvented in that files can now pass into the corporate network without going through router access controls, the intrusion detection system, or the firewall. This risk can also be mitigated through the use of a telephone firewall.

7.1.21 Cable Modems

The major technical difference and difference in risk between regular modems and cable modems is that when you dial into an Internet service provider with a regular modem, your computer is randomly assigned an Internet address. This address equates to the specific modem at the Internet service provider that you dialed into, and for that session, that is your Internet identity. On the next session, you will more than likely have a different address. However, when you have a cable modem, your address is always the same. Clients with cable modems often leave their connection active 24 hours a day, which creates a major security risk, leaving users more vulnerable to a hacker attack. Without additional client security, the user is only as secure as the network it is connected to, which can be problematic for home users. Any type of access that is engaged full time should have a traf-fic-filtering device to protect the endpoints behind it.

7.1.22   IP Phones

Another unique aspect of IP telephony is the IP phone, which has more intelligence than the dumb terminals used in traditional telephony. Unlike traditional phones in legacy systems, an IP phone can become an access point to the network. By compromising the IP phone, an attacker can potentially gain access to the switch to which it is connected. As discussed earlier, the SIP call control standard gives the IP phone enough intelligence to interact with servers and other components on the network, opening the door for attackers to access those components through the phone. Another risk results when the current LAN's physical infrastructure is used along with VoIP phones. If a separate addressing scheme that provides no routing path between networks is not used, less-skilled attackers can take advantage of this opportunity.

7.1.23   Core Routers

Network and service providers are now faced with deploying the critical next generation of IP services aimed at businesses, such as secure Virtual Private Networks (VPNs), with enriched voice, video, and multimedia content. These critical routers are not without their risks, and the requirement to protect these routers from a risk to DoS attacks is paramount for carriers. In order to manage a router over the Internet, you must permit at least some Internet hosts to have access to the router. It's possible that these hosts could be compromised or that their addresses could be spoofed. By permit-ting interactive access from the Internet, you make your security depend not only on your own antispoofing measures but also on those of the service providers involved. It's sometimes possible to hijack an unencrypted TCP connection (such as a Telnet session) and actually take control away from a user who is logged in. Although such hijacking attacks aren't nearly as com-mon as simple packet sniffing, and although they can be complex to mount, they are possible and might be used by an attacker who had your network specifically in mind as a target.

DoS attacks are relatively common on the Internet. If your network is being subjected to a DoS attack, you may not be able to reach your router to collect information or take defensive action. Even an attack on someone else's network may impair your management access to your own network.

VoIP may use services such as Digital Subscriber Line (DSL) that are installed with their own router. As with many network hardware appliances, the routers may be implemented without passwords, or a standard password may be used on all of the routers. Unfortunately, many organizations maintain this practice and even discourage users from changing their router passwords because it makes troubleshooting and supporting the service easier for a technician. Of course, this type of practice also makes it easier for an attacker to compromise the routers.

For those organizations that actually use passwords, many have bad password management practices. Poor passwords are common to many aspects of the Internet, and large-scale usage of default passwords is not unusual. In the broadband arena, DSL providers are the most common offenders of this practice, which is problematic because some of the larger commercial VoIP offerings are provided through DSL connections.

7.1.24 Media Gateways

H.323 is good for small VoIP implementations or someone making point-to-point Internet calls, but it does not scale very well into the carrier space. MGCP is mainly concerned with controlling larger-scale gateways and addresses more of the large-scale deployment needs of new and incumbent carriers of VoIP. The protocol also specifies that all call control should be handled away from the actual endpoints, centralizing management and billing functions. This keeps the intelligence at the center of the network, a model more closely related to the PSTN, and allows MGCP to work on gateways that are not as sophisticated as fully compliant H.323 gateways. MGCP's only support for encryption is in a lower-level protocol. As an upper-level protocol, MGCP provides no inherent encryption for securing calls, having been made with more specialized applications in mind—typically involving large rollouts of carrier-grade services, multiple gateways and many trunks.

These applications are typically used on very low-latency, high-bandwidth private networks that do not have any access points to the IP structure of the Internet, resulting in a low priority for the security of individual calls. A target of opportunity exists for a knowledgeable attacker if IPSec or a proprietary VPN tunnel is not implemented through this type of untrusted network.

7.1.25   SIP and SIP Proxies

SIP is not an easy protocol to secure. An SIP proxy behaves much like a normal data network proxy that forwards a request on your behalf. Advanced SIP services are handled by proxies, registrars, and redirectors, and SIP may go through one or more proxy or redirection servers when making a call. These are especially useful if you and the person you want to talk to do not have clients that are capable of using the same codec. An SIP transcoding proxy can speak to both sides of the call and provide the correct codecs to both parties. When a proxy receives the SIP message, it adds its address to the **Via** header information before forwarding the request. This ensures that the responses take the same path back to the initiator of the call. Proxies can also fork a single SIP Invite message to several recipients. This functionality is useful when trying to reach one person who has several possible addresses.

Zvon[5] has identified a few of the more common security risks found in most deployments of SIP, which are described as follows. This is not meant to be an all-inclusive list, but it illustrates the need to address particular security services that can potentially prevent an intruder or attacker from exploiting the SIP weaknesses. The primary security risks associated with SIP are the following:

- Hijacking registration
- Impersonation of the server
- Message body exploitation
- Mid-session exploitation
- Susceptibility to DoS attacks

Hijacking Registration

This risk exploits any absence of cryptographic assurance with a request's originator. Any network service of value (such as a gateway that processes SIP requests with traditional telephone calls) will likely want to control all access to its resources by conducting authentication requests. User Agents (UAs) should verify the identities of originators of requests before granting access. The SIP registration mechanism allows a UA to identify itself to a registrar as a device at which a user (designated by an address of record) is located. The identity, asserted in the **From** header field of a **REGISTER** message, is assessed by the registrar to determine whether this request can modify the contact addresses associated with the address-of-record in the **To** header field. These two fields are often the same, but there are many valid deployments in which a third party may register contacts on a user's behalf. The owner of a UA can arbitrarily modify the **From** header field of an SIP request, opening the door to malicious registrations. If attackers successfully impersonate any party authorized to change contacts associated with an address-of-record, they could deregister all existing contacts for a URL and then register their own device as the appropriate contact address, directing all requests for the affected user to the attacker's device.

Impersonation of the Server

The Request-URL usually specifies the domain to which a request is destined, and the UA request for delivery is commonly performed through direct contact with a server in this domain. It is possible that an attacker could impersonate the remote server in order to intercept the UA's request. In this case, a redirect server at one domain, ransome.com, could impersonate a redirect server at another domain, rittinghouse.com. A user agent sends a request to rittinghouse.com, but the redirect server at ransome.com answers with a forged response that has appropriate SIP header fields for a response from rittinghouse.com. The forged contact addresses in the redirection response could simply prevent requests for rittinghouse.com or it could direct the originating UA to inappropriate or insecure resources.

It is also possible for a registration sent to rittinghouse.com to be intercepted by ransome.com, which then replies to the intercepted registration with a forged 301 (moved permanently) response. This response might seem to come from rittinghouse.com, yet designate ransome.com as the appropriate registrar. All future **REGISTER** requests from the originating UA would then go to ransome.com. This is somewhat of a reverse of the hijacking registration risk described previously.

Message Body Exploitation

UAs route requests through trusted proxy servers. Although a UA may trust a proxy server to route a request, it does not have to inspect or modify the bodies contained in that request. Whenever a UA is using SIP message bodies to communicate session encryption keys for a media session, it may trust the proxy server of the domain it is contacting to deliver signaling properly, but it may not want the administrators of that domain to be capable of decrypting any subsequent media session. If there was active malicious activity on the proxy server, the session key could be modified to act as either a man-in-the-middle agent or to just change the security characteristics requested by the originating UA. This type of risk not only applies to session keys but also to all SIP-carried end-to-end content, such as MIME bodies. For example, an attacker might try to modify SDP bodies so that they point RTP media streams to a wiretapping device in order to eavesdrop on subsequent voice communications.

Mid-Session Exploitation

After initial messaging has established a dialog, subsequent requests that modify the state of the dialog and/or session can be sent. If these sessions are not secured properly, they can be forged by attackers. For example, a third-party attacker could capture initial messages in a dialog shared by two parties to obtain session parameters (such as the To and From tags) and then use the forged data to insert a BYE request into the session that appears to come from either participant. The session will be torn down prematurely after the BYE request is received by its target. Another mid-session risk involves the transmission of forged re-INVITEs that alter the session in order to reduce session security or redirect media streams as part of a wiretapping attack.

Susceptibility to DoS Attacks

SIP proxy servers commonly face the public Internet in order to accept requests from worldwide IP endpoints. SIP creates several potential opportunities for DDoS attacks that must be recognized and addressed by operators of SIP systems. For example, attackers can create bogus requests that contain a falsified source IP address and a corresponding **Via** header field that identify a targeted host as the originator of the request. The attacker will then send this request to many SIP network elements, thereby using SIP UAs or proxies to generate DoS traffic aimed at the target. Falsified route header field values can also be used in a request that identifies the target host, and then the attacker will send such messages to forking proxies that will amplify messaging sent to the target. A similar effect can be achieved by using Record-Route when the attacker is certain that the SIP dialog initiated by the request will result in numerous transactions originating in the backward direction.

REGISTER requests that are not properly authenticated and authorized by registrars can result in DoS attacks. Some or all users in an administrative domain could be deregistered by an attacker, preventing these users from being invited to new sessions. Many contacts could be registered that designate the same host for a given address-of-record in order to use the registrar and any associated proxy servers as amplifiers in a DoS attack. An attacker could also attempt to deplete available memory and disk resources of a registrar by registering huge numbers of bindings. As you can see, the use of multicast traffic to transmit SIP requests can greatly increase the potential for DoS attacks.

7.1.26   Gatekeepers

The VoIP gateway establishes the transition between the telephone network and the IP network. The gateway acts like a switchboard in a conventional telephone network and is controlled by the gatekeeper. A gatekeeper is a special H.323 server type that keeps a list of who is logged on and at what node they can be reached. It also monitors the availability of nodes to receive calls and performs authentication to decide if a node has the right to access the network. A gatekeeper typically interacts with both H.323 terminals and gateways. A gateway is a device that connects the PSTN to the H.323 network and allows H.323 calls to cross over into the PSTN world, allowing connections to normal phones. Occasionally, the gatekeeper becomes involved in situations where you do not make a direct point-to-point call because you do not know the direct IP address of the node you are trying to reach or that particular node is inaccessible directly, and you need to get authorization to make the call. A gatekeeper assumes the functions for address mapping, authentication, and bandwidth management. Gatekeepers also have the optional functions for call control signaling, reliable accounting, and ensuring the secure supply of supplementary services such as forwarding, diversion, consultation, and conferencing. The primary role of the gatekeeper is one of registration. If you are using a dynamically assigned IP address, using an alias and allowing the gatekeeper to store your current IP address makes it much easier for remote people to contact you.

Private IP addresses must use an Network Address Port Translation (NAPT) function to be mapped to a public IP address before the packets can be routed to another enterprise voice VPN. Most enterprise customers see this as a major security concern and mandate that all voice traffic transiting a public IP network must be encrypted. The use of Real-time Transfer Protocol (RTP) encryption and IPSec is an option, but it is complex and costly for the service provider to administer and maintain. Also, these technologies typically do not interoperate in the multivendor environments deployed within the enterprise networks. Service providers must address the security risk of how to ensure privacy when voice traffic must transit a public "nontrusted" network. VoIP network elements such as gatekeepers and media gateways must be protected from these types of attacks originating from a voice VPN customer's network as well.

7.1.27   VoIP Servers and Configuration Exploits

VoIP servers that handle call processing are arguably the most important components in a VoIP system. There are several risk areas where toll fraud can occur if an attacker gains access to the VoIP server. Call Detail Records (CDRs) are frequently stored in relational databases in VoIP systems. The database system is often an off-the-shelf application that comes with inherent security vulnerabilities. Access to the CDRs could allow a hacker to commit account fraud by changing the billing information to gain free calls. Some VoIP servers have a feature that you will want to disable for your day-to-day operations because it lets unknown phones download a generic configuration to get them started. Hackers can enable this feature if they gain unauthorized access to VoIP server configuration, making it possible to use an unknown phone to make calls. If an IP phone in your lobby has an incorrectly configured call routing plan, it could allow an unauthorized user to make international phone calls or allow calls to be made from certain locations to any other location. Routing plan configurations are usually configured on the VoIP server and stored in a database.

7.1.28   Switches

A switch is essentially an intelligent hub, deciding which ports to retransmit packets on rather than transmitting the packets to every connected device. For example, a Web request packet in a switched environment is only sent to the devices that need to see that packet, and in the case of a router, it will forward the Web request to the Internet. Sniffers placed on a switch are much less effective in collecting and analyzing traffic, because the other connected devices no longer see everyone else's traffic. However, most switches have special ports because of the need for network and traffic monitoring. These ports are normally called *monitoring* or *mirroring ports* and operate like a miniature hub. Because these ports receive a copy of any packet passing through the switch, they are an ideal place for a sniffer. Although switches are designed to provide defense against traditional sniffing attacks, advanced sniffers such as dsniff provide capabilities to perform sniffing in switched environments.

7.1.29   VoIP-Based Firewalls

Firewalls normally function by inspecting packets based on IP addresses and the transport layer protocol port numbers, applying any predefined policies and rule sets to those packets. Three significant problems related to a VoIP or IP telephony solutions result if a firewall operates in its traditional manner within or adjacent to a VoIP infrastructure:

1. A variety of protocols are used for a VoIP call session. The initial call setup is performed via static well-known ports through the use of either H.323 or SIP, while dynamically allocated ports are used for media and media control. Because ports are selected randomly in the range of 1,024 to 65,535, H.323 is particularly problematic, because it prevents stringent static policy rules specifically for these protocols in traditional firewalls that will open up large numbers of ports compromises overall network security.

2. Standard firewall configuration will not allow "unsolicited" call requests from outside the firewall. An IP telephony call can be initiated from both outside and inside the firewall.

3. Traditional Network Address Translation (NAT) functionality checks only the IP header; this is problematic for VoIP because IP phones communicating with each other imbed the IP address within the VoIP protocol (H.323 or SIP) and in the IP header.

A firewall application can overcome these problems by making it aware on an individual session basis. This would require that the firewall scan VoIP protocol messages and open ports dynamically only for calls approved by the call control server. The firewall would also have to close the session, as well as any open ports, at call disconnection. There is typically confusion concerning the number of protocol sessions involved in a VoIP call, during which several messages and specific message flow sequences must be recognized by the firewall. These sessions should be broken into a few distinct phases and analyzed based on activities in each phase.

The leading firewall vendors such as Cisco PIX, Check Point, and NetScreen have adequate H.323 support. Usage and call control are normally implemented via a gatekeeper in current IP telephony solutions, and the firewall should support gatekeeper-routed call handling. The non-PIX Cisco IOS and Secure Computing only support direct-routed calls and, therefore, do not meet the basic requirements. There are smaller firewall vendors, such as CyberGuard, WatchGuard, and BorderWare, that have limited VoIP support. Corporations that implement VoIP and have limited or no VoIP support on their firewalls will need to look at either the leading firewall vendors or emerging Application Layer Gateway vendors such as Kagoor and Ridgeway, for adequate firewall functionality for their VoIP infrastructures. Of course, depending on the actual firewall used, the use of VoIP inspection on traditional firewalls will have various levels of impact on performance.

7.1.30 Network Access Points

A network access point is any place in your network where an IP device can plug in, including the IP phone. During the reconnaissance phase of an attack, an attacker will look for exploitable areas where a firewall is not between your internal computer network and each external network access point to stop unauthorized users from gaining access to the internal network and company data. Because these phones generally use Dynamic Host Configuration Protocol (DHCP) to request an IP address, they could be exploited if those phones that can receive an address are not locked down by hardware address.

7.1.31 Wireless Access Points

Unsecured wireless network access points allow access to your corporate network by someone who is not physically inside your office. Depending on the range of equipment, someone down the hall, on another floor, or even outside the building could access your network. Hackers can intercept data packets, gathering sensitive information by having access to your internal network. Sensitive corporate data isn't the only—or necessarily the primary—interest of unauthorized wireless network users, because high-bandwidth Internet connectivity is a high-demand commodity.

An attacker using a laptop with scanning software can participate in "war driving," which is a method of locating open wireless networks in business and residential areas. The mapped results are often posted on the Internet to let others know where they can find an open high-speed connection to the Internet. In addition to the bandwidth drain resulting from unauthorized use, there is a legal concern with the content that may be transmitted to the Internet using your corporate network. Transmission of illegal copies of digital media and other inappropriate material could put your company at risk.

7.1.32 Remote-Access Points

Perhaps the best way to describe the level of risks of your remote access points is to present a sample checklist of questions that a potential attacker would use to assess your remote access vulnerability to exploitation. Some of those questions would be as follows:

- Is your Internet gateway protected with authentication and firewalls?

- Are intrusion-detection systems used to monitor traffic through your remote-access points?

- Do your information security personnel identify new vulnerabilities and install patches to security devices immediately upon release to the public?

- Do your information security personnel frequently review firewall logs, intrusion-detection alerts, and other data sources to identify potential security breaches?

- Do your information security personnel document instances of suspicious activity and/or security device malfunctions?

7.1.33 Voice-Mail Systems

Voice-mail systems are designed to make it easy for the intended recipient to retrieve messages from any phone anywhere, but that means anyone else who knows or can guess the user's password can gain access with equal ease. Modern voice-mail systems are basically just specialized server computers that store messages in digital form on a hard drive. A system administrator with physical access to the server could retrieve a message, even one deleted by the recipient, in essentially the same way that inadvertently erased word processing files can often be recovered. It is possible that tech-savvy company employees or an outside attacker who managed to penetrate an organization's internal data network could do the same thing.

Systems are often set up with an easily guessed default password (e.g., the user's extension or a simple sequence such as 1-2-3-4). Many users simply leave those passwords in place or switch them to something else an intruder would have a good chance of guessing, such as a birthday or home address. There is also the risk of voice-mail fraud, of which there are two types. The first type occurs when long-distance thieves attack voice-mail systems in much the same way as PBXs, and if successful, they can take over that particular mailbox and use it for their own purpose. Many stolen PBX remote-access authorization codes, stolen credit card numbers, computer passwords, and the telephone numbers and mailbox passwords of other compromised voice-mail systems are available to phreakers. They may use the mailboxes, or allow others to use the mailboxes, to conduct other illegal activities such as drug deals, gambling operations, and prostitution rings. They can access the voice-mail system remotely using either local telephone lines or toll-free lines. Phreaker tools include wardialers, cracker software, network sniffer software, and scanners. They also depend on social engineering to learn Telecom and Datacom system profiles, stolen passwords, and toll-free numbers and lines dedicated to modems and faxes. Important information is often obtained directly from company operators, administrators, or other employees. Voice-mail systems are also used by those engaged in industrial espionage, such as industrial spies who use voice-mail systems to pass or steal confidential messages and/or leave bogus messages to disrupt a company's operation.

Acquiring a PBX dial tone via the voice-mail system to facilitate transferring out of the voice-mail system to a phone on the PBX is a second type of abuse. If the PBX is not set up properly, the transfer can be made directly to dial tone or, in other instances, the call transfers to an extension. The extension may be on another PBX and require transmission over a tie line or T-1, and if the tie line or T-1 is not properly secured, a dial tone can be retrieved and fraudulent calls can be placed.

The greater the number of ways a voice-mail system is connected to a network, the more ways there are for someone to obtain unauthorized access. Increased security, such as effective password management and voice firewalls, is even more important because access to voice mail, faxes, e-mail messages, video mail, and other services can now occur in a single telephone call. A voice-mail system is only as secure as the least secure gateway into the network.

7.1.34   PBX Risks

As computers and telephone systems become integrated, it is vital that voice assets are secured properly. VoIP equipment, utilizing as it does IP technology, is much more likely to be subject to hacker attacks, worms, viruses, and other security hazards than conventional PBX gear, which is based on proprietary operating systems. If an IP PBX system is compromised, any external security measures in place on the data network are useless because the attacker already has access to the network. If the carrier network providing VoIP service is not sufficiently isolated from the Internet (or other access by the general public), then voice traffic could be susceptible to interception or disruption from DoS attacks. Security issues may be resolvable, but at the present time must be regarded as a risk area. If a company's security solutions and policies address voice and data separately, only half of each side of the picture is being observed. Thinking that voice and data are two separate entities in today's converged world is marking more and more companies as easy targets for attackers.

There are two primary reasons why an attacker will target PBX: (1) to gain access to the rest of the network and (2) for fraudulent reasons such as free long-distance calls and teleconferences, calling card schemes, and using the PBX as a diverter to cover their tracks. As VoIP becomes more popular, PBXs are becoming more integrated with the traditional data IP computer networks. In general, most companies are so worried about hackers and their data networks that they never turn to their voice assets to assess their security posture. For professional criminals, this is often the perfect weak link to gain access to the data network through the unsecured PBX. PBXs are vulnerable to attackers and scammers in several ways, and these methods are discussed in the following paragraphs.

Remote Access

In many situations, companies allow third-party vendors to have remote access to the PBX to maintain the system. One of the most commonly exploited vulnerabilities in PBXs revolves around the remote maintenance procedures and functions inherent in the system. Although this arrangement is ideal economically for all parties involved, it introduces a huge security risk. These companies often use well-known standards to set up your PBX for maintenance, and as a result they can be quickly compromised by an attacker. If attackers or disgruntled employees find out the phone number of the modem, all they have to do is simply log in using a default account or brute force their way into the PBX using an automated script to guess the administrative login and password. If successful, the attacker has literally taken control of the company's voice communications. Other ways attackers may obtain this type of data are through social engineering, dumpster diving, or wardialing. In dumpster diving, attackers go through the company's trash cans and dumpsters, looking for internal phone numbers, e-mails that contain UserIDs and possibly passwords, or information that may have been scribbled on a sticky note. Undertrained staff will always be the biggest and most easily exploited security threat to a company. Wardialing is also one of the most popular ways to gather potential PBX targets to compromise.

Accounts and Passwords

If attackers are successful in finding an account number, they will dial in to the PBX and attempt to log into a system account. PBX accounts allow various administrative accesses to the system for performing various tasks and configuration. Default passwords are by far the most commonly exploited vulnerability on a PBX. In addition to default passwords, weak passwords are also a danger and can be easily exploited through password-cracking programs. Administrators may overlook enabled default passwords when changing passwords or disable the various accounts, leaving the system open to unauthorized access. There is also the risk that a manufacturer has left some accounts open on purpose so it can dial in to change or configure certain features without having to request access from the administrator. There are circumstances where a manufacturer may do this so that an administrator doesn't have access to a special feature and will create a unique login, or back door, to the system to access the PBX and utilize the feature or tool.

Maintenance Features

Companies often prefer PBX system maintenance to be taken care of remotely by the product manufacturer. Vendors can simply dial in to the switch instead of traveling out to the location, and they prefer this because it is easier and faster to fix when a system goes down. Maintenance features require a login and password to perform a certain procedure. There are risks involved in a compromise of one of these features.

One of the most common maintenance features is the Debug utility. Its primary function is to troubleshoot faulty software and hardware. This function will normally require unlimited access to the switch so that anything on the system can be examined with the utility and, therefore, if this function is compromised, the attacker has virtual access to the entire PBX system. Another common maintenance feature that typically requires unlimited access to the PBX is called Flash. This entails updating software that has been embedded in read-only memory (ROM) and simply writes over or appends to the existing ROM software known as "firmware." The software update utility is a lot like the Flash program and allows the manufacturer to remotely update the system software. There is more risk to this feature being compromised than others, because in addition to allowing unlimited access to the switch, it will also allow the attacker to update the software. In other words, Trojan horses, hidden accounts, or system viruses could be uploaded and installed remotely, hidden in what appears to be the normal system software.

Databases are the nuts and bolts of the PBX system and its security. If a database is compromised, the entire switch has been compromised. Database manipulation utilities are common maintenance features for PBX databases that contain user accounts, user rights, passwords, and system configuration information. There are multiple utilities in place that allow a remote user to view, change, upload, or download the system databases. An attacker could use this information to crash, change, obtain access to, or manipulate different features or the entire system.

User Features

In addition to maintenance features, standard user features are susceptible to exploitation as well. A more dangerous scenario arises when employees can use authorization codes remotely. One feature is known as Dial-In System Access (DISA). The user types in his or her authorization code and, if the code is correct, the PBX simply gives the employee an outside line to place a long-distance call. This feature is used to avoid giving employees calling cards and allows employees to make business calls from home without incurring the expense. If a dishonest, disgruntled employee from another division were to gain access to another division's code, that person could charge all long-distance calls to the other division or just run up phone bills for the company.

Anyone who figures out a DISA authorization code can place long-distance calls from remote locations. Much like brute forcing a password, attackers can use computer programs to dial in to the PBX and guess random authorization codes until the correct one is found. Once compromised, these codes can be passed around to fellow hackers and groups of hackers, which can result in many attackers using your PBX for all of their long-distance needs. Bills in the tens of thousands can be run up if the attackers are not stopped quickly.

Automatic Call Distribution (ACD) is a common user feature found primarily in customer service call centers. Incoming calls are routed to the first available agent in a group assigned to handle the specific task with which the caller needs assistance. Each group can be configured to have a supervisor who can monitor the incoming calls for quality assurance. If ACD is compromised and an outside or internal attacker gains supervisor access, the attacker can drop calls, monitor calls, or in some cases, even speak to both the caller and the agent. In more extreme circumstances, the compromise of this feature could be used for industrial espionage.

The override feature, also called the intrude feature, is another user feature that may be abused if it is compromised. This feature allows a user who is normally the supervisor to break into a conversation that is already taking place on a line. Most PBX systems can also be configured to notify the administrator when an override is taking place. Just as with the ACD, if compromised, this feature could be used by an attacker to monitor a line or possibly harass the parties on the call.

Physical Security

Physical security is particularly important for PBX systems because they are vulnerable when an attacker has access to the system. With physical access to the PBX, an attacker could not only compromise the system, modify the software, or even crash the PBX, but also pull lines, change lines, or otherwise physically damage or destroy the machine. If physical access is gained to the attendant console by attackers, they would virtually have control of all the lines coming through the system.

Toll Fraud

A PBX can also be compromised to be used for fraudulent purposes. This could be for activities such as free long-distance or conference calls, or maybe to help someone make some extra money with a 900 number. It is also important to remember that if you are a victim of toll fraud, you are still responsible for the charges that are incurred.

7.2   VoIP Risk from Attacks

The convergence of the voice and data worlds has resulted in a risk that voice traffic on such networks has become just as vulnerable to exploitation as data traffic on IP networks. As the availability and complexity of networks that carry voice, video, and data have grown, so has the ingenuity and creativity of those who exploit network connections for malicious purposes. Although many attacks come from less technical individuals who leverage the work of others to achieve their goals, there is a more sophisticated element with an in-depth understanding of networks and the technology that powers them. This element prefers to perform their work in relative anonymity, as the intent of their efforts is usually more serious and often criminal. To achieve their goals, they must use a variety of attack techniques, and this section discusses some of the more advanced techniques used as they relate to VoIP.

7.2.1   Insertion and Evasion Attacks

Data insertion is the addition of new data to an existing data packet and, in some cases, the act of appending data so that the original data packet is not altered but is sent together with a data portion that has been created by the attacker. The lack of physical security in a VoIP infrastructure is a critical risk. If a VoIP network is not encrypted, anyone with physical access to the office LAN could potentially connect network monitoring tools such as sniffers and tap into telephone conversations. Physical access to VoIP servers and gateways may allow an attacker to monitor network traffic, even if the network is encrypted. A recently disclosed risk is the use of a tool called Voice Over Misconfigured Internet Telephones (VOMIT). The commands used to intercept VoIP traffic are trivial, and an example of such follows:[6]

```
arhontus:~# ./vomit -h

./vomit: [-h] [-d ] [-p ] [-r ] [filter]

-d use for sniffing (i.e. used on files captured
   with tcpdump or ethereal)
-p read this wav file for later insertion
-r use content of for sniffing
-h help
```

An attacker could insert a .wav file into an ongoing phone conversation on the network using VOMIT, which can open the .wav file for use in pranks and social engineering. Other types of cleartext traffic that are interesting to a potential attacker include Unix X-Window server cookies and Network File System (NFS) file handles. X-Window uses a "magic cookie" to authenticate connecting clients. Sniffing the cookie out and inserting it into the .Xauthority file in the attacker's home directory lets the cracker connect to the X-Window server used by the client whose cookie was intercepted. Sniffing the NFS handle allows attackers to contact the .nsfd daemon on a server and gain access to resources the handle describes. The best tool to sniff out NFS handles is Super Sniffer (ss –n flag).

If compromised, the security system for a VoIP infrastructure provides a powerful tool for almost virtually anonymous insertion and evasion attacks and general system abuse and misuse. The compromise of a security system not only allows system abuse but also allows the elimination of all traceability and the insertion of trapdoors for intruders to use on their next visit.

DHCP and Trivial File Transfer Protocol (TFTP) server insertion attacks are particularly problematic in the VoIP environment. It is possible to change the configuration of a target phone by exploiting the DHCP response when the IP phone boots. A rogue DHCP server can initiate a response with data fields containing false information as soon as the IP phone requests a DHCP response, making it possible for a man-in-the-middle attack on the IP-media gateway and connecting IP phones. The effects of this attack would be mitigated if static rather than dynamic IP addresses were used. This attack would also fail if a state-based intrusion detection system was used to filter out DHCP server packets originating from IP phone ports, allowing this traffic only from a legitimate server. Other methods can also be used to reboot the phone remotely, such as Medium Access Control (MAC) spoofing, ping flood, and social engineering. The configuration of a target phone can be changed by exploiting the TFTP response when the IP phone is resetting. In this case, spurious information would be supplied by a rogue TFTP server before the legitimate server is able to respond to a request. It would then be possible for an attacker to change the configuration of an IP phone.

7.2.2 User Identity Theft

User identity theft involves the unauthorized use of another person's identification or credentials that establish their access privileges to the network, devices, and software programs within a network infrastructure of the LAN. VoIP inherits both PBX phone and IP network vulnerabilities, which can lead to unauthorized access and privileges to the VoIP infrastructure through user identity theft, resulting in service theft and other malicious activity.

7.2.3 Device Identity Theft

Malicious devices on IP networks act like IP phones. They can be used for eavesdropping and may also reduce service availability. The same opportunity to eavesdrop will also provide the attacker with the ability to insert, delete, or modify the audio streams.

7.2.4 Session (Call) Hijacking

It is possible to hijack a call on a VoIP system midstream and redirect the media stream to another terminal. Although unlikely to be hijacked in mid-conversation, the phone routinely (approximately every 30 seconds) sends a "Hello"-type packet to the call manager. This is where it would be easy for a hacker to use *ettercap* (a man-in-the-middle tool set) to reset the Address Resolution Protocol (ARP) information on the phone and on its gateway router.

7.2.5   Monitoring (Eavesdropping)

In the analog POTS world, the most common way to eavesdrop on a telephone conversation is to simply tap the telephone line by attaching leads to the copper phone lines and attaching a speaker or a recording device. Although this procedure is simple, it requires physical access to the phone line, and you are limited to tapping only one phone line. When a voice call is converted to digital traffic on a T-1 or Integrated Services Digital Network (ISDN) trunk, it is much more difficult to eavesdrop because it is now a series of zeros and ones multiplexed with up to 24 other calls. It also requires knowledge of which time slot the call had been allocated to in order to tap a specific line and special equipment to monitor and decode the line without interrupting service and physical access to the trunk. Eavesdropping on Voice over Network media is somewhat easier, which also presents a new set of problems for Voice over Frame Relay, Voice over ATM, and Voice over IP. It involves the use of a specialized device designed to look for voice packets and, as alluded to earlier, it doesn't involve the resources and access typically only available to government and law enforcement organizations in the POTS environment.

7.2.6   Controlling a Conversation

Taking control of a VoIP conversation would be a significant technical challenge for most attackers, but it could be done and is still a risk. The RTP packets that transport the conversation each contain a sequence number. The previous sequence numbers are discarded if a higher sequence number is sent to a phone during a conversation. Attackers could play out their own conversation on the receiving phone. The challenge is to do this with a reasonable delay in order to intercept the real packets and forge the bogus packets. If the caller placed a call and the connection was made, the attackers could then step in and take control, basically breaking the real connection and forcing a new connection for themselves.

7.2.7   Call-Forwarding Control

IP phones can have vulnerabilities that allow for call-forwarding settings to be manipulated remotely. Once these settings have been manipulated, it would then be possible for an attacker to forward all calls to another location, and the user would not even be aware that the call was forwarded to someone else.

7.2.8 **Redirecting Control**

The kernel controls interactions between user programs and hardware, and it allocates resources such as CPU, memory, hard drive, and so on. User programs make calls into the system call table, which points to the kernel code for implementing the specific system call. *RootKits* are Trojan horse backdoor tools that modify existing operating system software on a computer so that an attacker can gain access to that machine. Furthermore, RootKits allow the attacker to hide his or her presence on the machine. User-mode RootKits modify programs and libraries, whereas kernel-mode RootKits modify the kernel. Kernal RootKits are far more efficient than user-mode RootKits because they actually alter the kernel, changing the underlying code that all of the user programs invoke. By changing the system call table, an attacker can wield great power by planting malicious code inside the kernel, implementing execution redirection. The unsuspecting user will think he or she is running one program, but the kernel is running a different one. This technique can also be used to hide files and processes. By implementing many careful changes to the system call table, the attacker can hide processes, files, and directories, and even hide which ports are being used, thereby achieving the ultimate hidden and undetectable execution redirection attack. Although a somewhat new method of attack to the public, there are currently five different methods of kernel RootKits being openly discussed and are available on both Linux and Windows.[7] It is also possible for a Stealth virus to be written with the ability to hide itself from detection, usually by either redirecting disk reads or by altering disk directory and file information to hide its presence.

7.2.9 **Message Integrity**

Message integrity attacks, in which someone could corrupt a message in transit, were of less concern in a POTS network than they were in a pure data network; however, that has all changed with the advent of the converged network, and administrators need to take preventive measures to guard against these attacks. There is also a risk of message integrity attacks in VoIP. How do you ensure that the message received is the same as the message sent? Redirected calls could potentially pass through an attacker's control, and the packets could be altered or manipulated in order to control the call. In addition, there is a risk of packet-spoofing, where someone intercepts a call by impersonating voice packets in a man-in-the-middle attack.

7.2.10   Manipulation of Accounting Data

The gatekeeper is the network device that administers VoIP calls and is responsible for gathering accounting data and for transmitting it to the back-end service where every call has to be accounted for. The back-end service collects and stores this data for later processing. The Call Detail Record (CDR) is the name for the accounting data structure. CDRs are sent on the connection between a gatekeeper and the back-end service. CDRs are used for billing accountability and have three primary components:

1.   The gatekeeper generates a value called "call duration" that consists of the start time and the end time of the call.

2.   A globally unique identifier generated by the gatekeeper, known as the "CallID," is assigned to each call, and all call-related data is indexed with it.

3.   A globally unique identifier, defined at the time of the subscription and called the "UserID," is used for each authorized user.

There is an active attack based on the data found in the CDR, and this data is used to modify the value of the call duration value in the CDR. An attacker must have access to the data packets sent between the back-end service and the gatekeeper in order to intercept the data as it is transported from the gatekeeper to the back-end service. Once intercepted, the attacker changes the value of the field containing the duration of the call and forwards the data packet to the back-end service.

7.2.11   Endpoint Impersonation

For an endpoint attack to be successful, the attacker must carry out a three-stage process as follows:

1.   An endpoint registration is sent

2.   Call admission

3.   Q.931 call setup message

The call admission process is defined as a part of the Remote Access Server (RAS) protocol. The RAS messages RRQ and RCF/RRJ take care of the registration process. The explicit messages for this procedure are ARQ, ACF, and ARJ, respectively. No real session takes place between the endpoint and the gatekeeper, because the transport protocol for both the registration process and the call admission process is UDP. This results in a risk that an attacker could insert data packets into the connection at will. Q.931 uses TCP to carry out call signaling. It is possible for an attacker to start an attack at different stages of the protocol. There are four endpoint impersonation protocol exploits that need to be explained:

1.   The gatekeeper accepts the attackers as the impersonated endpoint, allowing them to carry out the whole registration process, providing the attackers with an ability to use every service that the legitimate subscribed user could use. There are, however, two requirements for this attack to be possible: (1) the impersonated user cannot be registered at the moment of the attack, and (2) if the UserID that is used happens to be bound to a certain IP address, the attackers must reside on the network of the impersonated endpoint or on its network path from the endpoint to the gatekeeper. These two conditions are required because the attackers are attempting to establish a call and, therefore, need to receive the responses coming back from the gatekeeper.

2.   Attackers start an impersonation of a registered user by omitting the registration request and sending an admission request using the identifier (UserID) of the (victim) user they want to impersonate. The attackers must be on the same subnetwork the user is on or on the network path from the gatekeeper to the user in order to be able to receive responses from the gatekeeper.

3.   Attackers can also send the Q.931 message setup and skip the call precedent procedures. All Q.931 messages are identified by their CallID. Because all CallIDs used have to be valid, they are used to identify Q.931 messages and are generated during the call admission process. To accomplish this attack successfully, attackers have to take the CallID from a call that was already permitted. However, the attack will not be possible if the gatekeeper checks the validity of the CallID and whether it is already in use.

4.   Attackers who reside on the same network as the user can eavesdrop to gather setup messages and determine where there are weak or nonexistent authentication methods. This will allow an attacker to gain the ability to issue the Q.931 message setup with

the *preGrantedARQ* setting enabled. This is possible because endpoints skip the call admission procedure and do not request the permission of a call before trying to establish it by sending a setup message request. In this case, it is not possible for the gatekeeper to identify and assign setup requests to the corresponding user. This is why additional authentication methods are required to ensure a secure process.

All of these techniques assume that there are no security mechanisms, such as the binding of important messages to properties like UserID, and that source and destination IP address have been implemented. H.235[8] recommends the use of the HMAC function together with a password to secure the connection for all messages sent from an endpoint to the gatekeeper. The level of security would depend on the strength of the password and its resistance to dictionary attacks.

As a security professional, you may be asking yourself who would implement VoIP without security in mind. Well, look at current and future VoIP implementations and see how many have been rolled out without any regard to security or only as an afterthought. If nothing else, we hope this book educates IT professionals about the importance of security for VoIP implementations.

7.2.12 Gatekeeper Impersonation

At least two endpoints are required to make a VoIP call, typically involving one or more gatekeepers and the back-end service. One endpoint (EP1) establishes a call to another endpoint (EP2). The call is routed over the first gatekeeper (GK1), and if the second endpoint (EP2) is administered by a different gatekeeper than the calling one, then GK1 will have to forward the call establishment request to the second gatekeeper (GK2). GK2 then contacts EP2 with a Q.931 message call establishment request. The GK1 setup message finds out the "routing path" of the setup message by contacting the back-end service. The back-end service response will contain information about EP1, EP2, and GK2. An attacker can be successful at impersonating a gatekeeper through either impersonation against a second gatekeeper or against the back-end service.

When an attacker wants to impersonate a gatekeeper, the intent is that a gatekeeper will accept a call setup request as if it were sent by a valid gatekeeper, because there is no mechanism of authentication in Q.931 before actual call establishment. This attack scenario is possible when a setup message is sent to another gatekeeper that the original gatekeeper could not identify as coming from a registered endpoint and is assumed to be coming from another gatekeeper. This is a risky situation where the attacker only needs to send a setup message to establish a call. This scenario highlights the consequence of an attacker being located between two valid gatekeepers. The attacker will be able to impersonate one gatekeeper toward the other one where there is a lack of mutual authentication, or if the two gatekeepers are located on different networks where the lack of an application-level proxy server that only allows calls from authorized gatekeepers to access the other network would be in use. As stated earlier, it is also possible for an attacker to impersonate a gatekeeper against the back-end service. If the proprietary connection between the gatekeeper and the back-end service is not secured, it is possible for an attacker to discover UserIDs, IP addresses of endpoints, gatekeepers, and their passwords.

7.2.13 Back-End Service Impersonation

The back-end service protocol used is a proprietary client/server protocol that only communicates with gatekeepers. The gatekeeper requests information and the back-end service responds. The impersonation of the gatekeeper toward the back-end service attack described previously is also possible in the other direction because the attacker can impersonate the back-end service. As with the other impersonation attacks, it is assumed that there is no authentication from the back-end service to the gatekeeper. An attacker with the ability to intercept messages from the gatekeeper to the back-end service will then be able to send any kind of data to the gatekeeper as long as the protocol is respected. By intercepting and modifying a message from the gatekeeper to the back-end service, the attacker can forge his or her identity. In this case, the attacker would most likely target the field that contains the password of an endpoint in the back-end service's response or even invent a new endpoint identity and fill in the fields with the corresponding values. As in the previous section, these attacks exploit both the lack of mutual authentication between the gatekeeper and back-end service and no separation of the network into one subnetwork for the back-end service and the endpoints.

7.2.14 Packet Injection

The successful injection of IP spoofed packets into the local network of the target system results in what is called a TCP sequence number attack, allowing attackers to overcome a security system whose access control mechanisms are based on IP addresses. TCP offers a connection-oriented service. The progress of the TCP connection session is indicated by sequence numbers that appear to be a stream to the participants. The sequence numbers of consecutive packets must exactly match with the amount of data sent. Attackers are capable of inserting data packets into the stream with spoofing, so they are able to predict the sequence number. The first step of this attack is the examination of the behavior of the system sequence-number generator through the request of connections to harmless services. The attackers can only start the attack if they are successful in determining how the sequence number generator works and manages to predict sequence numbers. If the attackers are successful, the next step is to issue a request with a forged IP address to a critical TCP port on the target host, and the server will respond to the request by sending data to the system with the forged IP address. The computer with the forged IP address must then be disabled. Otherwise, it would respond to the server that it did not send that data packet and request termination of the connection. When the system is disabled, the attacker can then send messages. An attacker may use something like a DoS attack to disable the computer with the forged IP address.

7.2.15 Rogue VoIP Server or Gateway

It is possible for calls to be redirected to rogue VoIP servers or gateways if an attacker can get access to phone configurations. The attackers will set up a rogue VoIP server or gateway to potentially diverted and captured calls. They could also masquerade as a valid IP phone and intercept calls that were intended for the real phone. Unified messaging is appealing to VoIP users, but it is not without security problems. Unified messaging integrates closely with your e-mail servers. Your e-mail server stores voice mail as sound tiles that can be accessed as e-mail messages. If attackers are able to break into your e-mail server, they can obtain both private e-mail and voice-mail information.

7.2.16 Viruses and Other Malicious Software

As VoIP infrastructures become more common within enterprises, the risk of compromise of phone services through methods previously thought to only affect IP networks is on the rise. Viruses, worms, and other malicious software common to the IP world can now threaten users and providers of converged network phone services such as VoIP. Computer viruses and worms can now stop telephones from working and have become a whole new class of attacks that system administrators need to worry about. Everyone is looking at VoIP as a new technology for voice; although the way we're sending voice communications is absolutely new, the data is still riding on the same infrastructure that was significantly affected by recent problems such as Slammer and SoBig. The bottom line is that because VoIP runs over the same platforms that are currently affected by viruses, worms, and other malicious software, the situation with VoIP systems is not going to be any different and should be provided with the same levels of security protection. For example, the basic security of the IP PBX and phones should not be overlooked, because much of the VoIP gear on the market is based on commodity operating systems and commonly hacked software, making it vulnerable to Nimda and other threats. The lack of security patching and security fixes now common in the data world must also be overcome in the VoIP world to avoid the same risks.

7.2.17 Sniffing

Sniffers are software programs or hardware devices that monitor traffic flowing across a network connection and can be either pulling in everything that goes by or being selective by examining data to determine what to keep and what to discard based on predefined filters. Sniffers on TCP/IP networks are referred to as *packet sniffers* because they are used to examine the packets traversing a TCP/IP network. A sniffer typically has the following components:

- Hardware such as a Network Interface Card (NIC) to physically connect to the network segment
- Capture driver software with filtering capabilities to configure the NIC to pull in all packets from the physical network connection
- A temporary physical (on-disk) or virtual (in-memory) storage area (a buffer) for captured packets
- An analysis/decoder component

Some sniffers will stop capturing packets when the buffer fills up, whereas others will discard older packets, replacing them with newer ones when the buffer is full. Capture drivers usually contain filtering capabilities, although the types of filtering capabilities vary widely from one product to the next. Some of the more common filtering capabilities include the ability to filter by MAC address, IP address, protocol, port, data pattern, flags, and packet size. Sniffers can also vary widely in regard to their analysis/decode component. Some of the more common analysis/decode capabilities include decoding of IP addresses, Domain Name Server (DNS) resolution, decoding of data fields, protocol decoders, header information, sequence numbers, size, and flag decoders. Virtually any part of the packet can be decoded with a good analysis/decoder component and displayed in an easy-to-read format for the end user.

As you might guess, depending on your point of view, sniffers can be used for both legitimate and nefarious purposes. Traffic analysis and troubleshooting are the most common uses for sniffing in the commercial environment and they are considered to be an essential part of the system administrator's networking toolbox. Administrators and other network support staff typically use sniffers to accomplish many different tasks to monitor network traffic, such as traffic analysis, bandwidth analysis, and troubleshooting.

Sniffing can also be used for other purposes, which can be a risk to VoIP and converged network security. It is possible for an attacker to collect a tremendous amount of useful information from well-placed sniffers. Most attackers rely on software sniffers because they do not have the luxury of placing a commercial-grade, hardware-based sniffer on their target network. Software-based sniffers are placed on compromised hosts within the network to collect different types of sensitive information, and they can be extremely powerful, allowing the attackers to filter traffic and capture data. Some of the more common information targeted by attackers with sniffers includes account and password information, financial information, and other sensitive data such as payroll, client data, employee records, intellectual property, patient records, e-mail, and so on. This information could be used for personal or criminal gain, to damage a company's public image, for competitive advantage, corporate espionage, or to damage employee morale. Even more problematic is that, in many cases, attackers using sniffers are insiders who have a good working knowledge of what they are looking for in the system.

An attacker may use any of a number of freely available sniffers to conduct these attacks. Although these software sniffers are freeware, they are often highly sophisticated and can perform functions not found in commercial sniffers. The sophistication of freeware sniffers can be represented best by an overview of *dsniff*[9] and its capabilities. *dsniff* is available for virtually any Unix platform, and there is even a ported Windows version available. *dsniff* has some powerful capabilities, such as the collection of passwords from many services and applications, including FTP, Telnet, SMTP, HTTP, POP, poppass, NNTP, IMAP, SNMP, LDAP, Rlogin, RIP,

OSPF, PPTP MS-CHAP, NFS, VRRP, YPINIS, SOCKS, XII, CVS, IRC, AIM, ICQ, Napster, PostgreSQL, Meeting Maker, Citrix ICA, Symantec pcAnywhere, NAT Sniffer, Microsoft 5MB, Oracle SQL*Net, Sybase, and Microsoft SQL protocols. There are also some powerful subcomponents of *dsniff,* whose basic functionalities are as follows:

- *filesnarf.* Can conduct file collection by sniffing files from NFS sessions and saving them to a local directory.

- *mailsnarf.* Can conduct e-mail monitoring by collecting e-mail messages off the network and saving them in a local directory.

- *msgsnarf.* Can conduct message monitoring by collecting chat messages from applications such as AOL Instant Messenger, ICQ 2000, IRC, MSN Messenger, Yahoo Messenger, or standard chat sessions.

- *urlsnarf.* Can conduct Web traffic monitoring by collecting HTTP requests, which it stores in a common log format.

- *Webspy.* Can conduct real-time Web traffic monitoring by allowing one to monitor a target's Web surfing session and display that session to a browser in real time.

- *arpspoof.* Can redirect traffic on a switched network by allowing one to forge ARP replies and redirect packets intended for another host to the local system. arpspoof is often used to permit sniffing on a switched network.

7.2.18   Spoofing

Spoofing is the act of forging parts of packets or entire packets and making them appear as if they are coming from a legitimate source or concealing the actual source. Spoofing is most commonly used by attackers for DoS attacks, but it can also be used to modify data or to masquerade as someone else to gain access to a target system. DoS attacks such as TCP SYN floods, UDP floods, and ICMP broadcast attacks typically employ spoofing to hide the source of the attack. The attackers can use various tools to allow them to specify an alternate-source IP address to place in outgoing packets, making them appear to come from another source.

In spoofing attacks such as *smurf,* attackers send out packets to other networks with the target's address as the source address. The smurf attack is an ICMP-based broadcast DoS attack where the attackers create ICMP echo request packets to spoof the target's IP address as the source address of the packet. The echo request packets are then sent to a broadcast network address, and every active host in that network segment will then respond to the target host with an echo reply message. When the attackers spoof the source address, they can trick all of the active systems in a particular IP network range into sending response packets to the intended target, which will quickly become overwhelmed with packets it did not request.

IP source routing is another popular use of spoofing that uses source routing so the attackers can tell the victim what route to follow when sending reply packets. The attackers can try to redirect return packets to their system or at least send the packets past the attacking system so they can be sniffed by specifying a return route. Most routers prevent this type of attack because they are configured to discard packets that have source routing enabled.

DNS records, ARP entries, and routing tables can also be updated through spoofing. It is possible for an attacker to spoof DNS updates and convince a corporate DNS server to update all DNS entries for www.popularcompany.com with a different IP address so that the attacker can redirect all Web traffic bound for that Web site to another location. UserID/password login session combinations could be captured by attackers if they are successful in sending out spoofed ARP replies that identify their system as the Primary Domain Controller.

The Routing Information Protocol (RIP) can be compromised by spoofing RIP update packets and sending them to routers. If they are spoofed correctly and the spoofed RIP update "poisons" a route by indicating that it is unreachable, then the RIP packets may cause the routers to send network traffic to the wrong destination or not to deliver it at all. If attackers can use spoofing to transmit an authentication sequence identical to a victim's authentication sequence, they can conduct identity theft. Attackers can attempt a man-in-the-middle attack (see following section) to take the victim's place (identity theft) in the middle of an electronic conversation.

7.2.19 Man-in-the Middle Attacks

A man-in-the-middle attack is a spoofing attack that requires a fair degree of technical skill and understanding for attackers to attempt to inject themselves into an ongoing digital conversation and replace one of the two involved parties or to become an intermediary playing the role of both parties and relaying traffic back and forth. These attacks are often called *session hijacking* or *TCP hijacking* attacks because the digital conversation is interrupted, forcing it to go where the attackers want it to go.

An example of a man-in-the-middle attack is where the attack is directed at intercepting telephone traffic using known vulnerabilities of VoIP phones that contain remote-accessible code, which can be exploited to cause a Denial of Service and possibly leak information.[10] Like many IP devices, VoIP phones are also vulnerable to ARP spoofing, allowing man-in-the-middle attacks that may also include data interception and packet injection. It is possible that many VoIP phones can be tapped by anyone else with a phone on the same network. If an individual VoIP phone can be crashed easily, then many VoIP network infrastructures are heavily vulnerable to DoS attack. More disturbing is the thought that these attacks could be carried out remotely if a Trojan horse has been placed on the VoIP network.

Developers and end-user organizations are currently facing substantial problems trying to create security patches and bug fixes for relatively flexible IP devices such as PCs and servers. Fixed-purpose devices such as VoIP phones present far greater challenges in that bug fixes and software patches are likely to take longer to produce and, in many cases, hardware upgrades may be required.

7.2.20 Network Scanning

Attackers will use network scanning tools to gain information such as a network system's potential as a target, its susceptibility to attack, what types of packets the network will accept and send, and what services or applications it is providing. The attackers will then determine whether they have the right operating system, software, and tools to exploit those systems. To assist in these scanning efforts, a wide variety of good freeware tools can help attackers look for specific vulnerabilities. These tools are used by attackers to perform several network scanning activities that may include the following:

- Ping sweeps that look for any hosts that accept ICMP echo request packets and respond with an echo reply message

- Port scans that look for open services and applications on network systems

- Application scanning that looks for specific versions of an application, such as Sendmail

- Operating system scanning that looks for systems running a specific operating system such as Windows XP

- Vulnerability scanning that looks for problems or conditions on information systems that could be exploited

- Simple Network Management Protocol (SNMP) scans that look for systems that can be managed using SNMP or will respond to SNMP queries.

Scanning provides the attacker with a means to identify which systems warrant further investigation and which systems are not worth wasting time on. Scanning can provide the attacker with an enormous amount of useful information such as the details of active systems, open services, operating systems, applications, users, security status, patch status, possible holes, and confirmation of vulnerabilities. Scanning is important to serious attackers because it can provide them with a virtual blueprint of a remote network and a map of the systems residing on that network. It is used by attackers to gain the information needed to plan and execute an attack against a remote system. The information collected is also used to assist attackers in selecting the right area to attack, choosing the most effective tool or method for attacking a remote system, and determining the most attractive targets from a pool of target candidates.

Scanning does not guarantee success for attackers. They still need to know how to interpret the results of the scan, which tool takes advantage of what the scanning revealed, and what targets to pursue. Scanning tools sometimes produce "false positives," reporting results that prove to be invalid after further scrutiny. Unless performed carefully, scanning can also provide a clear warning and place potential targets on alert. If detected, attackers may be blocked from conducting further scanning activities.

In most cases, the risk from an internal scan is much greater than the risk from an external scan. Scans from remote locations typically have to cross a series of routers, firewalls, and other network devices and sensors before reaching the intended target. In contrast, internal scans are typically highly successful and return much more useful information without having to contend with access lists, firewalls, and intrusion detection systems. This occurs because most companies still do not understand and prepare for the internal threat. Many organizations plan their defenses at the network perimeter and design them to stop attacks from external sources. The insider also has the advantage of physical access to the network and, in most cases, inside knowledge of the network topology and direct access to other information that may be useful for malicious activity.

7.2.21 Password Cracking

A password cracker is a program that can decrypt passwords or otherwise disable password protection. It is important to understand that most password crackers need not decrypt anything. Most modern encryption processes are now one-way, and no process can be executed to reverse the encryption process that will reveal the password in plaintext. Many so-called password crackers are nothing but brute-force engines that are programmed to try word after word, often at high speeds, until one works. Simulation tools are actually used in real password crackers. They use the same algorithm as the original password program and, through a comparative analysis, these tools try to match encrypted versions of the password to the original. If a password is in the dictionary, it is vulnerable to being cracked. In fact, exploitation of ill-chosen and poorly protected passwords is one of the most common attacks used by attackers. Almost every multiuser system in operation uses passwords to protect against unauthorized logons, but comparatively few installations use them properly. The problem is universal in nature, not system-specific, and the solutions are simple, inexpensive, and applicable to any computer, regardless of operating system or hardware. It is interesting that one of the most common risks that is exploited on network systems is also the easiest to prevent.

7.2.22 Wardialers and Telephone Line Scanners

A wardialer is simply a computer program that will dial a series of phone numbers to see what answers and, on most phone lines, it will be a person, a fax machine, a voice mailbox, or no answer at all. If someone has left a computer with a modem connected to a phone line, it is possible that the computer will answer the call. Wardialers are generally designed to locate and exploit vulnerabilities for nefarious purposes and are readily available on the Internet, free for the downloading. They are less formal programs than telephone scanners or hacking tools that dial a sequence of telephone numbers with the intent of identifying any automated devices that might answer.

Penetrating a system discovered by wardialing is a real art because the scanner must attempt to log in as a valid user. These type of attempts are usually in the form of common or default accounts such as "Administrator" or "guest." If appropriately secure passwords are actually in use on the victim's system, a wardialing penetration attempt is not likely to succeed.

The term *wardialer* is often used interchangeably with telephone scanner. The term *telephone scanner* applies to those programs that are not only designed to dial a sequence of telephone numbers but also have the capability to potentially identify and penetrate the answering system, and these types of tools are sophisticated in nature. Although telephone scanners are generally commercial products designed for security professionals to protect their systems, they include specialized hardware and can cost thousands of dollars per copy. They are reliable, can scan thousands of phone numbers, identify and even penetrate the systems on the other end, and produce reports or compare previous scans with the current one to identify any differences. Although the basic applications are similar, telephone scanners and wardialers generally come with different tools and capabilities suited to the needs of the attacker.

Telephone scanners are generally configured to match specific modem characteristics and preferences, and the attacker defines these parameters before the scan is performed. Typically this will include the numbers or range of numbers to be scanned, the tests to be performed, such as identify or penetrate, how many times it should redial any busy signals encountered, numbers that should be excluded, and so on. After the data is collected, it must be analyzed by reviewing automated reports generated by the scanner.

Several telephone scanners and wardialers are available commercially and, depending on the value of the target, could also be affordable for an attacker to use for nefarious purposes. Two of the more popular commercial products are Xiscan from Xinetica Ltd. (www.xiscan.com) and PhoneSweep from Sandstorm Enterprises (www.sandstorm.net).

Although lacking the features of the commercial telephone scanners, freeware scanners are available at no cost and are suitable for small scans, and these products are most likely the ones you will have to face if someone targets your enterprise for malicious purposes. Some of the more popular freeware scanners are THC-Scan v2.0 from The Hacker's Choice (www.thehackerschoice.com) and Tone Loc Utilities from Packet Storm Security (http://www.securityfocus.com/tools/47).

Wardialers can also be implemented in hardware or on PDAs. For example, PocketDial (http://www.freewarepalm.com/communication/pocketdial.shtml) from PhreakMonkey enterprises is a self-contained, battery-powered, pocket wardialer, and TBA (www.atstake.com/research/tools) is a wardialer for the PalmOS platform that is available for download from @stake Corporation.

If an organization discovers that it is under attack and decides to shut off all Internet access, an attacker will attempt to use these techniques to exploit dial-up access through a terminal server if it is available. Dial-up lines are often overlooked by security administrators, and most likely they are managed by a separate group that has minimal security background or concern about security. The attacker leverages the fact that often little communication exists between this group and corporate security personnel. For those organizations that rely on remote dial-up access rather than Internet connections, an attacker will have a second avenue of approach if shut out of the corporate Internet connections. It is rare for an organization to have any significant monitoring capability for dial-up usage, and dial-up passwords are not typically changed as quickly as those protecting Internet access, if they are even changed at all. This gives a seasoned attacker an almost guaranteed means of penetration into a network. We all know there is at least one person in each large company who decides to set up his or her own remote access to a desktop machine using Symantec Corporation's pcAnywhere or a similar product without a password. Astute security staff should search these products out and eliminate them from use on the network.

7.2.23 Annoyances and Spam Calls

As was described earlier in this chapter, several attack methods can also be used to enhance the ability of an attacker to make prank calls anonymously or for spam calls to bypass VoIP control features such as call screening and anonymous call rejection. Unified messaging in VoIP implementations results in voice mail being more closely tied to e-mail. This can also make annoyance calls and spam more problematic until software becomes available to address this issue.

7.2.24 Caller ID Risks

In July 2004, hackers revealed some vulnerabilities within VoIP networks that make it easy to spoof Caller ID and to unmask blocked numbers.[11] They showed that they can also make phone calls appear to be from any number they want and even pierce the veil of Caller ID blocking to unmask an anonymous phoner's unlisted number.[12] Caller ID in POTS works as follows:

- Your local phone company or cell phone carrier sends your Calling Party Number (CPN) with every call, like a return address on an envelope.

- Transmitted along with your CPN is a privacy flag that tells the telephone switch at the receiving end of the call whether to share your number with the recipient.

- If you have call-blocking on your line, the phone company you are dialing into knows your number, but it won't share it with the person you are calling.

This arrangement relies on telephone equipment at both ends of the call being trusted. The phone switch providing you with a dial tone promises not to lie about your number to other switches, and the switch on the receiving end promises not to reveal your number if you have asked that it be blocked.

In the United States, that trust is backed by FCC regulations that dictate precisely how telephone carriers handle CPNs, Caller ID, and blocking. Most subscribers have come to take Caller ID for granted, and some financial institutions even use Caller ID to authenticate customers over the phone. The root of this vulnerability is based on what happens to a small piece of authentication data when it leaves the tightly regulated realm of traditional telephony and passes into the unregulated domain of the Internet. VoIP networks are currently outside FCC regulation, and that fact places unwanted capabilities in the hands of ordinary netizens.

Last year there was a similar risk in that Vonage's VoIP systems could allow a remote attacker to spoof a Vonage user's caller ID. By using SIP with enabled VoIP hardware, the attacker would begin by calling a vulnerable Vonage user and then spoof the victim's caller ID by placing the victim on hold. Once the victim answered the phone, the attacker would then call a third party using data that would allow the attacker to see and use the victim's caller ID information. The called party would simply assume that the attacker was the victimized Vonage user.[13]

Another VoIP CallerID vulnerability that exploited Asterisk by Structured Query Language (SQL) injection was found last year and identified by @stake.[14] Asterisk (www.asterisk.org) is a complete PBX implemented as a software product. It runs on Linux and provides all of the features one would expect from a PBX. Asterisk does VoIP with three protocols (i.e., SIP, IAXv1 and v2, and H323). It can interoperate with almost all standards-based telephony equipment using relatively inexpensive hardware. CDRs are generated by telephony systems in order to perform functions such as billing and rating. CDRs contain several fields that identify useful information about the call, including source, destination, and other items such as

CallerID. These records can be generated numerous times during the call to indicate the state of the call. @stake found an issue while conducting a source code review of the CDR logging functionality. It is possible to perform SQL injection if an attacker can supply a malformed CallerID string. The interesting thing to note about this vulnerability is that it can be launched not only via VoIP protocols but also through fixed-line connections (i.e., POTS).

7.2.25 Wi-Fi

The recent popularity of Wi-Fi and VoIP has occurred in part because converged voice/data network projects can be extremely tough to implement. Wi-Fi stands for "Wireless Fidelity" and is a set of standards for wireless local area networks (WLAN) based on the IEEE 802.11 specifications. Wi-Fi was intended to be used for wireless devices and LANs, but is now often also used for Internet access. It enables a person with a wireless-enabled computer or personal digital assistant (PDA) to connect to the Internet by moving within, for eaxample, 15 meters of an access point, called a "hotspot."[15] Although the adoption of wireless LANs isn't expected to outpace wired networks anytime soon, and land lines for voice are still the order of the day in most organizations, users who are willing to push the IT envelope are finding out that Wi-Fi VoIP is more than just a combination of two popular industry acronyms. Wireless Ethernet certainly isn't the first infrastructure enhancement that experts recommend for carrying VoIP, but many are finding out that 802.11 works just fine for satisfying most IP telephony requirements. The combination of these technologies is proving useful for keeping mobile employees, such as hospital workers, in touch with critical data or for linking IP phones in areas where Category 5 cabling is difficult to run. Voice quality can be a major issue because Wi-Fi LANs are comparatively slow at a mere 11 Mbit/sec. The IEEE is creating standards to increase security and quality of service on Wi-Fi. Such standards proposed include 802.11i and 802.11e, but widespread adoption of those technologies is still to come. VoIP over Wi-Fi inherits the risks of 802.11, of which there are many. The authors highly recommend readers to refer to their recently published book *Operational Wireless Security* for a detailed overview of the many risks that need to be addressed in relation to 802.11.

7.3   Summary

VoIP transports packetized voice over the LAN and may expose a company to security vulnerabilities that put its entire network at risk. Because most data network security devices were not designed for voice, IP telephony requires additional measures to protect networks from attacks. Many organizations initially install IP telephony systems at remote sites and fail to consider the additional network security that must be in place before implementation. This oversight can lead to expensive consequences caused by serious network attacks. VoIP security risks differ from those usually found with traditional PBX systems. Companies should not assume that vendors have taken adequate measures to eliminate security gaps within their products. End users bear the burden of addressing their network security issues and must proactively manage their VoIP and LAN voice traffic. The awareness of risk factors described in this chapter will help you prepare for VoIP and should help you mitigate potential security breaches and raise internal security awareness within your organization to significantly reduce risks from unwarranted attacks.

7.4 Endnotes

1. Gordon, L., Loeb, M., Lucyshyn, W., & Richardson, R. (2004). 2004 CSI/FBI Computer Crime and Security Survey. Retrieved July 26, 2004 from http://i.cmpnet.com/gocsi/db_area/pdfs/fbi/FBI2004.pdf

2. Office of the National Counterintelligence Executive. (2003). Annual Report to Congress on Foreign Economic Collection and Industrial Espionage—2003. Retrieved July 26, 2004 from www.fas.org/irp/ops/ci/docs/2003.pdf

3. Allen, P. (2002). VoIP Facing Fraud Threat. Retrieved on July 26, 2004 from www.pcw.co.uk/news/1133971

4. California Department of Corrections. (2003). Telephone Scams! Retrieved on July 26, 2004, from www.cdc.state.ca.us/InfoSecurity/Articles/ A_TELEPHONE_SCAM.asp

5. ZVON. (2004). RFC 3261: Security Considerations: Threat Model and Security Usage Recommendations. Retrieved August 3, 2004 from www.zvon.org/tmRFC/RFC3261/Output/chapter26.html

6. Monkey.ORG. (2004). VOMIT: Voice Over Misconfigured Internet Telephones. Retrieved on August 8. 2004 from http:// vomit.xtdnet.nl\

7.   Skoudis, E. (2004). The Evolution of Malware. ISSA Denver Chapter Presentation, June 8, 2004, Denver, CO.

8.   International Telecommunication Union. (2003). Security and Encryption for H-series (H.323 and other H.245-based) multimedia terminals—ITU-T Recommendation H.235. Retrieved August 8, 2004 from www.javvin.com/protocol/H235v3.pdf

9.   Song, D. (2004). Dsniff. Retrieved August 8, 2004 from http://monkey.org/~dugsong/dsniff

10. HNS. (2002). Multiple Vulnerabilities in CISCO VoIP Phones. Retrieved August 7, 2004 on www.net-security.org/vuln.php?id=1703

11. Abramson, A. (2004). VoIP Hackers Mean Business. Retrieved August 7, 2004 from http://andyabramson.blogs.com/VoIPwatch/2004/07/VoIP_hackers_me.html

12. Poulsen, K. (2004). VoIP Hackers Gut Caller ID. Retrieved. August 7, 2004 from www.theregister.co.uk/2004/07/07/hackers_gut_VoIP/

13. Internet Security Systems. (2003). Vonage VoIP Could Allow an Attacker to Spoof the Caller ID. Retrieved August 7, 2004 from http://xforce.iss.net/xforce/xfdb/12939

14. @stake. (2003). Security Advisory: Asterisk CallerID CDR SQL Injection. Retrieved August 7, 2004 from www.atstake.com/research/advisories/2003/a091103-1.txt

15. The FreeDictionary.Com. (2004). wIfI, 802.11. Retrieved September 22, 2004 from http://encyclopedia.thefreedictionary.com/WiFi,%20802.11

7.5   General References

Cisco. (2002). *Configuring H.323 Gatekeepers and Proxies*. Retrieved August 5, 2004 from http://noc.caravan.ru/ciscocd/cc/td/doc/product/software/ios122/122cgcr/fvvfax_c/vvf323gk.htm

FreeWarePalm. (2004). PocketDial v 1.0. Retrieved September 22, 2004 from http://www.freewarepalm.com/communication/pocketdial.shmtl

Hayden, R. (2004). Retrieved August 5, 2004 from www.rhyshaden.com/voice.htm

Networksorcery.com. (2004). *SIP, Session Initiation Protocol.* Retrieved August 4, 2004 from www.networksorcery.com/enp/protocol/sip.htm

Rosenberg, J. (2002). *SIP: Session Initiation Protocol.* Retrieved August 3, 2004 from www.jdrosen.net/papers/draft-ietf-sip-rfc2543bis-07.txt

SecurityFocus. (2004). THC-SCAN 2.0. Retrieved September 22, 2004 from http://www.securityfocus.com/tools/47

Shultz, T. (2000). *Voice over IP.* Retrieved August 5, 2004 from www.eicon.com/disv4bri/whtpap4.htm

ZVON. (2004). *RFC 3261: Security Considerations: Threat Model and Security Usage Recommendations.* Retrieved August 3, 2004 from www.zvon.org/tmRFC/RFC3261/Output/chapter26.html

8

VoIP Security Best Practices

Voice systems that encompass traditional PBXs, VoIP and multimedia servers, voice and unified messaging platforms, and voice gateways have evolved from closed and stand-alone installations to open and integrated systems in corporate networks. The evolution and increased complexity of these systems, combined with the migration to IP, has serious implications for security management. There are many issues to contend with when mitigating the VoIP security risks previously described in this book. We identified weaknesses an administrator must overcome in the previous chapter. Next, we need to identify the best practices for implementing software tools and hardware devices, combined with internal procedures providing the measures necessary to secure a network. A comprehensive strategy based on sound security best practices will ultimately provide the best practical measures for VoIP systems security management and control. The authors assume that the reader has a basic understanding of information systems security and will cover the aspects of security as they should be applied to VoIP infrastructures.

8.1   General

VoIP security risks present many challenges today. Of course, the benefits of VoIP are also many, and it is our job as security professionals to maximize the mitigation of risks so these benefits can be realized. Although there are a great many risks, don't let the sheer number of risks deter you from beginning a VoIP deployment. Careful planning, awareness, and proper management through adherence to VoIP security best practices can go a long way toward preventing, detecting, and reacting to security problems before they can impact your business.

8.1.1   Maintain Strong Physical Security

Many people go to great lengths to secure their network from the outside so
that intruders cannot get in, but they are often incredibly lax about ensuring that the servers are safe from direct attacks by people physically at the
machine. Physical security is important for securing the datacenter, the network and VoIP equipment, and the environment around the equipment.
Unless the VoIP network is encrypted, anyone with physical access to the
office LAN could potentially connect network monitoring tools and tap
into telephone conversations. Even if encryption is used, physical access to
VoIP servers and gateways may allow an attacker to monitor network traffic
or compromise the system in a matter of minutes. As described in several of
the risks in Chapter 7, if the proper physical countermeasures are not in
place to mitigate some of the biggest risks, such as insertion of sniffers or
other network monitoring devices, then the installation of a sniffer could
result in not just data but all voice communications being intercepted.
Therefore, it is important to ensure that adequate physical security is in
place to restrict access to VoIP network components. Physical security measures, including barriers, locks, access control systems, and guards, are the
first line of defense.

8.1.2   Secure the Datacenter

Small organizations often place their servers in limited control or publicly
accessible spaces. The crucial VoIP components, such as servers, gateways,
IP PBXs, databases, and routers, should be confined to a locked room and,
where possible, protected with electronic card access so that you can
record who enters and leaves the room. Most corporations maintain internal or outsourced datacenters, where they keep their important servers,
databases, network equipment, and management systems. Datacenters
enforce strict control over who can enter the datacenters, using badges,
cards, keys, or a keypad system, as well as log hooks and human security.
Physical access to your hardware in the datacenter or server room should
be limited to a select set of trustworthy administrators. Maintenance people should not be allowed to enter this area unaccompanied. Motion-sen-
sor alarms or surveillance cameras should be installed in these rooms for
mission-critical systems.

8.1.3 Secure the Equipment

In addition to locking the equipment in a controlled access area, network and desktop devices cases or locking lugs should be kept locked and the keys protected to keep intruders out. Copies of the case or device keys should be kept in a restricted location outside the datacenter. There should be no evidence of passwords or confidential information on notes stuck on the equipment or under the keyboards or voice devices. Documentation concerning LAN settings or network equipment settings should not be visible, and important user IDs and passwords should be kept in a restricted location. If the server room has both windows and mission-critical machines, they should be arranged in a way that people outside the room cannot see the keyboards, so they can't see user or administrator passwords as they are typed.

8.1.4 Secure the Environment around the Equipment

An attacker who can attach to your network can steal data in transit or mount attacks against computers on your network or on other networks. When possible, hubs and switches should be kept behind locked doors or in locked cabinets. You should also ensure that your external data connection points are kept locked and run cabling through walls and ceilings to make it harder to tap.

Security concerns should not override the environmental requirements of your hardware, and temperature and humidity controls should be provided to avoid any equipment damage. Although a critical server locked in a closet will prevent an attacker from accessing it, the lack of adequate ventilation will overheat the equipment and cause it to fail, thus rendering your security concerns useless. Uninterruptible power supplies should be used for the servers. This will keep the servers running or initiate a staged automatic server shutdown when a power outage occurs. Unused equipment that could be used to enhance an unauthorized user's stay should also be disconnected or eliminated. For example, any unused modem or Network Interface Card (NIC) connection should be disabled or removed.

8.1.5 Secure the Hardware

When possible, VoIP hardware should have an extra layer of security to help ensure against both unauthorized internal and external access and to accept connections from authorized users, applications, and locations. Some examples of the extra levels of security that can be provided for hardware are an additional password tier, modem control lists, access authentication, access control lists, session auditing, and session encryption. Hardware vendors have introduced hardware embedded with security controls, such as login authentication, and session encryption can be used to ensure internal network access control for administrators and applications.

8.1.6 Harden the Servers

The term *server hardening* is used to describe the process of making a server less susceptible to unwanted or unauthorized access, attacks, viruses, and other malicious software. Some aspects of network servers can make them tempting targets for attackers. Network server host identities can be redirected through IP and DNS spoofing, resulting in attackers presenting their servers to legitimate users as though they were those belonging to your organization. Servers usually actively listen for requests for services on known ports, and they try to process such requests. Servers are often configured to reboot automatically after some kinds of failures, which can offer opportunities for intruders. Public servers often have publicly known host names and IP addresses and may be deployed outside of an organization's firewall or other perimeter defenses. Servers do not usually have an attending administrative user who notices signs of unusual activity and are often remotely administered, so they willingly accept connections from privileged accounts.

Configuring the security of the servers to help maximize security will make them less vulnerable to attack and maintain their integrity. Host security is also a first line of defense against internal threats, which generally have a higher probability of occurrence than external threats, and provides a backup in case of failure of perimeter defenses. The security configuration of servers will include (1) regular operating system and application software security updates and patches; (2) restricting network and operating system services to only those that are essential to be on the server host machine; (3) user authentication, and appropriate object, device, and file access controls for the operating system; (4) secure remote administration; and (5) configuration for periodic file backups. The maintenance and management of logging and other data collection mechanisms must be ensured. Host and perimeter antivirus, intrusion detection, intrusion prevention, and firewalls should be used where appropriate, and their revisions should be updated regularly. Only appropriate physical access should be allowed to the servers.

VoIP servers may run multiple services that can be distributed across multiple devices to increase scalability and manageability. You can use the ability to run different applications on different computers to increase the level of security. Ensure that you turn off all unneeded services, disable any features on the servers that are not in use, and do not run any applications that are not needed on the server, such as an e-mail client or a Web server. By running these services on separate computers, you can harden each of them and avoid potential interaction among the applications. Also make sure that the services operate user or service accounts with only the privileges that are absolutely necessary to run normally. A compromised service should not provide root or administrative access.

8.1.7 Manage Your Storage Intelligently

One normally thinks of disaster recovery or business continuity practices—such as keeping the backed-up files in a restricted, off-site location so they are not wiped out by a storm or a fire, or making regular backups of the data and the configuration settings for each critical computer—when the subject of data storage integrity is brought up. Some may even use Redundant Array of Independent Disks (RAID) technology or disk mirroring on crucial hard drives. However, security practices must actually be considered when you want to intelligently ensure data storage integrity. Businesses cannot assume that a firewall or other network security solution will protect their confidential or proprietary data from disgruntled employees, so they should ensure that information housed in a Storage Area Network (SAN) is encrypted. The advent of SANs in recent years has made data security far more complex than it was when you only worried about securing the hard disk. SANs allow users to store information anywhere within an enterprise and access it from any point as well, rather than tying storage to specific servers. Although such a model boosts storage efficiency, it also raises questions about the security of sensitive data that is accessed over a network. Authentication, authorization, auditing, integrity, and confidentiality, along with firewalls and encryption, are used to secure SANs from both internal and external threats.

8.1.8 Create a Secure Build Image

You should never install an untested operating system and its applications on a computer and boot it up in the network. A secure image should be created that is tested against vulnerability-assessment software, antivirus software, a personal firewall, and Host-based Intrusion Detection System (HIDS) software and the base image replicated with each new installation of software on all computers related to your VoIP system: VoIP servers, DNS and DHCP servers, database servers, Web servers, gateways, and so on. To build and test a secure build image, you start with a computer with a hard disk that has been wiped clean and install the latest version of the operating system that you support. Next, you will apply the latest patches to the operating system, and then install your organization's applications and their latest patches. A vulnerability assessment will then be run against the system and report the potential holes in the system ranked in importance from critical to low, with the intention of identifying avoidable intrusions or exploits.

Next, either a host-based firewall for a server or a personal firewall for a client will be configured and installed. An HIDS for critical servers, with its early attack-mitigation capability, makes it the preferred choice for the high target value VoIP server because of the lag time involved in validating an application or operating system security patch for production use. HIDS may also be installed on mail servers, if they are being used to store voice mail, in addition to the installation of e-mail content filtering. Finally, antivirus software that has been updated to ensure that no viruses have been introduced during your build to the operating system will be installed on the operating system and will need to be updated remotely for each build install. This is the general process for developing a secure build image for your VoIP system.

8.1.9 Secure the System and Application Software

VoIP product evolution has focused more on enhancing telephony-specific features and improving the end-user quality of experience rather than on improving VoIP security. Dedicated security features have been limited to simple registration access control of users, with limited usage control and rudimentary fraud protection that are often based simply on real-time Call Detail Record (CDR) log files. As with any new technology, the constantly changing proprietary software and evolving standards have reduced opportunities for bug testing and software security hardening. VoIP security is finally being addressed by leading IP telephony vendors such as Cisco, Avaya, Alcatel, and Nortel, who have augmented support of security features in their products, including encryption of operations and maintenance (O&M), call control and voice traffic, authentication of users, devices, calls, and O&M personnel at different levels of authorization. Leading firewall vendors such as Check Point, NetScreen, and Cisco have also added VoIP security functionality to their products by providing support for SIP and H.323. In addition, niche VoIP firewall vendors are also appearing. Although this is a good start, there is still a ways to go in regards to the consistency level of VoIP software security feature support and the methods to implement it. Key software components of a VoIP network that must be secured typically reside in the call control center, voice gateway, and IP phone.

The call control server software is typically implemented on commercially available operating systems and is a critical network entity in a VoIP telephony solution. It contains all routing, service, and user information, and it can control access to servers containing this information. At a minimum, all unused services must be turned off, the operating system and services patching must be kept up-to-date, the system must only be used for the call control server and must be implemented on a secure hardened operating system, all user or device access to servers must be authenticated and authorized, and support of application-level hop-by-hop signaling message authentication on a per-packet basis and encryption of call setup information must be supported.

The voice gateway is a network entity that provides media and, in some cases, signaling conversion between the IP network and the Public Switched Telephone Network (PSTN). At a minimum, the voice gateway must support strong authentication for any configuration or software upgrades, provide IP interface denial-of-service protection, be configured to route calls only via the call control server, have both virus protection and HIDS configured on the voice gateway server component, support encryption of both call setup information and media, and support per-packet media protocol authentication.

The IP phone is an end-user device that provides voice and call signaling connections, and in some cases, advanced feature support such as Web browsing and wireless connectivity. At a minimum, the IP phone software must authenticate itself to the call control server or a proxy server upon initial registration, support strong authentication for any remote configuration or software upgrade, control any incoming traffic through the support of a configurable access control list, encrypt both call setup information and media, and have an implemented switching function combined with virtual LAN functionality for those phones required to support an additional Ethernet port for PC connectivity.

Additional protection that should be provided to VoIP software is standard virus protection and network intrusion detection at the domain boundary between the user device and the VoIP server domain for critical servers, such as the call control server or the message server. Firewalls, in particular application-aware firewalls, offer a significantly enhanced level of perimeter security, and it is recommended that they be deployed in conjunction with any VoIP implementation going across domain boundaries.

It is imperative that IT management evaluate software products and risks, as well as vendor product strategies and internal skill levels, to obtain a properly implemented security solution for VoIP software within your organization. In regards to the VoIP return on investment, if background research is not performed in the process, you may find that the purchased system is incompatible with the identified risks, thereby increasing costs beyond the initial budget.

8.1.10 Log Consolidation and Unusual Pattern Log Analysis

Voice security software has typically focused on specific areas of control, such as call traffic, or on point solutions that address only one type of platform and the management tools for voice platforms on managing the application layer for stand-alone systems only. The limited data available and proprietary nature of voice operating systems has made voice security—in particular, log consolidation and unusual pattern log analysis—a particularly difficult task. Call accounting systems provide the means to analyze call records and provide reports that identify suspicious call patterns, heavy usage, and, most important, toll fraud; but they offer only a small window into systems management. Alternative sources of information provided by voice security software are required to monitor system access information such as alarm and event data, and usage activity is required to gain a complete picture of overall system activity. The key voice security software requirements for the management of enterprise voice networks include the ability to support complex voice networks, provide 24×7 monitoring, and perform end-to-end analysis. Voice network security software should also provide robust reporting that provides control summary and detail information down to the transaction level; the ability to integrate and complement corporate standards; the ability to identify security issues and then close the loop to secure vulnerable areas; and immediate event notification to appropriate personnel such as the system administrator or network operations.

You also need to ensure that the machine that is logging has not been compromised, providing the attacker with the ability to erase the intrusion event by deleting the logs. Redundant logging can also be used to provide additional work for attackers. Where possible, an external log machine should be installed, such as behind a Network Address Translation (NAT) box where even nonlocal IPs can't see it. You can also use serial interface to connect to the logger, to exclude network connections so that the logger cannot be accessed for reading or resetting except through an interface that is not available via internal or external network.

8.1.11 Stay Up to Date with Your Network Equipment Vendors

An important part of VoIP infrastructure security is to keep an ongoing relationship with your VoIP equipment vendor to keep up with the latest security knowledge base related to their product, such as discovered security holes in their hardware and subsequent patches or remediation techniques, to mitigate or eliminate these risks within your environment and help you build defenses against the attacks or close the vulnerabilities. Your vendor is a rich source of information about the latest security alerts and product patches related to their products.

8.1.12 Stay Up to Date with Your Software Vendors

Specialized VoIP applications from vendors such as 3Com, Alcatel, Avaya, Cisco, and Nortel for VoIP servers and IP PBXs generally run on off-the-shelf server computers and on standard operating systems such as Windows, Linux, and Unix. As IP devices, their products have standard TCP/IP stacks with vulnerabilities and are susceptible to denial-of-service (DoS) or other attacks common to the IP networks and devices. In addition, applications that typically require a significant amount of patching for security holes and bugs, such as Microsoft Internet Information Server (IIS) and Apache Web server, are commonly used on VoIP servers. If your VoIP solution is dependent on Windows, you also inherit the risk that you have a heavily targeted operating system as part of the voice part of your converged infrastructure. Attackers typically target Windows rather than PBXs for the development and use of exploit tools, so your level of risk has increased by expanding the use of this operating system to another part of the network that is normally without this risk. Because the risk of attack is generally much higher to software than hardware, it is even more important to keep in contact with your software vendor for its knowledge of discovered security holes in software and subsequent patches or remediation techniques to mitigate or eliminate these risks within your environment and help you build defenses against the attacks or close the vulnerabilities.

8.1.13 Turn off Modem Support when Not Needed

Turning off modem support when it is not needed is a basic security practice that is often overlooked. This will prevent unnecessary risk from untrusted and/or unauthorized parties accessing your network.

8.1.14 Create a Well Educated Security Team

Part of a good security infrastructure is a well trained security team and a security-aware employee and contractor base. It is important to have thorough, in-depth, ongoing education for your security team in that they will most likely be educating the rest of the company and are the de facto go-to people for issues of security. With the proliferation of security news in the press and great online educational sites such as the SANS Institute[1] and CERT,[2] many of the general populace will "know more than enough to be dangerous" when they come to you for a question, concern, or technical review. It is important for the integrity of the security team, the solutions they deliver, and the policies they develop and enforce that they are well-educated in security and can hold their own on any topic related to security. The stakes are different for someone whose job now focuses on his or her knowledge of security. Various general and specialized security certifications are also available that will add to both the credibility and education of the security team.

8.1.15 Perform Security Incident Postmortems

It is important to go back and review a security incident for the lessons learned after it has occurred. Postmortems should be used as a mechanism to make improvements and to move your team forward, not as a mechanism to decide who to blame for the incident. Questions that need to be answered during a postmorten include the following:

- How did the intrusion occur?
- How could it have been prevented?
- How could it have been detected earlier, before it did too much damage?
- How could the users and the security team react better, to reduce the damage?
- What roles were not covered well, and which were?
- Was every action/anomaly that was observed logged as it occurred?

- Were incident logs exported to a secure server and backed up to mitigate the risk of tampering from the attacker?

- Was the reporting tool effective in correlating the incident data from the log data?

- Were the logs protected and handled in a manner that is legally admissible in court?

8.1.16 Implement Policy Management

Static policy configuration is no longer adequate, and network configurations may need to change throughout a day, week, or month. Policy servers are designed to remove you from these types of network configuration details. Policies are the rules and criteria for the devices, applications, and users of your network that can take effect at certain times of the day or days of the week, essentially doing custom configuration on the fly, which is a great improvement over manual configuration.

A structured database for holding the information about each policy is stored in a repository on the policy server. The policy console, the policy server, and policy clients communicate with one another by using a high-level protocol called Common Open Policy Service (COPS). COPS is an IETF standard that uses TCP to communicate policy information. In some cases, configuration proxies are used as an alternative to COPS to extend the useful life of the current network devices. Client policy management software makes it possible to create and change the user profiles for the users of a file server with a user-friendly graphical user interface, so that creating and changing policies looks and feels like other administrative tasks you already have in place. The policy server software converts its policies into actions to be taken at specified times or under certain conditions through the use of policy agents. The policy server pushes instructions to policy agents, which translate the policies into local device-specific configuration commands so that the actions are conveyed as configuration instructions to real devices in the network, such as switches, routers, and firewalls.

For reasons of usability and security, the policy repository will use a standard directory structure to store its information. Policy repositories will tie into existing enterprise directories to improve the consistency of the administration. Policy repositories are compatible with the Directory-Enabled Networks (DEN) schema, so they interface well with the directory services of the major vendors, such as Microsoft Active Directory, Novell NDS, Siemens X.500 Directory, and Sun Directory Services, and in the case of remote users, Lightweight Directory Access Protocol (LDAP) for remote communication administration. The policy servers provide the ability to maintain a uniform level of security because they work from the same central administrative directory as the rest of your network management.

8.2   PBX Network

8.2.1   Internal Control and Audit

In addition to VoIP audits, more organizations are seeing the benefits of offering security expert audits packaged with a converged solution to ensure internal control. Any new converged platform also needs to address existing PBX hacking methods, such as toll fraud. It also needs to be secure between Time Division Multiplexing (TDM) circuits (e.g., modem dial-in and the existing IP network); no signaling data path must exist between the two media. The audit should also ensure that new applications such as Web-enabled contact centers are not an open opportunity for hacking into the system via the Internet. To be thorough, PBX security audits should include a review of switches, voice-mail and automated attendants, wiring closets, microwave towers, test equipment such as line monitors and data scopes, and system documentation such as wiring schematics. An in-depth evaluation of PBX switch—and overall telecommunications—security involves many areas and at a minimum should include the following:

- Physical access security
- Logical access security
- Remote dial-in access security
- Automated attendant security
- Voice-mail security
- Trunk lines security
- Facility test call access code
- Backup and off-site rotation controls
- Disaster recovery/business continuity planning

There are numerous templates for PBX audit checklists available on the Internet, such as those found on the ISACA[3] or on the All.net[4] and Audit.net[5] Web sites.

8.2.2 Eliminate Unnecessary Modems

Uncontrolled and available modems pose a tremendous security risk and "back door," or both unauthorized internal access to external networks or computer systems and unauthorized external access to internal networks or computer systems. Uncontrolled means that if a user has a modem and can connect to other computer systems without going through the firewall, then the purpose and function of the firewall have been circumvented, and the corporation no longer controls what information is moving from its internal network to systems outside its network. The entire security infrastructure can be circumvented in that files can now pass into the corporate network without going through router access controls, the intrusion detection system (IDS), or the firewall.

The most effective way to control policies prohibiting unauthorized modems is through the use of telephone firewalls. Telephone firewalls have an analogous purpose in the telephone network in that they monitor and control traffic entering and exiting the network via the telephone system. There is also a risk of someone coming from outside the corporate network and using that modem to access internal networks or computer systems. Data can be transferred in both directions once a computer is connected via modem to a remote computer, providing an attacker with the ability to put files on an internal computer and possibly on the network without your permission. This risk can also be mitigated through the use of a telephone firewall.

8.2.3 Securing the IP PBX

A PBX is nothing more than a private switching system whose primary functions are to save costs and facilitate office communications. Criminals target PBXs to either gain access to the rest of the network or for fraudulent reasons, such as free long-distance and teleconferences, calling card scams, and using the PBX as a diversion to cover their tracks. As VoIP increases in popularity, traditional data IP computer networks are becoming more integrated with PBXs and, in many cases, security on the PBX is still somewhat of an afterthought. Attackers often take advantage of the fact that VoIP-enabled companies still focus most of their security resources on the data network rather than voice to gain access to the data network through the unsecured PBX. The bottom line is that in a converged network environment, you need to focus your security efforts equally on both your voice and data networks.

8.2.4   Remote Access

As discussed in Chapter 7, well-known standards are used by companies to set up your PBX for maintenance, and these can be easily compromised by an attacker. Remote maintenance procedures and functions inherent in the PBX system are some of its most commonly exploited risks. Attackers may take advantage of the fact that maintenance of a PBX can take place remotely by the vendor of the PBX or a third party contracted to maintain the system. For example, a vendor may instruct the company to install a modem on the maintenance port, giving the vendor a way to always have access to the PBX remotely. If attackers or disgruntled employees are able to acquire the phone number of the modem, they can simply log in using a default account or brute force their way into the PBX using an automated script to guess the administrative login and password and, if successful, they can literally taken control of the company's voice communications. As discussed previously, these numbers could be acquired rather easily by the attackers through social engineering, dumpster diving, or wardialing.

Telephone firewalls are one of the most comprehensive solutions to secure all remote-access activity, in that they can block access to all numbers and grant access to just those who need it, as well as detect wardialing attempts and prevent a rogue modem from getting set up within the company. Authentication solutions such as a smart card or token-based password authentication on the PBX (e.g., RSA SecurID by RSA Security Incorporated) can be an effective part of the security solution.

8.2.5   Accounts and Passwords

Most PBX systems have multiple accounts active on the system that allow various administrative access to the system for performing various tasks and configuration. Some systems have numerous default accounts enabled when they are first set up. There is also the possibility that when these default accounts are not documented, they will be overlooked when the administrator changes the passwords or disables the various accounts, leaving the system wide open to unauthorized access. A manufacturer may leave accounts open on purpose so it can dial in to change or configure certain features without having to request access from the administrator. Once the attackers have acquired the account number, they will dial in to the PBX and attempt to log in to the system. Default passwords are the most commonly exploited vulnerability on a PBX. Default passwords must be documented and tracked and verified for change, and newly created passwords must adhere to good password management practices and security (described elsewhere in this book).

8.2.6 Physical Security

It is just as important to address the physical security of a PBX as it is its logical security. PBX systems are particularly vulnerable when attackers have access to the system and could compromise, crash, physically damage, or destroy the PBX. They could also pull lines, change lines, or even monitor calls that are being placed. Some PBXs are configured using a dumb terminal that is attached directly to the PBX and may even be left logged into, so no username or password is required to start making changes to the configuration. If physical access were gained to the attendant console, the intruder would virtually have control of all lines coming through the system by accessing maintenance features, controlling call routing, making configuration changes, and setting up conference calls, and may also include an override. The PBX and attendant console should be locked away where only authorized, trusted employees have access to it. Employees who have access to the room should be required to log all of their activities in a shift log, and the shift log should be reviewed daily. This will not only help with maintaining system security, but it will also ease troubleshooting if an administrator makes a mistake.

8.2.7 Combating PBX and Voice-Mail Vulnerabilities

It is vital that voice assets are secured properly in a converged network environment. If an IP PBX system is compromised, any external security measures in place on the data network are useless because the attacker already has access to the network. The most critical assets to secure on the traditional voice side of the network are the PBX and voice-mail systems. Some of the best practices that must be considered to mitigate the security risks to these systems (identified in Chapter 7) are as follows:

- The best front line of defense against PBX social engineering is training your employees, operators, and administrators to verify the identity of any person requesting information about communication or data systems. In this regards, a good policy should include the following:

    - Verifying the employee number of the person asking for information

- Mandatory callbacks, which would ensure that the person has a company telephone number before any information is released
- A list of employees who are allowed to dial in remotely, ensuring that unauthorized employees or possible attackers do not obtain dial-in information
- Always contacting a supervisor if someone asks for usernames, passwords, or dial-in numbers

- The strongest countermeasures to social engineering are both policy compliance training and telecommunications fraud-monitoring software.

- The best way to mitigate your risk of being exploited by dumpster divers is by shredding company proprietary information, as well as locking up dumpsters, compactors, and other trash facilities.

- Wardialing remains one of the most popular ways to gather potential PBX targets to compromise. Because thousands of calls from a wardialer can last only a few seconds, switches that can detect whether someone is wardialing an exchange should be used. These types of systems have the ability to fire off an alert if a predetermined amount of short calls takes place or more than a preset number of extensions are dialed in order.

- Telephone firewalls are one of the most comprehensive solutions to apply to all remote-access activity. They can detect wardialing attempts and prevent a rogue modem from getting set up within the company by blocking access to all numbers and granting access to just those who need it.

- The use of good password practices, such as choosing a secure password, auditing passwords, changing passwords regularly, and changing default passwords, is very important to maintaining the integrity of the PBX.

- Another good practice is to install a smart card or token-based password authentication on the PBX, such as RSA SecurID by RSA Security Incorporated.

- Never patch or update system software without verifying its authenticity through the vendor. Additionally, after the software patch has been loaded, make sure that it didn't add any users or modify security settings.

- The Achilles heel of the PBX system and its security are its databases, because if they are compromised, the entire switch has been compromised.

- Disabling remote access to these features is the best way to protect them from being accessible to attackers. If remote access is required by a vendor for maintenance, then a strong password policy should be in place, as well as an access control list and telephone firewall.

- Dial-In System Access (DISA) abuse is another risk to the PBX. The only sure way to protect against this type of abuse is to disable the DISA feature all together. If this is not possible, the following best practices can be used to mitigate this risk:

  - The PBX should never answer with a steady tone; this is the first thing an attacker will listen for, because a steady tone simply lets the attacker know that he has what he is looking for and just needs the code. This also leaves you vulnerable to automatic dialing programs. The system should be configured to have no tone at all or to use a voice message to confuse or slow a potential attacker.

  - Programming a delay of more than four or five rings into the PBX before answering will appear to be a line that won't answer and will cause most attackers to move on to the next line.

  - Use an unlisted number instead of 800 or toll-free lines for DISA where possible.

  - All authorization codes given to employees who have been fired or who left the company should be deleted on the day they leave. You should also make sure to delete any codes that were used by guests or during testing on the PBX.

  - PBXs should be configured to block or limit the placement of international phone calls when they are not needed.

  - If possible, DISA should only be allowed during normal business hours.

- Choose a code in the same way you would a password, change it often, and disallow multiple attempts. The general rule of thumb is that the PBX program should be programmed to log and drop the caller if someone cannot type in the right access code after two failed attempts.

- Bills and logs associated with the line should always be monitored for a sudden, abnormal increase in calls. If this occurs, the feature should immediately be disabled, all codes should be changed, and checks should be made to make sure the PBX has not been compromised any further.

- The override feature may be used by an attacker to monitor a line or possibly harass the parties on the call, and when possible, should be disabled.

- Never transfer incoming calls outside of your PBX, and always verify employee ID numbers or supervisor contacts of any employee making an unusual request. If a technician ever asks for assistance in testing a line, always ask to call the technician back. A technician will rarely need assistance in diagnosing line problems.

- A voice-mail system is only as secure as the least secure gateway into the network. Voice mail, faxes, e-mail messages, video mail, and other services can now occur in a single telephone call and require increased security such as long passwords or voice firewalls.

- A voice-mail policy guideline needs to be written and enforced by any company and is only as good as the ability to enforce it. When developing a policy, many decisions will have to be made. A good voice-mail policy must consider the security levels, system administrator user levels, and superuser levels needed and be based on the capabilities of the voice-mail system, the connections and type of connections to the network, intranet, extranet, WAN, Internet, and the data network.

8.3   VoIP Network

8.3.1   Separate VoIP Traffic

VoIP traffic should be separated from other data traffic, and the VoIP components should be well isolated through the use of multiple layers. IP PBXs and VoIP servers should be isolated at Layer 2, on their own virtual LAN (VLAN), isolating them from lots of other traffic on the enterprise LANs, especially chatty protocols, multicasts, and broadcasts, which can cause delay, jitter, and some level of DoS attack. VLANs shouldn't be depended on entirely for VoIP security, but rather used as a good way to keep traffic separated without two physical networks. IP PBXs, VoIP servers, and gateways can also be separated on their own LAN in different Windows domains from other servers. When deploying VoIP, switches should be used and all hubs eliminated because switched networks are more secure than shared hubs and can help prevent hackers from just plugging in a device and capturing data. The use of private IP addressing inside your enterprise for the VoIP devices will also reduce the risk of DoS attacks. For example, as recommended in RFC 1918, the IP addresses in the private address ranges 10.0.0.0/8, 172.16.0.0/12, and 192.168.0.0/16 prohibit Internet-based attacks because private addresses are not routable on the Internet.

8.3.2 Encrypt VoIP Traffic

Sniffers are readily available as free software on the Internet, and many come with source code that can be easily modified for tapping. VoIP packets are vulnerable to snooping, which is as simple as an IP packet monitor sniffer placed on the network watching for VoIP packets and storing them on a hard drive for playback later. The encryption of the audio portion of the call is the only way to avoid this simple form of wiretapping. The effects of end-to-end delay and decline of the Mean Opinion Score (MOS) for the call must be considered before using on-the-fly encryption and decryption. Encryption is a component of the H.323v2 standard and is also available on many VoIP gateways but rarely used or typically one of the last features implemented.

Unencrypted IP voice over an unmanaged or public network should be avoided. End-to-end encryption and decryption of VoIP calls should be used wherever possible. However, when used for VoIP traffic over a public network, MOS testing for voice quality is important in device selection and calibration because many encryption devices are still too slow. The most cost-effective way to do VoIP encryption and decryption is to use an IPSec VPN, which lets you connect from one computer to another over any network. IPSec is standardized, widely implemented, supported by many vendors, and interoperates well among devices. IPSec VPNs offer assurance that the data cannot be observed by anyone capturing network packets, assurance that the data has not been modified, and device authentication. It is important to use monitoring tools to show you how VPN settings are affecting performance for different traffic types.

8.3.3 Isolate IP PBXs and VoIP Servers on a VLAN

VLANs are a good way to create "logical" networks on the same physical media. Restricting traffic flow between functional areas can help prevent sniffing and spoofing and isolate them from lots of other traffic on the enterprise LANs, especially chatty protocols, multicasts, broadcasts, and some level of DoS attack. IP PBXs and VoIP servers should be isolated at Layer 2 on their own VLAN.

8.3.4 Put Chatty Protocols on Their Own VLAN

Chatty network protocols such as DECnet, IPX, and NetBIOS (and their vulnerabilities) should be put on their own VLAN separate from the network with VoIP traffic. This not only reduces the risk of exploitation introduced by the vulnerabilities associated with these protocols but also the delay and jitter that can result from the chatter.

8.3.5 Isolate Voice Traffic on a Separate VLAN

VoIP traffic should be isolated onto a separate VLAN. Switches can be configured so that the voice and data traffic are carried on separate VLANs. Many IP phones contain a data port that enables computers to be plugged into the phone, which, although convenient for voice-mail and other functionalities, can be problematic from a security standpoint where separation of voice and data are required. If your IP phone supports both switching and bridging, then you could use the data port and the VLAN with the risk. VLANs are not a panacea for VoIP security, but rather a good way to keep traffic separated without two physical networks.

8.3.6 Unified Management Infrastructure

Unified policy management gives organizations the ability to allocate network resources according to business objectives and the tools to easily provision, enforce, and verify network policies across the network. In addition, it enables bandwidth management, QoS, application-level security, IP address management, dynamic configuration, fault management, provisioning, performance analysis, modeling, planning, and access-level security. Unified management solutions are composed of best-of-breed products that can be used either individually or as a tightly integrated solution set. Unified policy management can integrate campus, wide-area, and telephony management to create a unified network infrastructure that can enhance your ability to manage the complexities of converged network security.

8.3.7 Avoid Use of Voice on Shared Ethernet Segments

Avoiding the use of voice on shared Ethernet segments will prevent the threat of untrusted networks/segments, such as spoofing, sniffing, and unauthorized access.

8.3.8 Build Separate DHCP Servers

As with voice and data VLAN separation, separate DHCP servers should be used. For example, one DHCP server should be used for voice (IP phones) and one for data (PCs).

8.3.9 Put VoIP Devices on Different Windows Domains

When VoIP devices are used in Windows, IP PBXs, VoIP servers, and gateways should be separated on the LAN by putting the devices in different Windows domains from other servers. If they need to be in a Windows domain, they should be given their own domain. These core VoIP components should have different authorized administrators with different permissions and users from the other computers on your network.

8.3.10 Beware of Shared Drives

Computer viruses are spread through unsecured shared drives and by e-mail attachments. Although they are convenient and easy to use, it is best to avoid using shared drives if at all possible. Limiting access to read-only or ensuring that only authenticated users are granted full access will reduce your risk when you have to use shared drives.

8.3.11 Use Private IP Addressing Inside Your Enterprise

As per RFC 1918,[6] you should use private IP addressing inside your enterprise: 10.0.0.0/8, 172.16.0.0/12, and 192.168.0.0/16 to reduce external DoS attacks. Using IP addresses in the private address ranges 10.0.0.0/8, 172.16.0.0/12, and 192.168.0.0/16 prohibits Internet-based attacks, because private addresses are not routable on the Internet.

8.3.12 Use Switches Instead of Hubs

A switch is essentially an intelligent hub, deciding which ports to retransmit packets on rather than transmitting the packets to every connected device. Switched networks are more secure than shared hubs and can help prevent hackers from just plugging in a device and capturing data. Security risks aside, hubs are rather inefficient devices, and network congestion quickly becomes an issue as more devices compete for the limited network bandwidth available with a hub-based infrastructure. If your organization is deploying VoIP, you should eliminate all of your hubs. Because a hub retransmits to every other device connected to the hub, including other workstations and PCs, it is trivial to either connect a sniffer to another port on the hub or install a software-based sniffer on one of the other connected devices.

When switches are used, the other connected devices no longer see everyone else's traffic, making sniffers placed on a switch much less effective at collecting and analyzing traffic. However, switches have special ports, usually called *monitoring* or *mirroring ports*, because of the need for network and traffic monitoring that operates like a miniature hub. These parts receive a copy of any packet passing through the switch, making them an ideal place for a sniffer. Although switches provide a little more defense against traditional sniffing attacks than hubs, advanced sniffers such as *dsniff* are capable of sniffing in switched environments.

8.3.13 Secure the Voice Gateway

The voice gateway is a network device that provides media and, in some cases, signaling conversion between the IP network and the PSTN. The voice gateway's critical role in the VoIP infrastructure predicates the implementation of good security. The voice gateway server component should be configured with both virus protection and HIDS and should provide DoS protection on the IP interface. It must support strong authentication for any configuration or software upgrades and should support a media protocol authentication on a per-packet basis. Encryption of both call setup information and media should also be supported. It should be configured to route calls only via the call control server.

A basic level of security is afforded to networking systems that are deployed in a VoIP network. However, this is not absolute protection; it is possible to be subjected to internal attacks from a malicious user or simply from a media gateway that unknowingly continues to send RTP traffic after a call is complete. Increasingly, the need arises for more sophisticated tactics to detect and address VoIP security. Session controllers such as those from Netrake[7] address these issues with the following features:

- Rogue RTP detection
- DoS prevention/flood prevention
- Session admission control
- Topology hiding
- Header stripping

- Intrusion prevention

- Theft-of-service prevention

- The Federal Bureau of Investigation administers the Communications Assistance to Law Enforcement Act (CALEA), which was passed by Congress in 1994. CALEA was a response to advances in digital communications. It was a way for law enforcement and intelligence agencies to go beyond old-fashioned phone taps and listen in on mobile phone calls, pagers, the Internet and any other form of electronic messaging that might be used by enemies of the state. CALEA made the phone companies and pager companies and Internet companies responsible for building into their equipment the capability to tap all types of communications on the order of a judge or—in the case of foreign surveillance—of the U.S. Attorney General. Every telephone switch installed in the U.S. since 1995 is supposed to have this surveillance capability.

- Firewall and NAT traversal

8.3.14 Maintain Strong Security on All VoIP Servers

Whereas in the traditional voice network one has to tap into a specific circuit to eavesdrop, in an IP network any equipment connected to the corporate LAN can identify, store, and play back the VoIP packets that traverse that LAN. VoIP network security is not a network issue, but a server issue. Because there is no such thing as a secure IP network—only secure computing—one must secure the telephones, conversations, computers, and servers. Set up a chain of trust for authentication (encryption), control access (passwords and firewalls), encrypt for privacy, and employ call accounting software to establish accountability. Securing a VoIP network against employee abuse is achieved by assigning accountability. Distributing call accounting reports and charging back for usage, as in a telephone switch network, will accomplish this goal. Physical and network access to any VoIP server that is used to authenticate users, that controls access to the public telephone network, or that contains potentially confidential information should be locked down and treated with the same security precautions as any server containing a confidential database.

The common security requirements of confidentiality, integrity, and availability can be especially critical for network servers, in particular within a converged network environment. File servers and database servers are often used to store your organization's most important information resources, which must be kept strictly confidential. Servers may also store information that is used for management decisions or customer billing, which demands a high level of integrity. Authentication servers store information about user accounts and passwords; any disclosure could compromise all of the information on all of the hosts in your network.

Public servers (such as Web servers) can be a major component in the strategy your organization uses to represent itself to the public, so the integrity of the information on those servers is critically important. Servers used by customers for electronic commerce must be available and reliable to prevent loss of revenue.

8.3.15   Filtering on All Segments

Filtering on all segments will limit devices in unknown segments from connecting to IP PBXs, which will in turn prevent threats such as spoofing, sniffing, and unauthorized access from untrusted networks/segments.

8.3.16   Filter All Traffic

Egress filtering should be used to filter packets leaving the network, and only the packets with valid source IP addresses that belong to the network should be allowed to pass. This will prevent attacks that rely on the ability to send spoofed source packets to cover their tracks and create bogus network traffic. This precaution will greatly reduce the chance that the network will be used as the source of a spoofed attack. Most routers have the option to check the source address of a packet against the routing table to ensure that the return path of the packet is through the interface on which it was received.

Antispoofing filtering should be applied on your border routers for ingress and egress routes. This is important because once a spoofed packet is allowed past the border, catching it is nearly impossible. Depending on the direction of traffic, it is egress when leaving the network or ingress when entering the network. Most routers have built-in antispoofing features. Ingress filtering will filter packets attempting to come into the network, and egress filtering should be applied to outbound traffic from the network to prevent spoofed packets from leaving the network. It is also advisable to make sure your upstream provider also applies ingress and egress filtering. Only noncustomer network block source address traffic should be accepted by the customer network, and the Internet service provider's edge router should only accept traffic with source addresses belonging to the customer network. Filtering for spoofed packets makes it much harder to covertly stage a DDoS attack, but it does not eliminate the potential for attacks.

However, the elimination of spoofed attacks will limit the threat to direct attacks from valid hosts, making it easier to track the source of attack and, therefore, increasing your chances of stopping it.

Several blocks of IP address space that are reserved for private networks should never be used as a source IP address. You should filter all RFC 1918 and Reserved IP address space using access control lists on firewalls or routers. The following list of Private RFC 1918 and Reserved Source IP Addresses should be filtered because these IP addresses should never be a source IP:

```
0.0.0.018                Historical Broadcast
10.0.0.0/8               RFC 1918 Private Network
127.0.0.0/8              Loopbacks
169.254.0.0/16           Link Local Networks
172.16.0.0/12            RFC 1918 Private Network
192.0.2.0/24             TEST-NET
192.168.0.0/16           RFC 1918 Private Network
224.0.0.0/4              Class D Multicast
240.0.0.0/5              Class E Reserved
248.0.0.0/5              Unallocated
255.255.255.255/32       Broadcast
```

Spoofed attacks commonly use these address blocks. These are not valid source IP addresses to be used over the Internet, and the IP address blocks should be filtered. Blocking these IP addresses will help prevent spoofed packets that are not checked by upstream providers from entering the network.

8.3.17 Deploy Firewalls

Firewalls should be deployed on both the telecommunications and data networks at the same time in order to eliminate the largest number of threats. After both networks are protected, the next layer of security can be addressed. As the movement toward convergence of the data and telephone networks progresses, the two separate layers of defenses will combine to become a single set of layers.

Firewalls simplify security management in VoIP networks by consolidating security measures at the firewall gateway, instead of requiring all of the endpoints to maintain up-to-date security policies. The firewall is the ultimate bottleneck for network traffic because, when properly designed, no traffic can enter or exit the LAN without passing through the firewall, which provides a central location for deploying security policies and takes an enormous burden off the VoIP network infrastructure. Unfortunately, this also comes at a price in that in complicates several aspects of VoIP, most notably dynamic port trafficking and call setup procedures.

In VoIP and other media streaming protocols, this information can also be used to distinguish between the start of a connection and an established connection. There are two types of packet filtering firewalls: stateless and stateful. *Stateless firewalls* retain no memory of traffic that has occurred earlier in the session. *Stateful firewalls* do remember previous traffic experience and can also investigate the application data in a packet. Thus, stateful firewalls can handle application traffic that may not be destined for a static port. Streaming voice traffic generally flows on dynamically assigned, even UDP port numbers greater than 16,384. The ports to be used in a phone conversation are specified in the call setup flows (i.e., in the H.323 or SIP transactions). To tie a port number to a conversation, a firewall needs to look for the port numbers inside the call: setup frames. Without stateful inspection, a firewall would have to open a wide range of UDP ports (which does not help when it is trying to block undesirable traffic). Firewalls generally add some delay, because they hold each frame while they look at it, deciding what to do. Most VoIP traffic travels across UDP ports. Firewalls typically process such traffic using a technique called *packet filtering*. Packet filtering investigates the packet headers of each packet attempting to cross the firewall and uses the IP addresses, port numbers, and other flags contained therein to determine the packet's legitimacy.

In many cases, firewalls deployed in VoIP networks must employ not only standard firewall practices but also the added responsibility of brokering the data flow between the voice and data segments of the network. All voice traffic emanating from or traveling to PC-based IP phones would have to be explicitly allowed in if no firewall was present, because RTP uses dynamic UDP ports, of which there are thousands, and this results in a security nightmare. Therefore, PC-based phones should be placed behind a stateful firewall to broker VoIP media traffic; otherwise, a UDP DoS attack could compromise the network by exploiting any number of open ports. There are other cases where firewalls should be used to provide a barrier between voice and data sectors, such as the following identified by Halpern (2002):[8]

- PC-based IP phones (data) require access to the (voice) segment to place calls, leave messages, and so on
- IP phones and call managers (voice) accessing voice mail (data)
- Users (data) accessing the proxy server (voice)
- The proxy server (voice) accessing network resources (data)
- Traffic from IP phones (voice) to the call processing manager (voice) or proxy server (voice) must pass through the firewall, because such contacts use the data segment as an intermediary

Although fiscally and physically unacceptable for most organizations, because one of the prime benefits of VoIP is voice and data sharing the same physical network, firewalls should also be used to broker traffic between physically segmented traffic where possible: one network for VoIP, one network for data.

8.3.18 Use a Telecommunications Firewall

Telecommunications firewalls are placed between the telephone company's central office and the company's PBX system so it can monitor every call on every telephone line used by the company and ensure that it can block intrusion attempts before damage can occur. The telecommunications firewall has many capabilities, including the following: (1) enforces the security and usage policy, (2) characterizes call traffic, (3) logs call progress, (4) controls the remote maintenance facility and port access, (5) reports resource utilization, (6) detects fraud through use and analysis of logs, (7) monitors trunk line and equipment status and utilization, (8) provides emergency alert notification and 911 location, and (9) provides record logs that are invaluable for audits and investigations. Specific to its use for security, telecommunications firewalls allow for the following:

- The development, storage, and execution of telecommunication security policies
- Identification of the types of calls occurring, and taking actions based on the call type and the time of day, to include controlling after-hours use of fax, voice, and modem lines
- Restriction of fax lines to fax traffic only

- Prevention of outbound or long-distance calls from lines that are intended for inbound use only, such as in a call center, to protect intellectual property and corporate data by restricting inbound and outbound modem activity

- Blocking of harassing or malicious inbound calls

- Blocking of long-distance and modem calls on unused lines

- Logging of calls, termination of calls, sending pager alerts, sending e-mail alerts, and triggering Simple Network Management Protocol (SNMP) traps in real time

- Serves both functions analogous to data firewall and intrusion detection systems by monitoring and controlling the type of traffic allowed onto each telephone line, according to predefined rules and identification of potential intrusions of the telephone network, and warns the administrator if any traffic violating the policy is detected on the telephone lines

- Automatic logging of the intruder attempt calls, terminating the call, notifying the system administrator that a policy has been violated, and logging the time, source, and destination of the intrusion attempt

- Enforcement of policies regulating the use of modems and telecommunication resources

- Distributed administration and control

Although current PBX systems may have the capability to be configured to collect data similar to that collected by a telecommunications firewall, they lack user-friendly tools for data manipulation and reporting. In a large corporate network with various types of PBX systems, the collection of this data becomes labor intensive and costly. It is difficult to consistently configure PBXs in this type of environment to monitor and control the types of calls going across all of the company's phone lines.

Telecommunications firewalls are an invaluable tool to protect, detect, respond to intrusions, and secure the back door in a converged network environment. Because of its capabilities and placement, the telecommunication firewall can be used to centrally manage all corporate telecommunications resources. With some straightforward data analysis and reporting tools, it can also be shown that the telecommunications firewall can possibly pay for itself by aiding in the identification of fraud and abuse of telecommunications resources. One of the more popular telecommunications firewalls currently available on the market is the TeleWall@Telecommunications Firewall (www.securelogix.com/firewall).

8.3.19 Intrusion Detection and Prevention Systems

Network Intrusion Detection Systems (NIDS) provide a comprehensive, real-time warning system that proactively identifies and isolates real security attacks. Rather than looking at one frame at a time, as with firewalls, NIDS usually don't add delay because they look across a broad collection of frames flowing in either direction, looking for patterns that signify an attack. These are known as *attack signatures,* and patterns of packets and their flows for many network attacks have been identified. NIDS will raise events when they detect attack signatures. A technique known as *NIDS shunning* can block traffic from sources that have generated traffic that matches one of the attack signatures. Once an attack signature is detected on a LAN segment, shunning can be used to dynamically change the Layer 3 filtering configuration of a network device to drop all additional traffic from the source on that segment. Resets can be used to tear down a TCP session that triggers an attack signature. NIDS shunning could be used to block UDP flood attacks sourced from the data segment against the voice segment. However, this tool must be deployed carefully because, like any automatic detection system, you need to be aware of false positives.

Both firewalls and NIDS are typically used collaboratively on the network for security. Research as to the capabilities of NIDS with respect to recognizing and protecting VoIP traffic for both the call setup and the actual call flows should be done before implementation. You should also examine how much delay and jitter a firewall adds to the VoIP traffic that it passes. By intelligently placing intrusion detection sensors on a network, monitoring for security violations or misuse that originate from inside or outside the network can be achieved and can enhance the organization's firewall protection. NIDS generally reside in switches.

VoIP systems pose several new challenges to NIDS because the VoIP employs multiple protocols for call management (e.g., SIP) and data delivery (e.g., RTP). Also, VoIP systems are distributed in nature and employ distributed clients, servers and proxies; the attacks to such systems span a large class, from DoS to billing fraud attacks. Additionally, the systems are heterogeneous and typically under several different administrative domains.[9]

Host-based Intrusion Detection Systems (HIDS) can also be a good addition to a layered defense, in addition to NIDS, and can prevent as well as detect attacks. HIDS work to detect attacks originating within individual computers. They can detect intrusions by monitoring the actions within a computer, such as file accesses or login attempts. This involves identifying attacks as they occur, by the sequence and timing of bytes or system calls (the attack signature) or by correlating information in event logs. HIDS can also use heuristic techniques to prevent or detect attacks as they occur.

8.3.20   Monitoring and Logging

Logging information about user calls may be useful for billing or tracking purposes, but these logs can also become a target for hacking. If this kind of information becomes compromised, it can be a serious concern to the organization. Servers containing VoIP call log information need to be physically secured. These servers should not be running any unneeded services or daemons. In addition, logins to the VoIP servers should be strictly limited. Many operating systems, such as Windows and most varieties of Unix, have logging built in. Several services, including FTP, HTTP, mail, and countless others, also provide logging features. Logging provides audit trails that assist in the detection of intrusive activities. These audit trails provide information and evidence of attacks or penetrations. In terms of security, the logging should contain the following information: the date and time of the event, the unique identifier of the user or program generating the event, the type of event, the success or failure of the event, and the origin of the request.

8.3.21   Router Security

Routers provide services that are essential to the correct, secure operation of the networks they serve. The compromise of a router can lead to various security problems on the network served by that router or even on other networks with which that router communicates. In general, well-configured secure routers that at a minimum have secured their remote access (i.e., SSH), disabled unneeded IP services, and use and closely manage their access control lists (ACLs) and logging will greatly improve the overall security posture of a network. The *NSA/SNAC Router Security Configuration Guide, Version 1.1* cites five primary areas of focus[10] for router security best practices that include:

1. Create and maintain a written router security policy that includes the identification of who is allowed to log in to the router and who is allowed to configure and update it, and that outlines the practices and management for logging

2. Comment and organize offline master editions of your router configuration files and keep the offline copies of all router configurations in sync with the actual configurations running on the routers for use in diagnosing suspected attacks and recovering from them

3. Implement access lists that allow only those protocols, ports, and IP addresses required by network users and services, and that deny everything else

4. Run the latest available General Deployment IOS version

5. Test the security of your routers regularly, especially after any major configuration changes

The NSA/SNAC Router Security Configuration Guide, Version 1.1 (2004) also includes the following Router Security Checklist, which will be invaluable in checking the overall security of the routers within your converged network environment:

- Router security policy written, approved, distributed

- Router IOS version checked and up to date

- Router configuration kept off-line, backed up, access to it limited

- Router configuration is well-documented, commented

- Router users and passwords configured and maintained

- Password encryption in use, enable secret in use

- Enable secret difficult to guess, knowledge of it strictly limited (if not, change the enable secret immediately)

- Access restrictions imposed on Console, Auxiliary (AUX) ports, and Virtual TTYs (VTYs)

- Unneeded network servers and facilities disabled

- Necessary network services configured correctly (e.g., DNS)

- Unused interfaces and VTYs shut down or disabled

- Risky interface services disabled
- Port and protocol needs of the network identified and checked
- Access lists limit traffic to identified ports and protocols
- Access lists block reserved and inappropriate addresses
- Static routes configured where necessary
- Routing protocols configured to use integrity mechanisms
- Logging enabled and log recipient hosts identified and configured
- Router's time of day set accurately, maintained with NTP
- Logging set to include consistent time information
- Logs checked, reviewed, archived in accordance with local policy
- SNMP disabled or enabled with good community strings and ACLs

8.3.22 Use Existing Firewalls/IDS to Highlight Attempted Attacks

Whether or not the VoIP traffic rides a traditional data network or a segregated, voice-only network, the IP network is vulnerable to all of the same IP security concerns as well as VoIP-specific issues. When deploying a VoIP infrastructure that uses an existing IP infrastructure, it is important not to forget about and to utilize existing security within the IP network to enhance the security of the VoIP infrastructure and the converged network as a whole. In this regard, it is particularly important to use existing firewalls/IDS to highlight attempted attacks.

8.3.23 Use Authentication to Exclude Requests from Unknown Hosts

Authentication helps prevent ID spoofing, toll fraud, unauthorized access, and so on that can result from unknown hosts that would otherwise have access to your network.

8.3.24 Use Dedicated VoIP Firewalls to Prevent Attacks

Firewall security for voice differs greatly from firewall security for data. Most firewalls today are designed to protect data networks, but data firewalls cause latency in real-time communications such as voice and video transmissions. As a result, many voice transmissions travel unprotected from port to port to prevent delays and disruptions, which leaves the door open for hackers and DoS attacks. Currently, most VoIP traffic occurs in private networks, but as it transitions to the public Internet, more firewalls geared specifically toward VoIP will be needed.

8.3.25 Use a VoIP-Aware Firewall/IDS to Monitor Untrusted VoIP Traffic

H.323 relies on dynamic port allocation that requires the firewall to do some type of packet inspection so that the return ports can be allowed. Without specific H.323 handling, a firewall would not necessarily allow the negotiated port.

8.3.26 Security Issues with the Use of H.323, SIP, H.235v3, MGCP, and MEGACO/H.248

VoIP systems currently use either a proprietary protocol or one of two standards: H.323 or the Session Initiation Protocol (SIP). Neither of these protocols has become dominant in the market yet, so it often makes sense to incorporate components that can support both. The H.235 security recommendation may also be used. In addition to SIP and H.323, there are also two further standards: Media Control Gateway Protocol (MGCP) and MEGACO/H.248, which may be used in large deployments for gateway decomposition and to ease message handling with media gateways or to implement terminals without any intelligence. As you implement security best practices within your VoIP environment, it is important to understand the security role and interrelation of H.323, SIP, H.235, MGCP, and MEGACO/H.248.

H.323

H.323 is a multimedia conferencing protocol, which includes voice, video, and data conferencing, for use over packet-switched networks. All H.323 traffic is routed through dynamic ports, with the exception of the "Q.931-like" H.225, which is particularly problematic for firewalls within a H.323 VoIP network. The ad hoc method of securing channels does not lend itself well to a static firewall configuration, particularly those cases of stateless firewalls that cannot comprehend H.323 traffic because these simple packet filters cannot correlate UDP transmissions and replies. This will necessitate punching holes in the firewall to allow H.323 traffic to traverse the security bridge on any of the transient ports it might use. Of course, this action will result in an unacceptable security risk because it would leave 10,000 UDP ports and several H.323-specific TCP ports wide open. In order to solve this firewall problem in the VoIP environment, vendors are developing firewalls that can understand the VoIP and H.323 environment so they can read H.323 messages and dynamically open the correct ports for each channel as the protocol moves through its call setup process.

It should be noted that even with a VoIP-aware firewall, parsing H.323 traffic will not be a trivial matter because H.323 traffic is encoded in a binary format based on ASN.1. Special code generators are needed because ASN.1 has a level of complexity that does not allow for simple parsing tools or uncomplicated scripts to decode the traffic, which is not available on traditional packet filtering firewalls or even simple stateful firewalls. Although the complex parsing necessary to discern the contents of the ASN.1-encoded packets can be done in the newer VoIP-aware gateways, it will introduce latency into an already speed-sensitive system.[11] The H.323 call setup protocol in VoIP systems can be a problem with NAT because the external IP address and port specified in the H.323 headers and messages themselves are not the actual address/port numbers used internally. The "setup next" procedure used by each protocol within the H.323 suite, such as H.225 setting up H.245, is disrupted by this process. The firewall must be able to understand this process, and the VoIP application receiving these H.323 communications must receive the correct translated address/port numbers. The NAT device must be able to reconfigure the addresses in the control stream in order for H.323 to traverse a NAT gateway. NAT requires that H.323 traffic be read and modified so that the correct address/port numbers are sent to each of the endpoints.

H.235 provides comprehensive security architecture for the H.323 protocol suite, and as discussed elsewhere in this section, it provides several different alternatives for authentication and encryption. Because the use of Transport Layer Security (TLS) in a predefined port 1300 establishes the Call Connection Channel, it is considered to be a constraint because it is predefined and no other security mechanisms can be used for the first connection. Dynamically allocated sockets are used by H.323-compliant applications for audio, video, and data channels requiring a firewall to allow H.323 traffic through on an intelligent basis. An H.323-enabled firewall requires an H.323 proxy or the ability to snoop to determine which dynamic sockets are in use for H.323 sessions and allow traffic during the period when the control channel is active.

SIP

The Session Initiation Protocol (SIP)—RFC 3261 uses elements called *proxy servers* to help route requests to the user's current location, authenticate and authorize users for services, implement provider call-routing policies, and provide features to users. SIP also provides a registration function that allows users to upload their current locations for use by proxy servers.[12] SIP runs on top of several different transport protocols and has five security mechanisms that are currently supported: TLS, HTTP Digest, IPSec with IKE, manually keyed IPSec without IKE, and S/MIME. Some of them have been built into the SIP protocol directly, such as HTTP authentication, whereas others have alternative algorithms and parameters. The 3rd Generation Partnership Project (3GPP) (www.3gpp.org) provides a tool for selecting which security mechanisms to use between two entities, but RFC 3261 does not provide any mechanism agreement options.

There are incompatibility issues regarding the use of SIP with RTP and NAT. In a SIP environment, stateful firewalls are required and must be able to monitor SIP traffic to determine which RTP ports are to be opened and made available to which addresses. Although similar to that required for firewalls within an H.323-based network, the call setup and header parsing is much simpler. NAT inhibits SIP's registration and communication mechanisms because within a SIP-based network, the SIP proxy is normally outside the NAT device, which requires innovative solutions to resolve. A SIP proxy is typically used within the corporate LAN with the telecommuter connect from outside, at the telecom side from the clients (i.e., smaller companies connecting to this proxy for VoIP service), or as two administrative domains that are connected and both have their own proxy. The communication bartering between a proxy server that deals with global IP addresses and a machine that has been assigned a private network address results in requests, receiving requests, and handling RTP problems within this type of SIP architecture.

There are also issues that NAT presents to the call setup process. A caller only needs to send an INVITE message to initialize a session from behind the NAT. NAT will preserve the outgoing port number, which is 5060, but the response communication could be disturbed. SIP is protocol independent, and if it is implemented over UDP, the proxy server must send the UDP response to the address and port on which the request arrived. By using a standard practice of routing SIP communication over TCP, the response from the callee will come over the same channel as the original INVITE, and NAT will not present a problem.

Another problem with SIP occurs during the registration process and incoming calls. When users contact the registrar, they provide their IP address as their reachable address, and this is stored in the location server, which is also their private IP address. The proxy server deals only with global IP addresses, so when a message comes in for a particular address, it will attempt to route this call to the registered address, but in the public domain. This address is unreachable for the proxy server, and the connection will be refused. The delicate manipulation of IP addresses and an expansion of the responsibilities of the SIP proxy server will help mitigate this risk associated with SIP and incoming calls associated with the registration process.

Because SIP is a session control protocol, IP addresses and TCP ports appear in the body of the protocol. It is therefore imperative to secure the traversal of SIP and its signaled sessions through NAT and the firewall. If you use NAT on your network, translation of internal network addresses to external addresses will be required. SIP operations requires that the body not be encrypted when a NAT device is used for translation because this imposes a security constraint that also results in difficulties in NAT and firewall traversal.[13] SIP encryption is based on the use of Pretty Good Privacy (PGP) and, to be useful, requires Public Key Infrastructure (PKI). Encryption does not cover many critical headers, such as the "To" and "From" headers, and the PGP-based model assumes advance knowledge of the recipient's public key and does not work with forwarding.[14] When HTTP digest authentication is used for both request and response, a reflection attack may occur. When the same shared secret is used in both directions, an attacker can obtain credentials by reflecting a challenge in a response back in request. The risk from this attack can be eliminated by using different secrets in different directions or through the use of PGP.[15]

The challenge-response mechanism used within SIP does not work with forking, and only B1 rings in cases where challenge-response is used. *Forking* is when A calls to B and the call invitation request forks to B1 and B2, which are different terminals that user B has specified they are using, with the result being that both terminals B1 and B2 are ringing. The use of signed requests without challenge-response would require the use of PKI to solve this problem.[16]

H.235v3

H.235 is the security recommendation for the H.3xx series systems. In particular, H.235 provides security procedures for H.323-, H.225.0-, H.245-, and H.460-based systems. H.235 is applicable to both simple point-to-point and multipoint conferences for any terminals that utilize H.245 as a control protocol. The scope of H.235 is to provide authentication, privacy, and integrity for H.323-based systems. H.235 provides a means for a person, rather than a device, to be identified.[17] Before we discuss H.235v3, it is important to discuss the baseline functionality of H.235v2, because H.235v3 inherits some of its baseline functionality.

Version 2 of H.235 superseded H.235 version 1 that was approved in November 2000. With the establishment of the H.235v2 standard, the ITU-T took a step toward interoperability by defining different security profiles. This was necessary because the standard does not mandate particular features. The defined profiles provide different levels of security and describe a subset of possible security mechanisms offered by the considered security standard H.235 as mandatory. They comprise different options for the protection of communication (e.g., by using different options of H.235), which results in different implementation impact. H.235v2 provides several security improvements over H235v1, such as elliptic curve cryptography, security profiles (simple password-based and sophisticated digital signature), new security countermeasures (media antispamming), support for the Advanced Encryption Algorithm (AES), support for back-end service, object identifiers defined, and changes incorporated from the H.323 implementer's guide. Several security profiles are defined to support product interoperability, and they are defined in annexes to H.235v2 as follows:

- **Annex D:** Shared secrets and keyed hashes
- **Annex E:** Digital signatures on every message
- **Annex F:** Digital signatures and shared secret establishment on first handshake, afterward keyed hash usage
- **Annex G:** Support for H.235v3, Annex G describes a profile to support Secure Real-time Transport Protocol (SRTP). Version 3 of H.235 supersedes H.235 version 2, featuring:
  - A procedure for encrypted DTMF (touch-tone) signals
  - Object identifiers for the AES encryption algorithm for media payload encryption
  - The Enhanced OFB (EOFB) stream-cipher encryption mode for encryption of media streams
  - An authentication-only option in Annex D for smooth NAT/firewall traversal
  - A key distribution procedure on the RAS channel

- Procedures for more secure session key transport and more robust session key distribution and updating
- Procedures for securing multiple payload streams
- Better security support for direct-routed calls in a new Annex I
- Signaling for more flexible error reporting
- Clarifications and efficiency improvements for fast-start security and for Diffie-Hellman signaling, along with longer Diffie-Hellman parameters
- Changes incorporated from the H.323 implementer's guide

- **Draft H.235v3 Annex H:** RAS Key Management, which amends the basic idea formulated in H.235 Annex H for key management negotiation during the RAS gatekeeper discovery phase.

- **H.235v3 Annex I:** H.235 Annex D for Direct-Routed Scenarios. Both Annex D and Annex F are to be used in gatekeeper-routed environments.

Annex I of H.235 enhances the Baseline Security Profile (Annex D) as well as the Hybrid Security Profile (Annex F), with the option to be applied in an environment where direct-routed calls (endpoint to endpoint) are performed using the gatekeeper for address resolution.

MGCP

There are no security mechanisms designed into the MGCP protocol. The informational RFC 2705 refers to the use of IPSec (either AH or ESP) to protect MGCP messages.[18] Without this protection, a potential attacker could set up unauthorized calls or interfere with ongoing authorized calls. Besides the usage of IPSec, MGCP allows the call agent to provide gateways with session keys that can be used to encrypt the audio messages, protecting against eavesdropping. The session key can be used later on in RTP encryption, as described in RFC 1889,[19] which may be applied. Session keys may also be transferred between the call agent and the gateway by using the Session Description Protocol (SDP)—RFC 2327.[20] Issues with security constraints of MGCP and the related standards are similar to the presented constraints of H.323 and SIP, with the exception that according to RFC 3525, security issues should be solved by using external security protocols and especially IPSec.[21] If IPSec is required to be used, it is assumed that, up to a point, the security issues of IPSec determine the security constraints for MGCP.

MEGACO/H.248

MEGACO (RFC 3525)[22] is a gateway control protocol that recommends security mechanisms that may be underlying transport mechanisms such as IPSec. H.248 actually requires that implementations of the H.248 protocol implement IPSec if the underlying operating system and the transport network support IPSec. Implementations of the protocol using IPv4 are required for the interim AH scheme. H.248 states that implementations employing the AH header shall provide a minimum set of algorithms for integrity checking using manual keys that are compliant to RFC 2402.[23] MEGACO assumes a manual key management, and the replay protection as defined for IPSec may not be used in this scenario because the sequence number in the AH may overrun when using manual key management, since rekeying is not possible.

The H.248 protocol header defines an optional AH header in the interim AH scheme. The H.248 header fields are identical to those of the SPI: SEQUENCE NUMBER and DATA fields as defined in RFC 2402. With the exceptions of the calculation of the Integrity Check Value (ICV), the semantics of the header fields are the same as the transport mode of RFC 2402. Protection against eavesdropping and replay attacks is not provided by the interim AH scheme. H.248 states that implementations employing the ESP header shall provide a minimum set of algorithms for integrity checking and encryption as compliant to RFC 2402. These implementations should use IKE (RFC 2409) to permit more robust keying options. Implementations employing IKE *should* support authentication with RSA signatures and RSA public key encryption.[24]

At the voice gateway, which interfaces with the PSTN, disallow H.323, SIP, or MGCP or MEGACO/H.248 connections from the data network. Use strong authentication and access control on the voice gateway system, as with any other critical network management component. Strong authentication of clients toward a gateway is often difficult, and access control mechanisms and policy enforcement are the rule of thumb.

8.3.27 Network Address Translation (NAT)

Network Address Translation (NAT) is a powerful mechanism that can provide security and network scalability. NAT allows the several endpoints within a LAN to hide behind the same IP address. This provides a layer of security from outside attackers because the individual internal IP is hidden. NAT also allows practically an unlimited number of private addresses to be routed across the Internet using one public IP.

Typical implementations of NAT would be more correctly called Network Address and Port Translation (NAPT) because strictly speaking, in NAT the outgoing IP headers are changed from private LAN addresses to the router's global IP. In NAPT, the TCP/UDP headers are converted. For the purpose of this discussion, the term NAT will really refer to NAPT. The benefits of NATs come at a price. Because NATs hide the real IP of one end of the communications path, certain kinds of traffic become problematic. This design has significant implications for VoIP, especially for inbound traffic where a call comes into the network. This situation is similar to sending a letter to an address where several people with the same name live. Complicating this situation are the problems introduced when trying to secure the media by using IPSec to encrypt the traffic.

At first glance, the easiest way to get around these problems is to eliminate NATs entirely, but NATs have benefits and are used extensively in most networks. It is unlikely that network owners would be able or willing to abandon these benefits.

NAT and VoIP Issues

Two problems that impact VoIP interoperability with firewalls and NATs are QoS and how incoming calls are to be received by a system behind the firewall or NAT. Both of these problems are nonprotocol-specific issues.

Incoming Calls   Regardless of the protocol used for call setup, NAT presents considerable difficulties for incoming calls. To facilitate these incoming connections, a firewall administrator might leave several ports open, but these might be exploited by attackers. Alternative solutions exist without such holes, including application-level gateways and firewall control proxies. NAT creates even more tribulations for incoming calls. Complicating this problem further is the need for any IP application, including VoIP, trying to make a connection from an external network to a system behind a NAT device, to know the internal system's external IP and port number assigned by the NAT device. This NAT device maintains a table of internal addresses and ports to external addresses and ports. This makes the inbound call nearly impossible because the source doesn't know the recipient's address/port.

NAT and QoS   NAT can degrade QoS in a VoIP system by introducing latency and jitter. NAT devices can also act as a bottleneck on the network, because all traffic is routed through this single node. VoIP is highly sensitive to QoS issues, especially latency. A NAT device needs to be able to process traffic with a minimum time penalty, even one that would go unnoticed with simple data traffic. This isn't just a network issue but a processor problem as well.

VoIP requires the NAT device to delve into the packet to determine the traffic's validity. This increases the exposure to a DoS attack. A flood of call request packets, whether from an increase in call volume or a malicious attack, can have a tremendous impact on the processor. NAT compounds this issue because the payload of the packet must then be changed at the application level to correspond to the NAT-translated source or destination address and ports.

The other aspect of VoIP that puts a strain on a firewall CPU is the small but plentiful number of RTP packets that make up a VoIP conversation. Network devices are rarely concerned with the size of a packet, but because each packet must be inspected, a large number of packets can stress the firewall. The throughput of a firewall may support 100 Mbits/sec (based on the assumption of large packets), but would likely be overloaded by a flood of small 50-byte packets long before the 100 Mbits/sec rate is reached. Once again, NAT complicates matters because RTP encapsulates the source and destination IP addressing in Layer 7 headers, which have to be found and changed.

NAT and RTCP

In addition to the need to "NAT-correct" the RTP traffic, the control side of the voice link has to be processed as well. RTP traffic is dynamically assigned an even port number in the range of UDP ports (1,024 to 65,534). The RTCP port controlling this stream must flow through the next-highest-numbered odd port. Again, opening a vast number of ports by default would leave the system highly exposed. That requires firewalls to be aware of not only which ports media is using, but the control port as well. For this reason, only stateful firewalls that can process H.323 and SIP should be incorporated into the network to open and close ports. Typical stateful inspection firewalls employing NAT assign new port numbers at random, and this breaks the pair relationship of RTP and RTCP ports. The translation of IP addresses and ports by NAT and the relationship of RTP and RTCP ports is also problematic for the reception of VoIP packets. If the NAT router does not properly process the traffic, the new addresses/ports will not correspond to those negotiated in the call setup process. In this scenario, the VoIP gateway may not properly deliver the RTP packets. The problem is exacerbated if both call participants are behind NATs.

Call Setup Considerations with NAT

The call setup process corresponds to lifting the receiver and dialing in a traditional system. Users may be annoyed with a setup process that requires more than a few seconds. Several factors can influence the setup time of a VoIP call, including network topology, the location of both endpoints, and the presence of a firewall or NAT. Additionally, the degree or lack of authentication and other data security measures and the choice of protocol used to set up the call can dramatically alter the time necessary to prepare a VoIP connection.

Mechanisms to Solve the NAT Problem

Real-time communication protocols such as H.323 and SIP are extremely sensitive to NAT because these protocols include IP addresses in their messages. If integrity protection is used, the NAT device would have to be a trusted intermediate host so that the integrity sum could be recalculated. This is not recommended, but there are mechanisms available to address the NAT problem. STUN, TURN, and ICE are protocols that all try to deal with the problems introduced by NAT. An alternative approach is to employ Application-Level Gateways (ALGs). A firewall and ALG can work together to parse and understand H.323 or SIP and dynamically open and close the necessary ports. When NAT is employed, the ALG needs to open the VoIP packets and reconfigure the header information to correspond to the correct internal IP addresses on the private network, or on the public network for outgoing traffic. Finally, the ALG can configure the RTP and RTCP ports to support proper VoIP traffic.

8.3.28 VoIP Proxies

VoIP proxies and firewalls take on the processing burden for multimedia traffic. These devices tell the enterprise firewall which ports to open and how to handle other issues such as NAT. A working group within the IETF is developing a protocol known as the Middlebox Communication Architecture and Framework (MIDCOM) to enable such devices to better integrate with traditional firewalls. In this section, we first describe the concepts of firewall control proxies and middleboxes and then discuss the use of internal and external proxies within the VoIP environment.

Firewall Control Proxies and Middleboxes

ALGs are a type of firewall that is designed to manage specific protocols. Where a simple firewall looks at just the source and destination address and port, an ALG looks deeper into the packet. Each ALG has its own set of parameters that are used to control its operation.

One drawback to ALGs is that this additional firewall function adds to the latency and throughput slowdown of all traffic through the firewall. This is aggregated and then compounded by the VoIP call volume. One way to alleviate this malady is by placing an extra device, a middlebox, outside the firewall that performs many of the functions associated with an ALG. The middlebox, sometimes called a Firewall Control Proxy (FCP), is considered to be a trusted system that parses incoming VoIP traffic and instructs the firewall to open or close ports as required by the VoIP traffic. Offloading this function provides some isolation between the technology specifics of VoIP and the firewall. This means that if the VoIP protocol changes, the firewall does not have to change. Additionally, the processing requirement is removed from the firewall, alleviating that overhead.

Of course, the firewall must be configured for control by the FCP. A second drawback is that even though the firewall is isolated from VoIP protocol changes, the middlebox would have to be replaced every time the protocol for VoIP changed. Finally, the middlebox requires protection from attackers. Because the middlebox is a trusted system, if an intruder took control of the FCP, he or she could open any ports in the firewall and then gain access to the private network, so the middlebox may require a firewall.

Internal and External Proxies

Proxy servers are another solution to the firewall/NAT traversal issue. The proxy comprehends both the private network and the public sector, and its placement has a major impact on VoIP operations. Acting as a middleman, the proxy receives messages from the outside and relays them to the correct internal address and vice versa. This model does require that an H.323 gatekeeper or SIP registrar must communicate with the proxy so that addresses can be bound correctly. The importance of this communication means that it is imperative that the phone's whereabouts and user are kept up to date.

One radical approach to using proxy servers to resolve the firewall/NAT issue places them completely outside of the firewall and NAT. This approach is specific to SIP, and although it is more complex than other solutions, it offers the benefit of not requiring change to the internal structure of the firewall/NAT system. This solution is particularly attractive for users who do not have control over the firewall or cannot afford the expensive hardware required in other approaches. Even though this solution does not require changes to the existing internal network, it is also the most complex and least secure mechanism.

The outside proxy architecture works well during call setup but does require workarounds when dealing with the actual RTP media traffic if NAT is used. Because NAT translates and controls the ports in the media traffic, it is essential that the user inside the NAT send the first packet and that the return RTP packet comes in on the same port pair. To provide this function, a bidirectional RTP can be used. Bidirectional RTP functions like TCP, but over UDP ports and without a handshake. All traffic goes to the same port in both directions. Additionally, the requirement that the machine behind the NAT sends the first RTP packet is satisfied by the use of an "ACTIVE" or "PASSIVE" tag in the SDP. During setup, if a proxy detects that the machine it is representing is behind a NAT, it tags its communication as Active, meaning this machine must initiate communication. This solution is fine unless both communicants are behind a NAT. In this case, an RTP forwarding device (RTP translator) must be integrated into the architecture between the proxy and one of the endpoints. This device will act as a middleman, translating active traffic to passive so both endpoints can work in active mode.

RTP translators are inefficient bottlenecks. They also need to be bundled with the proxies, because no standardized protocol is available for communication between the two or even simply addressing the RTP translator. Finally, the RTP translator can introduce significant latency. There are other sources of QoS degradation. A decrease in voice quality will result if both traffic streams must traverse the same port. This means that the pseudo-simultaneous delivery of voice at both ends (facilitated by the bidirectional RTP) will not be possible. Another QoS impact comes from results if TCP is needed to traverse the firewall (all UDP ports blocked), and then even a small amount of packet loss will cause a downturn in QoS.

The placement of the proxy server completely outside the private network is often not by choice. Usually, this is a limitation placed on a user (e.g., a caller from home might need to register with an SIP proxy at their place of business). Security must be considered for this connection and the proxy. The proxy and RTP translator must be protected by a firewall and standard security measures. Because these devices act as middlemen in multiple conversations, their compromise would be a disastrous breach of security. Also, a persistent connection between the endpoint and this proxy could be secured in a TLS connection over the recommended SIP over TLS, port 5061. Despite all of these security concerns and constraints and the complexity of their solution, there are steps that will help users and other VoIP clients who do not have control over their network configuration or firewall/NAT administration to increase the security of their systems.

8.3.29 Virtual Private Networks (VPNs) and IP Security (IPSec) in VoIP

VPNs

Virtual Private Networks (VPNs) are tunnels between two endpoints that allow data to be securely transmitted between the nodes. In a white paper on Virtual Private Networking,[25] Pawel Golen stated that most typical VPN-related documents define a VPN as the extension of a private network. Golen believes that this type of definition is meaningless and only characterizes the VPN concept as a determinant of a private network. His point is that the concept of a VPN is still somewhat unclear.

A private network is one on which all data paths are hidden from all except a limited group of people, generally the customers or employees of a company. In theory, the simplest way to create such a private network would be to isolate it entirely from the Internet. However, for a business with remote location needs, this is clearly not a practical solution. Although it is technically possible to create a private network using Frame Relay, ATM, or some other form of leased-line solution, that solution could easily become cost prohibitive. Also, that solution may not even provide the required degree of security needed for the organization's remote-access users. When using leased lines to establish a private network, another consideration to factor into the mix is what happens when (not if) the line goes down. This outage situation would cause all connected nodes in the private network to go "COMM OUT" until the leased line came back up. Clearly, this is not a practical solution either. What if we wanted to share resources on the private network with customers? That would not be possible over a physically separated or isolated network. A remote dial-up server may solve the problem, but then we would have to question the concept of "virtual" in our VPN.

Nowadays, a VPN uses existing infrastructure, public or private. This may encompass the use of both LANs and WANs. The transfer of data over a public network is accomplished by using what is referred to as a *tunneling technology* (further explained as follows) to encrypt data for secured transmission. The preferred definition of a VPN, as used in this text, is "a dedicated private network, based on use of existing public network infrastructure, incorporating both data encryption and tunneling technologies to provide secure data transport."

There are several good reasons why organizations choose to use VPNs. Data security is undoubtedly a prime consideration, but we must also understand the risks and corresponding trade-offs involved when using remote-access technologies. For example, if a company can provide remote access to its employees, it is an assumed benefit that they will be able to access the network and be productive regardless of where they happen to be physically located when connecting to the VPN. The risk of providing such remote access is that if the data the employees are attempting to transmit or access is not secured in some fashion, it could become compromised through a variety of means. This may or may not be a devastating issue to that particular company, but each organization must make such determinations as a matter of deciding the level of risk they are willing to take for providing a remote-access capability.

Most companies today choose to use a technology that fully supports data protection. This generally means that in order to gain access to the company network, a remote-access user must first authenticate to the remote host server. Additionally, once an authenticated connection is established, the client and host machines jointly establish a shared secure channel (often referred to as *establishing a tunnel*) from which to communicate. The advantage of using this secure channel for communication is that all subsequent data packets transmitted and received are encrypted in order to minimize the risk of data compromise.

The current VPN growth that has emerged in the industry in the last couple of years is mostly centered on IP-based networks such as the Internet. One of the major problems of VPN technologies is that there are a wide variety of implementation styles and methods, which cause a lot of confusion when trying to develop a strategy for their use in a company. Currently, the following methods of VPN implementations are in use:

- Router-to-router VPN-on-demand "tunnel" connections between sites

- Router-to-router VPN-on-demand multiprotocol "tunnel" connections between sites over an IP network

- Router-to-router VPN-on-demand encrypted session connections between sites

- Firewall-to-firewall VPN-on-demand "tunnel" connections between sites

- Firewall-to-firewall VPN-on-demand "tunnel" connections between sites
- Client-to-firewall IP tunnel VPN facilities
- Client-to-server IP tunnel VPN facilities
- Client and server firewall implementation with full VPN capabilities
- Dedicated VPN "box"
- Nonsecure VPNs

There can be a bewildering array of VPN choices and solutions available to the customer, depending on need and fiscal resources. With these implementations, however, there is the need to interoperate with existing protocol suites in network environments that are used in companies. Nearly all companies use more than one protocol suite to transport network information (such as IP, IPX, AppleTalk, SNA, DECnet, and many others). Although many routers can offer a site-to-site VPN capability, the capability is often limited to IP-only traffic or, if non-IP, it must be a routable protocol with a routing layer and that layer must be implemented on the router. In sites where nonroutable protocols such as NetBEUI and LAT are used, bridging must be used, and it is not implemented as a VPN connection in most bridge/router combinations.

Tunneling is a technique that leverages an internetworked infrastructure (such as the Internet or a corporate WAN) to transfer data from one network over another network. The tunneling process consists of payload encapsulation, transmission, decoding of packet data, and routing to an endpoint. The data (referred to as a *payload*) to be transmitted can be sent in packets that are built using another protocol. The data is wrapped with a header that provides routing information. Instead of sending a packet produced by the originator in its original form, a tunneling protocol encapsulates the packet with a new packet header (thus, wrapping the old header in the new header). The additional header provides routing information so the encapsulated payload can traverse the intermediate internetwork. The encapsulated packets are then routed between established tunnel endpoints over the internetwork.

The logical path through which the encapsulated packets travel the internetwork is referred to as a *tunnel*. Once the encapsulated frames reach their destination on the internetwork, the packet is decoded into its original form and forwarded to its final destination. Tunneling technology has been around for some time. Current tunneling technologies include PPTP,

L2TP, and IPSec. Older tunneling technologies such as SNA tunneling over IP and IPX tunneling for Novell will not be discussed here. Each of the current technologies is discussed later in this section.

Tunnels can be created in one of two ways: voluntary or compulsory. With voluntary tunnels a user or client computer can issue a VPN request to configure and create a tunnel. In this case, the user's computer is a tunnel endpoint and acts as the tunnel client. For compulsory tunnels, a VPN-capable dial-up access server configures and automatically creates a tunnel. With a compulsory tunnel, the user's computer is not a tunnel endpoint. The dial-up access server, which sits between the user's computer and the tunnel server, is considered the tunnel endpoint and acts as the tunnel client.

When creating a VPN connection, several security features come into play, including authorization, authentication, encryption, and filtering. Any organization considering implementing a VPN must take each of these features into account during their planning process. We briefly discuss each feature in the following paragraphs.

Authorization

VPN connections are only created for users and routers that have been duly authorized. In most cases, the authorization of a VPN connection is determined by the connect properties for the user account and the organizational remote-access policies. If a user or router is not properly authorized to make such remote-access connections, the server will disable access at that point, and the user will not gain entry to the network.

Authentication

Authentication is a prime concern in the process of connecting remote-access users. Authentication takes place at two levels: machine-level (or certificate-based) and password-level (or user-based). For machine-level authentication, a secure protocol (e.g., IPSec) is used to establish a VPN connection. The machine-level authentication is then performed by forcing an exchange of machine-level digital certificates during establishment of a tunnel. Password-level authentication requires a user to respond to a login prompt by presenting a login ID and password. If either is incorrect, access is denied. Let's look at both types of authentication in greater detail.

Certificate-Based Authentication

This is often accomplished using digital certificates and the SSL protocol. In order to authenticate a client to a server, the client is required to digitally sign a randomly generated piece of data and send both the certificate and the digitally signed data across the network. The server would then authenticate the user's identity and evaluate the digitally signed data. The results of this evaluation would determine whether final access is granted based on the strength of the evidence presented by the user.

Certificate-based authentication is usually preferred to password-based authentication because it is based on what the user has (the private key) as well as what the user knows (the password that protects the private key). These assumptions are valid only if the following conditions are met:

1. Unauthorized personnel have not gained access to the user's machine or password.

2. The password for the client software's private key database has been set.

3. The software requests the password at reasonably frequent intervals.

Packet Filtering

In order to enhance security of the VPN server, packet filtering must be configured so that the server only performs VPN routing. Routing and Remote Access Service (RRAS) filters may be used (only on Windows 2000/XP) for the Internet interface of the VPN. This is sometimes referred to as the "poor man's firewall," and while RRAS greatly expands the system-level security capabilities of Windows 2000/XP Server (by allowing packet filtering based on source and destination IP address and port numbers), it falls far short of the feature set provided with a typical hardware-based router. Where possible, use the hardware solution.

VPN Encryption

In the article entitled "What is VPN Encryption?"[26] the (anonymous) author points out that in order to ensure that your VPN remains secure, it is not enough to simply limit access. Once a user has been authenticated, the data needs to be protected. Data sent through the communications channel will be transmitted in cleartext, which is easily viewed with a packet sniffer. To prevent this, modern VPNs use cryptographic solutions to create ciphertext. This ciphertext is decrypted by the recipient and read as plaintext or cleartext.

Data Encryption

The protocols used to create VPN connections allow encrypted data to be sent over a network. Although it is possible to have a nonencrypted connection, this is not recommended. Note that data encryption for VPN connections does not provide end-to-end security (encryption), but only security between the client and the VPN server. In order to provide a secure end-to-end connection, the IPSec protocol can be used once a VPN connection has been established. See the following section on VPN encryption for a detailed explanation of data encryption over VPN.

For cryptographic solutions, the longer the encryption keys are, the stronger they are. Strength of the crypto solution is measured in bit length. The bit length of the algorithm determines the amount of effort that is required to crack the system using a brute-force attack, where computers are combined to calculate all of the possible key permutations. Currently, some countries have governmental restrictions on encryption strength in a VPN, such as Japan, which may require multiple key lengths in an international tunneling solution.

Two basic cryptographic systems exist today: symmetric and asymmetric. Symmetric cryptography is commonly used to exchange large packets of data between two parties who know each other and use the same private key to access the data. Asymmetric systems are far more complex and require a pair of mathematically related keys. One key is a public version, and the other a private version. This method is commonly used to transmit more sensitive data. It is also used during the authentication process. Both of these systems are discussed in greater detail later in this section.

Many different encryption schemes are available today in the United States. Data Encryption Standard (DES) is more than 20 years old and has been thoroughly tested. It is considered a venerable benchmark encryption scheme. It uses a highly complex symmetric algorithm, but, even with that, it is considered less secure than more recent systems that have appeared. Triple DES uses multiple passes of the original version to increase the key length and strengthen its level of security. Although theoretically possible, an unbreakable algorithm has not been developed to date.

In establishing a standard for using VPNs over the Internet, RFC 2764[27] has defined the basic framework for getting VPNs running across the IP backbones. VPN tunneling means establishing and maintaining the connection of two VPN endpoints. An IP tunnel operates similarly, as an overlay across the IP backbone infrastructure. All of the traffic sent through the IP tunnel is indecipherable to the IP backbone, which, in this scenario, has been used as a virtual link layer. The tunnel over IP establishes a point-to-point link, which is sometimes referred to as a "wire in the cloud." Many different IP tunneling mechanisms, such as Generic Routing Encapsulation (GRE), Layer 2 Tunneling Protocol (L2TP), IPSec, and Multiprotocol Label Switching (MPLS) exist, but IPSec is considered the best choice, whenever there is a requirement for strong encryption or strong authentication.

Although L2TP and PPTP are the main tunneling protocols used in Windows, an IPSec VPN implementation can also be used. IPSec is considered more secure and uses Layer 3 (OSI model) data tunneling with a specific mode set, ESP Tunnel mode. This mode offers strong IP datagram encapsulation and encryption for packets sent over a public IP network. In ESP Tunnel mode, whole IP datagrams are encapsulated and encrypted using IPSec ESP. The IP datagram is then encapsulated with a new IP header, and the new IP datagram obtained is sent over a network. Upon receipt of the L2TP datagram, the recipient processes the data-link frame to authenticate the content and forward the data to the destination site.

VPN VoIP Considerations

VPN tunnels within a corporate LAN or WAN are much more secure and generally faster than the IPSec VPNs across the Internet because the data never traverses the public domain. The IPSec ESP tunnel is a specific kind of VPN used to traverse a public domain, such as the Internet, in a private manner. Because the LAN/WAN VPNs are not scaleable, we will concentrate our focus on the discussion of IPSec VPNs with regard to VoIP. Many implementations of VoIP have attempted to use other VPN techniques, including VPN tunneling within an organization's intranet. This sort of implementation has a physical limit at the size of the private network. Although VPN tunneling will alleviate many of the VoIP firewall issues by tunneling straight through the firewalls, tunneling all VoIP traffic over VPNs will prohibit firewalls from investigating incoming and outgoing packets for malicious traffic, and the centralization of security at the firewall will be lost.

IPSec

We have discussed how a variety of network security devices and software can help keep intruders from compromising a network. Another layer of defense is to protect the data by encrypting the packets at the IP level using IPSec, rendering any VoIP traffic packets that are intercepted unintelligible to the attacker. The IPSec suite of security protocols and encryption algorithms is the standard method for securing packets against unauthorized viewers over data networks and will be completely supported by the protocol stack in IPv6. Unfortunately, it is not as simple as leaving the data encrypted end-to-end in a VoIP environment, because devices such as routers and proxies must be able to read the VoIP packets in order to traffic the packets properly within the network. The process of IPSec encryption and decryption within the network and the lack of QoS in its crypto-engine can also cause an excessive amount of latency in the VoIP packet delivery, leading to voice-quality degradation and reducing the QoS. NIST-sponsored testing has shown that IPSec can be incorporated into an SIP network with roughly a three-second additional delay in call setup times—an acceptable delay for many applications.[28]

In an overview of VPNs,[29] Radoslav Ratchkov points out that:

Originally, IPSec was conceived as an extension for IPv4 with added security features. Now IPSec is an Internet standard framework for the establishment and management of data privacy between network entities, based on the architecture model defined in RFC 2401. IPSec VPNs use the services defined within IPSec to ensure confidentiality, integrity, and authenticity of data communications across public networks. A group of standards starting from RFC 2402 to 2412 and numerous other protocols define all the IPSec-based VPN solutions existing in the industry.

Every IPSec-based VPN solution includes the following components:

- Security associations (SAs)
- Authentication, digital certificates, and signatures
- Nonrepudiation
- Key generation and management
- Data integrity
- Encryption

IPSec operates in a peer-to-peer relationship and refers to SAs similarly to a contract between two parties. The establishment of such a contract facilitates an IP-based conversation between the two communicating parties. Each party must agree on the rules of their conversation by negotiating with their potential peer. Every SA is uniquely identified by an IP destination address, a security protocol (AH or ESP) identifier, and a unique Security Parameter Index (SPI). There are two types of SAs: Internet Security Association Key Management Protocol (ISAKMP) SAs (also known as IKE SAs) and IPSec SAs. The valid authenticating methods used in IPSec are preshared key, Digital Signature Standard (DSS) signatures, RSA signatures, encryption with RSA, and revised encryption with RSA. Nonrepudiation prevents a party involved in a communication from later denying having participated, requires proof of identity of the sender, and is based on digital signatures and mathematical algorithms.

IPSec Protocols

RFC 2401[30] provides the foundations for development of an IP-based security architecture. IPSec provides security services at the IP layer by enabling a system to select required security protocols, determine the algorithm(s) to use for the service(s), and provide any cryptographic keys that may be required to provide requested services. IPSec can be used to protect one or more paths between a pair of hosts, between a pair of security gateways, or between a security gateway (a router or a firewall implementing IPSec) and a host. The set of security services IPSec provides includes access control, connectionless integrity, data origin authentication, rejection of replayed packets, confidentiality (encryption), and limited traffic flow confidentiality. Because these services are provided at the IP layer, they can be used by any higher-layer protocol such as TCP, UDP, ICMP, BGP, and so on.

IPSec uses two protocols to provide traffic security: Authentication Header (AH) and Encapsulating Security Payload (ESP). The AH provides connectionless integrity, data origin authentication, and an optional antireplay service. ESP protocol provides the confidentiality (via encryption) and limited traffic flow confidentiality. It can also provide connectionless integrity, data origin authentication, and an antireplay service. Both AH and ESP are used for access control. Access control is based on the distribution of cryptographic keys and the management of traffic flows relative to the security protocols. These protocols may be applied alone or in combination with each other to provide security services in IPv4 and IPv6.

Each protocol supports two modes: transport mode and tunnel mode. In transport mode, the protocols provide protection primarily for the upper-layer protocols. In tunnel mode, the protocols are applied to tunneled IP packets. IPSec also allows an administrator to control the granularity at which a security service is offered. He or she can create a single encrypted tunnel to carry all traffic between two security gateways or a separate encrypted tunnel for each TCP connection between each pair of hosts communicating across these gateways. IPSec management must incorporate facilities for specifying which security services to use and in what combinations, the granularity at which a given security protection should be applied, and the algorithms used to effect cryptographic-based security. Because these security services use shared secret values (i.e., cryptographic keys, used for authentication and encryption), IPSec relies on a separate set of mechanisms to implement them.

Authentication Header

The IP AH is discussed in RFC 2402.[31] It is used to provide connectionless integrity, data authentication for IP datagrams, and protection against replays. The AH provides authentication for as much of the IP header as possible, as well as for upper-level protocol data. However, some IP header fields may change in transit, and the value of these fields, when the packet arrives at the receiver, may not be predictable by the sender. The values of such fields cannot be protected by AH. Thus, the protection provided to the IP header by AH is occasionally fragmented.

AHs may be applied alone or in combination with the IP ESP. Security services can be provided between a pair of communicating hosts, between a pair of communicating security gateways, or between a security gateway and a host. ESP may be used to provide the same security services, and it also provides a confidentiality (encryption) service. The primary difference between the authentication provided by ESP and AH is the extent of the coverage. Specifically, ESP does not protect any IP header fields unless those fields are encapsulated by ESP (tunnel mode).

Authentication Header Format

The protocol header immediately preceding the AH will contain the value 51 in its Protocol (IPv4) or Next Header (IPv6) field. The following subsections define the fields that comprise the AH format. All of the fields described here are mandatory. They are always present in the AH format and are included in the Integrity Check Value (ICV) computation.

Next Header

The Next Header is an 8-bit field that identifies the type of the next payload after the AH. The value of this field is chosen from the set of IP Protocol Numbers defined in RFC 32328, which defines the "Assigned

Numbers" database managed by the Internet Assigned Numbers Authority (IANA).

Payload Length

This is an 8-bit field used to specify the length of the AH in 32-bit words (4-byte units), minus 2. For the normal 96-bit authentication value and the three 32-bit-word fixed segments, this length field will be set to four. A null authentication algorithm may be used for debugging purposes. This is indicated by a one value for this field for IPv4 or a two for IPv6.

Reserved

This 16-bit field is reserved for future use. It *must* be set to 0.

Security Parameters Index (SPI)

The SPI is an arbitrary 32-bit value used in combination with the destination IP address and AH to uniquely identify the SA for the datagram. SPI values from 1 through 255 are reserved by the IANA for future use. An SPI value of 0 is reserved for local use and *must not* be sent out on the Internet.

Sequence Number

An unsigned 32-bit field, the sequence number field, contains a monotonic (consistently increasing and never decreasing) counter (the sequence number). It is mandatory and always present, even if the receiver does not choose to enable antireplay services. Processing of the Sequence Number field is at the discretion of the receiver, but the sender *must* always transmit this field. The sender's counter and the receiver's counter are initialized to 0 when an SA is established. If antireplay services are enabled (default setting), the transmitted Sequence Number must never be allowed to cycle. What this means is that the sender's counter and the receiver's counter must be reset by establishing a new SA and a new key before packet number (232) is sent on the current SA.

Authentication Data

This variable-length field contains the ICV for the packet. The field length must be an integral multiple of 32 bits. This field may include explicit padding to ensure that the length of the AH is an integral multiple of 32 bits (IPv4) or 64 bits (IPv6). All implementations must support padding. The authentication algorithm specification must specify the length of the ICV, along with the comparison rules and the necessary processing steps used for validation.

Encapsulated Security Payload (ESP)

The ESP header, which is described in RFC 2406,[32] is designed to provide a mixed complement of security services available in both IPv4 and IPv6. ESP may be applied in combination with the IP AH or by itself. Security services can be provided between a pair of communicating hosts, between a pair of communicating security gateways, or between a security gateway and a host. The ESP header is inserted after the IP header and before the upper-layer protocol header (in transport mode) or before an encapsulated IP header (in tunnel mode). ESP is used to provide confidentiality, data origin, authentication, connectionless integrity, an antireplay service (a form of partial sequence integrity), and limited traffic flow confidentiality.

The set of services provided depends on options selected at the time of SA establishment and the placement of the implementation. Confidentiality may be selected independent of all other services. However, use of confidentiality without integrity/authentication (either in ESP or separately in AH) may subject traffic to certain forms of active attacks that could undermine the confidentiality service. Data origin authentication and connectionless integrity are joint services that are offered optionally in conjunction with confidentiality. The antireplay service may be selected only if data origin authentication is selected, and its election is solely at the discretion of the receiver. Traffic flow confidentiality requires selection of tunnel mode and is most effective if implemented at a security gateway, where traffic aggregation may be able to mask true source-destination patterns.

ESP Packet Format

The protocol header that immediately precedes the ESP header will contain the value 50 in its Protocol (IPv4) or Next Header (IPv6) field. The following sections define the fields used in the ESP header format. Optional means the field is omitted if the option is not selected. Whether an option is selected is defined as part of SA establishment. Thus, the format of ESP packets for an SA is fixed for the duration of the SA.

Payload Data

Payload Data is a variable-length field containing data described by the Next Header field. The Payload Data field is mandatory and is an integral (32-bit) number of bytes in length. If the algorithm used to encrypt the payload requires cryptographic synchronization data (e.g., an Initialization Vector), then this data can be carried explicitly in the Payload field.

Padding (for Encryption)

Several factors would necessitate use of the Padding field. If an encryption algorithm is employed that requires plaintext used to be a multiple of some number of bytes (e.g., the block size of a block cipher), then the Padding field is used to fill the plaintext to the proper length required by the algorithm. Padding also may be required, irrespective of encryption algorithm requirements, to ensure that the resulting ciphertext terminates on a 4-byte boundary. Specifically, the Pad Length and Next Header fields must be right-aligned within a 4-byte word. Padding beyond that required for the algorithm or alignment reasons cited previously may be used to conceal the actual length of the payload, in support of traffic flow confidentiality. However, inclusion of such additional padding has adverse bandwidth implications, and it should be used with caution. The sender may add 0 to 255 bytes of padding. Inclusion of the Padding field in an ESP packet is optional, but all implementations *must* support generation and consumption of padding.

Pad Length

The Pad Length field indicates the number of pad bytes immediately preceding it. The range of valid values is 0 to 255, where a value of 0 indicates that no Padding bytes are present. The Pad Length field is mandatory.

8.3.30 IPSec VoIP Considerations

Secure VoIP key management and distribution is included under the umbrella of IPSec in the Internet Key Exchange (IKE) and Internet Security Association Key Management Protocols (ISAKMP). Most implementations will likely rely on some variant of Diffie-Hellman public key exchange.

IPSec can be used to protect both what is being spoken and the identity of who is being spoken to when it uses ESP as the tunneling method. ESP is used to secure the identities of both endpoints of the call, and the voice data being carried by the packets will mitigate against risks such as packet sniffers, voice traffic analysis, and man-in-the-middle attacks. Some protocols will need to continue to rely on their own security features because IPSec isn't always the best fit for some applications.

You should also be aware that connections to single users in low-bandwidth areas such as modems may become infeasible with VoIP IPSec deployments because of the increase in the header size as a result of the encryption and encapsulation of the old IP header and the introduction of the new IP header and encryption information, which decreases the effective bandwidth by as much as 63%.[33] The increase in packet size caused by IPSec does not result in an increased payload capacity.

VPN tunneling with IPSec is incompatible with NAT. There is no way to authenticate the true sender of the data when using IPSec and NAT because NAT traversal completely invalidates the purpose of AH, as the source address of the machine behind the NAT is masked from the outside world. This also results in the inoperability of source authentication in ESP. If both endpoints are behind NAT, IKE negotiation can be used for NAT traversal, with UDP encapsulation of the IPSec packets, and will also be less problematic if one of the endpoints is behind NAT.[34]

8.3.31 Security Association (SA)

The concept of a Security Association (SA) is fundamental to IPSec. Both AH and ESP use SAs, and a major function of IKE is the establishment and maintenance of SAs. All implementations of AH or ESP must support the concept of an SA. The remainder of this section describes various aspects of SA management, the required characteristics for SA policy management, traffic processing, and SA management techniques.

What Is a Security Association?

An SA is a process used to provide security services to the traffic carried by a network. Security services are provided to an SA by using either the AH or ESP. If both AH and ESP protection is applied to a traffic stream, two (or more) SAs need to be created to afford protection to the data stream. For typical, bidirectional communication between two hosts, two SAs (one in each direction) are required.

An SA is uniquely identified by the Security Parameter Index (SPI), the IP Destination Address, and a security protocol (AH or ESP) identifier. As noted earlier, two types of SAs are defined: transport mode and tunnel mode. A transport-mode SA is one between two hosts. In IPv4, a transport-mode security protocol header appears immediately after the IP header and any options, and before any higher-layer protocols (e.g., TCP or UDP). In IPv6, the security protocol header appears after the base IP header and extensions, but may appear before or after destination options, and before higher-layer protocols. In the case of ESP, a transport-mode SA provides security services only for these higher-layer protocols, not for the IP header or any extension headers preceding the ESP header. In the case of AH, the protection is also extended to selected portions of the IP header, selected portions of extension headers, and selected options (contained in the IPv4 header, IPv6 hop-by-hop extension header, or IPv6 destination extension headers).

A tunnel-mode SA is essentially an SA applied to an IP tunnel. Whenever either end of an SA is a security gateway, the SA must be in tunnel mode. Thus, an SA between two security gateways is always a tunnel-mode SA, as is an SA between a host and a security gateway. Note that where traffic is destined for a security gateway (e.g., SNMP commands), the security gateway is acting as a host and transport mode is allowed. But in that case, the security gateway is not acting as a gateway (i.e., not transiting traffic). Two hosts may establish a tunnel-mode SA between themselves. The requirement for any (transit traffic) SA involving a security gateway to be a tunnel SA arises because of the need to avoid potential problems with regard to fragmentation and reassembly of IPSec packets, and in circumstances where multiple paths (e.g., via different security gateways) exist to the same destination behind the security gateways.

For a tunnel-mode SA, an "outer" IP header specifies the IPSec processing destination, plus an "inner" IP header specifies the (apparently) ultimate destination for the packet. The security protocol header appears after the outer IP header and before the inner IP header. If AH is employed in tunnel mode, portions of the outer IP header are afforded protection (as above), as well as all of the tunneled IP packet (i.e., all of the inner IP header is protected, as well as higher-layer protocols). If ESP is employed, the protection is afforded only to the tunneled packet, not to the outer header. In summary: (1) A host *must* support both transport and tunnel mode; and (2) a security gateway is required to support only tunnel mode. If it supports transport mode, that should be used only when the security gateway is acting as a host as in the case of network management.

8.3.32 Enhanced 911 (E911) VoIP Considerations

Special consideration should be given to Enhanced 911 (E911) service communications, because E911 automatic location service is not available with VoIP in some cases. VoIP's packet-switched technology allows a particular number to be anywhere, unlike traditional telephone connections that are tied to a physical location. Calls can be automatically forwarded to their locations for the convenience of the users, but this flexibility severely complicates the provision of E911 service that normally provides the caller's location to the 911 dispatch office.

Many VoIP vendors have workable solutions for E911 service, but government regulators and vendors are still working out standards and procedures for 911 service in a VoIP environment. Lots of work still needs to be done in regard to the IP security risk inheritance for a VoIP risk specific side of the house. You must carefully evaluate E911 issues in planning for VoIP deployment. In the mean time, it is even more important that adequate physical security is in place and ensured to restrict access to VoIP network components to mind the gap. Physical controls are especially important in a VoIP environment and, unless the VoIP network is encrypted, anyone with physical access to the office LAN could potentially connect network monitoring tools and tap into telephone conversations. As alluded to in Chapter 7, there are cases when encryption is used and physical access to VoIP servers and gateways may still allow an attacker to monitor network traffic. Physical securities measures include barriers, locks, access control systems, and guards as the first line of defense. Proper physical countermeasures should be in place to mitigate risks such as insertion of sniffers or other network-monitoring devices; otherwise, the installation of a sniffer could result in not just data but all voice communications being intercepted, which is particularly disturbing in a VoIP E911 environment.

As with any VoIP system, organization security policy that includes VoIP-ready firewalls, other appropriate protection mechanisms, security features, and protocols described elsewhere in this book should be employed and enforced as per policy, standards, and procedures.

8.4   VoIP Phones

The IP phone will typically have numerous parameters that need configuration, as well as software that needs to be maintained. Usually, it will require the following configurations to ensure security:[35]

- Must authenticate itself to the call control server or a proxy server upon initial registration

- Must support strong authentication for any remote configuration or software upgrade

- Should support a configurable access control list to control any incoming traffic (e.g., H.323/SIP, RTP, HTTP, FTP, DHCP)

- (Some) should support an additional Ethernet port for PC connectivity; the IP phones that provide this support should have an implemented switching function combined with virtual LAN functionality

- Should support encryption of both call setup information and media (an additional end-to-end delay on each media packet of approximately 5 ms should be expected)

8.4.1 Set up the IP Phones Securely

Incorrect configurations of IP phones create vulnerabilities that can enable hackers to take control of the phone, redirect calls, or even possibly eavesdrop on conversations. You must change all default passwords and ensure the use of good password creation, management, and enforcement techniques. It is important to identify and properly secure IP phones that contain Web, Telnet, or FTP Servers. Many IP phones and softphones now have Web, Telnet, and FTP servers embedded in them with many associated business benefits and, in the case of internal Web servers, diagnostic gathering and debugging information. Unfortunately, Web servers are susceptible to every known Web-based attack, and some phones require no authentication to get to their Web pages. An attacker who gets through can cause damage by manipulating the call-setup signaling, rebooting the phone, or getting information about calls made from the phone. Lock down the phone and its internal servers as its manufacturer recommends, and continue to update regularly any patches released to correct vulnerabilities as they are identified.

8.4.2 Manage Phone Passwords Carefully

IP phones may be shipped from their manufacturer with no administrative password, which allows easy access for attackers, who can then gain both remote and local administrative access to the phone. As stated previously, find and change all default passwords after implementation. Anytime someone changes departments or leaves the organization, passwords should be changed again.

8.4.3 Limit the Functions Available in Publicly Available Phones

A VoIP phone can be a direct route into your network. This makes those IP phones located in an unprotected lobby of a public building or in a windowless office or closet a significant security risk. Where possible, security should be applied uniformly across all of your VoIP phones. Treat the phone in the lobby as an even greater risk because it is used in a public area. It should be used only for room-to-room calls within the building or local area. Make sure the call routing tables are specifically configured so that toll, long-distance, and international calls are disallowed.

8.4.4 Allow Limited Administrative Access

Create security policies that describe what can be remotely accessed and what permissions are required to obtain remote access. Record all occasions when sanctioned remote access takes place, and make sure alerting mechanisms are in place to provide notifications when unsanctioned access occurs. If Telnet is not the mechanism used for remote access, disable the Telnet server.

8.4.5 Identify Users

IP phones authenticate with their MAC address. If a phone with an unknown MAC address attempts to download a network configuration from the VoIP server, then that IP phone will not receive a configuration package. Some IP phones support simple user authentication, forcing a user to log in to a phone. By providing either a valid password or personal identification number (PIN), the attacker is granted access to the phone and given a custom configuration. Again, the use of strong authentication and good password management will mitigate this threat and reduce the attacks against the VoIP network. Enabling call control logging on the VoIP server will provide records of placed calls and aid in nonrepudiation. Some softphones provide Windows-based authentication, whereas others use a combination of username and password/PIN. A combination of username and password/PIN may be used to identify the user to the VoIP server. This feature lets users access their custom configuration settings after successfully authenticating. It is also recommended to require users to undergo strong authentication if they want to change their custom settings.

8.4.6 Disable Automated Phone Registration

Where possible, disable the Automated Phone Registration feature to prevent rogue IP phones from grabbing a directory number from the IP PBX. Any detected IP phone registration attempts should be rejected if the IP server address used by the phone does not exactly match the source address. Be careful to check default settings that disable strict IP address checking during the registration process.

8.4.7 Maintain Vulnerability Assessments, Antivirus, and Firewall on Softphone Computers

Softphones that run on regular computers are not as resilient as their IP phone counterparts. That fact makes them more susceptible to attacks because of the wide variety of vulnerabilities that can be exploited in the IP environment, to include operating system vulnerabilities, application vulnerabilities, service vulnerabilities, worms, and viruses. Therefore, it is imperative that VoIP administrators implement and maintain vulnerability assessment, antivirus, and firewall software on all installed softphone computers.

8.5 Summary

We have covered a lot of ground in describing best practices that will mitigate the security risks described in the previous chapter to include the need to:

- Craft and implement voice security policies and procedures

- Maintain strong security on all VoIP hosts

- Harden and maintain patches for operating system on voice servers

- Prevent any inbound/outbound VoIP for campus VoIP

- Use existing firewalls/IDS to highlight attempted attacks

- Use VLANs to separate voice from other traffic

- Use authentication to exclude requests from unknown hosts

- Avoid use of voice on shared Ethernet segments

- Deploy dedicated VoIP firewalls to prevent attacks

- Use a VoIP-aware firewall/IDS to monitor all untrusted VoIP traffic

- Put dedicated VoIP firewalls/proxies in front of servers/between VLANs

- Use VPN technology to protect voice calls over untrusted networks and proxies to deflect DoS attacks

- Consider host-based security for voice servers

- Examine logs on voice servers and integrity

- Be aware of the challenges of E911

■ Know the implications and proper use of NAT, proxies, and VPNs in a VoIP infrastructure and the implementation issues associated with the use of H.323, SIP, H.235v3, MGCP, and MEGACO/H.248 in a VoIP environment

Best practices in network security start with a top-down policy that begins with understanding what you need to protect and what you need to protect against. The levels of responsibility need to be understood, and that implies that security is everyone's job, as each employee understands how he or she contributes to the organization. Best practices in network security are more about the what and why of securing the organization's information assets than about the how. The security policy is a formal definition of an organization's stance on security, meaning what is allowed and what is not allowed. IT executives and managers faced with a myriad of technology choices become quickly overwhelmed at the daunting task of securing the enterprise. The first stage in securing your VoIP infrastructure is the implementation of a three-step framework of preparation, organization, and execution of a VoIP security best practices program for your converged network infrastructure.

8.6   **Endnotes**

1.   SANS Institute. (2004). SANS Institute Web page. Retrieved August 9, 2004 from www.sans.org

2.   CERT Coordination Center. (2004). Carnegie Mellon Software Engineering Institute. CERT Coordination Center Web page. Retrieved August 9, 2004 from www.cert.org

3.   www.isaca.org/gir/catDspl.cfm?catID=11&catName=Telecommunications#subcat97

4.   www.all.net/books/audit/pbx/general.html

5.   www.auditnet.org/docs/pbxaudit.txt

6.   Rekhter, Y. et al. (1996). RFC 1918—Address Allocation for Private Internets. Retrieved August 12, 2004 from www.faqs.org/rfcs/rfc1918.html

7.   Netrake. (2004). Netrake Web site. Retrieved August 12, 2004 from www.netrake.com

8. Halpern, J. (2002). IP Telephony Security in Depth. White Paper, Cisco Systems. Retrieved August 13, 2004 from www.cisco.com/warp/public/cc/so/cuso/epso/sqfr/safip_wp.pd

9. Wu, Y. et al. (2004). SCIDIVE: A Stateful and Cross Protocol Intrusion Detection Architecture for Voice-over-IP Environments. Retrieved August 14, 2004 from http://dynamo.ecn.purdue.edu/~sbagchi/Research/Papers/scidive_dsn04_submit.pdf

10. National Security Agency. (2004). NSA/SNAC Router Security Configuration Guide, Version 1.1. Retrieved August 13, 2004, from http://nsa1.www.conxion.com/cisco/guides/cis-1.pdf

11. NIST. (2004). Security Considerations for Voice Over IP Systems—Special Publication 800-58 (DRAFT). Retrieved August 16, 2004 from http://csrc.nist.gov/publications/drafts/NIST_SP800-58-040502.pdf

12. Rosenberg, J. (2002). RFC 3261—SIP: Session Initiation Protocol. Retrieved August 17, 2004 from www.faqs.org/rfcs/rfc3261.html

13. Anonymous, "Voice Over IP Via Virtual Private Networks: An Overview." White Paper, AVAYA Communication, Feb. 2001

14. Ibid.

15. Ibid.

16. Ibid.

17. Javvin Company. (2004). Protocol Dictionary—H.235: Security and encryption for H.323 (and other H.245-based) multimedia terminals. Retrieved August 17, 2004 from www.javvin.com/protocolH235.html

18. Arango, M., Dugan, A., Huitema, C., & Pickett, S. (1999). RFC 2705—Media Gateway Control Protocol (MGCP) Version 1.0. Retrieved August 16, 2004 from www.faqs.org/rfcs/rfc2705.html

19. Schulzrinne, H., Casner, S., Frederick, R., & Jacobson, V. (1996). RFC 1889—RTP: A Transport Protocol for Real-Time Applications. Retrieved August 17, 2004 from www.faqs.org/rfcs/rfc1889.html

20. Handley, M. & Jacobson, V. (1998). RFC 2327—SDP: Session Description Protocol. Retrieved August 17, 2004 from www.ietf.org/rfc/rfc2327.txt

21.   Groves, C., Pantaleo, M., Anderson, T., & Taylor, T. (2003). RFC 3525: Gateway Control Protocol—Version 1. Retrieved August 16, 2004 from http://ietfreport.isoc.org/rfc/rfc3525.txt

22.   Ibid.

23.   Kent, S. & Atkinson, R. (1998). RFC 2402—IP Authentication Header. Retrieved August 17, 2004 from www.faqs.org/rfcs/rfc2402.html

24.   Packetizer. (2004). H.248. Retrieved August 17, 2004 from www.packetizer.com/iptel/h248/

25.   Golen, P. (2002). Virtual Private Networking. Retrieved August 18, 2004 from www.windowsecurity.com/articles/ Virtual_Private_Networking.html

26.   Web Host Industry Review, Inc. (2002). What is VPN Encryption? Retrieved August 18, 2004 from http://findvpn.com/articles/encryption.php

27.   Gleeson, B., Heinanen, J., Armitage, G., & Malis, A. (2000). RFC 2764—A Framework for IP-Based Virtual Private Networks. Retrieved August 25, 2004 from www.faqs.org/rfcs/rfc2764.html

28.   Telcordia Technologies. (2004). Performance and Security Analysis of SIP Using IPsec. National Institute of Standards and Technology.

29.   Ratchkov, R. Overview of VPN. Retrieved on August 18, 2004 from www.ratchkov.com/vpn

30.   Kent, S. & Atkinson, R. (1998). RFC 2401—Security Architecture for the Internet Protocol. Retrieved August 18, 2004, from www.faqs.org/rfcs/rfc2401.html

31.   Kent, S. & Atkinson, R. (1998). RFC 2402—IP Authentication Header. Retrieved August 18, 2004, from www.faqs.org/rfcs/rfc2402.html

32.   Harkins, D. & Carrel, D. (1998). RFC 2409—The Internet Key Exchange (IKE). Retrieved August 19, 2004, from www.faqs.org/ rfcs/rfc2409.html

33.   Sinden, R. (2002). "Comparison of Voice over IP with Circuit Switching Techniques." Department of Electronics and Computer Science, Southampton University, UK.

34.   National Institute of Standards and Technology. (2004). NIST Special Publication 800-58: Security Considerations for Voice Over IP Systems Recommendations of the National Institute of Standards and Technology. Retrieved August 3, 2004 from http://csrc.nist.gov/publications/drafts/NIST_SP800-58-040502.pdf

35.   Munch, B. (2003). VoIP Security: Part 3—Product Status. Retrieved August 14, 2004 from http://techupdate.zdnet.com/techupdate/stories/main/0,14179,2914628,00.html

8.7   General References

All.net. (2004). *A PBX Audit Checklist*. Retrieved August 9, 2004 from www.all.net/books/audit/pbx/general.html

Archer, K. at al. (2001). *Voice and Data Security*. Indianapolis, IN: SAMS Publishing.

Cavanagh, J. (2002). *Secure Business Telephony With VoIP: A Technical White Paper*. Retrieved August 3, 2004 from www.consultant-registry.com/delivery/TSWP1.pdf

Cisco. (2002). *Configuring H.323 Gatekeepers and Proxies*. Retrieved August 5, 2004 from http://noc.caravan.ru/ciscocd/cc/td/doc/product/software/ios122/122cgcr/fvvfax_c/vvf323gk.htm

CERT Coordination Center. (2004). Carnegie Mellon Software Engineering Institute CERT Coordination Center Web page. Retrieved August 9, 2004 from www.cert.org

Cloud, B. (2000). *PBX Audit Review and Questionnaire: Key Areas to Review During a PBX Audit*. Retrieved August 9, 2004 from www.auditnet.org/docs/pbxaudit.txt

Gleeson, B., Heinanen, J., Armitage, G., & Malis, A. (2000). *RFC 2764—A Framework for IP Based Virtual Private Networks*. Retrieved August 25, 2004 from www.faqs.org/rfcs/rfc2764.html

Halpern, J. (2002). *IP Telephony Security in Depth*. White Paper, Cisco Systems. Retrieved August 13, 2004 from www.cisco.com/warp/public/cc/so/cuso/epso/sqfr/safip_wp.pdf

ISACA.org. (2004). *Telecommunications*. Retrieved August 9, 2004 from www.isaca.org/gir/catDspl.cfm?catID=11&catName=Telecommunications#subcat97

Le, T. (2004). *Internet Firewalls: The Thin Red Line*. Retrieved August 9, 2004 from www-sal.cs.uiuc.edu/~steng/cs497_01/presentation.pdf

Munch, B. (2003). *VoIP Security: Part 3—Product Status*. Retrieved August 14, 2004 from http://techupdate.zdnet.com/techupdate/stories/main

National Security Agency. (2004). *NSA/SNAC Router Security Configuration Guide, Version 1.1*. Retrieved August 13, 2004 from http://nsa1.www.conxion.com/cisco/guides/cis-1.pdf

Netrake. (2004). Netrake Web site. Retrieved August 12, 2004 from www.netrake.com

National Institute of Standards and Technology. (2004). *NIST Special Publication 800-58: Security Considerations for Voice Over IP Systems Recommendations of the National Institute of Standards and Technology*. Retrieved August 3, 2004 from http://csrc.nist.gov/publications/drafts/NIST_SP800-58-040502.pdf

Rekhter, Y. et al. (1996). *RFC 1918—Address Allocation for Private Internets*. Retrieved August 12, 2004 from www.faqs.org/rfcs/rfc1918.html

SANS Institute. (2004). SANS Institute Web page. Retrieved August 9, 2004 from www.sans.org

SecureLogix Corporation. (2004). *TeleWall: Telecommunications Firewall 4.1*. Retrieved August 3, 2004 from www.securelogix.com/applications/telewall.htm

Thalhammer, J. (2002). *Security in VoIP—Telephony Systems*. Master's Thesis. Retrieved August 3, 2004 from www.iaik.tu-graz.ac.at/../teaching/11_diplomarbeiten/archive/thalhammer.pdf

Vitel Software, Inc. (2003). *Voice Network Security: Strategies for Control*. Retrieved August 9, 2004 from www.ivize.com/pub/security_wp401.pdf

Walker, J. & Hicks, J. (2004). *Taking Charge of Your VoIP Project*. Indianapolis, IN: Cisco Press.

Wu, Y. et al. (2004). *SCIDIVE: A Stateful and Cross Protocol Intrusion Detection Architecture for Voice-over-IP Environments*. Retrieved August 14, 2004 from
http://dynamo.ecn.purdue.edu/~sbagchi/Research/Papers/scidive_dsn04_submit.pdf

ZVON. (2004). *RFC 3261: Security Considerations: Threat Model and Security Usage Recommendations*. Retrieved August 3, 2004 from www.zvon.org/tmRFC/RFC3261/Output/chapter26.html

9

VoIP Security and the Law

Internet telephony, an inexpensive alternative to traditional telephone service, has been facing regulatory backlash that could slow adoption of the fast-growing technology, raise prices, and put financially shaky start-ups out of business. The Federal Communications Commission (FCC) could adopt new rules for VoIP operators, signaling the end of the honeymoon for an industry that's operated to date with no official oversight. Many believe that if a company is operating as a phone company, then it must follow requirements regardless of whether the calls are made over the Internet or not. Most significant of these requirements is the concern over VoIP emergency 911 services that has been raised by several states. Higher prices, slower introductions of new Internet telephony services, and the demise of some of the same start-ups will more than likely result if regulations force VoIP providers to offer essential 911 services.

As U.S. IP telephony subscribers have dramatically increased in numbers, a growing number of states and the FCC have begun exploring whether to put VoIP providers on their regulatory radar. As a telecommunications service, IP telephony providers such as Vonage and Packet8 would likely have to carry the monstrous load of common-carrier regulations, including contributions to the federal universal-service funds and per-minute access charges levied on calls that terminate on the networks of other phone carriers, which are mostly likely to be the Baby Bells. There remain many questions about whether the Internet Tax Freedom Act exempts IP telephony providers from federal excise tax. Telephone regulators in several states are in various stages of drafting some IP telephony regulations. A good Web site to access to stay up to date on state-specific regulatory issues is www.cybertelecom.org/voip.states.htm.

The Federal Bureau of Investigations (FBI) has recently put pressure on regulators to seek rules requiring VoIP and broadband Internet service providers (ISPs) to ensure the ability of law enforcement to conduct wiretaps on VoIP subscribers. The FBI wants the FCC to bring Internet calling under provisions of the 1994 Communications for Law Enforcement Act (CALEA), which requires phone carriers to provide the FBI with direct access to phone lines. Because voice calls over the Internet travel in digital packets, it is relatively easy to encrypt conversations, or to use secure tunnels, making them difficult for law enforcement to access.

IP telephony providers face an uphill effort against the lobbying machines of the local-telephone companies. The Baby Bells, with their huge war chests and political influence, will prove to be an ominous opponent. Cable providers have taken serious steps toward launching VoIP telephone services and are considered a major challenge to the dominance of phone companies. This competition has driven telephone companies—most notably, BellSouth and SBC Communications—to argue that it's time for regulators to level the competitive landscape. Earlier this year, Qwest Communications International broke ranks with the other Bells, in that it wants IP telephony to be regulated but believes the FCC should draft separate, lighter rules for the start-up services compared with those traditional telephone companies must follow.[1] AT&T was the second major phone company to break ranks this year and join those rallying against IP telephony regulations as well. In April 2004, the FCC rejected a petition from AT&T Corp. that would have allowed the company to avoid paying its telecommunications competitors access charges on telephone calls partly carried on IP networks.[2] Interestingly enough, on August 23, 2004, AT&T announced that the retail chain Best Buy will be among the first national retailers to offer AT&T's residential VoIP phone service, AT&T CallVantage^SM Service, in its 628 stores nationwide and online at www.bestbuy.com.[3]

9.1   Regulatory Issues

To date, the most significant national-level legislation has been the VoIP Regulatory Freedom Act of 2004 (S. 2281). On July 22, 2004, the Senate Commerce, Science, and Transportation Committee passed this VoIP Bill, which requests a report from the General Accounting Office (GAO) that will do the following:

- Assess the technical capability of law enforcement to intercept and analyze IP transmissions

- Assess problems encountered by law enforcement when intercepting communications over the Internet or using IP

- Assess options for law enforcement agencies to acquire the skills and equipment necessary to analyze Internet communications

- Assess the impact of the first 10 years of CALEA implementation and compliance along with a cost-benefit analysis

The bill also requires a study from the FCC to assess the first 10 years of CALEA; however, the bill does not affect VoIP telephony provider obligations under CALEA. The Act regulates VoIP at the federal level and preempts state law with three major exceptions:

1. States may still enforce laws and regulations of general applicability, including consumer protection laws and prohibitions against fraud and unfair trade practices.

2. States and local governments may still require 911 and E911 services.

3. States may still regulate transmission facilities and require VoIP providers to pay compensation to incumbent carriers for the use of facilities and contribute to the universal service fees.[4]

Recent increase in the popularity of VoIP services has accelerated the pace at which lawmakers are moving to define IP telephony's place within the larger scheme of telecommunications regulation, but there remains considerable disagreement in Congress over the roles federal and state regulators should play. Earlier this year, the FBI and the Justice Department renewed their efforts to wiretap voice conversations carried across the Internet. They asked the FCC to order companies offering VoIP service to rewire their networks to guarantee police the ability to eavesdrop on subscribers' conversations. They predicted, in a letter that was signed by the Drug Enforcement Administration (DEA) to the FCC in December 2003, that without such mandatory rules, criminals, terrorists, and spies (could) use VoIP services to avoid lawfully authorized surveillance.[5]

In July 2004, commerce committee senators approved the VoIP Regulatory Freedom Act after amending it to preserve some authority for the states. However, the absence of a solid consensus makes it unclear whether the measure will be brought to a vote in the full Senate later in 2004. Sen.

John Sununu, R-N.H., who authored the bill, wants to not only prevent state regulators from meddling in the emerging technology but also restrict the FCC's authority. Sununu and Sens. Maria Cantwell, D-Wash., and Ron Wyden, D-Ore., warned the FCC this month to resist pressure from the FBI and the DEA to impose wiretap requirements on the Internet application. Cautioning that applying wiretap rules to VoIP would put law enforcement "in the role of mandating design features for Internet applications," the senators urged the FCC to reject law enforcement's request.[6]

The FBI has pressured regulators to seek rules requiring VoIP and broadband ISPs to ensure the ability of law enforcement to conduct wiretaps on VoIP subscribers. The FBI wants the FCC to bring Internet calling under provisions of CALEA, which requires phone carriers to provide them with direct access to phone lines. Internet privacy advocates, such as the San Francisco–based Electronic Frontier Foundation, are backing Pulver who launched Free World Dial-Up (FWD). Jeff Pulver, the President and CEO of FWD. FWD is the largest open network service provider for person-to-person, advanced, real-time IP communications. Earlier this year, the FCC ruled that FWD VoIP service is an information service, not a telecommunications service. But even requiring FWD to provide access to voice communications will probably be of little use to the FBI if a caller is determined to block eavesdropping. Because voice calls over the Internet travel in digital packets, it is relatively easy to encrypt conversations, or to use secure tunnels, making them inaccessible to law enforcement.[7]

The current lack of definitive regulatory requirements or guidelines specific to VoIP security and the law do not negate the legal requirements for security that currently exist within the IP domain. As with the IP security risks inherited by VoIP, the laws appropriate for both IP and the plain old telephone service (POTS) are also inherited by VoIP. With the rash of cyber-incidents that have taken a huge financial toll on governments and businesses within the last decade, legislators began to see that laws needed to be enacted to control the Wild West environment that existed in cyberspace. Laws have been enacted to protect privacy, infrastructure, people, companies, and just about anything or anyone that uses a computer or any form of computer technology. We will discuss the most significant of those laws and how they impact corporate security operations in the remaining parts of this chapter.

9.2   The 1996 National Information Infrastructure Protection Act

In 1996, when this law was passed, legislators were presented with some startling statistics. For example, the Computer Emergency and Response Team (CERT) at Carnegie-Mellon University in Pittsburgh, Pennsylvania, reported *a 498% increase in the number of computer intrusions and a 702% rise in the number of sites affected with such intrusions* in the three-year period from 1991 through 1994.[8] During 1994, approximately 40,000 Internet computers were attacked in 2,460 incidents. Similarly, the FBI's National Computer Crime Squad opened more than 200 hacker cases from 1991 to 1994.[9]

Before passing this law, legislators realized that there are two ways, conceptually, to address the growing computer crime problem. The first would be to comb through the entire U.S. Code, identifying and amending every statute potentially affected by the implementation of new computer and telecommunications technologies. The second would be to focus substantive amendments on the Computer Fraud and Abuse Act to specifically address new abuses that spring from the misuse of new technologies. The new legislation adopted the latter approach for a host of reasons, but the net effect on this approach was a revamp of our laws to address computer-related criminal activity. The full text of the legislative analysis can be found at the following Web address: www.usdoj.gov/criminal/cybercrime/1030_anal.htm.

With these changes, the United States stepped into the forefront of rethinking how information technology crimes must be addressed—simultaneously protecting the confidentiality, integrity, and availability of data and systems. By choosing this path, the hope was to encourage other countries to adopt a similar framework, thus creating a more uniform approach to addressing computer crime in the existing global information infrastructure.

9.3   President's Executive Order on Critical Infrastructure Protection

Following the terrorist attacks on the World Trade Center and the Pentagon that occurred on the morning of September 11, 2001, there was a growing realization in our government and across industry sectors that our national infrastructure was vulnerable and that we had become (almost completely) dependent on such critical elements that they needed specific protection. On October 16, 2001, President Bush issued an Executive Order[10] to ensure protection of information systems for critical infrastructure, including emergency preparedness communications, and the physical assets that support such systems.

The President's Executive Order established policy that reflects the fact that the IT revolution has changed the way business is transacted, government operates, and national defense is conducted. Those three functions now depend (almost wholly) on an interdependent network of critical information infrastructures. The protection program authorized by this Executive Order requires continuous efforts to secure information systems for critical infrastructure. Protection of these systems is essential to the telecommunications, energy, financial services, manufacturing, water, transportation, health care, and emergency services sectors. The official statement of policy, excerpted from the Executive Order, follows:

It is the policy of the United States to protect against disruption of the operation of information systems for critical infrastructure and thereby help to protect the people, economy, essential human and government services, and national security of the United States, and to ensure that any disruptions that occur are infrequent, of minimal duration, and manageable, and cause the least damage possible. The implementation of this policy shall include a voluntary public-private partnership, involving corporate and non-governmental organizations.

Ten days after this Executive Order was issued, the 107th Congress of the United States of America passed H.R. 3162, which became Public Law 107-56, the USA PATRIOT Act of 2001.[11]

9.4   The USA PATRIOT Act of 2001

Public Law 107-56, formally titled as "Uniting and Strengthening America by Providing Appropriate Tools Required to Intercept and Obstruct Terrorism (USA PATRIOT) Act of 2001" was enacted on October 26, 2001. A result of the terrorist attack against the United States on September 11, 2001 carried out by members of Osama Bin Laden's Al Qaeda organization, this legislation made broad and sweeping changes that created a federal antiterrorism fund and directed law enforcement, military, and various government agencies to collectively develop a national network of electronic crime task forces throughout the United States. These task forces were designed to prevent, detect, and investigate various forms of electronic crimes, including potential terrorist attacks against critical infrastructure and financial payment systems.

Title II of this bill amends the federal criminal code to authorize the interception of wire, oral, and electronic communications for the production of evidence of (1) specified chemical weapons or terrorism offenses and (2) computer fraud and abuse. This section of the law authorizes law enforcement and government personnel who have obtained knowledge of the contents of any wire, oral, or electronic communication or evidence derived therefrom, by authorized means, to disclose contents to such officials to the extent that such contents include foreign intelligence or counterintelligence.

Title III of this law amends existing federal law governing monetary transactions. The amended document prescribes procedural guidelines under which the Secretary of the Treasury may require domestic financial institutions and agencies to take specified measures if there are reasonable grounds for concluding that jurisdictions, financial institutions, types of accounts, or transactions operating outside or within the United States are part of a primary money-laundering concern. The intent of this section is to prevent terrorist concerns from using money-laundering techniques to fund operations that are destructive to national interests.

Title IV is targeted at tightening the control of our borders and immigration laws. In addition to waiving certain restrictions and personnel caps, it directs the Attorney General and the Secretary of State to develop a technology standard to identify visa and admissions applicants. This standard is meant to be the basis for an electronic system of law enforcement and intelligence sharing that will be made available to consular, law enforcement, intelligence, and federal border inspection personnel. Among the many provisions of Immigration Naturalization Service changes, this section of the law includes within the definition of *terrorist activity* the use of any weapon or dangerous device. The law redefines the phrase *engage in terrorist activity* to mean, in an individual capacity or as a member of an organization, to:

1. Commit or to incite to commit, under circumstances indicating an intention to cause death or serious bodily injury, a terrorist activity

2. Prepare or plan a terrorist activity

3. Gather information on potential targets for terrorist activity

4.   Solicit funds or other things of value for a terrorist activity or a terrorist organization (with an exception for lack of knowledge)

5.   Solicit any individual to engage in prohibited conduct or for terrorist organization membership (with an exception for lack of knowledge)

6.   Commit an act that the actor knows, or reasonably should know, affords material support, including a safe house, transportation, communications, funds, transfer of funds or other material financial benefit, false documentation or identification, weapons (including chemical, biological, or radiological weapons), explosives, or training for the commission of a terrorist activity; to any individual who the actor knows or reasonably should know has committed or plans to commit a terrorist activity; or to a terrorist organization (with an exception for lack of knowledge)

Title IV of this law also defines *terrorist organization* as a group:

1.   Designated under the Immigration and Nationality Act or by the Secretary of State

2.   Of two or more individuals, whether related or not, which engages in terrorist-related activities

It also provides for the retroactive application of amendments under this Act and stipulates that an alien shall not be considered inadmissible or deportable because of a relationship to an organization that was not designated as a terrorist organization before enactment of this Act. A provision is included to account for situations when the Secretary of State may have identified an organization as a threat and has deemed it necessary to formally designate that organization as a "terroristic organization." This law directs the Secretary of State to notify specified congressional leaders seven days before formally making such a designation.

Title V, "Removing Obstacles to Investigating Terrorism," authorizes the Attorney General to pay rewards from available funds pursuant to public advertisements for assistance to the Justice Department to combat terrorism and defend the nation against terrorist acts, in accordance with procedures and regulations established or issued by the Attorney General, subject to specified conditions, including a prohibition against any such reward of

$250,000 or more from being made or offered without the personal approval of either the Attorney General or the President.

Title VII, "Increased Information Sharing for Critical Infrastructure Protection," amends the Omnibus Crime Control and Safe Streets Act of 1968 to extend Bureau of Justice Assistance regional information-sharing system grants to systems that enhance the investigation and prosecution abilities of participating federal, state, and local law enforcement agencies in addressing multijurisdictional terrorist conspiracies and activities. It also revised the *Victims of Crime Act of 1984* with provisions regarding the allocation of funds for compensation and assistance, location of compensable crime, and the relationship of crime victim compensation to means-tested federal benefit programs and to the September 11th victim compensation fund. It established an antiterrorism emergency reserve in the *Victims of Crime Fund*.

Title VIII, "Strengthening the Criminal Laws Against Terrorism," amends the federal criminal code to prohibit specific terrorist acts or otherwise destructive, disruptive, or violent acts against mass transportation vehicles, ferries, providers, employees, passengers, or operating systems. It amends the federal criminal code to:

1. Revise the definition of "international terrorism" to include activities that appear to be intended to affect the conduct of government by mass destruction

2. Define "domestic terrorism" as activities that occur primarily within U.S. jurisdiction, that involve criminal acts dangerous to human life, and that appear to be intended to intimidate or coerce a civilian population, to influence government policy by intimidation or coercion, or to affect government conduct by mass destruction, assassination, or kidnaping

The specific issue of information sharing that came up in many discussions of the "talking heads" around the Washington, D.C. area after the September 11th attacks is addressed in Title IX, "Improved Intelligence." Herein, amendments to the National Security Act of 1947 require the Director of Central Intelligence to establish requirements and priorities for foreign intelligence collected under the Foreign Intelligence Surveillance Act of 1978 and to provide assistance to the Attorney General to ensure that information derived from electronic surveillance or physical searches is disseminated for efficient and effective foreign intelligence purposes. It also requires the inclusion of international terrorist activities within the scope of foreign intelligence under such Act.

Part of this section expresses the sense of Congress that officers and employees of the intelligence community should establish and maintain intelligence relationships to acquire information on terrorists and terrorist organizations. The law requires the Attorney General or the head of any other federal department or agency with law enforcement responsibilities to expeditiously disclose to the Director of Central Intelligence any foreign intelligence acquired in the course of a criminal investigation.

By now, it should be abundantly clear that the 107th Congress viewed the threat of terrorist activities as a huge security concern. Steps taken to close loopholes in money transaction processes, immigration and border control changes, and the hundreds of other specifics found in Public Law 107-56 reflect the determination of a nation victimized by terrorism to prevent reoccurrences using any means necessary and available. Citizens of the United States rallied around a cause like few other times in history, and the will of the people was reflected in these congressional actions.

9.5   The Homeland Security Act of 2002

Nine months after the attacks on September 11, 2001, President Bush proposed creation of a cabinet-level Department of Homeland Security. This new department was formed to unite essential agencies to work more closely together. The affected agencies consisted of the Coast Guard, the Border Patrol, the Customs Service, Immigration officials, the Transportation Security Administration, and the Federal Emergency Management Agency. Employees of the Department of Homeland Security would be charged with completing four primary tasks:

1.   To control our borders and prevent terrorists and explosives from entering our country

2.   To work with state and local authorities to respond quickly and effectively to emergencies

3.   To bring together our best scientists to develop technologies that detect biological, chemical, and nuclear weapons, and to discover the drugs and treatments to best protect our citizens

4.   To review intelligence and law enforcement information from all agencies of government, and produce a single daily picture of

threats against our homeland; analysts will be responsible for imagining the worst, and planning to counter it

On November 25, 2002, President Bush signed the "Homeland Security Act of 2002" into law. The Act restructures and strengthens the executive branch of the federal government to better meet the threat to our homeland posed by terrorism. In establishing a new Department of Homeland Security, the Act created a federal department whose primary mission will be to help prevent, protect against, and respond to acts of terrorism on our soil. The creation of this new cabinet-level department was an historic event in American history, and it will have long-lasting repercussions on the global community as well. For security professionals, it adds yet another dimension to the complexity of securing infrastructure from malcontents.

9.6   US Patriot Act and Changes to Computer-Related Laws

Since the tragic events of September 11, 2001, the U.S. Congress has enacted legislation in the USA PATRIOT Act that has strengthened or amended many of the laws relating to computer crime and electronic evidence. In this section, we review some of the more important changes that have been made to the laws[12] in the United States, and we will discuss the topics of investigations and ethics.

9.6.1   Authority to Intercept Voice Communications

Under previous law, investigators could not obtain a wiretap order to intercept wire communications (those involving the human voice) for violations of the Computer Fraud and Abuse Act (18 U.S.C. § 1030). For example, in several investigations, hackers have stolen teleconferencing services from a telephone company and used this mode of communication to plan and execute hacking attacks. The new amendment changed this situation by adding felony violations of the Fraud and Abuse Act (18 U.S.C. § 1030) to the list of offenses for which a wiretap could be obtained. However, this provision will expire by December 31, 2005, unless Congress mandates otherwise.

9.6.2   Obtaining Voice-Mail and Other Stored Voice Communications

The Electronic Communications Privacy Act (ECPA) governed law enforcement access to stored electronic communications (such as e-mail), but not stored wire communications (such as voice-mail). Instead, the wiretap statute governed such access because the legal definition of *wire communication* included stored communications, requiring law enforcement to use a wiretap order (rather than a search warrant) to obtain unopened voice communications. Thus, law enforcement authorities were forced to use a wiretap order to obtain voice communications stored with a third-party provider, but they could use a search warrant if that same information were stored on an answering machine inside a criminal's home. This procedure created an unnecessary burden for criminal investigations. Stored voice communications possess few of the sensitivities associated with real-time interception of telephones, making the extremely burdensome process of obtaining a wiretap order unreasonable.

Moreover, the statutory framework largely envisions a world in which technology-mediated voice communications (such as telephone calls) are conceptually distinct from nonvoice communications (such as faxes, pager messages, and e-mail). To the limited extent that Congress acknowledged that data and voice might coexist in a single transaction, it did not anticipate the convergence of these two kinds of communications typical of today's telecommunications networks. With the advent of Multipurpose Internet Mail Extensions (MIME) and similar features, an e-mail may include one or more attachments consisting of any type of data, including voice recordings. As a result, a law enforcement officer seeking to obtain a suspect's unopened e-mail from an ISP by means of a search warrant had no way of knowing whether the inbox messages included voice attachments (i.e., wire communications), which could not be compelled using a search warrant. This necessitated changes to be made to the existing wiretap procedures.

9.6.3   Changes to Wiretapping Procedures

An amendment was written that altered the way in which the wiretap statute and the ECPA apply to stored voice communications. The amendment deleted "electronic storage" of wire communications from the definition of *wire communication* and inserted language to ensure that stored wire communications are covered under the same rules as stored electronic communications. Thus, law enforcement can now obtain such communications using the procedures set out in section 2703 (such as a search warrant) rather than those in the wiretap statute (such as a wiretap order). This provision will expire by December 31, 2005, unless Congress mandates otherwise.

9.6.4   Scope of Subpoenas for Electronic Evidence

The government must use a subpoena to compel a limited class of information, such as the customer's name, address, length of service, and means of payment under existing law. Before the amendments enacted with the USA PATRIOT Act, however, the list of records investigators could obtain with a subpoena did *not* include certain records (such as credit card number or other form of payment for the communication service) relevant to determining a customer's true identity. In many cases, users register with ISPs using false names. In order to hold these individuals responsible for criminal acts committed online, the method of payment is an essential means of determining true identity. Moreover, many of the definitions used within were technology-specific, relating primarily to telephone communications. For example, the list included "local and long-distance telephone toll billing records," but did not include parallel terms for communications on computer networks, such as "records of session times and durations." Similarly, the previous list allowed the government to use a subpoena to obtain the customer's "telephone number or other subscriber number or identity," but did not define what that phrase meant in the context of Internet communications.

Amendments to existing law expanded the narrow list of records that law enforcement authorities could obtain with a subpoena. The new law includes "records of session times and durations," as well as "any temporarily assigned network address." In the Internet context, such records include the Internet Protocol (IP) address assigned by the provider to the customer or subscriber for a particular session, as well as the remote IP address from which a customer connects to the provider. Obtaining such records will make the process of identifying computer criminals and tracing their Internet communications faster and easier.

Moreover, the amendments clarify that investigators may use a subpoena to obtain the "means and source of payment" that a customer uses to pay for an account with a communications provider, "including any credit card or bank account number." While generally helpful, this information will prove particularly valuable in identifying users of Internet services where a company does not verify its users' biographical information.

9.6.5   Clarifying the Scope of the Cable Act

Previously, the law contained several different sets of rules regarding privacy protection of communications and their disclosure to law enforcement: one governing cable service,[13] one applying to the use of telephone service and Internet access,[14] and one called the pen register and trap and trace statute.[15] Before the amendments were enacted, the Cable Act set out an extremely restrictive system of rules governing law enforcement access to most records possessed by a cable company. For example, the Cable Act did not allow the use of subpoenas or even search warrants to obtain such records. Instead, the cable company had to provide prior notice to the customer (*even if he or she were the target of the investigation*), and the government had to allow the customer to appear in court with an attorney and then justify to the court the investigative need to obtain the records. The court could then order disclosure of the records only if it found by "clear and convincing evidence"—a standard greater than probable cause or even a preponderance of the evidence—that the subscriber was "reasonably suspected" of engaging in criminal activity. This procedure was completely unworkable for virtually any criminal investigation.

The restrictive nature of the Cable Act caused grave difficulties in criminal investigations because today, unlike in 1984 when Congress passed the Cable Act, many cable companies offer not only traditional cable programming services but also Internet access and telephone service. In recent years, some cable companies have refused to accept subpoenas and court orders pursuant to the pen/trap statute and ECPA, noting the seeming inconsistency of these statutes with the Cable Act's harsh restrictions. Treating identical records differently depending on the technology used to access the Internet made little sense. Moreover, these complications at times delayed or even ended important investigations.

When this restrictive legislation was amended in the USA PATRIOT Act, it clarified the matter, stating that the ECPA, the wiretap statute, and the pen/trap and trace statute all govern disclosures by cable companies that relate to the provision of communication services such as telephone and Internet service. The amendment preserves the Cable Act's primacy with respect to records revealing what ordinary cable television programming a customer chooses to purchase, such as particular premium channels or "pay per view" shows. Thus, in a case where a customer receives both Internet access and conventional cable television service from a single cable provider, a government entity could use legal process under the ECPA to compel the provider to disclose only those customer records relating to Internet service but not those relating to viewer television usage of premium channels or "adult" channels.

9.6.6 Emergency Disclosures by Communications Providers

Previous law relating to voluntary disclosures by communication service providers was inadequate for law enforcement purposes in two respects. First, it contained no special provision allowing communications providers to disclose customer records or communications in emergencies. If, for example, an ISP independently learned that one of its customers was part of a conspiracy to commit an imminent terrorist attack, prompt disclosure of the account information to law enforcement could save lives. Because providing this information did not fall within one of the statutory exceptions, however, an ISP making such a disclosure could be sued in civil courts. Second, before the USA PATRIOT Act, the law did not expressly permit a provider to voluntarily disclose noncontent records (such as a subscriber's login records) to law enforcement for purposes of self-protection, even though providers could disclose the content of communications for this reason. Moreover, as a practical matter, communications service providers must have the right to disclose to law enforcement the facts surrounding attacks on their systems. For example, when an ISP's customer hacks into the ISP's network, gains complete control over an e-mail server, and reads or modifies the e-mail of other customers, the provider must have the legal ability to report the complete details of the crime to law enforcement.

The USA PATRIOT Act corrected both of these inadequacies. The law was changed to permit, but not require, a service provider to disclose to law enforcement either content or noncontent customer records in emergencies involving an immediate risk of death or serious physical injury to any person. This voluntary disclosure, however, does not create an affirmative obligation to review customer communications in search of such imminent dangers. The amendment here also changed the ECPA to allow providers to disclose information to protect their rights and property. All of these changes are scheduled to expire by December 31, 2005, unless Congress mandates otherwise.

9.6.7 Pen Register and Trap and Trace Statute

The pen register and trap and trace statute (known as the "pen/trap" statute) governs the prospective collection of noncontent traffic information associated with communications, such as the phone numbers dialed by a particular telephone. Section 216 of the USA PATRIOT Act updates the pen/trap statute in three important ways: (1) the amendments clarify that law enforcement may use pen/trap orders to trace communications on the Internet and other computer networks; (2) pen/trap orders issued by federal courts now have *nationwide* effect; and (3) law enforcement authorities must file a special report with the court whenever they use a pen/trap order to install their own monitoring device on computers belonging to a public provider.

9.6.8   Intercepting Communications of Computer Trespassers

Under prior law, the wiretap statute allowed computer owners to monitor the activity on their machines to protect their rights and property. This changed when Section 217 of the USA PATRIOT Act was enacted. It was unclear whether computer owners could obtain the assistance of law enforcement in conducting such monitoring. This lack of clarity prevented law enforcement from assisting victims to take the natural and reasonable steps in their own defense that would be entirely legal in the physical world. In the physical world, burglary victims may invite the police into their homes to help them catch burglars in the act of committing their crimes. The wiretap statute should not block investigators from responding to similar requests in the computer context simply because the means of committing the burglary happen to fall within the definition of a "wire or electronic communication" according to the wiretap statute.

Because providers often lack the expertise, equipment, or financial resources required to monitor attacks themselves, they commonly have no effective way to exercise their rights to protect themselves from unauthorized attackers. This anomaly in the law created, as one commentator has noted, a "bizarre result," in which a "computer hacker's undeserved statutory privacy right trumps the legitimate privacy rights of the hacker's victims." To correct this problem, the amendments in Section 217 of the USA PATRIOT Act allow victims of computer attacks to authorize persons "acting under color of law" to monitor trespassers on their computer systems. Also added was a provision where law enforcement may intercept the communications of a computer trespasser transmitted to, through, or from a protected computer. Before monitoring can occur, however, four requirements must be met:

1. The owner or operator of the protected computer must authorize the interception of the trespasser's communications.

2. The person who intercepts the communication must be lawfully engaged in an ongoing investigation. Both criminal and intelligence investigations qualify, but the authority to intercept ceases at the conclusion of the investigation.

3. The person acting under color of law must have reasonable grounds to believe that the contents of the communication to be intercepted will be relevant to the ongoing investigation.

4. Investigators must intercept only the communications sent or received by trespassers. Thus, this section would only apply where the configuration of the computer system allows the interception of communications to and from the trespasser and not the interception of non-consenting users authorized to use the computer.

The USA PATRIOT Act created a definition of a *computer trespasser*. Such trespassers include any person who accesses a protected computer without authorization. In addition, the definition explicitly *excludes* any person "known by the owner or operator of the protected computer to have an existing contractual relationship with the owner or operator for access to all or part of the computer." For example, certain ISPs do not allow their customers to send bulk unsolicited e-mails (or "spam"). Customers who send spam would be in violation of the provider's terms of service, but would *not* qualify as trespassers because they are authorized users and because they have an existing contractual relationship with the provider. These provisions will expire by December 31, 2005, unless Congress mandates otherwise.

9.6.9 Nationwide Search Warrants for E-mail

Previous law required the government to use a search warrant to compel a communications provider or ISP to disclose unopened e-mail less than six months old. Rule 41 of the Federal Rules of Criminal Procedure required that the "property" (the e-mails) to be obtained must be "within the district" of jurisdiction of the issuing court. For this reason, some courts had declined to issue warrants for e-mail located in other districts. Unfortunately, this refusal placed an enormous administrative burden on districts where major ISPs are located, such as the Eastern District of Virginia and the Northern District of California, even though these districts had no relationship with the criminal acts being investigated. In addition, requiring investigators to obtain warrants in distant jurisdictions slowed time-sensitive investigations.

The amendment added in the USA PATRIOT Act has changed this situation in order to allow investigators to use warrants to compel records outside of the district in which the court is located, just as they use federal grand jury subpoenas and orders. This change enables courts with jurisdiction over investigations to compel evidence directly, without requiring the intervention of agents, prosecutors, and judges in the districts where major ISPs are located. This provision will expire by December 31, 2005, unless Congress mandates otherwise.

9.6.10 Deterrence and Prevention of Cyberterrorism

Several changes were made in Section 814 of the USA PATRIOT Act that improve the Computer Fraud and Abuse Act. This section increases penalties for hackers who damage protected computers (from a maximum of 10 years to a maximum of 20 years). It clarifies the *mens rea* required for such offenses to make explicit that a hacker need only *intend* damage, not necessarily *inflict* a particular type of damage. It also adds a new offense for damaging computers used for national security or criminal justice and expands the coverage of the statute to include computers in foreign countries so long as there is an *effect* on U.S. interstate or foreign commerce. It now counts state convictions as "prior offenses" for the purpose of recidivist sentencing enhancements, and it allows losses to several computers from a hacker's course of conduct to be aggregated for purposes of meeting the $5,000 jurisdictional threshold. We discuss the most significant of these changes in the following sections.

Raising Maximum Penalty for Hackers

Under previous law, first-time offenders could be punished by no more than five years' imprisonment, whereas repeat offenders could receive up to ten years. Certain offenders, however, can cause such severe damage to protected computers that this five-year maximum did not adequately take into account the seriousness of their crimes. For example, David Smith pled guilty to releasing the "Melissa" virus that damaged thousands of computers across the Internet. Although Smith agreed, as part of his plea, that his conduct caused more than $80 million worth of loss (the maximum dollar figure contained in the Sentencing Guidelines), experts estimate that the real loss was as much as 10 times that amount. Had the new laws been in effect at the time of Smith's sentencing, he would most likely have received a much harsher sentence.

Eliminating Mandatory Minimum Sentences

Previous law set a mandatory sentencing guideline of a minimum of six months' imprisonment for any violation of the Computer Fraud and Abuse Act, as well as for accessing a protected computer with the intent to defraud. Under new amendments in the USA PATRIOT Act, the maximum penalty for violations for damaging a protected computer increased to 10 years for first offenders and 20 years for repeat offenders. Congress chose, however, to eliminate all mandatory minimum guidelines sentencing for section 1030 (Computer Fraud and Abuse Act) violations.

Hackers' Intent versus Degree of Damages

Under previous law, an offender had to "intentionally [cause] damage without authorization." Section 1030 of the Computer Fraud and Abuse Act defined "damage" as impairment to the integrity or availability of data, a program, a system, or information that met the following criteria:

1.   Caused loss of at least $5,000

2.   Modified or impairs medical treatment

3.   Caused physical injury

4.   Threatened public health or safety

The question arose, however, whether an offender must intend the $5,000 loss or other special harm, or whether a violation occurs if the person only intends to damage the computer, that in fact ends up causing the $5,000 loss or harming the individuals. Congress never intended that the language contained in the definition of "damage" would create additional elements of proof of the actor's mental state. Moreover, in most cases, it would be almost impossible to prove this additional intent. Now, under new law, hackers need only intend to cause damage, not inflict a particular consequence or degree of damage. The new law defines "damage" to mean "any impairment to the integrity or availability of data, a program, a system or information." Under this clarified structure, in order for the government to prove a violation, it must show that the actor caused damage to a protected computer and that the actor's conduct caused *either* loss exceeding $5,000, impairment of medical records, harm to a person, or threat to public safety.

Aggregating Damage Caused by a Hacker

Previous law was unclear about whether the government could aggregate the loss resulting from damage an individual caused to different protected computers in seeking to meet the jurisdictional threshold of $5,000 in loss. For example, an individual could unlawfully access five computers on a network on ten different dates—*as part of a related course of conduct*—but cause only $1,000 loss to each computer during each intrusion.

If previous law were interpreted not to allow aggregation, then that person would not have committed a federal crime at all because he or she had not caused more than $5,000 of damage to any particular computer. Under the new law, the government may now aggregate "loss resulting from a related course of conduct affecting one or more other protected computers" that occurs within a one-year period in proving the $5,000 jurisdictional threshold for damaging a protected computer.

Damaging Computers Used for National Security or Criminal Justice Purposes

Previously, there were no special provisions in the Computer Fraud and Abuse Act that would enhance punishment for hackers who damage computers used in furtherance of the administration of justice, national defense, or national security. Thus, federal investigators and prosecutors did not have jurisdiction over efforts to damage criminal justice and military computers where the attack did not cause more than $5,000 loss (or meet one of the other special requirements). Yet these systems serve critical functions and merit felony prosecutions even where the damage is relatively slight. Furthermore, an attack on computers used in the national defense that occur during periods of active military engagement are particularly serious—even if they do not cause extensive damage or disrupt the war-fighting capabilities of the military—because they divert time and attention away from the military's proper objectives. Similarly, disruption of court computer systems and data could seriously impair the integrity of the criminal justice system. Under new provisions, a hacker violates federal law by damaging a computer "used by or for a government entity in furtherance of the administration of justice, national defense, or national security," even if that damage does not result in provable loss over $5,000.

"Protected Computer" and Computers in Foreign Countries

Before the law was changed, *protected computer* was defined as a computer used by the federal government or a financial institution, or one "which is used in interstate or foreign commerce." The definition did not explicitly include computers outside of the United States. Because of the interdependency and availability of global computer networks, hackers from within the United States are increasingly targeting systems located entirely outside of this country. The old statute did not explicitly allow for prosecution of such hackers. In addition, individuals in foreign countries frequently route communications through the United States, even as they hack from one foreign country to another. In such cases, their hope may be that the lack of any U.S. victim would either prevent or discourage U.S. law enforcement agencies from assisting in any foreign investigation or prosecution.

The USA PATRIOT Act amends the definition of *protected computer* to make clear that this term includes computers outside of the United States so long as they affect "interstate or foreign commerce or communication of the United States." By clarifying the fact that a domestic offense exists, the United States can now use speedier domestic procedures to join in international hacker investigations. Because these crimes often involve investigators and victims in more than one country, fostering international law enforcement cooperation is essential. In addition, the amendment creates the option of prosecuting such criminals in the United States. Because the United States is urging other countries to ensure that they can vindicate the interests of U.S. victims for computer crimes that originate in their nations, this provision will allow the United States to reciprocate in kind.

Counting State Convictions as "Prior Offenses"

Under previous law, the court at sentencing could consider the offender's prior convictions for state computer crime offenses. State convictions, however, did not trigger the recidivist sentencing provisions of Section (a)(5) of the Computer Fraud and Abuse Act, 18 U.S.C. § 1030, which double the maximum penalties available under the statute.

The new law alters the definition of *conviction* so that it includes convictions for serious computer hacking crimes under state law (i.e., state felonies where an element of the offense is "unauthorized access, or exceeding authorized access, to a computer").

Definition of Loss

Calculating loss is important where the government seeks to prove that an individual caused more than $5,000 in loss in order to meet the jurisdictional requirements found in the Computer Fraud and Abuse Act. Yet the existing law had no definition of *loss*. The only court to address the scope of the definition of loss adopted an inclusive reading of what costs the government may include. In *United States v. Middleton*, 231 F.3d 1207, 1210-11 (9th Cir. 2000), the court held that the definition of *loss* includes a wide range of harms typically suffered by the victims of computer crimes, including costs of responding to the offense, conducting a damage assessment, restoring the system and data to their condition prior to the offense, and any lost revenue or costs incurred because of interruption of service. In the new law, the definition used in the Middleton case was adopted.

Development of Cybersecurity Forensic Capabilities

The USA PATRIOT Act requires the Attorney General to establish such regional computer forensic laboratories as he considers appropriate, and to provide support for existing computer forensic laboratories, to enable them to provide certain forensic and training capabilities. The provision also authorizes the spending of money to support those laboratories.

9.6.11 Investigations

During the conduct of any investigation following a bona fide incident, a specific sequence of events is recommended. This sequence of events should generally be followed as a matter of good practice for all incidents unless special circumstances warrant intervention by law enforcement personnel. This section is meant to provide an overview of the process taken when an investigation is needed. The sequence of events for investigations is as follows:

- Investigate report
- Determine crime committed
- Inform senior management
- Determine crime status
- Identify company elements involved
- Review security/audit policies and procedures
- Determine need for law enforcement
- Protect chain of evidence
- Assist law enforcement as necessary
- Prosecute

9.6.12   **Ethics**

Internet RFC 1087,[16] "Ethics and the Internet" may have been the first document that addressed ethical behavior for the access to and use of the Internet. It stated that it is a privilege and should be treated as such by all users. An excerpt from the RFC follows:

> The IAB strongly endorses the view of the Division Advisory Panel of the National Science Foundation Division of Network, Communications Research and Infrastructure which, in paraphrase, characterized as unethical and unacceptable any activity which purposely: (a) seeks to gain unauthorized access to the resources of the Internet, (b) disrupts the intended use of the Internet, (c) wastes resources (people, capacity, computer) through such actions, (d) destroys the integrity of computer-based information, and/or (e) compromises the privacy of users. The Internet exists in the general research milieu. Portions of it continue to be used to support research and experimentation on networking. Because experimentation on the Internet has the potential to affect all of its components and users, researchers have the responsibility to exercise great caution in the conduct of their work. Negligence in the conduct of Internet-wide experiments is both irresponsible and unacceptable. The IAB plans to take whatever actions it can, in concert with Federal agencies and other interested parties, to identify and to set up technical and procedural mechanisms to make the Internet more resistant to disruption. Such security, however, may be extremely expensive and may be counterproductive if it inhibits the free flow of information which makes the Internet so valuable. In the final analysis, the health and well-being of the Internet is the responsibility of its users who must, uniformly, guard against abuses which disrupt the system and threaten its long-term viability.

Since the wide acceptance and use of the Internet, the blending of technologies has made it a bit more difficult to distinguish a "research-based" Internet of 1989 from the intra/extra/Internet businesses in use today. With such evolved networks come evolved ideas of how to behave. In the next chapter, we extend the security realm to coverage of wireless issues and discuss the ramifications of setting up WLANs in your business environment.

9.7   Summary

This chapter has covered security and the law, with an overview of some recently passed government statuary requirements that have far-reaching effects into every part of our network infrastructures and practices. We have made the point that laws have been enacted to protect privacy, infrastructure, people, companies, and just about anything that uses a computer or any form of computer technology. We have also provided some discussion of the most significant of these laws and they affect VoIP operations.

9.8   Endnotes

1.   Bartash, J. (2004, April 30). "Qwest CEO Breaks Ranks with Bells: Says phone industry must change how it does business." Retrieved August 26, 2004 from http://cbs.marketwatch.com/news/story

2.   IDG News Service. (2004, April 22). "FCC rejects AT&T VoIP petition." Retrieved August 27, 2004 from www.itworld.com/Man/2697/040422fccatt/

3.   AT&T. (2004, August 23). "AT&T CallVantage Service to be Available in More Than 600 Best Buy Stores Nationwide." Retrieved August 27, 2004 from www.att.com/news/item/0%2C1847%2C13214%2C00.html

4.   IPTAlog.org. (2004, July 23). Regulating VoIP. Retrieved August 27, 2004 from www.iptablog.org/legislation

5.   McCullagh, D. (2004). "Feds seek wiretap access via VoIP." Retrieved August 26, 2004 from http://zdnet.com.com/2100-1105_2-5137344.html

6.   Carlson, C. (2004). "Will States or Feds Control VoIP Regulations?" Retrieved August 26, 2004 from www.eweek.com/print_article/0,1761,a=132098,00.asp

7.   Towne, R. (2004). VoIP. Retrieved August 26, 2004 from www.rogertowne.com/VoIP.htm#Technology

8.   CERT Coordination Center. (1994). CERT Coordination Center web document, www.cert.org. Also see CERT Annual Report to ARPA for further information.

9. United States Dept. of Justice, "The National Information Infrastructure Protection Act of 1996 Legislative Analysis," Web document at: www.usdoj.gov/criminal/cybercrime/1030_anal.html

10. United States of America Executive Order, issued October 16, 2001, by President George W. Bush. www.whitehouse.gov

11. Public Law 107-56, electronic document available from the Library of Congress, ref: H.R. 3162, www.thomas.loc.gov

12. More information on these changes can be found at the U.S. Department of Justice Web site, www.usdoj.gov

13. Known as the "Cable Act," 47 U.S.C. § 551

14. Known as the "Wiretap Statute," 18 U.S.C. § 2510 et seq.; ECPA, 18 U.S.C. § 2701 et seq.

15. Known as the "Pen/Trap Statute," 18 U.S.C. § 3121 et seq.

16. RFC 1087, "Ethics and the Internet", Internet Activities Board, January 1989, www.ietf.org

10

The Future of VoIP

A sharp increase in broadband connections to the home has generated renewed interest in VoIP among consumers as a result of improvements in quality of service and hookups that provide more viable service, allowing VoIP calls over ordinary telephone handsets rather than clumsy PC microphone systems. Broadband Internet connections allow for low-cost telephone appliances to attach to any home computer network and use IP telephony to make phone calls to any phone number in the world using an IP home telephone. Features include advanced voice-mail management, individual call-handling methods configured over the Internet, and sophisticated call-blocking schemes that the traditional telephone companies are not even able to offer and at costs that are a fraction of the typical residential phone bill. Cable operators can provide VoIP services over managed networks with end-to-end quality of service (QoS) that is significantly greater than that of Internet telephony.

10.1 The New Breed of VoIP: Internet Telephony

Although Internet telephony calls are delivered via the public Internet using a customer's high-speed data connection, they are unmanaged and susceptible to the same slowdowns as data traffic on the Internet, leaving them at risk to network and power outages. Currently, voice quality and reliability is not as good as carrier-grade standards for IP telephony services. Providers have little control over the quality of the transmissions once they transit the Internet, even when Session Initiation Protocol (SIP) and H.323 are used, because voice transmissions are treated the same as data transmissions. Internet telephony does not offer QoS guarantees, operator services, or emergency 911 services, and it should, therefore, be considered an enhanced feature of an Internet service similar to Web access or e-mail rather than being relied on for primary-line service. IP is utilized to carry voice in the long-distance transport network because of its transport efficiency. Major international phone carriers such as Sprint and AT&T have been converting much of their international telephone traffic to the Internet, which is a much cheaper method of transport. Once the remaining pieces of technology that will ensure quality transport in the last mile are in place, service providers will be able to provide wide commercial and residential deployment to individual homes and businesses with an equivalent level of service as found in traditional delivery of voice.

Vonage, Packet8, and VoicePulse are currently three of the most popular broadband IP telephony services. Through the use of an existing high-speed connection, such as broadband, these technologies enable anyone to make and receive phone calls worldwide with a touch-tone telephone, offering an innovative, feature-rich, and cost-effective alternative to traditional telephony services. As part of this type of service, customers install an analog adaptor (such as the Cisco ATA 186) between their home telephone and the high-speed data connection and connect to the Internet using the SIP, which is widely believed to be the cornerstone of Internet-based phone calling. After call transmission has begun, it is routed in the form of packets to one of the provider's regional data centers, and the gateways there redirect the call to either the public Internet or the Public Switched Telephone Network (PSTN). Although Vonage is currently the most popular of the broadband IP telephony solutions, it is not without its issues.

The whole point of the Internet is to enable unforeseen innovation at the endpoints, and they are still trying to copy PSTN on IP rather than doing something PSTN cannot do, such as integration with encryption, higher voice quality, and voice mail stored at the endpoints. The inflexibility and limited functionality of the current breed of devices may make this transition difficult or impossible. The future of telephony may, in fact, belong to a centralized directory service provider such as MSN, Yahoo!, AOL, or possibly a decentralized system such as Skype. It is likely that cable TV providers and phone companies will eventually move calls over their private digital networks, which would allow them to guarantee higher sound quality.

Traditional phone companies and cable television providers are fast taking note of the opportunities and challenges they face with the popularity of Internet telephony. The fact that international communications carriers that once charged hundreds of dollars for international calls that can now be made for nothing has definitely caught the attention of the traditional telephony carriers. The Baby Bells are fighting back, and AT&T, Qwest, Verizon, and other phone companies are also looking at ways to tap into the market and bundle IP telephony services along with local and long-distance service to their customers with Digital Subscriber Line (DSL) service.

Established telephone companies have been threatened so much from the competition of IP telephony that they are petitioning officials in several states to impose the same regulations on VoIP providers that they now face. Ironically, these regulations were put in place when the phone companies had a monopoly over local-phone service, and now they want to regulate VoIP out of the market. IP telephony will more than likely accelerate the losses that Baby Bells are incurring because of competitive wireless calling plans offered to consumers. Of course, the consumer is now benefiting from this new competition, because the local phone companies are being forced to drop prices.

More than 20 million U.S. homes receive broadband Internet access through cable or DSL providers, and this number will likely continue to increase and evolve because IP telephony services rely on such high-speed connections. Analysts at Frost & Sullivan have predicted that VoIP will account for approximately 75% of world voice services by 2007,[1] and other firms predict that VoIP will grow steadily over the next four years, rising from 6.5 million lines in 2004 to 19.2 million lines in 2007, following the growth of broadband projected to be used in 46.9% of U.S. households by 2007 up from 21.9% in 2004.[2]

10.2   The Internet Telephony Providers

A handful of providers are currently offering IP telephony service. These include Free World Dial-Up, Net2Phone, Packet8, VoicePulse, and Vonage. We will discuss each enterprise briefly in the following paragraphs.

10.2.1   Free World Dial-Up

Free World Dial-Up, originally found on the Internet at http://pulver.com, launched Free World Dial-Up (FWD) on November 11, 2002, as a free "community service." FWD allows you to make free phone calls with any broadband connection using devices that follow Internet standards. This can be a regular telephone connected to a packetizer, an IP Phone, or any number of free softphones. The service is a peer-to-peer SIP system using an SIP proxy server infrastructure that links FWD members to other members exclusively, but not out to the PSTN. A free system can't afford to route calls to the traditional phone system, where local telcos charge fees to use their lines; therefore, both the caller and receiver must be FWD customers.[3]

10.2.2   Net2Phone

Net2Phone offers cable operators the ability to deliver a viable cable telephony service to their video and high-speed data customers. VoIP over cable has matured as a viable communications solution, as various VoIP-related companies have spearheaded the development of standards and protocols for cable telephony. Net2Phone, a pioneer in VoIP, has now developed this technology for consumer deployment, offering operators substantial cost savings and the opportunity to provide a competitive quality phone service. Their system uses PacketCable technology, an evolving specification for VoIP services for the cable industry. Net2Phone is also backed by investments from Liberty Media Corp. Although they offer the same kind of service as Vonage, they partner with cable operators exclusively, where its service can be branded under the operator's umbrella.[4]

10.2.3   Packet8

Packet8 is an affordable and easy-to-use broadband telephone and videophone service. They manufacture their own telephony hardware through their parent company. Designed with both residential and business customers in mind, Packet8 allows anyone with broadband (high-speed) Internet access to use their regular phone to make unlimited calls to anywhere in the United States and Canada. Packet8 subscribers with videophones can also make video calls for a higher monthly rate than the general service. All Packet8 subscribers get worldwide unlimited calling to other Packet8 subscribers at no extra charge. Calls to non-Packet8 international numbers (outside the United States and Canada) are charged at a very low per-minute rate. Similar to Vonage, Packet8 is not only selling to homes and businesses, but also trying to partner with cable companies.[5]

10.2.4   VoicePulse

VoicePulse is hoping to carve out a niche as the technology leader, offering richer features than either of its VoIP competitors and the local phone companies. VoicePulse launched its broadband phone service in April 2003, and six months later its engineers duplicated each of the "big five" calling features consumers had come to expect from traditional telephony, specifically caller ID, call waiting, caller ID with name, call forwarding, and call return

(*69). Whereas traditional phone companies continue to charge extra for each of these features, VoicePulse includes them at no additional charge. In the months following this feat, VoicePulse raised the bar by offering customers a suite of new and innovative features that just weren't possible with traditional telephone service. Currently, VoicePulse customers enjoy enterprise-like functions such as Call Hunt / Find Me, Multi-Ring, Anonymous Call Block, Do Not Disturb with Prompting, Enhanced Voicemail, Call Filters, Three-way Calling, and Call Transfer, and VoicePulse includes all of these features at no additional charge.[6]

10.2.5 Vonage

Vonage is the current leader of the telephone-based VoIP market and has offered its service since April 2002. Using an existing high-speed Internet connection, Vonage technology enables anyone to make and receive phone calls worldwide with a touch-tone telephone. Offering quality phone service bundled with enhanced IP communications services, their interactive communications portal is a gateway to advanced features that were previously only available through digital telephone service. Utilizing a global network and advanced routing technologies, Vonage offers an innovative, feature-rich, and cost-effective alternative to traditional telephony services. Vonage has marketed its products extensively in online, print, and television advertising, and those features have become competitive with VoicePulse. In addition to selling to homes and small businesses, Vonage seeks partnerships with cable providers and ISPs, and at present Vonage is working with telecom companies to resell their services.[7]

10.3 VoIP over Wireless LAN (VoWLan)

Several market factors have converged to bring VoIP and the 802.11 wireless LAN (WLAN) together as an exciting emerging technology. Cellular phone usage has been steadily growing for years, and users have become accustomed to the flexibility and freedom of movement. At the same time, Internet usage and the number of people with home PCs has continued to grow. Consumers are now looking to combine the freedom of cellular phones with their growing acceptance and reliance on the Internet.

Businesses are also looking at VoIP and VoIP over WLAN (VoWLAN) to increase productivity while reducing telecommunications costs. How VoWLAN will be deployed in business will vary. Some businesses will be satisfied with a "walkie-talkie" type service, relying on 802.11b, VoWLAN, and personal digital assistants (PDAs). Other business users will have greater demands that will tie the VoWLAN service to the company private branch exchange. This integration will provide anytime, anywhere communications within corporate facilities. Such usefulness will greatly increase the technology's appeal and rate of adoption.

Current VoIP implementations are providing all of the functions and features that users have come to expect from their wired digital telephone systems. Call forwarding, call waiting, paging, and call conferencing are baseline features that are enhanced by unified messaging. VoWLAN communications on wireless handsets, softphones, and PDAs are supported by the following protocols: H.323, Cisco's SKINNY, or SIP.

Many solution providers are making significant technological advances in an effort to gain market share. Companies such as Avaya, Cisco, Nortel, and Motorola are the bigger names, but smaller companies are casting an even newer light on this emerging technology. Although most solutions recognize the importance of capacity, QoS, and security, the merging of VoIP and WLAN complicates these concerns. Cisco, for example, is capitalizing on its Lightweight Encrypted Authentication Protocol (LEAP), 802.1x network access control, and 802.1q VLAN technology to provide VoWLAN security. Motorola is taking this issue a step further by combining VoWLAN functionality and Global System for Mobile communications (GSM) cellular access. This will provide seamless roaming of VoIP calls when the user traverses his or her own corporate WLAN access points, but will switch to cellular when the 802.11 network is out of range. Another company, Vocera, is even marketing a Star Trek communicator-like device that adds voice recognition to the list of features supported with VoWLAN.

What's in the future for VoWLAN? Some things will continue to be a concern to manufacturers and network users: QoS and security are key factors. The market will undoubtedly continue to create new technology demands (and opportunities) to add even more functionality and a greater range of services. One of these innovations is WiMAX, which is an IEEE-approved standard (IEEE 802.16). This wireless Metropolitan Area Network standard will provide broadband wireless access with a much larger footprint than previous innovations have been able to accomplish. WiMAX has a range of several miles and will certainly allow VoWLAN to compete with traditional cellular services.

10.4 The Need for VoIP Security

Most users implementing VoIP these days are primarily concerned about voice quality, latency, and interoperability. These are all fundamental QoS considerations that companies need to deal with before they can even begin justifying the move to VoIP. Most implementers are not generally concerned as much about security. One reason for this attitude is that companies that are implementing VoIP are preoccupied with simply making it work and booking the revenue for successfully turning it on for the buyer/customer. It is also not easy to connect VoIP with existing phone networks and existing security solutions. For example, some existing network technologies, such as network address translators and most existing firewalls, aren't very VoIP-friendly, and firewalls that aren't VoIP-aware can keep VoIP calls from getting through. As a result, companies are grappling with how to make VoIP work to enterprise and industry standards rather than worrying about security. Without a sharp focus on security during VoIP planning and implementation, the corporate use of VoIP will become expensive and problematic at best when security is addressed after the fact.

A basic level of security is afforded to networking systems that are deployed in a VoIP network, but this does not provide absolute protection. It is still possible to be subjected to internal attacks from a malicious user or simply from a media gateway that unknowingly continues to send Real-time Transport Protocol (RTP) traffic after a call is complete. There is an increasing need for more sophisticated tactics to detect and address VoIP security. If IP telephony is going to prevail, there will have to be some better way for average users to set up and adjust all of the pertinent pieces needed to make their VoIP networks secure. To properly secure VoIP, security and defense measures must be implemented in every layer of the architecture. VoIP security education and technical assistance must be more readily available. In addition, the need for better tools and user interfaces that allow administrators to globally set security parameters is a strong driving force for development in many organizations.

Given the budgetary constraints and pressure to deliver everything yesterday, there is a fear within many organizations to bring up the topic of security during a VoIP implementation because it will slow down the process and add expense to an already lean budget. Again, the best way to handle security matters is during the review process, starting from the evaluation stage, through the proposal stage, during implementation, and beyond. Perhaps the recent prediction by analysts that most enterprises will outsource 90% of security operations by 2010[8][9] will alleviate the issue. If nothing else, an outsourced security organization, particularly in the case of VoIP, can provide access to security expertise they might not be able to afford in-house.

Even if you have rock solid security internally, you are still only as secure as your weakest link. There is also the risk that your IP telephony provider may be your weak link. For example, last year Vonage discovered that users had figured out a way to crack their provisioning encryption. Early this year, many IP telephony products using the H.323 protocol were found to have buffer overflows, creating potential security issues. In February 2004, a routing issue brought down Free World Dial-Up for several hours. And in March 2004, Broadvox Direct users discovered that an entire directory containing sensitive configuration files was open to any Web browser. These security concerns not only affect the technology's rate of adoption among consumers, but fraud and abuse concerns also threaten to eat into already slim profit margins, further slowing VoIP deployments. The good news is that the industry as a whole, from the service providers to hardware manufacturers, is taking significant steps to ensure that communications over the Internet are safe and secure. The goal is to make IP telephones as trustworthy and reliable as those that were connected to the plain old telephone service. Although we are not there yet, using the information provided in this book will help you maximize the performance, reliability, and security of your company VoIP infrastructure.

10.5 Endnotes

1. IPDeliver. (2004). VoIP Knowledgebase. Retrieved August 27, 2004 from http://www.ipdeliver.com/.voip_k_future.php

2. eMarketeer. (2004, June). Flurry of Activity in VoIP Market over Coming Years. Retrieved on August 26, 2004 from http://www.emarketeer.com/Article.aspx?1002871

3. FreeWorldDialup. (2004). Welcome to FWD! Retrieved on August 27, 2004 from http://www.pulver.com/fwd/

4. Net2Phone. (2004). Net2Phone homepage. Retrieved on August 27, 2004 from http://web.net2phone.com/cable/

5. Packet8. (2004). Packet8 Homepage. Retrieved on August 27, 2004 from http://www.packet8.net/about/index.asp

6. VoicePulse. (2004). About VoicePulse Inc. Retrieved on August 27, 2004 from http://www.voicepulse.com/corporate/default.aspx

7. Vonage. (2004). About Vonage. Retrieved on August 27, 2004 from http://www.vonage.com/corporate/aboutus_index.php

8.   Source: Haley, S. (2004, August 23). Security Outsourcing to Soar. Retrieved August 27, 2004 from http://news.earthweb.com/ent-news/article.php/3398471

9.   Mears, J. (2004, August 23). Is security ripe for outsourcing? Retrieved on August 27, 2004 from http://www.nwfusion.com/news/2004/082304outsecure.html?fsrc=rss-security

Appendix

A.1   Abbreviations

1000Base-T—1000-Mbps Ethernet over twisted-pair copper cable

100Base-T—100-Mbps Ethernet over twisted-pair copper cable

10Base-T—10-Mbps Ethernet over twisted-pair copper cable

ACD—Automatic Call Distribution

ACELP—Algebraic-Code-Excited Linear Prediction

AH—Authentication Header

AIB—Authenticated Identity Body

ADPCM—Adaptive Differential Pulse Code Modulation

AMIS—Audio Messaging Interchange Specification

ANI—Automatic Number Identification

ARP—Address Resolution Protocol

ASIC—Application-Specific Integrated Circuit. A chip designed to perform a specific function or functions, with the purpose to offload a central processor and perform the function(s) faster.

AS—Autonomous System

ATM—Asynchronous Transfer Mode

BGP—Border Gateway Protocol

BIR—Burstable Information Rate

CAC—Call Admission Control

CAS—Common Associated Signaling

CBR—Constant Bit Rate

CBWFQ—Class-based Weighted Fair Queuing

CCS—Common Channel Signaling

CES—Circuit Emulation Service

CIDR—Classless Interdomain Routing

CIR—Committed Information Rate

CLI—Calling Line ID

CO—Central Office of a telecommunications operator

Codec—Coder/Decoder

COPS—Common Open Policy Service

CoS—Class of Service

CR-LDP—Constraint-based Routing–Label Distribution Protocol

CRM—Customer Relationship Management

CSMA/CD—Carrier Sense Multiple Access/Collision Detection

CSU—Channel Service Unit

CVSD—Continuously Variable Slope Delta modulation

D4—A T-1 framing scheme

DBCES—Dynamic Bandwidth Circuit Emulation Service

DES—Data Encryption Standard

DiffServ—Differentiated Services

DLCI—Data Link Connection Identifier

DNS—Domain Naming System. A service that translates domain names into IP addresses.

DoD—Department of Defense

DS-0—64-Kpbs channel

DS-1—Equal to 1.544 Mbps, which is equal to throughput of a T-1 (24 x 64-Kbps channels)

DS-3—Equal to 44.736 Mbps or throughput of a T-3 (28 x T-1s or 672 x 64-Kbps channels)

DSCP—Differential Services Code Point

DSI—Digital Speech Interpolation

DSL—Digital Subscriber Line

DSP—Digital Signal Processor

DSS/BLF—Direct Station Select / Busy Lamp Field (Attendant Console)

DTMF—Dual-Tone Multi-Frequency

DWDM—Dense Wavelength Division Multiplexing

E.164—The international public telecommunications numbering plan

EGP—Exterior Gateway Protocol

ESF—Extended Super Frame, a T-1 framing scheme

ESP—Encapsulating Security Payload

FCP—Firewall Control Proxy

FEC—Forwarding Equivalence Class

FRAD—Frame Relay Assembler/Disassembler

FTN—FEC to NHLFE Map

FTP—File Transmission Protocol

FXO—Foreign Exchange Office

FXS—Foreign Exchange Station

G.711—Pulse code modulation (PCM) of voice frequencies

G.723.1—Dual-rate speech coder for multimedia communications, capable of transmitting at either 5.3 or 6.3 kbit/s

G.729a—Coding of speech at 8 Kbps using Conjugate-Structure Algebraic-Code-Excited Linear-Prediction (CS-ACELP)

GMPLS—Generalized Multiprotocol Label Switching

GRE—Generic Route Encapsulation

GSM—Global System for Mobile communications

H.225.0—Call signaling protocols and media stream packetization for packet-based multimedia communication systems.

H.245—Control protocol for multimedia communication

H.248—ITU equivalent of IETF MEGACO

H.320—Narrow-band visual telephone systems and terminal equipment

H.323—Packet-based multimedia communications systems

H.450—Generic functional protocol for the support of supplementary services in H.323

HDLC—High-level Data Link Control

HIDS—Host-based Intrusion Detection System

ICV—Integrity Check Value

IEEE—Institute of Electrical and Electronics Engineers

IETF—Internet Engineering Task Force

IGP—Interior Gateway Protocol

ILM—Incoming Label Map

IP—Internet Protocol

ISDN—Integrated Services Digital Network

ISP—Internet Service Provider

ITU—International Telecommunication Union

L2—Layer 2

L3—Layer 3

LAN—Local Area Network

LCD—Liquid Crystal Display

LDP—Label Distribution Protocol

LEC—Local Exchange Carrier

LED—Light-Emitting Diode

LER—Label Edge Router

LIB—Label Information Base

LFI—Link Fragmentation and Interleaving

LLQ—Low-Latency Queuing

LPC—Linear Predictive Coding

LSP—Label Switch Path

LSR—Label Switch Router

MAN—Metropolitan Area Network

MBE—Multi-Band Excitation

MEMS—Micro-Electric Mechanical System

MG—Media Gateway Control Protocol

MIPS—Million Instructions Per Second

MOS—Mean Opinion Score

MPE—Multiprotocol Extension

MP*Lambda*S—Multiprotocol *Lambda* Switching

MPLS—Multiprotocol Label Switching

MP-MLQ—Multipulse Maximum Likelihood Quantization

MPOA—Multiprotocol over ATM

MTU—Maximum Transmission Unit

NANP—North American Numbering Plan

NAT—Network Address Translation

NCS—Network Call-Signaling protocol

NFS—Network File System

NHLFE—Next Hop Label Forwarding Entry

NI2—Standard ISDN Signaling scheme

NIDS—Network Intrusion Detection System

NLRI—Network Layer Reachability Information

NTP—Network Time Protocol

OC-1—51.840 Mbps

OC-3—155 Mbps

OC-12—622 Mbps

OC-48—2.4 Gbps

OEO—Optical-Electrical-Optical

OSI—Open Systems Interconnection

OSPF—Open Shortest Path First

OXC—Optical Cross-Connect

P.831—Subjective performance evaluation of network echo cancellers

PABX—Private Automatic Branch Exchange

PBX—Private Branch Exchange

PCM—Pulse Code Modulation

PDF—Probability Distribution Function

PDU—Protocol Data Unit

PNNI—Private Network-to-Network Interface

PoS—Packet over Sonet

POTS—Plain Old Telephone Service

PSTN—Public Switched Telephone Network

PVC—Permanent Virtual Circuit

Q.931—ISDN user-network interface layer 3 specification for basic call control

QoS—Quality of Service

RAS—Remote Access Server

RIP—Routing Information Protocol

RPC—Remote Procedure Call

RSVP—Resource Reservation Protocol

RTP—Real-time Transport Protocol

SAD—Speech Activity Detector

SAN—Storage Area Network

SCCP—Skinny Client Control Protocol

SCP—Session Control Point

SCTP—Stream Control Transmission Protocol

SDH—Synchronous Digital Hierarchy (European Equivalent of Sonet)

SDP—Session Description Protocol

SIP—Session Initiation Protocol (RFC-2543)

SLA—Service-Level Agreement

SNA—Systems Network Architecture

SNR—Signal-to-Noise Ratio

Sonet—Synchronous Optical Network

SRTP—Secure Real-time Transfer Protocol

STP—Signal Transfer Point

STS—Synchronous Transport Signal (Sonet)

STS-1/STM-1—Equal to throughput of 51.840 Mbps

STS-3/STM-3—Equal to throughput of 155.52 Mbps

STS-12/STM-12—Equal to throughput of 622.08 Mbps

STS-48/STM-48—Equal to throughput of 2.488 Gbps

SVC—Switched Virtual Circuit

SVP—Switched Virtual Path

T-1— Equal to throughput of 1.544 Mbps, which is equal to a DS-1 (24 × 64-Kbps channels)

T-3— Equal to throughput of 44.736 Mbps, which is equal to a DS-3 (28 x T-1s or 672 × 64-Kbps channels)

TAPI—Telephony Application Programming Interface

TCO—Total Cost of Ownership

TCP/IP—Transmission Control Protocol/Internetworking Protocol

TCP—Transmission Control Protocol

TE—Traffic Engineering

TFTP—Trivial File Transfer Protocol

TLS—Transport Layer Security

TTL—Time-To-Live

UA—User Agent

UBR—Unspecified Bit Rate

UDP—User Datagram Protocol

VCI—Virtual Circuit Identifier

VC—Virtual Circuit

VoIP—Voice over IP

VP—Virtual Path

VPI—Virtual Path Identifier

VPIM—Voice Profile for Internet Messaging

VPN—Virtual Private Network

WAN—Wide Area Network

WFQ—Weighted Fair Queuing

WRED—Weighted Random Early Detection

A.2 Glossary

NOTE: Some of the material presented here was taken from the *Wireless Operational Security* book written by the authors and published in February 2004 by Digital Press of New York, NY. Reprinted with permission.

Access Control Lists (ACLs)—Data typically comprising a list of principals, a list of resources, and a list of permissions.

ACL-based authorization—A scheme where the authorization agent consults an ACL to grant or deny access to a principal. See *centralized authorization*.

Address spoofing—A type of attack in which the attacker steals a legitimate network address of a system and uses it to impersonate the system that owns the address.

Administrator—A person responsible for the day-to-day operation of a system and network resources. This is most often several individuals or an organization.

Advanced Mobile Phone Service (AMPS)—The standard system for analog cellular telephone service in the United States. AMPS allocates frequency ranges within the 800–900 MHz spectrum to cellular telephones. Signals cover an area called a *cell*. Signals are passed into adjacent cells as the user moves to another cell. The analog service of AMPS has been updated to include digital service.

Agent—A program used in Distributed Denial-of-Service (DDoS) attacks that sends malicious traffic to hosts based on the instructions of a handler.

Alert— Notification that a specific attack has been directed at the information system of an organization.

Alphanumeric—Text consisting of numbers and letters of the alphabet.

Amplitude—The magnitude or strength of a waveform. The greater the amplitude, the greater the energy.

Analog—Pertaining to data that is transmitted in the form of a continuously varying electrical signal. The pitch and volume of the caller's voice is represented by the analog signal.

Anonymity—Anonymity is the fact of being anonymous. To provide anonymity, a system will use a security service that prevents the disclosure of information that leads to the identification of the end users. An example is anonymous e-mail that has been directed to a recipient through a third-party server that does not identify the originator of the message.

Application gateway firewall—A type of firewall system that runs an application, called a *proxy*, that acts like the server to the Internet client. The proxy takes all requests from the Internet client and, if allowed, forwards them to the intranet server. Application gateways are used to make certain that the Internet client and the intranet server are using the proper application protocol for communicating. Popular proxies include Telnet, FTP, and HTTP. Building proxies requires knowledge of the application protocol.

Application-level firewall—A firewall system in which service is provided by processes that maintain complete TCP connection state and sequencing; application-level firewalls often readdress traffic so that outgoing traffic appears to have originated from the firewall, rather than the internal host. In contrast to packet filtering firewalls, this firewall must have knowledge of the application data transfer protocol and often has rules about what may and may not be transmitted.

Application Program Interface (API)—The specific method prescribed by a computer operating system or by an application program by which a programmer writing an application program can make requests of the operating system or another application. An API can be a set of standard software interrupts, calls, and data formats that application programs use to initiate contact with network services, mainframe communications programs, telephone equipment, or program-to-program communications.

Application proxy—An application that forwards application traffic through a firewall. Proxies tend to be specific to the protocol they are designed to forward and may provide increased access control or audit.

Area code—The first three digits of a 10-digit telephone number. Designates a geographic area within which station numbers are subgrouped. Three-digit code designating a geographic division within the North American Numbering Plan.

ARPANET (Advanced Research Projects Agency Network)—One of the earliest networks. It provided a vehicle for networking research centers and universities. ARPANET was the basis for the evolution of the Internet.

ASCII (pronounced as-key)—The American Standard Code for Information Interchange is a universally recognized format used mainly for text file exchange. ASCII uses bits to represent different alphanumeric symbols (e.g., ABC, xyz, !, @, +) and control codes (e.g., tab, backspace, carriage return).

Assurance—A measure of confidence that the security features and architecture of a secured site correctly mediate and enforce the security policy in place for that site.

Asymmetric algorithm—An encryption algorithm that requires two different keys for encryption and decryption. These keys are commonly referred to as the public and private keys. Asymmetric algorithms are slower than symmetric algorithms. Furthermore, speed of encryption may be different from the speed of decryption. Generally, asymmetric algorithms are either used to exchange symmetric session keys or to digitally sign a message. RSA, RPK, and ECC are examples of asymmetric algorithms.

Asynchronous Transfer Mode (ATM)—A fast cell-switched technology based on a fixed-length 53-byte cell. All broadband transmissions (whether audio, data, imaging or video) are divided into a series of cells and routed across an ATM network consisting of links connected by ATM switches.

Attack——Intentional action taken to bypass one or more computer security controls.

Attribution—A determination based on evidence of probable responsibility for a computer network attack, intrusion, or other unauthorized activity. Responsibility can include planning, executing, or directing the unauthorized activity.

Audit—(1) A service that keeps a detailed record of events. (2) The independent review of data records and processes to ensure compliance with established controls, policy, and operational procedures. Followed up with formal recommendations for improvements in controls, policy, or procedures.

Authenticate—To verify the identity of a user, user device, or other entity, or the integrity of data stored, transmitted, or otherwise exposed to unauthorized modification in an information system, or to establish the validity of a transmission.

Authentication—A secure process used to establish the validity of a transmission, message, message sender, or an individual's authorization to gain access to or receive specific information.

Authentication Header (AH)—An IP device used to provide connectionless integrity and data origin authentication for IP datagrams.

Authentication token—See *token*.

Authorization—The process of determining what a given principal can do.

Availability—The timely access to data and information services for authorized users.

Back door—A hidden mechanism in software or hardware that is used to circumvent security controls (a.k.a. *trap door*).

Bandwidth—The maximum units of data that can be transmitted per second through a channel. Measured in hertz in an analog system and in bits per second (bps) in digital systems.

Baselining—Monitoring resources to determine typical utilization patterns so that significant deviations can be detected.

Bastion host—A host system that is a "strong point" in the network's security perimeter. Bastion hosts should be configured to be particularly resistant to attack. In a host-based firewall, the bastion host is the platform on which the firewall software is run. Bastion hosts are also referred to as *gateway hosts*.

Binary—Pertaining to a numbering system with a base of two (as compared to tens in the decimal system), consisting of the values 0 and 1.

Biometrics—A method of generating unique, replicable authentication data by digitizing measurements of physical characteristics of a person, such as their fingerprint, hand size and shape, retinal pattern, voiceprint, or handwriting (a.k.a. *biometric authentication*).

Blended attack—Malicious code that uses multiple methods to spread.

Boot sector virus—A virus that plants itself in a system's boot sector and infects the master boot record.

Breach—Detected circumvention of established security controls that result in penetration of the system.

Broadband—A high-capacity communications circuit/path. It usually implies a speed greater than 1.544 Mbps.

Buffer overflow—A condition that occurs when data is put into a buffer or holding area that exceeds the capacity the buffer can handle. This condition often results in system crashes or the creation of a back door leading to system access.

Carrier-1—A telecommunications provider that owns its own switching equipment, which it rents, leases, or sells to the public for a set fee.

Carrier-2—A radio wave that is modulated by another signal for transmission over the airways (see also *modulation*).

Centralized authorization—A scheme in which a central, third-party authorization agent is consulted for access control. All access control rules are defined in the database of the central authorization agent.

Central Office (CO)—A telephone company switching center, in which is found a telephone switch that connects to customers' telephone lines.

Central Processing Unit (CPU)—The "brain" of a computer, which contains the circuitry that interprets information and executes instructions.

Certification Authority (CA)—A trusted agent that issues digital certificates to principals. Certification authorities may have a certificate that is issued to them by other certification authorities. The highest certification authority is called the Root CA.

Channel—A path used to send signals in a communications system.

Channel bank—The terminal equipment used to combine 12 or 24 voice channels together.

Coax—The abbreviation for coaxial cable.

Code Division Multiple Access (CDMA)—CDMA refers to any of several protocols used in wireless communications. As the term implies, CDMA is a form of multiplexing, which allows numerous signals to occupy a single transmission channel, optimizing the use of available bandwidth. The technology is used in ultra-high-frequency (UHF) cellular telephone systems in the 800-MHz and 1.9-GHz bands.

Common Channel Signaling (CCS)—A network of high-speed links, connecting Digital Multiplex Systems (DMS). Information such as on-hook, off-hook, and telephone numbers are carried over common channels.

Common Criteria (CC)—The Common Criteria represents the outcome of a series of efforts to develop criteria for evaluation of IT security that are broadly useful within the international community. The Common Criteria is an International Standard (IS 15408) and is a catalog of security functionality and assurance requirements.

Compromise—A situation where secured information is disclosed to unauthorized persons either intentionally or unintentionally.

Compromised Key List (CKL)—A list with the Key Material Identifier (KMID) of every user with compromised key material; key material is compromised when a card and its personal identification number (PIN) are uncontrolled or the user has become a threat to the security of the system.

Computer Emergency Response Team (CERT)—A federally funded research and development center at Carnegie-Mellon University in Pittsburgh, Pennsylvania. They focus on Internet security vulnerabilities, provide incident-response services to sites that have been the victims of attack, publish security alerts, research security and survivability in WAN computing, and develop site security information. They can be found at www.cert.org.

Computer forensics—The practice of gathering and retaining computer-related data in a manner that makes the data admissible in a court of law.

Computer intrusion—An incident of unauthorized access to data or an Automated Information System (AIS).

Computer security incident—See *incident.*

Computer Security Incident Response Team (CSIRT)—A capability set up to assist in responding to computer security-related incidents; also called a Computer Incident Response Team (CIRT) or a Computer Incident Response Center, Computer Incident Response Capability (CIRC).

Countermeasure—An intentional action taken to reduce the vulnerability of an information system to compromise.

Credential—A credential is what one principal presents to another to authenticate itself. For mutual authentication, both parties exchange credentials. Credentials are issued by an authentication agent or a certification authority. Depending on the model for authentication, credentials may only be valid for a session, or they may have longer validity periods. Digital certificates are credentials that typically last for a year or two. Tickets are credentials that are only good for a session, which typically does not last more than several hours.

Critical infrastructures—Those physical and cyber-based systems necessary for the continued maintenance of a minimum level of operations supporting the economy and government.

CryptoAPI—The Cryptographic Application Programming Interface available from Microsoft Corporation.

Cryptographic functions—A set of procedures that provide basic cryptographic functionality. The functionality includes using various algorithms for key generation, random number generation, encryption, decryption, and message digesting.

Customer—The party, or his or her designee, responsible for the security of designated information. The customer works closely with Information Systems Security Engineering (ISSE). Also referred to as the *user.*

Cut-and-paste attack—An attack conducted by replacing sections of ciphertext with other ciphertext, making the altered result appear to decrypt correctly, but in reality the message decrypts to plaintext that is used by the attacker for unauthorized purposes.

Cyberterrorist—An individual, or group of individuals, engaged in malicious activities against targeted computing infrastructure and/or resources, usually in the name of or on behalf of an entity the participants have considered to be greater than or serving a purpose greater than the specific individual(s) that are actually performing the malicious acts.

Data confidentiality—See *data privacy*.

Data diddling—An attack in which the attacker changes the data while en route from source to destination.

Data-driven attack—An attack encoded in what appears to be ordinary data and is initiated by either a user or a process trigger. Such an attack may pass through the firewall in data form undetected and subsequently launch itself against system resources located behind the firewall.

Data Encryption Standard (DES)—The most common encryption algorithm with symmetric keys.

Data integrity—The reasonable assurance that data is not changed while en route from a sender to its intended recipient.

Data privacy—The reasonable assurance that data cannot be viewed by anyone other than its intended recipient.

Decision maker—A person who makes or approves policy. These are often the same people who are responsible for or own the resources to be protected.

Decoded—Converted (as in data) back to its original state (i.e., before having been encoded).

Defense-in-depth—An approach for establishing an adequate IA posture whereby (1) IA solutions integrate people, technology, and operations; (2) IA solutions are layered within and among IT assets; and (3) IA solutions are selected based on their relative level of robustness. Implementation of this approach recognizes that the highly interactive nature of information systems and enclaves creates a shared risk environment; therefore, the adequate assurance of any single asset depends on the adequate assurance of all interconnecting assets.

Delegation—The ability to empower a principal to act on behalf of another principal.

Denial-of-Service (DoS) attack—(1) An attack where an attacker floods the server with bogus requests, or tampers with legitimate requests. Although the attacker does not benefit, service is denied to legitimate users. This is one of the most difficult attacks to thwart. (2) The result of any action or series of actions that prevents any part of an information system from functioning normally.

Diaphragm—A vibrating disk.

Dictionary attack—(1) A crude form of attack in which an attacker uses a large set of likely combinations to guess a secret. For example, an attacker may choose one million commonly used passwords and try them all until the password is determined. (2) A brute-force technique of attacking by successively trying all of the variations of words found in a (usually large) list.

Diffie-Hellman—A public key algorithm in which two parties, who need not have any prior knowledge of each other, can deduce a secret key that is known only to them and secret from everyone else. Diffie-Hellman is often used to protect the privacy of a communication between two anonymous parties.

Digital—Pertaining to data in the form of a sequence of ones and zeros (bits), which is stored and interpreted by a network.

Digital certificate—A structure for binding a principal's identity to its public key. A Certification Authority (CA) issues and digitally signs a digital certificate.

Digital electronic signature—A process that operates on a message to ensure message source authenticity and integrity, and may be required for source nonrepudiation.

Digital Signal Processor (DSP)—A processor specifically designed to convert analog information into digital form, typically applying some form of compression as well.

Digital signature—A method for verifying that a message originated from a principal and that it has not changed en route. Digital signatures are typically performed by encrypting a digest of the message with the private key of the signing party.

Digital Signature Algorithm (DSA)—This algorithm uses a private key to sign a message and a public key to verify the signature. It is a standard proposed by the U.S. government.

Distributed Denial of Service (DDoS)—A denial-of-service technique that uses numerous hosts.

Distributed Computing Environment (DCE)—Open Group's integration of a set of technologies for application development and deployment in a distributed environment. Security features include a Kerberos-based authentication system, Generic Security Services (GSS) API interface, ACL-based authorization environment, delegation, and audit.

Distributed tool—A tool deployed to multiple hosts that can be directed to anonymously perform an attack on a target host at some time in the future.

DNS Spoofing—The action of assuming the DNS name of another system by either corrupting the name service cache of the victim or by compromising a DNS for a valid domain.

Downgrade—The change of a classification label to a lower level without changing the contents of the data. Downgrading occurs only if the content of a file meets the requirements of the sensitivity level of the network for which the data is being delivered.

Dual-homed gateway—A firewall consisting of a bastion host with two network interfaces, one of which is connected to the protected network and the other of which is connected to the Internet. IP traffic forwarding is usually disabled, restricting all traffic between the two networks to whatever passes through some kind of application proxy.

Dynamic Host Configuration Protocol (DHCP)—A protocol for dynamically assigning IP addresses to devices on a network. Simplifies network administration by allowing software to keep track of devices rather than requiring an administrator to manage the task.

Eavesdropping—An attack in which an attacker listens to a private communication. The best way to thwart this attack is by making it very difficult for the attacker to make any sense of the communication by encrypting all messages.

Effective key length—A measure of strength of a cryptographic algorithm, regardless of actual key length.

Egress filtering—The process of blocking outgoing packets that use obviously false IP addresses, such as source addresses from internal networks.

Electro-Magnetic Interference (EMI)—Interference (noise) induced on a system by energy radiating from an electrical source such as a motor.

Elliptic Curve Cryptosystem (ECC)—A public key cryptosystem where the public and the private key are points on an elliptic curve. ECC is purported to provide faster and stronger encryption than traditional public key cryptosystems (e.g., RSA).

Encapsulating security payload—This message header is designed to provide a mix of security services that offer confidentiality, data origin authentication, connectionless integrity, an antireplay service, and limited traffic flow confidentiality.

Entrapment—Deliberate placement of seemingly apparent holes or flaws in an information system in order to aid in detection of attempted penetrations.

Evaluation Assurance Level (EAL)—One of seven increasingly rigorous packages of assurance requirements from CC (Common Criteria (ISO 15408)) Part 3. Each numbered package represents a point on the CC's predefined assurance scale. An EAL can be considered a level of confidence in the security functions of an IT product or system.

Event—An occurrence that has yet to be assessed but may affect the performance of an information system.

False negative—A condition whereby an intrusion has actually occurred but the system allowed it to pass as if no intrusion ever occurred.

False positive—A condition whereby the system deems an action to be anomalous (indicating a possible intrusion) when it is actually an authorized, legitimate action.

File infector virus—A virus that attaches itself to a program file, such as a word processor, spreadsheet application, or game.

File integrity checker—Software that generates, stores, and compares message digests for files to detect changes to the files.

Fishbowl—Describes a scenario whereby specific actions are taken in order to contain, isolate, and monitor an unauthorized user found in a system so information about the user can be obtained.

Flooding—The unauthorized insertion of a large volume of data into an information system, resulting in a denial-of-service (DoS) condition.

Forensics—See *computer forensics.*

Frequency—Amount of times per second that an electromagnetic wave completes a full cycle. One Hertz (Hz) equals one cycle per second.

Frequency Division Multiple Access (FDMA)—The division of the frequency band allocated for wireless cellular telephone communication into 30 channels, each of which can carry a voice conversation or, with digital service, carry digital data. FDMA is a basic technology in the analog Advanced Mobile Phone Service (AMPS), the most widely installed cellular phone system installed in North America. With FDMA, each channel can be assigned to only one user at a time. FDMA is also used in the Total Access Communication System (TACS).

Future Narrow-Band Digital Terminal (FNBDT)—An end-to-end secure signaling protocol that will allow establishment of communications interoperability among communications devices that share the same communications capabilities, but are not configured to communicate with each other. FNBDT sets the common configuration. It is a network-independent/transport-independent message layer. FNBDT operates in the narrowband portion of the STE spectrum (64 kbps and below).

Gateway—A combination of hardware and software that bridges two different communications networks, permitting users on each network to exchange information.

Generic Security Services API (GSS API)—A programming interface that allows two applications to establish a security context independent of the underlying security mechanisms. GSS API is used to hide the details of the security mechanism. Typically, both applications use the same mechanism at any given time. The security context is used to mutually authenticate the parties as well as to protect the privacy and integrity of the communication. Some mechanisms also allow nonrepudiation and delegation. The GSS API is fully defined in Internet RFCs 1508 and 1509. Various RFCs and proposed RFCs define the implementation of the GSS API using a specific mechanism.

Gigahertz (GHz)—1,000 MHz, 1 billion Hertz.

Global Command and Control System (GCCS)—A comprehensive, worldwide network of systems that provide the NCA, joint staff, combatant and functional unified commands, services, and defense agencies, joint task forces and their service components, and others with information processing and dissemination capabilities necessary to conduct C2 of forces.

Global Information Grid (GIG)—A globally interconnected, end-to-end set of information capabilities, associated processes, and personnel for collecting, processing, storing, disseminating, and managing information on demand to war fighters, policy makers, and support personnel.

Global Network Information Environment (GNIE)—A composition of all information system technologies used to process, transmit, store, or display Department of Defense (DoD) information. GNIE has been superceded by the Global Information Grid (GIG).

Ground-start—A way of signaling initiation of a call from a private branch exchange (PBX) to the central office (CO) by briefly grounding one side of a line.

Guard(s)—A set of processes designed to limit the exchange of information between systems. A device used to defend the network boundary by being subjected to a high degree of assurance in its development; supports few services; services at application level only; may support application data filtering; may support sanitization of data and is often used to connect networks with differing levels of trust.

Hacker—An unauthorized user who attempts to or succeeds in gaining access to an information system.

Handler—A type of program used in DDoS attacks to control agents distributed throughout a network. Also refers to an incident handler, a person who performs incident response work.

Hertz (Hz)— Named after the German physicist Heinrich R. Hertz, a unit of frequency equal to one cycle per second.

Hierarchy—Data arranged in an organized series consisting of graded levels.

Hijacking—See *IP splicing.*

Honey pot—(1) A system or a network resource designed to be attractive to potential crackers and intruders, analogous to honey being attractive to bears. (2) A host that is designed to collect data on suspicious activity and has no authorized users other than its administrators.

Host—A centralized computer that supplies data to PCs on a network, or a centralized telephone switch that provides switching services to several smaller remotes.

Host-based firewall—A firewall where the security is implemented in software running on a general-purpose computer of some sort. Security in host-based firewalls is generally at the application level, rather than at a network level.

Host-based security—The technique of securing an individual system from attack; host-based security is operating system and version dependent.

Hubs—A device used to centralize where all nodes are wired in a local area network (LAN).

Hybrid—A device used in communication networks that converts a four-wire voice circuit into a two-wire circuit.

Identification—The process of identifying a principal.

Identification & Authentication (I&A)—Identification of an entity with some level of assurance.

Impersonation—See *delegation*.

Inappropriate usage—A user violates acceptable computing use policies.

Incident—(1) A violation or imminent threat of violation of computer security policies, acceptable-use policies, or standard computer security practices. (2) An occurrence that has been assessed and found to have adverse or potentially adverse effects on an information system.

Incident handling—The mitigation of violations of security policies and recommended practices.

Incident response—See *incident handling*.

Indication—A sign that an incident may have occurred or may be currently occurring.

Information infrastructure—An infrastructure comprising communications networks, computers, databases, management, applications, and consumer electronics that can exist at the global, national, or local level.

Information protection policy—See *security policy*.

Information system—The collection of infrastructure, organization, personnel, and components used for transmission, handling and disposal of information.

Information Systems Security Engineering (ISSE)—The art and science of discovering user information protection needs and then designing and making information systems, with economy and elegance, so they can safely resist the forces to which they may be subjected.

Information Technology (IT)—The hardware, firmware, and software used as part of the information system to perform DoD information functions. This definition includes computers, telecommunications, automated information systems, and automatic data processing equipment as well as any assembly of computer hardware, software, and/or firmware configured to collect, create, communicate, compute, disseminate, process, store, and/or control data or information.

Ingress filtering—The process of blocking incoming packets that use obviously false IP addresses, such as reserved source addresses.

Insider attack—An attack originating from inside a protected network, usually initiated from inside the security perimeter by an authorized user attempting to gain access to system resources in an unauthorized manner.

Interface—A common boundary between two pieces of equipment where they join together, enabling them to exchange information.

International Data Encryption Algorithm (IDEA)—A symmetric encryption algorithm that is popular outside of the United States and Canada. However, DES is still the most popular symmetric algorithm anywhere.

Internet—A collection of myriad networks linked by a common set of protocols that make it possible for users in any one of the networks to gain access to or use resources located on any of the other networks.

Internet Control Message Protocol (ICMP)—A message control and error-reporting protocol between a host server and a gateway to the Internet. ICMP is used by a device, often a router, to report and acquire a wide range of communications-related information.

Intrusion—(1) The act of bypassing the security mechanisms of a system without authorization in an attempt to obtain resources or to compromise the integrity, confidentiality, or availability of a resource. (2) An unauthorized act of circumventing security mechanisms enabled for protection of a system.

Intrusion detection—Detection of break-ins or break-in attempts either manually or via software expert systems that operate on logs or other information available on the network.

Intrusion detection system—(1) Software that looks for suspicious activity and alerts administrators. (2) A system that detects and identifies unauthorized or unusual activity on the hosts and networks; this is accomplished by the creation of audit records and checking the audit log against the intrusion thresholds.

IPSec—A security standard for protecting the privacy and integrity of IP packets.

IP splicing—A situation whereby a network session is intercepted and taken over by an unauthorized user. IP splicing often happens after a user has already authenticated. This allows the hijacker to assume the role of an already authorized user. Protection is effected by using strong encryption (a.k.a. *hijacking*).

Kerberos—A third-party trusted host authentication system devised at the Massachusetts Institute of Technology (MIT) within Project Athena. The Kerberos authentication server is a central system that knows about every principal and its passwords. It issues tickets to principals who successfully authenticate themselves. These tickets can be used to authenticate one principal (e.g., a user) to another (e.g., a server application). Moreover, Kerberos sets up a session key for the principals that can be used to protect the privacy and integrity of the communication. For this reason, the Kerberos system is also called a Key Distribution Center (KDC).

Key Management Infrastructure (KMI)—Framework established to issue, maintain, and revoke keys accommodating a variety of security technologies, including the use of software.

Keystroke monitoring—A type of software used to record every key pressed by a user and every character that the system returns to the user.

Labeling—Process of assigning a representation of the sensitivity of a subject or object.

Layered solution—The judicious placement of security protections and attack countermeasures that can provide an effective set of safeguards that are tailored to the unique needs of a customer's situation.

Leapfrog attack—The use of illicitly obtained logon ID and password on one host in order to compromise another host. Using Telnet to go through multiple hosts in order to avoid a trace.

Letterbomb—An e-mail containing data intended to do malicious acts to the recipient's system.

Local Area Network (LAN)—A limited-distance, high-speed data communication system that links computers into a shared system (two to thousands) and is entirely owned by the user. Cabling typically connects these networks.

Logical—The electronics involved with adding and subtracting ones and zeros is called binary logic. A one or a zero generated by the electronics is called a logical one or zero.

Loop-start—A way of signaling call initiation by creating a loop across the two wires of a telephone pair.

Macro virus—A virus that attaches itself to documents and uses the macro programming capabilities of the document's application to execute and propagate.

Malicious code—A virus, worm, Trojan horse, or other code-based entity that infects a host, typically with malicious intent.

Man-in-the-middle-attack—An attack in which an attacker inserts itself between two parties and pretends to be one of the parties. The best way to thwart this attack is for both parties to prove to each other that they know a secret that is only known to them. This is usually done by digitally signing a message and sending it to the other party as well as asking the other party to send a digitally signed message.

Masquerading—An attack in which an attacker pretends to be someone else. The best way to thwart this attack is to authenticate a principal by challenging it to prove its identity.

MD5—A message digest algorithm that digests a message of arbitrary size to 128 bits. MD5 is a cryptographic checksum algorithm.

Medium Access Control (MAC)—Internationally unique hardware identification address that is assigned to the Network Interface Card (NIC), which interfaces the node to the LAN.

Message digest—The result of applying a one-way function to a message. Depending on the cryptographic strength of the message digest algorithm, each message will have a reasonably unique digest. Furthermore, the slightest change to the original message will result in a different digest. Message digest functions are called "one-way" because knowing the message digest, one cannot reproduce the original message. Encrypted message digests give rise to integrity-protected messages.

Mimicking—See *spoofing*.

Mission Needs Statement (MNS)—Describes the mission need or deficiency; identifies the threat and projected threat environment.

Mobile code—Software transferred across a network and executed on a local system without explicit installation or execution by the recipient. Such code usually has the intention of compromising performance or security, or it is used to grant unauthorized access in order to corrupt data, deny service, or steal data resources; examples of mobile code software are Java, JavaScript, VBScript, and ActiveX.

Modulate—To vary the amplitude, frequency, or phase of a carrier wave in order to transmit information.

Motivation—The specific technical goal that a potential adversary wants to achieve by an attack (e.g., gain unauthorized access; modify, destroy, or prevent authorized access).

Multiple-component incident—A single incident that encompasses two or more incidents.

Multiplex—To transmit more than one message at one time on a single communications channel.

Multipurpose Internet Mail Extensions (MIME)—A specification for formatting non-ASCII messages so they can be sent over the Internet. MIME enables graphics, audio, and video files to be sent and received via the Internet mail system. In addition to e-mail applications, Web browsers also support various MIME types. This enables the browser to display or output files that are not in HTML format. The Internet Engineering Task Force (IETF) defined MIME in 1992. See *Secure Multipurpose Internet Mail Extensions (S/MIME).*

NAK attack—A penetration action leveraging a vulnerability in operating systems that cannot handle asynchronous interrupts properly, in order to expose the system during the occurrence of such interrupts *(a.k.a. negative acknowledgment).*

National Information Assurance Partnership (NIAP)—A collaboration between the National Institute of Standards and Technology (NIST) and the National Security Agency (NSA) with a goal of helping increase the level of trust consumers have in their information systems and networks through the use of cost-effective security testing, evaluation, and validation programs.

National Science Foundation Network (NSFnet)—A high-speed network that forms part of the Internet backbone.

Network—A framework of several telephone switches, which together permit seamless transmission of telephone calls.

Network processor—A centrally located computer that monitors national voice traffic.

Network weaving—See *leapfrog attack.*

Nonrepudiation—(1) The reasonable assurance that a principal cannot deny being the originator of a message after sending it. Nonrepudiation is achieved by encrypting the message digest using a principal's private key. The public key of the principal must be certified by a trusted certification authority. (2) Assurance that the sender of data has provided a proof of delivery and the recipient has provided proof of the sender's identity so neither party can deny having electronically processed the data.

Nontechnical countermeasure—A security measure, which is not directly part of the network information security processing system, taken to help prevent system vulnerabilities. Nontechnical countermeasures encompass a broad range of personnel measures, procedures, and physical facilities that can deter an adversary from exploiting a system.

Octet—A byte composed of eight binary characters (bits).

Open System Interconnection model (OSI)—A reference model of how messages should be transmitted between any two endpoints of a telecommunication network. The process of communication is divided into seven layers, with each layer adding its own set of special, related functions. The seven layers are the application, presentation, session, transport, network, data, and physical layers. Most telecommunication products tend to describe themselves in relation to the OSI model. The OSI model is a single reference view of communication that provides a common ground for education and discussion.

Operations security—Process of denying information to others by identifying, controlling, and protecting seemingly generic activities or information that could be used by someone outside the organization to piece together usable, potentially damaging information about operations or intentions (a.k.a. *OPSEC*).

Optical Carrier (OC)—The speed rate of an optical transmission, according to the Sonet standard.

Orange Book—A Department of Defense (DoD) publication, Series 5200.28-STD, "Trusted Computer System Evaluation Criteria," that is now superceded by the Common Criteria.

Packet—A grouped set of data sent over the network adhering to a specific protocol.

Packet filter—(1) A tool used to inspect each data packet transmitted in a network for user-defined content, such as an IP address. (2) A type of firewall in which each IP packet is examined and either allowed to pass through or rejected. Normally, packet filtering is a first line of defense and is typically combined with application proxies for more security.

Packet filtering—The act of limiting the flow of data based on preset rules for processing the data, such as source, destination, or type of service being provided by the network. Packet filters allow administrators to limit protocol-specific traffic to one network segment, isolate e-mail domains, and perform many other traffic control functions.

Packets—An accumulation of bits, made up of data and control information, which are grouped together and treated by the network as a single unit. The packet is sent by one node to another across the network. The terms *packet* and *frame* are often interchanged.

Packet sniffer—(1) Software that observes and records network traffic. (2) A device or program that monitors the data traveling between computers on a network.

Password cracking—The act of attempting penetration of a network, system, or resource with or without using tools to unlock a resource secured with a password.

Patch management—The process of acquiring, testing, and distributing patches to the appropriate administrators and users throughout the organization.

Perimeter-based security—The technique of securing a network by controlling accesses to all entry and exit points of the network.

Peripheral—Equipment or facilities connected to but not in the same building as the local switch.

Phase—A variation in a signal, measured in degrees, from one reference point to another.

Piggyback—The act of gaining unauthorized access to a system via another user's legitimate connection.

Port scanning—Using a program to remotely determine which ports on a system are open (e.g., whether systems allow connections through those ports).

Precursor—A sign that an attacker may be preparing to cause an incident.

Pretty Good Privacy (PGP)—A software package that uses public/private and secret keys for sending private mail messages as well as storing files securely. A de facto standard used for securing e-mail and file encryption on the Internet. Its public key cryptography system allows for secure transmission of messages and guarantees authenticity by adding digital signatures to messages.

Principal—Any entity that uses a security system. Users, systems, client, and server applications are all principals.

Private Communication Technology (PCT)—A standard created by Microsoft Corporation for establishing a secure communication link using a public key system.

Private key—A key that belongs to a principal and is never revealed to anyone. It is used by a principal to decrypt messages that are sent to it and are encrypted with the principal's public key. It is also used to encrypt a message digest sent by the principal to anyone else. This provides nonrepudiation, because anyone can use the principal's public key to decrypt the digest and be sure that the message originated from that principal.

Probe—An attempt to gather information about an information system for the apparent purpose of circumventing its security controls. Access a target in order to determine its characteristics.

Profile—Patterns of a user's activity, which can detect changes in normal routines. In computer security, a description of the characteristics of an entity to which access is controlled.

Profiling—Measuring the characteristics of expected activity so that changes to it can be more easily identified.

Protection Needs Elicitation (PNE)—A process of discovering a customer's prioritized requirements for the protection of information.

Protection Profile (PP)—A Common Criteria term for a set of implementation-independent security requirements for a category of Targets of Evaluation that meet specific consumer needs.

Proxy—Software agent that performs a function or operation on behalf of another application or system while hiding the details involved.

Public key—A key that belongs to a principal and is revealed to everyone. In order for everyone to trust that the public key really belongs to the principal, the public key is embedded in a digital certificate. The public key is used to encrypt messages that are sent to the principal as well as to verify the signature of a principal.

Public Key Cryptographic Standards (PKCS)—A set of standards proposed by RSA Data Security Inc. for a public-key based system.

Public Key Infrastructure (PKI)—Public and private keys, digital certificates, certification authorities, certificate revocation lists, and the standards that govern the use and validity of these elements make up an infrastructure where principals can engage in private and nonrepudiable transactions.

Pulse code modulation—A four-step process that converts an analog signal to a digital signal by sampling the signal, quantizing it, encoding it, and multiplexing it with many other signals. The signal is converted back to its original analog state at the receiving end.

QSig—Signaling system for use at the Q reference point in narrow-band private integrated service networks; QSig operates at the Q reference point between Private Integrated Services Network Exchanges (PINXs) connected together within a 64-kbit/s–based PISN.

Quality of Protection (QoP)—Quality of protection refers to the set of security functions that are applied to what needs to be protected. The QoP can consist of any combination of authentication, privacy, integrity, and nonrepudiation.

Raike Public Key (RPK)—A public key cryptosystem invented by Bill Raike.

Regenerated—In reference to a digital signal that has been reconstructed to return it to its original form.

Replay attack—An attack in which an attacker captures a message and communicates that message to a principal at a later time. Although the attacker cannot decrypt the message, it may benefit by receiving a service from the principal to whom it is replaying the message. The best way to thwart a replay attack is by challenging the freshness of the message. This is done by embedding a time stamp, a sequence number, or a random number in the message.

Replicator—Any program that acts to produce copies of itself (e.g., worm, fork bomb, or virus). It is even claimed by some that Unix and C are the symbiotic halves of an extremely successful replicator.

Retrovirus—A retrovirus is a virus that waits until all possible backup media are infected too, so that it is not possible to restore the system to an uninfected state.

Risk—The probability that one or more adverse events will occur.

Risk management—Process of identifying and applying countermeasures, commensurate with the value of the assets protected based on a risk assessment.

Risk plane—A graphic technique for depicting the likelihood of particular attacks occurring and the degree of consequence to an operational mission.

Rivest Cipher 2 (RC2) and Rivest Cipher 4 (RC4)—Symmetric encryption algorithms developed by Ron Rivest (the R in RSA).

Robustness—A characterization of the strength of a security function, mechanism, service, or solution, and the assurance (or confidence) that is implemented and functioning correctly.

Root CA—The Certification Authority that is trusted by everyone. The root CA issues digital certificates to other CAs.

Rootkit—A hacker security tool that captures passwords and message traffic to and from a computer. A collection of tools that allows a hacker to provide a back door into a system, collect information on other systems on the network, mask the fact that the system is compromised, and much more. Rootkit is a classic example of Trojan horse software. Rootkit is available for a wide range of operating systems.

Router-based firewall—A firewall on which the security is implemented using screening routers as the primary means of protecting the network.

Routing—Assigning the most economical and quickest transmission path on a network, by which information will reach its destination.

Routing control—The application of rules during the process of routing so as to choose or avoid specific networks, links, or relays.

RSA—Rivest, Shamir, Adleman; a public key cryptosystem invented by Ron Rivest, Adi Shamir, and Leonard Adleman.

Sandboxed environment—The enforcement of access control by a native programming language such that an applet can only access limited resources. Java applets run in a sandboxed environment where an applet cannot read or write local files, cannot start or interact with local processes, and cannot load or link with dynamic libraries. Although a sandboxed environment provides excellent protection against accidental or malicious destruction or abuse of local resources, it does not address the security issues related to authentication, authorization, privacy, integrity, and nonrepudiation.

Sanitization—The changing of content information in order to meet the requirements of the sensitivity level of the network to which the information is being sent.

Scan—Software that performs an access check against a set of targets sequentially in order to identify which targets have specific characteristics is said to perform a scan.

Scanning—Sending packets or requests to another system to gain information to be used in a subsequent attack.

Screened subnet—A firewall architecture in which a "sandbox" or "demilitarized zone" network is set up between the protected network and the

Internet, with traffic between the protected network and the Internet blocked. Conceptually, this is similar to a dual-homed gateway, except that an entire network, rather than a single host, is reachable from the outside.

Screening router—A router that is used to implement part of the security of a firewall by configuring it to selectively permit or deny traffic at a network level.

Secret key—A key used by a symmetric algorithm to encrypt and decrypt data.

Secure hash—A hash value such that it is computationally infeasible to find a message that corresponds to a given message digest, or to find two different messages that produce the same digest.

Secure Hash Algorithm (SHA)—A message digest algorithm that digests a message of arbitrary size to 160 bits. SHA is a cryptographic checksum algorithm.

Secure Hyper Text Transfer Protocol (S-HTTP)—An extension to the HTTP protocol to protect the privacy and integrity of HTTP communications.

Secure Multipurpose Internet Mail Extensions (S/MIME)—A version of the MIME protocol that supports encrypted messages. S/MIME is based on RSA's public key encryption technology. See also *multipurpose internet mail extensions (MIME)*.

Secure Single Sign-On (SSSO)—A sign-on methodology that satisfies three related sets of requirements: (1) From an end-user perspective, SSSO refers to the ability of using a single user ID and a single password to log on once and gain access to all resources that one is allowed to access. (2) From an administrative perspective, SSSO allows management of all security-related aspects of one's enterprise from a central location. This includes adding, modifying, and removing users, as well as granting and revoking access to resources. (3) From an enterprise perspective, SSSO provides the ability to protect the privacy and the integrity of transactions, as well as to engage in auditable and nonrepudiable transactions.

Secure Socket Layer (SSL)—A standard for establishing a secure communication link using a public key system.

Security administrator—Person responsible for the security of information and information technology. Sometimes this function is combined with administrator.

Security Management Infrastructure (SMI)—A set of interrelated activities providing security services needed by other security features and mechanisms; SMI functions include registration, ordering, key generation, certificate generation, distribution, accounting, compromise recovery, rekeying, destruction, data recovery, and administration.

Security mechanism—A piece of software that provides any combination of security functionalities, including authentication, privacy, integrity, non-repudiation, delegation, auditing, and authorization. A mechanism uses cryptographic functions and exports its services using an API.

Security policy—What security means to the user; a statement of what is meant when claims of security are made. More formally, it is the set of rules and conditions governing the access and use of information. Typically, a security policy will refer to the conventional security services, such as confidentiality, integrity, availability, and so on, and perhaps their underlying mechanisms and functions.

Security Support Programming Interface (SSPI)—A standard programming interface developed by Microsoft Corporation in which two applications can establish a security context independent of the underlying security mechanisms. SSPI is very similar to GSS API.

Security target—A set of security requirements and specifications drawn from the Common Criteria for Information Technology Security Evaluation (CC) to be used as the basis for evaluation of an identified ToE.

Session key—A temporary symmetric key that is only valid for a short period. Session keys are typically random numbers that can be chosen by either party to a conversation, by both parties in cooperation with one another, or by a trusted third party. Also see *Kerberos*.

Signature—A recognizable, distinguishing pattern associated with an attack, such as a binary string in a virus or a particular set of keystrokes used to gain unauthorized access to a system.

Signed applet—An applet that is digitally signed by the source that provides it. Signed applets are integrity-protected and cannot be tampered with while en route from the server to the browser.

Simple Key Management for IP (SKIP)—A protocol for protecting the privacy and integrity of IP packets.

Smart card—A tamper-resistant hardware device on which sensitive information can be stored. Typically, a smart card stores the private key(s) of a principal. Smart cards can also be used to encrypt or decrypt data on the card directly. This has the desirable effect of not exposing the private keys, even to the owner of the key. Smart cards are password protected; in order for an application to use the keys and functions of a smart card, the user must enter the correct password to open the card.

Smurfing—A denial-of-service attack in which the attacker spoofs the source address of an echo request using an Internet Control Message Protocol (ICMP, e.g., a ping) packet, altering it to a broadcast address for a network, causing the machines in the network to respond en masse to the victim, thereby flooding its network with ICMP traffic.

Sniffer—A software tool used to audit network traffic packets. Designed to capture data across a computer network, it is often used by hackers to capture user ID names and passwords.

Social engineering—(1) An attempt to trick someone into revealing information (e.g., a password) that can be used to attack systems or networks. (2) An attack based on deceiving users or administrators at the target site, typically carried out by an adversary telephoning users or operators and pretending to be an authorized user to attempt to gain illicit access to systems.

SOCKS—A networking proxy protocol that enables full access across the SOCKS server from one host to another without requiring direct IP accessibility. The SOCKS server authenticates and authorizes the requests, establishes a proxy connection, and transmits the data. SOCKS is commonly used as a network firewall that enables hosts behind a SOCKS server to gain full access to the Internet, while preventing unauthorized access from the Internet to the internal hosts.

Spam—The act of indiscriminately sending unsolicited, unwanted, pornographic, or otherwise inappropriate messages en masse over a network, usually for advertising purposes.

Spoofing—Unauthorized use of legitimate logon data in order to mimic a subject and mask the existence of an attacker *(a.k.a. impersonating, masquerading, piggybacking,* and *mimicking).*

Strength of encryption—The strength of encryption is measured by the amount of effort needed to break a cryptosystem. Typically, this is measured by the length of the key used for encryption. The strength of encryption is algorithm-dependent. For example, the minimum acceptable key length for DES is 56 bits, while the minimum acceptable length for RSA is 512 bits.

Strength of Mechanism (SML)—A scale for measuring the relative strength of a security mechanism hierarchically ordered from SML 1 through SML 3.

Subscriber/Termination—A common eight-wire bus to which all devices connect.

Subversion—A scenario that occurs when an intruder subverts the operation of an Intrusion Detection System (IDS) to force false negatives to occur.

Switching system—Communications equipment on which each user has a unique address represented by his or her phone number. In response to a telephone number, the switching system or switch selects the transmission path or circuit used to connect one user to another.

Symmetric algorithm—An algorithm where the same key can be used for encryption and decryption.

Synchronized—Referring to a communications transmission system where input and output signals are timed at intervals that keep them operating in step with one another.

Synchronous—Occurring at the same time with regard to transmission systems; all locations are running off the same clock source.

Tamper—Unauthorized modification that alters the proper functioning of cryptographic or automated information system security equipment in a manner that degrades the security or functionality it provides.

Target of Evaluation (ToE)—A Common Criteria term for an IT product or system and its associated administrator and user guidance documentation that is the subject of a security evaluation.

Technical countermeasure—A security feature implemented in hardware and/or software that is incorporated into the network information security processing system.

Technology gap—A technology that is needed to mitigate a threat at a sufficient level but is not available.

Terminal adapter—Electronic interface that makes non-ISDN devices look like ISDN.

Third-party trusted host model—An authentication model in which a trusted third party authenticates principals to each other. The trusted third party shares a secret (password) with each principal. It uses a key derived from the password to issue tickets to these principals. Also see *Kerberos*.

Threat—An event with the potential to adversely impact an information system via unauthorized access. The potential source of an adverse event.

Threat agent—Entities used to exploit vulnerabilities in an information system, operation, or organizational or governmental infrastructure.

Threat assessment—A process that formally defines and evaluates the degree of threat to which an information system may be exposed in an attack scenario.

Ticket—A credential used in a third-party trusted host model. A ticket is encrypted with the password of the principal to whom the ticket is presented. A ticket contains a session key as well as the identity of the principal to whom the ticket is issued. Tickets have an expiration time.

Time-Division Multiplexing (TDM)—A method of combining and transmitting several digital signals over a single line.

Time-Division Multiple Access (TDMA)—A technique to interweave multiple conversations into one transponder so as to appear to get simultaneous conversations.

Tinkerbell program—A program that operates in the background, monitoring network traffic in order to generate alerts when calls are received from particular sites, or when logins are attempted using certain IDs.

Token—A token is an object that represents something else, such as another object (either physical or virtual). A security token is a physical device, such as a special smart card, that together with something that a user knows, such as a PIN, enables authorized access to a computer system or network.

Token ring—A type of LAN with nodes connected in a ring. Each node constantly passes a "token" or control message on to the next one. Only the node with the token can send a message.

Topology—Describes the physical layout and interaction of different facilities and services.

Trace packet—Used in packet-switching networks, a special type of packet that forces a report to be generated and sent to a Network Control Center (NCC) during each stage of its progression across the network.

Traceroute—An operation that uses trace packets and records the sequence of addressing obtained from UDP packets sent from the local host to a remote host. The output record normally displays time, address of the route taken, and a sequence number or "hop ID" used to reach its destination address.

Transmission—The process of sending data from one place to be received at another.

Trojan horse—(1) A program that performs a desired task, but that also includes unexpected (and undesirable) functions. Consider as an example an editing program for a multiuser system. This program could be modified to randomly delete one of the users' files each time they perform a useful function (editing), but the deletions are unexpected and definitely undesired. (2) A software application containing hidden code that enables the unauthorized collection, alteration, or destruction of information. (3) A non-self-replicating program that seems to have a useful purpose, but in reality has a different, malicious purpose.

Trunk—A high-capacity communications connection between two switching systems that provides outgoing, incoming, or both services to telephone subscribers.

Trusted applet—See *signed applet*.

Trusted computer system—"A system that employs sufficient hardware and software integrity measures to allow its use for processing simultaneously a range of sensitive or classified information." *[taken from page 112 of the Orange Book]*

Trusted Computing Base (TCB)—The totality of protection mechanisms within a computer system—including hardware, firmware, and software—the combination of which is responsible for enforcing a security policy. A TCB consists of one or more components that together enforce a unified security policy over a product or system. The ability of a trusted computing base to correctly enforce a security policy depends solely on the mechanisms within the TCB and on the correct input by system administrative personnel of parameters (e.g., a user's clearance) related to the security policy. *[taken from Page 112 of the Orange Book]*

Trusted gateway—A firewall that uses a very secure, hardened operating system. These types of operating systems are typically rated B1 or better according to the Trusted Computing Base Evaluation Criteria (referred to as the Orange Book). The firewall system is divided into three software compartments: (1) that which interacts with the Internet, (2) that which interacts with the enterprise, and (3) a trusted gateway that mediates communications between the other two compartments. The operating system prevents applications that run in one compartment from accessing resources outside of that compartment. Any application that runs on the Internet compartment (e.g., a Web server) can only have access to resources in the Internet compartment (e.g., public HTML pages), or else it must use the trusted gateway to ask for information from the enterprise compartment.

Trusted operating system—A part of a Trusted Computer Base (TCB) that has been evaluated at an assurance level necessary to protect the data that will be processed. See *trusted computing base* and *trusted computer system*.

Tunneling—A term used to describe a connection process whereby both sender and receiver begin encapsulating a network protocol within packets carried by another network.

Tunneling router—A router or system capable of routing traffic by encrypting it and encapsulating it for transmission across an untrusted network, for eventual deencapsulation and decryption.

Unauthorized access—A user gains access without permission to a network, system, application, data, or other resource.

Vaccine—A program that injects itself into an application in order to perform a signature check and provide warning if alterations are detected.

Victim—A machine that is attacked.

Virtual network perimeter—A network that appears to be a single protected network behind firewalls, which actually encompasses encrypted virtual links over untrusted networks.

Virtual Private Network (VPN)—A way of using a public network (typically the Internet) to link two sites of an organization. A VPN is typically set up by protecting the privacy and integrity of the communication line using a secret session key. The secret session key is usually negotiated using the public keys of the two principals.

Virus—Malicious code that self-replicates and attaches itself to an application or other executable and leaves no obvious signs of its presence. The new copy of the virus is executed when a user executes the new, copied host program. The virus may include an additional "payload" that triggers when specific conditions, such as time of day or specific date, are met. For example, some viruses display a text string on a particular date. There are many types of viruses, such as variants, overwriting, resident, stealth, and polymorphic.

Virus hoax—An urgent warning message about a nonexistent virus.

Vulnerability—A weakness in a system, application, or network that is subject to exploitation or misuse. An exploitable flaw or weakness in an information infrastructure.

Vulnerability assessment—A complete, orderly examination of an information system and/or infrastructure to determine the adequacy of security measures, identify any security vulnerabilities, gather data that will be used to predict the effectiveness of any proposed security measures, and confirm the adequacy of such measures post-implementation.

Wardialer—A program that autodials a list of numbers and records those that answer with handshake responses indicating possible entry points to networked systems.

War driving—The process of using a wardialer in a wireless or mobile environment, where the hacker is often moving from location to location scanning for vulnerable computer systems and cataloging those numbers that return a handshake response so a crack can be attempted at a later time to try to infiltrate the system.

Wide Area Network (WAN)—A data communications network that spans any distance and is usually provided by a public carrier. Users gain access to the two ends of the circuit and the carrier handles the transmission and other services in between.

Worm—(1) A self-replicating, self-propagating, self-contained program that uses networking mechanisms to spread itself. (2) An insidious, self-contained program that replicates from machine to machine across network connections, often clogging networks as it spreads. (3) A self-replicating program, self-contained executable, able to propagate without need of a host program. The program creates a copy of itself and causes the copy to execute without user intervention. Worms commonly use network services to propagate to other host systems.

A.3   Related Web Sites

Links related to Computer Crime and Hacking

http://www.cybercrime.gov/
CYBERCRIME

http://www-106.ibm.com/developerworks/security/library/s-crack/
Security Hacking techniques

http://www.eccouncil.org/312-50.htm
Ethical Hacking Course Outline EC-Council 312-50

http://www.infosyssec.net/
Hacking and Hackers - Computer Security Portal

http://www1.ifccfbi.gov/strategy/statistics.asp
Internet Fraud Complaint Center

http://www.interpol.int/Public/TechnologyCrime/CrimePrev/
ITSecurity.asp Crime Prevention Methods

Links related to General Networking and Security

ftp://coast.cs.purdue.edu/pub/tools/unix/
Unix security tools download site

http://www.packetstormsecurity.org/
.[packet storm]. - http--packetstormsecurity.org

http://www7.nationalacademies.org/cstb/topic_security.html
CSTB Topic Security, Assurance & Privacy

http://www.esecurityplanet.com/
eSecurity Planet

http://www.govexec.com/homeland/
GovExec.com - Homeland Security

http://www.it-director.com/index.php
IT-Director.com Expert IT analysis, news and research.

http://networking.ittoolbox.com/
ITtoolbox Networking

http://www.nwfusion.com/research/manage.html
Network Management

http://www.thecouncils.com
The Councils of Advisors - Home

http://bob.nap.edu/html/trust/trustsum.htm
Trust In Cyberspace Executive Summary

Links related to Security Focused Businesses

http://www.aphanes.net/
Aphanes ProServe - Professional Security Consulting

http://www.atstake.com/research/lc/index.html
L0phtCrack LC4

http://www.comptia.com/
Welcome to CompTIA - The Computing Technology Industry Association

http://www.securityfocus.com/
SecurityFocus Corporate Site

http://www.ssh.com/support/cryptography/index.html
SSH Support Cryptography A-Z

http://www.intellnet.org/
The Intelligence Network

Links related to online reference material

http://www.cromwell-intl.com/security/Index.html
Computer System and Network Security

http://csrc.nist.gov/publications/nistpubs/index.html
NIST Computer Security Special Publications

http://www.securitystats.com/tools/default.asp
Security Stats - Awareness Tools

http://www.whitehouse.gov/homeland/book/index.html
The National Strategy For Homeland Security

http://www.cio.gov/index.cfm?function=links
The U.S. Chief Information Officers Council

http://library.disa.mil/
Standards Document Library - DISA Interoperability (IN) Directorate

http://rfc.sunsite.dk/
RFC Hypertext Archive @ SunSITE Denmark

http://www.whitehouse.gov /
Welcome to the White House

http://www.nswc.navy.mil/ISSEC/
WWW Information System Assurance Site

http://www.iec.org/
International Engineering Consortium (IEC)

http://www.iec.org/online/tutorials /
Web ProForum Tutorials from IEC

http://www.ciao.gov/
CIAO Home Page

http://cin.earthweb.com/
CIO Information Network (CIN)

http://www.nstissc.gov/html/library.html
CNSS Library

http://itpapers.techrepublic.com/
Tech Republic

http://www.secinf.net/
Network Security Library

http://www.itpapers.com/cgi/SubcatIT.pl?scid=281
Network Security

http://www.nric.org/
NRIC Homepage

http://www.commoncriteria.org/
The Common Criteria Home Page

http://www.nswc.navy.mil/ISSEC/Docs/Ref/GeneralInfo/
NSWC Information System Assurance Site

http://www.radium.ncsc.mil/tpep/library/rainbow/index.html
Rainbow Series Library

http://irm.cit.nih.gov/security/sec_policy.html
Security Policies, Guidelines, and Regulations

http://www.iatf.net/framework_docs/version-3_1/index.cfm
IATF Docs

http://www.ietf.org/home.html
IETF Home Page for RFCs

http://www.information-security-policies-and-standards.comInformation
 Security Policies Directory

http://www.c3i.osd.mil/org/sio/ia/diap/otherialinks.html
Defense Information Assurance Program

http://www.disa.mil/
Defense Information Systems Agency

http://www.alaska.net/~research/Net/whatnew.htm#msg
Networking Tutorials

http://csrc.nist.gov/publications/nistpubs/index.html
NIST Computer Security Special Publications

http://wwwoirm.nih.gov/policy/aissp.html
INFORMATION SYSTEMS SECURITY PGM HANDBOOK

http://www.c4i.org/
C4I.org - Computer Security and Intelligence

http://www.cerias.purdue.edu
CERIAS Home Page

http://www.cert.org/
CERT Coordination Center

http://www.naic.org/1privacy/
NAIC Privacy

A.4   References

All.net. (2004). *A PBX Audit Checklist.* Retrieved August 9, 2004 from www.all.net/books/audit/pbx/general.html

Ananthapadmanabha, T. V. & Fant, G. (1982). "Calculation of true glottal flow and its components." *Speech Communication,* 1(3-4):167–184.

Arango, M. et al. (1999). *RFC2705: Media Gateway Control Protocol (MGCP) Version 1.0.* Retrieved July 26, 2004 from http://rfc.sunsite.dk

Archer, K. et al. (2001). *Voice and Data Security.* Indianapolis, IN: SAMS Publishing.

Bellovin, S., Ioannidis, J., Keromytis, A., & Stewart, R. (2003). *RFC 3554: On the Use of Stream Control Transmission Protocol (SCTP) with IPsec.* Retrieved July 18, 2004 from www.ietf.org/rfc/rfc3554.txt

Biran, G. (2004). *Voice over Frame Relay, IP and ATM: The Case for Cooperative Networking.* Retrieved July 12, 2004 from www.protocols.com/papers/voe.htm

Cavanagh, J. (2002). *Secure Business Telephony With VoIP: A Technical White Paper.* Retrieved August 3, 2004 from www.consultant-registry.com/delivery/TSWP1.pdf

CERT Coordination Center. (2004). Carnegie Mellon Software Engineering Institute, CERT Coordination Center Web page. Retrieved August 9, 2004 from www.cert.org

Cisco. (2002). *Configuring H.323 Gatekeepers and Proxies*. Retrieved August 5, 2004 from http://noc.caravan.ru/ciscocd/cc/td/doc/product/software/ios122/122cgcr/fvvfax_c/vvf323gk.htm

Cloud, B. (2000). *PBX Audit Review and Questionnaire: Key Areas to Review During a PBX Audit*. Retrieved August 9, 2004 from www.auditnet.org/docs/pbxaudit.txt

Coene, L. (2002). *RFC 3257: Stream Control Transmission Protocol Applicability Statement*. Retrieved July 18, 2004 from www.faqs.org/rfcs/rfc3257.html

Dudley, H. (1950). "The speaking machine of Wolfgang von Kempelen." *Journal of the Acoustical Society of America*, 22(2):151–166.

Dudley, H. (1936). "Synthesizing speech." *Bell Laboratories Record*, 15:98–102.

Dudley, H., Riesz, R. R., & Watkins, S. S. A. (1939). "A synthetic speaker." *Journal of the Franklin Institute*, 2227(6):739–764.

Emmerson, B. (2004). *Convergence: the Business Case for IP Telephony*. Retrieved July 13, 2004 from www.acaimc.com/downloads/business-case.pdf

ENSC. (2004). *ENSC 835 Final Project Report*. Retrieved July 12, 2004 from www.ensc.sfu.ca/~ljilja/ENSC835/Projects/e.chan/Report.pdf

Franks, J. et al. (1999). *RFC 2617: HTTP Authentication: Basic and Digest Access Authentication*. Retrieved July 26, 2004 from http://rfc.sunsite.dk

Fuller, V. et al. (1993). *RFC 1519: Classless Inter-Domain Routing (CIDR): an Address Assignment and Aggregation Strategy*. Retrieved July 26, 2004 from http://rfc.sunsite.dk

Gartner. (2003). *Business Planning for VoIP and IP-Telephony—train wreck or smooth ride?* Retrieved July 13, 2004 from www.gartner.com/teleconferences/asset_9148.jsp

Gersho, A. & Gray, R. M. (1992). *Vector Quantization and Signal Compression*. Germany: Kluwer Academic Publishers.

Groves, C. et al. (2003). *RFC 3525: Gateway Control Protocol Version 1*. Retrieved July 18, 2004 from ftp://ftp.isi.edu/in-notes/rfc3525.txt

Halpern, J. (2002). *IP Telephony Security in Depth*. White Paper, Cisco Systems. Retrieved August 13, 2004 from www.cisco.com/warp/public/cc/so/cuso/epso/sqfr/safip_wp.pdf

Handley, M. et al. (1998). *RFC 2327: SDP: Session Description Protocol*. Retrieved July 26, 2004 from http://rfc.sunsite.dk

Harkins, D. & Carrel, D. (1998). *RFC 2409—The Internet Key Exchange (IKE)*. Retrieved July 18, 2004 from www.faqs.org/rfcs/rfc2409.html

Haden, R. (2004). *Voice*. Retrieved August 5, 2004 from www.rhyshaden.com/voice.htm

Hedrick, C. et al. (1988). *RFC 1058: Routing Information Protocol*. Retrieved July 26, 2004 from http://rfc.sunsite.dk

ISACA. (2004). *Telecommunications*. Retrieved August 9, 2004 from www.isaca.org/gir/catDspl.cfm?catID=11&catName=Telecommunications#subcat97

Jungmaier, A., Rescoria, E., & Tuexen, M. (2002). *RFC 3436: Transport Layer Security over Stream Control Transmission Protocol*. Retrieved July 18, 2004 from www.ietf.org/rfc/rfc3436.txt

Kent, S. et al. (1998). *RFC 2402: IP Authentication Header*. Retrieved July 26, 2004 from http://rfc.sunsite.dk

Kiser, C. (2003). *Regulatory Considerations for Cable-Provided IP Telephony*. Retrieved July 12, 2004 from www.mintz.com/images/dyn/publications/Kiser-IPTelephony.pdf

Krawczyk, H. et al. (1997). *RFC 2104: HMAC: Keyed-Hashing for Message Authentication*. Retrieved July 26, 2004 from http://rfc.sunsite.dk

Le, T. (2004). *Internet Firewalls: The Thin Red Line*. Retrieved August 9, 2004 from www-sal.cs.uiuc.edu/~steng/cs497_01/presentation.pdf

Lemmetty, S. (1999). *Review of Speech Synthesis Technology*. Master's Thesis, Helsinki University of Technology, Finland.

Management Information Base. Retrieved July 12, 2004 from www.ietf.org/internet-drafts/draft-ietf-ccamp-gmpls-lsr-mib-05.txt

McDermott, R. (1999). *Voice over IP*. Research Paper. Retrieved July 12, 2004 from http://people.bu.edu/rjm123/VoIP.htm

Moorer, J. A. (1978). "The use of the phase vocoder in computer music applications." *Journal of the Audio Engineering Society*, 26(1):42–45.

National Cable and Telecommunications Association. (2004). *Balancing Responsibilities and Rights: A Regulatory Model for Facilities-Based VoIP Competition—An NCTA Policy Paper.* Retrieved July 12, 2004 from www.ncta.com/PDF_files/VoIPWhitePaper.pdf

NexTone Communications, Inc. (2003). *Enterprise Voice Services.* Retrieved July 12, 2004 from www.nextone.com/pdfs/enterprise.pdf

Munch, B. (2003). *VoIP Security: Part 3—Product Status.* Retrieved August 14, 2004 from http://techupdate.zdnet.com/techupdate/stories/main

Nadeau, T. et al. (2004). Internet Draft: *Generalized Multiprotocol Label Switching (GMPLS) Label Switching Router (LSR)*

National Institute of Standards and Technology. (2004). *NIST Special Publication 800-58: Security Considerations for Voice Over IP Systems Recommendations of the National Institute of Standards and Technology.* Retrieved August 3, 2004 from http://csrc.nist.gov/publications/drafts/NIST_SP800-58-040502.pdf

National Security Agency. (2004). *NSA/SNAC Router Security Configuration Guide, Version 1.1.* Retrieved August 13, 2004, from http://nsa1.www.conxion.com/cisco/guides/cis-1.pdf

NetIQ. (2001). *A Handbook for Successful VoIP Deployment: Network Testing, QoS, and More.* Retrieved July 13, 2004 from http://itpapers.zdnet.com/abstract.aspx?docid=29619&tag=tu.tk.6587.f1

Netrake. (2004). Netrake Web site. Retrieved August 12, 2004 from www.netrake.com

Networksorcery.com. (2004). *SIP, Session Initiation Protocol.* Retrieved August 4, 2004 from www.networksorcery.com/enp/protocol/sip.htm

Ong, L. & Yoakum, J. (2002). *RFC 3286: An Introduction to the Stream Control Transmission Protocol (SCTP).* Retrieved July 18, 2004 from www.faqs.org/rfcs/rfc3286.html

Oppenheim, A. V. & Schafer, R. W. (1989). *Discrete-Time Signal Processing.* Englewood Cliffs, NJ: Prentice-Hall.

Pisello, T. (2003). *Ask the Expert: Questions and Answers—ROI and IT Investment.* Retrieved July 21, 2004 from http://searchcio.techtarget.com/ateQuestionNResponse

Rekhter, Y. et al. (1996). *RFC 1918: Address Allocation for Private Internets.* Retrieved July 26, 2004 from http://rfc.sunsite.dk

Roinetworks.com. (2004). *Business Case for VoIP, Remote Agents, and Converged Communications*. Retrieved July 13, 2004 from www.roinetworks.com/businessdiscussion.htm

Rosenberg, J. et al. (2002). *RFC 3261: SIP: Session Initiation Protocol*. Retrieved July 26, 2004 from http://rfc.sunsite.dk

Rosenberg, J. (2002). *SIP: Session Initiation Protocol*. Retrieved August 3, 2004 from www.jdrosen.net/papers/draft-ietf-sip-rfc2543bis-07.txt

Samhassan.com. (2004). *Voice-Over-IP*. Retrieved July 12, 2004 from www.samhassan.com/Voice-Over-IP.htm#latency

SANS Institute. (2004). SANS Institute Web page. Retrieved August 9, 2004 from www.sans.org

Schulzrinne, H. et al. (1996). *RFC 1889: RTP: A Transport Protocol for Real-Time Applications*. Retrieved July 26, 2004 from http://rfc.sunsite.dk

SecureLogix Corporation. (2004). *TeleWall: Telecommunications Firewall 4.1*. Retrieved August 3, 2004 from www.securelogix.com/applications/telewall.htm

Shultz, T. (2000). *Voice over IP*. Retrieved August 5, 2004 from www.eicon.com/disv4bri/whtpap4.htm

Spanias, A. (1994). "Speech coding: A tutorial review." *Proceedings of the IEEE*, 82:1539–1582.

Stewart, R. et al. (2004). *RFC 3758: Stream Control Transmission Protocol (SCTP) Partial Reliability Extension*. Retrieved July 18, 2004 from http://rfc.sunsite.dk/rfc/rfc3758.html

Stone, J., Stewart, R., & Otis, D. (2002). *RFC 3309: Stream Control Transmission Protocol (SCTP) Checksum Change*. Retrieved July 18, 2004 from www.ietf.org/rfc/rfc3309.txt

Techabulary. (2004). *Voice over IP (VoIP)*. Retrieved July 13, 2004 from www.techabulary.com/v/voip.html

Thalhammer, J. (2002). *Security in VoIP—Telephony Systems*. Master's Thesis. Retrieved August 3, 2004 from www.iaik.tu-graz.ac.at/../teaching/11_diplomarbeiten/archive/thalhammer.pdf

Villalona, S. & Lee, C. (2002). *Voice Over IP*. Retrieved July 12, 2004 from http://webcomposer.pace.edu/CL78352N/IPTelePP.ppt

Vitel Software, Inc. (2003). *Voice Network Security: Strategies for Control.* Retrieved August 9, 2004 from www.ivize.com/pub/security_wp401.pdf

Walker, J. & Hicks, J. (2004). *Taking Charge of Your VoIP Project.* Indianapolis, IN: Cisco Press.

Walker, J. & Hicks, J. (2002). *The Essential Guide to VoIP Implementation and Management.* Retrieved July 13, 2004 from www2.cs.uh.edu/~sujeetv/projects/Ad-Hoc/NetIQ_VoIP_Chapter1.pdf

Wu, Y. et al. (2004). *SCIDIVE: A Stateful and Cross Protocol Intrusion Detection Architecture for Voice-over-IP Environments.* Retrieved August 14, 2004 from http://dynamo.ecn.purdue.edu/~sbagchi/Research/Papers/scidive_dsn04_submit.pdf

ZVON. (2004). *RFC 3261: Security Considerations: Threat Model and Security Usage Recommendations.* Retrieved August 3, 2004 from www.zvon.org/tmRFC/RFC3261/Output/chapter26.html

Index